D1356425

Estimative Intelligence in
European Foreign Policymaking

Intelligence, Surveillance and Secret Warfare

Series Editors: Richard J. Aldrich, Rory Cormac, Michael S. Goodman, Hugh Wilford and Daniela Richterova

This series explores the full spectrum of spying and secret warfare in a globalised world.

Intelligence has changed. Secret service is no longer just about spying or passively watching a target. Espionage chiefs now command secret armies and legions of cyber warriors who can quietly shape international relations itself. Intelligence actively supports diplomacy, peacekeeping and warfare: the entire spectrum of security activities. As traditional inter-state wars become more costly, covert action, black propaganda and other forms of secret interventionism become more important. This ranges from proxy warfare to covert action; from targeted killing to disruption activity. Meanwhile, surveillance permeates communications to the point where many feel there is little privacy. Intelligence, and the accelerating technology that surrounds it, have never been more important for the citizen and the state.

Titles in the *Intelligence, Surveillance and Secret Warfare* series include:

https://edinburghuniversitypress.com/series-intelligence-surveillance-and-secret-warfare.html

Estimative Intelligence in European Foreign Policymaking

Learning Lessons from an Era of Surprise

Edited by

Christoph O. Meyer, Eva Michaels, Nikki Ikani, Aviva Guttmann and Michael S. Goodman

EDINBURGH
University Press

Edinburgh University Press is one of the leading university presses in the UK. We publish academic books and journals in our selected subject areas across the humanities and social sciences, combining cutting-edge scholarship with high editorial and production values to produce academic works of lasting importance. For more information visit our website: edinburghuniversitypress .com

Edinburgh University Press Ltd
The Tun – Holyrood Road
12(2f) Jackson's Entry
Edinburgh EH8 8PJ

Typeset in11/13 Sabon LT Pro
by Cheshire Typesetting Ltd, Cuddington Cheshire, and
printed and bound by CPI Group (UK) Ltd, Croydon, CR0 4YY

A CIP record for this book is available from the British Library

ISBN 978-1-399-50551-2 (hardback)
ISBN 978-1-399-50553-6 (webready PDF)
ISBN 978-1-399-50554-3 (epub)

Contents

Contents

List of Contributors

Gerhard Conrad is a former director of the European Union Intelligence and Situation Centre (EU INTCEN, 2016–2019) and a former senior member of the German Federal Intelligence Service (BND, 1990–2016). He was, among other things, the BND's Damascus bureau chief and Chief of Staff to two BND Presidents while also acting as a key mediator between conflict parties in the Middle East. He holds a PhD in Islamic Studies and is currently a Visiting Professor at King's College London and Lecturer on Intelligence Studies at the Federal University of Applied Administrative Sciences at Berlin. He has published his findings on European intelligence cooperation in J.-H. Dietrich et al. (eds) *Reform der Nachrichtendienste zwischen Vergesetzlichung und Internationalisierung* (Mohr Siebeck, 2019) and in 'Situational Awareness for EU Decision Making' in the *European Foreign Affairs Review*.

Michael S. Goodman is a Professor of Intelligence and International Affairs, Head of the Department of War Studies and Dean of Research Impact, King's College London. He is also a Visiting Professor at the Norwegian Defence Intelligence School and at Sciences Po Paris. He has published widely in the field of intelligence history, including *The Official History of the Joint Intelligence Committee, Volume I: From the Approach of the Second World War to the Suez Crisis* (Routledge, 2015). He has recently finished a secondment to the Cabinet Office where he has been the Official Historian of the Joint Intelligence Committee.

Aviva Guttmann is a Lecturer in Strategy and Intelligence at Aberystwyth University. Before joining Aberystwyth, she was a

Marie Curie Senior Researcher at the Center for War Studies at Southern Denmark University (Project: LINSEC) and a Research Associate at King's College London, where she contributed to the INTEL project. Aviva is the founder and chair of the Women's Intelligence Network (WIN), which connects and promotes women scholars and practitioners in the field of intelligence studies. Her research focuses on the international relations of intelligence agencies and covert actions in Europe and the Middle East during and after the Cold War. She has published a monograph on *The Origins of International Counterterrorism* (Brill, 2018) and has contributed several articles in three languages to refereed academic journals of history, intelligence, international and strategic studies.

Nikki Ikani is an Assistant Professor in Intelligence and Security at the Leiden University Institute of Security and Global Affairs. She is also a Visiting Research Fellow at the War Studies Department at King's College London. She previously held a position as Research Associate at the King's College London Department of European and International Studies between 2018 and 2021, where she contributed to the INTEL project. She conducts her research at the intersection of intelligence studies, public policy studies and EU foreign policy. Her findings on strategic surprises in the UK, Germany and the European Union during the Arab uprisings and the Ukraine conflict have been published in *Geopolitics* and the *Journal of European Integration*. She is the author of *Crisis and Change in European Union Foreign Policy* (Manchester University Press, 2021), which investigates foreign policy change at the European level.

Andreas Lutsch is Junior Professor of Intelligence Analysis at the Hochschule des Bundes für öffentliche Verwaltung, Berlin, and a Visiting Professor at Sciences Po Paris. An historian by training, he was a Research Fellow at the University of Mainz, an Assistant Professor at the University of Würzburg and a Postdoctoral Fellow at the Center for International Security and Cooperation at Stanford University.

Christoph O. Meyer is a Professor of European and International Politics at King's College London and Fellow of the Academy of Social Sciences. He has worked extensively on European foreign and security policy and is the author of *The Quest for European Strategic Culture* (Palgrave, 2006), the co-editor of *Forecasting, Warning and Responding to Transnational Risks* (Palgrave, 2011) and the lead author of *Warning about War: Conflict, Persuasion and Foreign Policy* (Cambridge University Press, 2020) – winner of the ISA and ISA-ICOMM Best Book Awards for 2021. He was PI of the FORESIGHT project funded by the European Research Council and with Michael Goodman led the ESRC-funded project on intelligence and learning in European foreign policy (INTEL) which forms the basis for this book.

Eva Michaels is a Beatriu de Pinós Fellow at the Institut Barcelona d'Estudis Internacionals where she leads a project on the acceptability of EU crisis response initiatives in African conflicts. She is also a Visiting Research Fellow in the Department of War Studies at King's College London. She previously worked in various research and teaching capacities at KCL. Earlier experience includes working as a foreign policy and conflict analyst with think tanks in London, Paris, Berlin, Brussels, Vienna and Johannesburg. Eva holds a PhD in War Studies from KCL (2016). Her research focuses on the theory and practice of European foreign policy with an emphasis on crisis response. Eva's work has appeared in *Intelligence & National Security, Journal of Common Market Studies* and *Media, War & Conflict*.

Paul Rimmer served for thirty-seven years in the UK Ministry of Defence, retiring as Deputy Chief of Defence Intelligence in May 2020. An experienced intelligence analyst, he was a member of the Joint Intelligence Committee for nearly thirteen years. In Defence, the Cabinet Office and elsewhere in government he has briefed various high-level committees dealing with security matters and helped to inform and advise the Prime Minister, Cabinet Ministers and senior military and civilian personnel. He has also been a customer for intelligence in jobs ranging from Principal Private Secretary to two Defence Secretaries to being senior civilian at the Permanent Joint Headquarters, responsible for providing policy, legal, media and financial advice for military operations and contingency planning. Paul is Honorary Colonel of 3 Military Intelligence Battalion Intelligence Corps and Honorary Air Commodore of 7010(VR) Intelligence Squadron RAF, a Visiting Professor at King's College London and a Senior Adviser to the International Institute for Strategic Studies.

Ulrich Schlie is Henry Kissinger Professor for Security and Strategic Studies as well as Director of the Center for Advanced Security, Strategic and Integration Studies (CASSIS) at the University of Bonn. Between 1993 and 2020, he was a member of the German Foreign Service, from 2012 to 2014 Director General for International Security and Defence Policy, and from 2005 to 2012 Head of Policy Planning at the Federal Ministry of Defence.

Acknowledgements

This book has benefited from the contribution of many others beyond the named editors and authors since 2018. The editors would like to acknowledge the funding by the UK Economic and Social Research Council for the INTEL project led by Christoph Meyer and Michael Goodman (ES/R004331/1). Furthermore, the research team has benefited from the contribution of three research assistants whom we would like to gratefully acknowledge: Ana Maria Albulescu (on Ukraine and the Arab uprising as viewed from Germany), Katherine Crofts-Gibbons (on Ukraine as viewed from the UK) and Bahar Karimi (on ISIS from the perspective of the UK and EU) helped to co-author the timelines with knowledge claims and government responses for our three cases and polities. These are publicly available on our project website. A warm thank you goes to Anna Unger for her meticulous work on the index of the book. We would also like to acknowledge the support of professional service staff Anthony Senior, John Fogarty and Daniel Mansfield at King's College London.

The project team was superbly supported by the members of the INTEL Advisory Board composed of the following eminent experts from the world of practice and academia: Gerhard Conrad, Tim Dowse, Charlie Edwards, Lawrence Freedman, Joelle Jenny, Christian Haas and David Omand. They contributed their advice at various meetings, but also through hands-on comments on work in progress, including some of the draft chapters of this book. Furthermore, we are grateful to Christian Haas, Charlie Edwards, Gerhard Conrad and Steven Blockmans for their invaluable assistance in helping to set up virtual or in-person workshops with practitioners of the German, UK and EU foreign policy communities respectively. These workshops provided invaluable opportunities to road-test our findings and to identify suitable lessons yet to be learnt. More broadly, our post-mortem exercise would not have been possible without the support of numerous practitioners who kindly agreed to contribute through interviews or comments during the workshops. Their strong interest in understanding what, if anything, went wrong in these cases and how to improve the production of and receptivity to estimative intelligence was indispensable for getting closer to 'the truth' which will hopefully facilitate future research and tangible improvements. We are also grateful to the participants and the discussant when we presented our first findings at the Annual Convention of the International Studies Association in 2021. As usual, the authors remain solely responsible for any shortcomings or judgements in each of the chapters.

Finally, we would like to express our gratitude to the commissioning editors at Edinburgh University Press as well as the anonymous reviewers whose perceptive comments and suggestions helped to improve our arguments.

December 2021

Introduction: Estimative Intelligence and Anticipatory Foreign Policy

Aviva Guttmann, Nikki Ikani, Christoph O. Meyer and Eva Michaels[1]

In January 2011, the anti-government protests which had started in Tunisia in the previous month were spreading to Egypt. To the astonishment of decision-makers and commentators alike, the protests could not be suppressed by the long-standing autocratic leaders in both countries, culminating in the downfall of both Ben Ali of Tunisia and Mubarak of Egypt within the span of a month. Not long after, the protests spread across many parts of the Middle East and North Africa (MENA) in another unforeseen development. Three years later, a chain of events that had erupted after the Euromaidan protests in Ukraine in 2013 evolved into a full-blown violent conflict after Russia violated Ukraine's sovereignty and territorial integrity by annexing Crimea in March 2014. This move caught both experts and decision-makers in the West by surprise, with Putin openly admitting in April that Russian servicemen had indeed backed the 'little green men' in Crimea, fighters without military insignia that had initially caused confusion in the West.[2] Weeks later, in June 2014, the so-called 'Islamic State of Iraq and al-Sham' (ISIS) seized Mosul and its international airport while Iraqi security forces failed to counter the offensive and withdrew. The collapse of the Iraqi army at Mosul and the fall of the city to ISIS surprised many expert observers and reportedly even ISIS.[3] Similarly unforeseen was the group's rapid expansion beyond Mosul, which cemented ISIS's rise as a powerful and destructive actor in Iraq and Syria.

Each of these events represented a moment of 'peak surprise' for Western professional analysts and decision-makers in three partly overlapping crises erupting in the European neighbourhood in the first half of the 2010s. In the aftermath, intelligence communities and policymakers were accused of failing to anticipate, warn, listen or prepare for these eventualities. In response, some intelligence professionals claimed that some of these events had been 'inherently [. . .] unpredictable' because 'there were no sort of secrets there which could have told us they were going to happen' as the British Chief of SIS (MI6) argued in relation to the Arab uprisings.[4] Strategic documents and reviews issued in Washington, London, Berlin or Brussels in subsequent years painted the picture of a new era of uncertainty. For instance, the European Union (EU) proclaimed: '[w]e live in a world of predictable unpredictability. We will therefore equip ourselves to respond more rapidly and flexibly to the unknown lying ahead.'[5] In response to these surprises and alleged failures, different public bodies in the United Kingdom (UK), Germany and the EU have conducted performance reviews relating to the Arab uprisings,[6] the EU's approach to Russia,[7] the 2003 invasion of Iraq[8] and the confluence of different crises.[9] Lessons identified rightly or wrongly from these episodes are likely to shape future foreign policy for years to come, just as lessons from the 1930s shaped the thinking of a generation of US and European policymakers, for good or for worse.[10] Yet, the few existing inquiries differ substantially in their depth, scope, level of independence, their criteria for judging success and failure, how they handle problems such as hindsight bias and, crucially, which lessons they advocate for intelligence and foreign policy. More fundamentally, it is doubtful whether the right lessons have been learned in a lasting way by European governments, ministries and agencies, foreign policy communities, and societies.

This is why the present volume sets out an academically rigorous post-mortem approach to learn lessons from the way in which three major European polities – the UK, Germany and the EU – handled estimative intelligence in relation to these three salient crises of the Arab uprisings, ISIS's rise to power in Syria and Iraq, and the Russian annexation of parts of Ukraine. Did European foreign political analysts and decision-makers see these crises coming or were they surprised by key events? If the latter, were these near complete 'Black Swan' moments or were they more limited and potentially even avoidable surprises? How well did the intelligence community and other relevant knowledge producers perform in identifying, explaining and forecasting these developments? How receptive were decision-makers to any assessments or warnings given the cognitive constraints and political conditions at the time? If knowledge producers or decision-makers should have done better, what were the most significant underlying causes of any performance problems? And which are the lessons that individuals, organisations, governments and foreign policy communities should learn for the future to be less frequently and completely surprised about major foreign threats and opportunities? As such, the book responds to calls to improve 'the knowledge base' for anticipatory foreign policy at a time of growing complexity in the interplay between political, economic, social, environmental and health risks. Unlike other writings on strategic surprise, the contributors to this volume do not stop with assessing the quality and timeliness of the intelligence process and products, but seek to take communication, credibility, receptivity and prioritisation challenges seriously too.

A post-mortem approach focused on learning lessons remains highly relevant. At the time of writing, Western policymakers again acknowledged their surprise at the speed of the collapse of the Afghan national army in the summer of 2021.[11] Less than six weeks prior to the fall of Kabul and the Western-backed government of Ashraf Ghani, US President Joe Biden had argued confidently that the Afghan army was 'as well-equipped as any army in the world' and that the Taliban were not sufficiently capable to conquer the country: he assessed the likelihood of 'the Taliban overrunning everything and owning the whole country' as 'highly unlikely'. Biden also denied reports that the US intelligence community had warned about such a scenario.[12] Similar statements were made by UK and German leaders and questions were raised about the quality of the intelligence they received. Yet, one can see striking parallels to the ineffectiveness of the numerically and technologically superior US-trained Iraqi army against ISIS in 2014, which should have prompted critical questions about whether the same or similar problems also apply to the Afghan army. Furthermore, it highlights similarities in the political climate for intelligence production and use shaped in both cases by a high-level US decision to withdraw and a degree of domestic political fatigue with these interventions. This book draws attention not just to lessons apparently not learned about specific intelligence challenges, but also argues that the typical blame attribution contests between intelligence analysts and policymakers during crises miss the more subtle underlying problems behind surprises and the frequently lamented warning-response gap.

Readers should also note that the manuscript was finalised in autumn 2021 before Russia's full-scale invasion of Ukraine. Despite the 2014 Ukraine–Russia crisis discussed in this volume and the vocal warnings by the USA, many observers, particularly in Germany, but also in Ukraine itself, were caught by surprise. So the era of surprise continues and many important lessons are yet to be identified, let alone learned.

The Approach

This volume provides the first comparative assessment of the performance of intelligence producers and external experts vis-à-vis three major contemporary cases of foreign policy surprise in three different European settings. The overriding aim is to identify lessons that European knowledge producers and decision-makers can embrace, internalise, and remember to better forecast and mitigate the effects of future foreign policy surprises. The normative reference points for this endeavour are four fundamental aspirations of European foreign policy: to be well-informed, collaborative, reflexive, and anticipatory. From these principles flow more specific performance criteria for assessing the quality of intelligence and the way such knowledge is communicated, received and processed by decision-makers. The theoretical framework used to assess the performance of practitioners and organisations in each of the cases aims to proceed on the basis of realistic yardsticks that take into account the most significant enabling or hindering conditions prevalent at the time. The core task of a post-mortem is to determine whether any errors that were made are excusable given the challenges of each case or situation, whether they are due to severe failings of individual practitioners, or whether they point to broader structural problems and shortcomings in the intelligence process as well as the interface with policy. It is true that evaluators cannot forget how and why a past threat or crisis developed and are therefore susceptible to misjudging what practitioners should have known or prioritised. Yet, we seek to mitigate this in our framework developed in Chapter 1 where we set out case-, actor- and environment-specific factors that could either lower or increase our expectations. In each case practitioners face variable levels of limited, contradictory or unreliable information, attempts of deception or pressures of time and competing policy agendas. We should hold governments that devote considerable resources to a high-priority country or threat to higher standards than those who had set lower intelligence requirements and devoted fewer resources to detecting and assessing threats and opportunities in this region. Only by setting our expectations fairly is it possible to identify underlying problems that can realistically be tackled through 'lessons to be learned'.

This book approaches the processes of knowledge production and use for foreign policymaking in a holistic way, thereby distinctly extending its focus beyond the traditional realm of intelligence production and extant conceptualisations of the intelligence-policy nexus. We propose to broaden the term estimative intelligence to contain forecasts by different experts who through various channels and products support decision-making by governments or the leadership of international or supranational bodies such as the EU. In addition to members of intelligence agencies, this includes desk officers from various ministries dealing with foreign affairs or from the European External Action Service (EEAS), as well as diplomats posted to national embassies or one of the 140 EU delegations abroad. We use the term estimative intelligence to highlight the forward-looking aspect of intelligence provision, with an emphasis on the questions of what may happen next and/or where, while current intelligence refers to past and present developments with a focus on what, when, where, who, why and what for.[13] We understand estimative intelligence to include threat and risk assessments as well as warnings which can be of tactical and/or strategic nature.[14] We understand that a warning should, as a minimum, include a knowledge claim about future harm, but could also include political relevance and action claims as detailed in our previous work.[15]

Our approach is unusual as we do not just focus on governmental knowledge producers, but also systemically include non-governmental experts such as journalists, think tank analysts or staff at non-governmental organisations (NGOs). While external experts differ from knowledge producers in the service of governments in their organisation's mandates, the main audiences they target, or the format and length of their outputs, they share the aspiration to understand and often also to anticipate foreign events, instability and security threats. They use both qualitative and quantitative research methods, collect data and employ country experts on the ground who may have access to more granular, reliable and up-to-date information and can sometimes arrive at more accurate analytical judgements than intelligence analysts or diplomats. As such, their products are a potentially very valuable ingredient of open-source intelligence (OSINT). Yet, such sources may be seen by governmental analysts simultaneously as competitors for the attention and credibility with decision-makers and therefore prompt efforts of being better or different. Furthermore, some of these NGOs and news media are influential actors in foreign policy discourses in their own right so they can shape political receptivity to intelligence and warning in more or less helpful ways. We contend that a holistic view on the entire foreign policy process allows for a more comprehensive investigation of all potential producers of estimative and warning intelligence for our three cases and three polities at hand, enabling us to understand in more detail which actors, procedures and features of the process shape receptivity to intelligence or impact producer-consumer interactions and relationships. This, in turn, facilitates the discussion in many chapters of this book of how to improve intelligence and foreign policy for the three polities.

The study is focused on intelligence and 'foreign policy knowledge' production in Europe, which has received far less attention among scholars of strategic surprise who tend to focus on cases and studies involving the US,[16] rather than European countries (with the exception of the UK). Amid growing efforts to build a European intelligence community,[17] it is worth reiterating the significant differences between US and European contexts – diverse as they are internally – in both intelligence production and decision-making. In the US, the intelligence community is a vast and complex institutional structure, currently consisting of eighteen highly professionalised organisations that is overseen by the National Intelligence Council and the Director of National Intelligence. These various agencies often compete with each other for the attention of a small circle of top decision-makers with the Commander-in-Chief as the prime customer. The intelligence production by this vast and well-resourced community serving a superpower with diverse interests and enemies brings with it a substantial level of scrutiny, further reinforced by partisan polarisation in Washington. In contrast, intelligence structures in Europe have evolved along different historical paths.[18] Not only is the institutional infrastructure devoted to intelligence (generally speaking) much smaller and less professionalised and coordinated than across the Atlantic, but also more knowledge related to national security from foreign threats is produced by analysts from outside the traditional intelligence community. There is less specialisation and doctrine surrounding foresight and warning than in the US. Furthermore, power in foreign policy is usually less centralised in Europe compared to the US, with coalition governments often resulting in smaller parties holding the foreign ministry and larger ones the office of the head of government or state.[19] This has substantial implications for who can direct intelligence and knowledge requirements, who is to be informed and warned how, and how to deal with potentially divergent political interests on foreign policy issues throughout the intelligence process. The framework we propose offers greater flexibility in tracing the interplay between forward-looking knowledge production and use and involves a variety of different institutional, political and diagnostic factors. It is likely to be more widely applicable beyond Europe than models based on the rather distinct and in many respects unusual case of the United States.

Another innovative feature of this volume is our more nuanced conceptualisation of 'surprise' that allows us to look closer for each specific case at the degree of cognitive dissonance experienced, the scope of such surprise in terms of key aspects or events, and the spread among and within groups of analysts and decision-makers. This enables a more fine-grained analysis of who was surprised to what degree, about what and at which point in time. This helps to improve the basis for judging actors' performance, understanding the underlying reasons and informing any lessons to be learned.

Furthermore, we expand beyond the preoccupation of the strategic surprise literature with military or terrorist attacks. Over the past decade, the actors under study have been confronted with slower-burning, indirect and non-kinetic threats by state as well as non-state actors which are not covered well by this body of literature. We thus extend our notion of surprise to cover these threats which have manifested themselves in more gradual and indirect ways. This book focuses on three crises which, particularly in the case of the Arab uprisings and ISIS's rise to power, cannot be considered traditional 'bolts from the blue', but whose root causes developed relatively subtly and over a longer period of time. We believe there are some striking parallels to recent research on 'creeping crises', including COVID-19.[20]

A final important objective of this study is to develop a more sophisticated approach to learning the most realistic and impactful lessons from episodes of surprise. Such an endeavour must be rooted in an accurate analysis of the most consequential causes of underperformance and failings. Our review of the literature and previous research on the communication of warnings in earlier cases and somewhat different actors led us to identify as a starting point a set of common causes that affect intelligence producers, decision-makers or both. These include information, research and expertise shortcomings, such as out-of-date information sources, inter- and intra-organisational pathologies such as blind spots and policy silos, cognitive and professional biases such as reluctance to investigate unintended consequences of government or allied policies, problems in the intel-politics nexus and relations such as a tendency for blame games, and issues with decision-making arrangements such as confusion over who decides, or delays due to bottlenecks. Yet, even if one can pinpoint right underlying causes, it is far from trivial to set out lessons that can realistically be learned as our review of the relevant literatures in public administration and IR shows. We distinguish between instrumental, organisational and social learning. We highlight some of the most significant obstacles that hinder organisations from identifying, learning and remembering more demanding lessons. Our approach acknowledges that more than one 'solution' exists for the same underlying problem and that practitioner knowledge is key to generating impactful yet feasible recommendations for change. This is why the contributors not only talked to practitioners in a series of workshops, but also asked former senior officials from the EU, Germany and the UK to reflect on the findings and set out lessons each of these polities should learn.

Contribution to Strategic Surprise and Learning in Foreign Policy

This book offers a novel theoretical and methodological approach to an old puzzle that has occupied scholars of intelligence studies and foreign policy for decades. Some post-mortems devote considerable attention to questions of what should have been done or not done in terms of political judgement about policy, such as the Chilcot Inquiry's discussion of the premature abandonment of deterrence,[21] whereas other post-mortems are more focused on the accuracy of intelligence products and the performance of their producers, such as the 9/11 inquiry.[22] Several post-mortem inquiries that were conducted after alleged failures to warn about and react to crises concluded that intelligence needs 'to think smarter, put things together better, and stick with only the preconceptions that are accurate'.[23] One can distinguish between public or semi-public officials reviews and those done by academics not officially commissioned in any ways. A review of public post-mortem inquiries by Farson and Phythian highlights how they can vary regarding their degree of openness and transparency of investigative processes, their autonomy from the executive as well as regarding the speed with which they deliver results.[24]

Yet despite the growth in academic as well as public or state-commissioned post-mortem exercises, little is still known about the theoretical assumptions behind them, including the definition of appropriate performance criteria to be used or the micro-foundations in terms of a sound model of desirable knowledge use in foreign policy.[25] For instance, strong disagreement exists over what policymakers 'should' accept from analysts and where to draw the line between intelligence and policy failures – if this line needs drawing in the first place.[26] This has implications for the lessons advocated such as the prospect of institutional reorganisations to address the distorting effects of politicisation on analytical judgements.[27] The orthodox school of US intelligence has cautioned against unrealistic expectations of what warning intelligence can achieve in terms of accuracy and timeliness.[28] In return, it has been criticised for not taking enough responsibility for making sure intelligence is actually listened and responded to.[29] One of this volume's key conclusions is that the vigorous debates over policy versus intelligence failures are often unproductive to understanding and meeting the challenges of estimative intelligence. Particularly, warning intelligence as a sub-strand needs to be recognised as an exception from the normal intelligence process and treated as such in terms of dedicated responsibilities, mechanisms and modalities for expressing analytical dissent, and ringfencing bureaucratic and political resources for dealing with it. For instance, while the UK's norms of aiming for a consensus among intelligence agencies expressed in writing makes sense in terms of avoiding politically motivated cherry picking, it can also stifle the articulation of minority views that typically drive early warnings whilst a written rather than an oral culture of reporting can reduce the accessibility, clarity and impact of what is being communicated to decision-makers. Our findings also raise difficult issues regarding the minimum necessary degree of autonomy for intelligence practitioners to shift attention to countries or topics not currently deemed priorities or, alternatively, about a mechanism for quick political authorisation to surge resources to monitor potentially troublesome and fast-moving situations as we have seen in the case of ISIS in Iraq and Syria in 2012–14.

The approach chosen in this book considers that both knowledge producers and decision-makers need to be held accountable for the performance in their core domain, but that these domains are more interlinked than is commonly acknowledged. For instance, the role of distinct policy agendas and national public mood on potentially risky foreign policy including interventions often sets soft boundaries within which intelligence producers and users operate. It also shapes perceptions of which answers will be welcome and which questions are so uncomfortable that they are not being asked or at best half-heartedly. The findings presented in this book raise questions not just about the appropriate training and expertise of analysts, diplomats and other experts, but also about administrative and leadership cultures and career (dis)incentives for civil servants and the interplay between the most powerful players within any given foreign policy system. Our emphasis thus differs somewhat from the preoccupation of the US-focused strategic surprise with the inter-agency challenges of 'connecting the dots' or with drawing the line between intelligence or policy failures amidst relationships shaped by politicisation pressures.[30]

While the UK has substantial experience with post-mortems of strategic surprise,[31] there has been little research on estimative intelligence related to either Germany or the EU. In the case of Germany, intelligence studies has been an undeveloped field for largely historical reasons as Krieger noted and explained in 2004.[32] Even in 2020 expert outsiders such as François Heisbourg wrote that 'intelligence remains an unloved stepchild in the German system'.[33] Only recently have there been more publications specifically on the history of the German foreign intelligence service, but very little on contemporary cases and indeed the ones we cover in this book. This can partly be explained by a more restrictive legal framework for the release of government documents for public interest reasons, weakly developed and used parliamentary mechanism for scrutiny and accountability, and an underdeveloped culture of learning through genuinely independent, bipartisan and well-resourced public inquiries. Beyond the idiosyncrasies of the German case, foreign policy in Europe is not simply the sum of national foreign policies but emerges out of complex system with a substantial involvement of EU institutions, and it is reliant on EU regulatory, financial and operational instruments. The rapid emergence and expansion of intelligence capacities and networks linking Brussels and national capitals has attracted only little attention until very recently.[34] Understanding the specific challenges arising in these European settings is vital for the ongoing debate about alleged intelligence failures at the national and European level and how to best address them. For instance, to what extent are officials seconded from member states to the European External Action Service likely to ask questions or reach conclusions that contradict insights and policies pursued by their member states?

One of the lessons from the era of surprise is that intelligence services and indeed knowledge producers more generally need to become much better at tackling two interlinked analytical problems: firstly, to better decipher the strategies, capability- and coalition-building, and tactical operations, of highly secretive and closed state and non-state actors such as Russia and ISIS; secondly, to anticipate or at least accurately trace and explain bottom-up developments and protests leading to instability and potentially regime change. For the first challenge, Western intelligence needs to become more imaginative, resourceful, innovative and probably also risk-tolerant in how signal, communication and human intelligence is being developed and used. For the second challenge, rather than accepting defeat prematurely as the previously mentioned quote from the British Chief of SIS seems to indicate, government knowledge producers need to become better at exploiting the huge potential of open-source intelligence to complement and indeed challenge secret intelligence. Reputable NGOs and news media can play a key role in this regard as they are not subject to the same filtering mechanisms as government analysts, can talk to a wider set of actors on the ground, and employ different lenses and methods given their diverse mandates and missions. We found that experts reporting for NGOs or news media from the ground did often spot some surprising developments early, but that their reporting was either not noticed by officials at all or discounted as politically biased or unreliable for other reasons. Furthermore, analysts need to understand better how new communication and surveillance technologies, as they become more widely available, are changing political mobilisation and suppression dynamics in different contexts – with tensions and trade-offs over freedom of speech, protection of independent media, privacy and the regulations of tech and media companies.

Regardless of the collection method or type of intelligence, a key challenge emerging from our research is that all Western-trained or socialised analysts suffer from a degree of institutional mirror-imaging whereby familiar sounding institutions or actors in foreign countries work in quite different ways than in those consolidated Western democracies. This creates significant analytical and policy errors when it is not clear who really wields the power in a country, who is considered legitimate and why, and who may join coalitions with whom for what reason. One frequently mentioned but not easily implemented lesson is to diversify the ethnic, socio-economic, age, sex and disciplinary mix of diplomats and analysts to ensure, inter alia, a better understanding of social media impact on diaspora communities. Even more importantly, estimative intelligence needs a far stronger local 'grounding' and more mutual challenges among analysts from different countries and institutions to overcome transnational Western homogeneity in political thought. It also requires dedicated training in forecasting and estimative analysis as a specific mode of thinking and analysis, which requires some practice and time to improve. Academic work on forecasting as well as forecasting tournaments can help in this regard as long as it remains clear that improving 'batting averages' can get in the way of 'surprise-sensitive' forecasting. It is particular striking that estimative intelligence did not benefit from lessons that could have been learned from previous historical episodes of surprise, including the 1968 Soviet invasion of Czechoslovakia or the 2005 Russia-Georgia war. These were either not learned at all, quickly forgotten as officials move on, or were kept within narrowly defined country silos or communities. In line with some of the literature on public inquiries,[35] our research suggests that more attention should be devoted to obstacles to both learning and remembering and how to best tread the line between being open to learning lessons from previous cases that look similar for the future whilst realising that each country, region and political context have their own unique challenges. These cannot tell us how things will play out, but they can help us to ask the right questions. Post-mortems cannot provide us with a reliable recipe for dishes that all consumers will like, but they can sensitise the intelligence 'master chefs' to the most common mistakes in the cooking process as well as broaden their imagination in using some ingredients and techniques.

Research Design

The research design revolves around a dual comparison of the performance of three ambitious and capable actors with each other as well as across three cases of surprise with major impact. This allows for a very thorough and comprehensive analysis going beyond the single-case and national levels. Through the comparison between cases of different kinds of surprise we aim to identify the most influential underlying causes of performance problems. The comparison between actors can help with better identifying and specifying lessons to be learned, including opportunities for better collaboration between the three actors at the heart of our study. This book focuses on the UK, Germany and the EU as each of them pursues ambitious foreign and security policies beyond individual countries in their immediate neighbourhood. This is visible in their respective security agenda and global strategies. They have significant capacities for conflict prevention and crisis management and devote considerable resources to knowledge production, not just within conventional intelligence agencies, but also in their broader diplomatic services and relationships with external experts.

While the UK stands out in the breadth and depth of its own intelligence capabilities and its access to US intelligence, Germany combines strong technical expertise with substantial knowledge related to Eastern Europe and Russia. Even though the EU is legally limited in what kind of intelligence it may gather, it can draw on the expertise of a large number of country and issue experts in Commission and External Action Service, reporting from its 137 delegations, fifteen civilian and military missions, and some of the diplomatic reporting and intelligence from member states. Together with national diplomats, EU officials form a close-knit professional network underpinned by frequent meetings as well as a shared communication infrastructure (COREU). As such, the EU's intelligence and foreign policy staff constitute an epistemic community in foreign affairs and strategic intelligence.[36]

The selection of the three cases at the heart of the book – the Arab uprisings with an emphasis on developments until 2011, the rapid rise and expansion of ISIS in 2013–14, and Russia's invasion and annexation of parts of Ukraine in 2014–15 – is justified by their frequent classification as strategic surprises. These are unpredicted and often unimagined developments with wide-ranging effects that threaten a state's vital security interests and typically prompt a substantial rethink and revision of its policies. All three of them subsequently developed into crises, defined as a situation deriving from a change in the external or internal environment which surprises the members of a decision-making unit, induces a sense of uncertainty, threatens vital goals and values and restricts the amount of time available for a response.[37]

The empirical basis for the research is twofold. First, in order to determine what governmental and non-governmental experts could have known at the time, the research team has undertaken a thorough and systematic open-source analysis of knowledge claims and policy responses that were issued in the months preceding each crisis. This was done by creating historical timelines which reconstructed key developments for each case for a particular time-frame.[38] In these timelines, we created an overview of the threat evolution and response. We did this with the benefit of hindsight but used data that had been made available while each crisis emerged and eventually escalated. We proceeded systematically by reviewing all open-source data by selected experts and policymakers that a keyword search yielded and that had been published during the specified timeframes. Subsequently, we mapped what claims were made by key authoritative expert sources about the evolution of the threat and potential risks. We searched in particular for knowledge claims about likely future risk-related developments, namely judgements about actor intentions and capabilities as well as underlying structural vulnerabilities, including their relevance to Western actors and, if available, any claims about what should be done. We searched for these claims in sources by key non-governmental actors (think tanks, NGOs and quality media sources) and key governmental actors in intelligence products and diplomatic reporting. Finally, we looked at the impact these claims have made at the senior political level, namely whether they led to a form of learning at the decision-making level, visible in a shift in attitudes, prioritisation and change in behaviour or policy, for example during meetings held of senior committees, summits, declarations, policies adopted and action taken. The inclusion of open-source data in our empirical research ensured that the authors had a strong sense of the contexts in which analysts operated and thus helped to see more clearly which aspects prevented or facilitated the production of estimative intelligence and warnings by external experts.

The timelines did more than retrospectively reconstruct key events and dynamics by setting out which knowledge claims were made and accepted about the evolving situation, consequences for actor interests, and options to act within the three polities over time.

Second, the research team was able to draw on a total of seventy-six semi-structured interviews, particularly with practitioners from Germany, the UK and the EU. These included members of the intelligence community in the respective polities, but also knowledge producers in various institutions dealing with foreign policy, relevant members of parliament, and external experts. During these interviews, the goal was to reconstruct the case at hand with the interviewee, asking for their insights on the threat revolution, any warnings they may have issued, whether and how these warnings travelled up the organisational hierarchy and what the receptivity has been to these warnings. The research team has also organised three practitioner workshops with a total of thirty-six officials from the EU, UK and Germany working in foreign affairs, security and intelligence, which helped us to test and refine our accounts of the nature and causes of surprises as well as potential lessons to be learned. The goal was to learn more about these case episodes by jointly reconstructing the events, getting a clear sense of what knowledge was available at the time, what was known about the threat evolution, and what happened to these knowledge claims as they entered the policy process.

At the same time, it is important to acknowledge some of the limitations of the empirical basis. As was to be expected from such recent and partly still politically sensitive cases, we could not access classified documents produced by the intelligence services and documents except for those already in the public domain or summarised by the news media. In this regard, a well-resourced public inquiry or expert task force with rights to access documents and call key witnesses could go deeper and wider. Furthermore, our interview coverage of each case and actor was not as symmetric as we would have hoped, partly as a result of COVID-19 limiting face-to-face interviews, with somewhat fewer interviews in relation to the UK and Germany compared to the EU. Yet, our empirical findings, including the timelines based on open sources, offer a sound basis for future investigations of the same cases involving the same as well as other European countries and for further testing the theories we have developed in more recent cases such as the botched Western withdrawal from Afghanistan in 2021. As a result of our frequent interactions with practitioners, we are confident about the identification of underlying problems and the lessons that may flow from these.

Indeed, a key strength of the research design is that it allows for and fosters a dialogue between academics and practitioners. The underlying project has been supported from the start by an advisory board composed of seven highly experienced current and former officials and two academics who have a track record of working closely with analysts and policymakers. This has helped to inform the research design of the project and eased access to practitioners for interviews and workshops. Of the six empirical chapters, three are written by practitioners who held senior government positions in intelligence, foreign and public policy in Germany, the UK, or the EU. The authors combine the research findings presented in Chapters 2–4 with their own extensive experience of the cases under study. We hope the inclusion of former practitioners opens up the discussion of this book to a wider range of audiences.

Structure of the Book

Chapter 1 lays the theoretical research framework for the following chapters. Drawing on literature from public policy, disaster as well as intelligence studies, it sets out a normative model of informed, collaborative, reflexive and anticipatory foreign policy from which specific performance indicators such as accuracy, timeliness, convincingness and open-mindedness are derived. The chapter then discusses the challenges for estimative intelligence when seeking to minimise surprise in foreign affairs. It provides a taxonomy of different degrees and types of surprise involving dissonance, spread and scope to enable a more nuanced measurement of who was surprised to what extent and about what. To arrive at fair performance judgements, we set out various case-specific, actor-specific and situational factors that would lower or increase expectations on practitioners and organisations. The chapter then sets out the most important underlying causes of underperformance related to lack of information, organisational features, cognitive and motivational biases, and characteristics of consumer–producer relations and decision-making processes. Finally, we look at the specific challenge of identifying and learning the right lessons and how to prioritise among recommendations for change and reform.

The first empirical part of this book (Chapters 2–4) takes an in-depth look at the Arab uprisings, ISIS's rise to power and the Ukraine crisis from the perspective of actors in the UK, Germany and the EU. It includes discussions of diagnostic difficulties that were inherent to the threat itself, or to enabling conditions, and that were challenging for all three actors. Each chapter is guided by the same questions: what were knowledge producers and/or decision-makers surprised about as the crisis unfolded, how did they perform, and what were the underlying reasons for performance problems?

Chapter 2 unpacks the surprising nature of the Arab uprisings and the performance of the EEAS, INTCEN and DG NEAR, challenging some of the extant explanations in the literature. To this aim, it dissects surprise into the three dimensions set out in Chapter 1, drawing on thirty-two interviews with EU policy officials working across the studied institutions, complemented by knowledge claim tracing using open-source data. By unpacking who was surprised (the spread of the surprise), on what (the scope of the surprise) and to what degree (the dissonance of the surprise), this chapter complements the extant literature which prioritises the explanation of 'surprisingness' over an in-depth investigation of the specific characteristics which made the Arab uprisings so surprising. It subsequently probes which factors negatively affected the EU's performance such as the scattering of relevant knowledge across the institutions and across hierarchical levels and the lack of receptivity of senior officials in Brussels to warnings, particularly from EU delegations. This analysis prepares the ground for identifying lessons to be learned such as creating analytical dissent channels for staff.

Chapter 3 explores and compares how well intelligence and expert communities in the UK and Germany anticipated ISIS's expansion in Syria and Iraq and its reach into Europe during an early phase of the crisis, from July 2013 to June 2014. Knowledge producers in both countries experienced partial surprise about ISIS's rise to power and its development into a foreign policy crisis. Important diagnostic difficulties were a lack of access to sources on the ground as well as the complexity and speed of parallel developments across Syria and Iraq. Cross-country developments contrasted with intelligence and expert communities' traditional organisation along country foci. The chapter identifies four underlying reasons for performance shortcomings in Germany and the UK. First, German policymakers showed limited interest in Iraq and the Middle East prior to the summer of 2014 and were not sufficiently receptive to expert warnings about the evolving crisis. In the UK reigned a desire for disengagement after the withdrawal of its remaining forces from Iraq in May 2011, and Iraq was thus a lower priority. Second, structures for efficient inter-institutional cooperation were not yet in place during this early phase of the crisis. Third, British and German intelligence analysts experienced professional-cultural biases which hindered their performance. Fourth, both countries faced agenda competition during the period under study.

Chapter 4 focuses on how the EU's foreign policy machinery anticipated and handled the events leading from the summer of 2013, when Russia first exerted real pressure and sanctions on the Eastern Partnership states, to the annexation of Crimea by force and the military intervention in Donbas in the late summer of 2014. It finds that some aspects were less surprising, such as the U-turn of President Yanukovych before the Vilnius summit, whereas the Russian annexation of Crimea came as a complete surprise to officials in the EU institutions, if not in all member states. The EU should have performed better when anticipating events in Ukraine but was not well enough equipped in terms of legal authority, collection capacities, and organisation of diplomatic and assessed intelligence to anticipate Russia's actions, which represented a major discontinuity. The EU machinery suffered from geopolitical and security blind spots regarding the role of Russia, disregarded some warnings because of suspicions of national bias, and some political agendas limited receptivity in relation to events in Ukraine. This chapter discusses potential lessons such as bringing together analytical resources to analyse the Russian threat, analytical dissent procedures and structural reforms relating to the decision of labour between the Commission and EEAS.

The second empirical part (Chapters 5–7) looks at each actor separately and compares how each handled the three crises. For these chapters, the authors combine the research findings presented in Chapters 2–4 with their own extensive experience. They focus on how each political actor has tried to learn lessons from these crises, where they have been successful, and which lessons are yet to be learned to improve crisis anticipation and preparedness in foreign policy.

Chapter 5 examines the production of intelligence assessments and their impact on policy decision-making in the UK. It focuses principally on the Joint Intelligence Committee and Defence Intelligence as the leading sources of analysis in the UK intelligence community on the Arab Spring, ISIS's rise to power and the Russian annexation of Crimea. Comparing the three cases in terms of surprise, Chapter 5 finds that only in the last case did the intelligence community fail to warn. A core reason was that the policy community in the UK was concerned with improving relations with Russia and focused more on issues like counterterrorism, Syria, and Afghanistan. It finds that surprises happen more often in low-priority areas for intelligence collection and assessment. It also highlights the unavoidability of surprise in foreign policy. The chapter concludes with a review of lessons learned and offers three recommendations. First, warning can only happen effectively through a long-term and deep understanding of a region or issue. Second, early warning deserves to be treated as a discipline in its own right, with intelligence products that are marked as such for the customer. Third, one should not underestimate the importance of open-source intelligence as a means to complete the overall picture, and intelligence analysis should not rely on secret sources alone.

Chapter 6 concentrates on lessons learned from the Ukraine crisis 2013–14 and its impact on the organisation of foreign and security policy in the German political system. It puts the Ukraine crisis into the larger context of political power shifts and the ability of policymakers and analysts to anticipate crises and wars. Several political crises in the 2010s, most notably the Ukraine crisis, have highlighted the need for an adjustment of the foreign and security policy structures in Germany. Discrepancies between rhetoric and practice remain. Despite a more clearly articulated demand for crisis-proof structures and far-sighted policy, little progress has been made in the discussion about new government structures or strengthening existing ones. Consequently, Germany is lagging far behind almost all partners in the coordination of foreign and security policy. The growing need for a more strategic whole-of-government approach will increasingly become a problem for German foreign and security policy. Only a real change in awareness, as well as structural and organisational adaptations, in particular a new relationship between the armed forces and other instruments of security policy such as secret intelligence, could ensure that Germany will be better prepared for strategic surprises.

Chapter 7 focuses on learning lessons for estimative intelligence production and use by the EU from all three cases. It explores political, structural and procedural deficiencies in producing and disseminating estimative intelligence within the EEAS and beyond with a focus on the setting up of the EEAS in 2010–11 and later developments. Among the shortcomings and problems identified were a lack of infrastructure for the secure access to and sharing of classified information and analysis with relevant parts of the EEAS, a lack of procedure around the production of all-sources authoritative warning intelligence, and limitations as to how the EU's Intelligence Assessment and Situation Centre (INTCEN) was plugged into high-level decision-making fora such as the Political and Security Committee. In addition, Chapter 7 discusses the cooperation between civilian and defence intelligence, the intelligence support provided by member states, and the politicisation problems arising from the mixing of operational/policy and situational/intelligence perspectives. The EU has been seeking to address shortcomings since 2014, for instance through the EU Early Warning System (EWS) and creation of a fusion cell for hybrid threats. However, further steps are necessary for emancipating and professionalising the build-up and promotion of all sources comprehensive situational awareness and forecasting.

The final chapter answers the research-guiding questions by drawing on the evidence and arguments presented in the previous chapters, and it pushes the overall argument further. Chapter 8 is structured into three sections: the first is case study centred and asks which aspect made each of them particularly challenging to track, explain and forecast. It highlights as a common feature the unexpected and rapid interplay of three factors: (1) the growth in public resentment against corrupt and authoritarian governments, (2) the impact of new communication technologies and media platforms, and (3) the willingness and capacity of revisionist state and non-state actors to embrace bold strategies to challenge Western powers and liberal norms. The second section compares the performance of the three polities and explores distinct and common strengths and weaknesses. The third section identifies lessons that are yet to be learned such as diversifying expert input and strengthening its local grounding, to design and improve specialised warning capacities, and the creation of more rigorous, independent and sustainable learning mechanisms. This chapter concludes by discussing the implications for the literature in areas such as professional and cultural biases in analysis, the differences between the US and European intelligence policy-nexus, politicisation and attribution of blame, and processes and preconditions for learning.

Notes

1. All authors have contributed equally and are therefore listed in alphabetical order. The manuscript was finalised in December 2021.
2. Vladimir Putin, 'Direct Line with Vladimir Putin' (Kremlin web page, 2014), 14.
3. Hassan Abu Hanieh and Mohammad Abu-Rumman, 'The "Islamic State" Organization: The Sunni Crisis and the Struggle of Global Jihadism' (Amman: Friedrich Ebert Stiftung, 2015), 178; Tallha Abdulrazaq and Gareth Stansfield, 'The Enemy Within: Isis and the Conquest of Mosul', *The Middle East Journal* 70, no. 4 (2016).
4. HMG, Intelligence and Security Commitee, 'Annual Report 2011–2012' (London: UK Stationary Office, 2012), 14.
5. EU High Representative, 'Shared Vision, Common Action: A

Stronger Europe. A Global Strategy for the European Union's Foreign and Security Policy' (Brussels: European Union, 2016), 46.

6. House of Commons Foreign Affairs Committee, 'British Foreign Policy and the "Arab Spring". Second Report of Session 2012–13' (London, 2012).

7. House of Lords, European Union Committee, 'The Eu and Russia: Before and Beyond the Crisis in Ukraine' (London: House of Lords, 2015).

8. Chilcot Inquiry, 'Iraq Inquiry': http://www.iraqinquiry.org.uk

9. German Foreign Office, 'Review 2014: Außenpolitik Weiter Denken: Krise – Ordnung – Europa' (Berlin: Auswärtiges Amt, 2014).

10. Richard Ned Lebow, 'Generational Learning and Conflict Management', *International Journal* 40, no. 4 (1985).

11. Isaac Chotiner, 'How America Failed in Afghanistan' (*The New Yorker*, 2021).

12. The White House, 'Remarks by President Biden on the Drawdown of U.S. Forces in Afghanistan' (2021).

13. David Omand, 'Reflections on Intelligence Analysts and Policymakers', *International Journal of Intelligence and CounterIntelligence* 33, no. 3 (2020): 475–6.

14. While we draw on David Omand's model of intelligence analysis, we alter his model by including strategic warning under estimation.

15. Christoph O. Meyer, Chiara De Franco and Florian Otto, *Warning About War: Conflict, Persuasion and Foreign Policy* (Cambridge: Cambridge University Press, 2020), 28–9.

16. Richard K. Betts, *Surprise Attack: Lessons for Defence Planning* (Washington, DC: The Brookings Institution, 1982); Erik J. Dahl, *Intelligence and Surprise Attack: Failure and Success from Pearl Harbor to 9/11 and Beyond* (Washington, DC: Georgetown University Press, 2013); Robert Jervis, *Perception and Misperception in International Politics* (Princeton, NJ: Princeton University Press, 1976); Ephraim Kam, *Surprise Attack: The Victim's Perspective* (Cambridge, MA: Harvard University Press, 2013); Janice Gross Stein, 'Building Politics into Psychology: The Misperception of Threat', *Political Psychology* (1988).

17. Damien Van Puyvelde, 'European Intelligence Agendas and the Way Forward', *International Journal of Intelligence and CounterIntelligence* 33, no. 3 (2020); Yvan Lledo-Ferrer and Jan-Hendrik Dietrich, 'Building a European Intelligence Community', ibid.

18. Bob De Graaf and James M. Nyce, eds, *The Handbook of European Intelligence Cultures* (London: Rowman & Littlefield, 2016).
19. Nikki Ikani, Aviva Guttmann and Christoph O. Meyer, 'An Analytical Framework for Postmortems of European Foreign Policy: Should Decision-Makers Have Been Surprised?', *Intelligence and National Security* 35, no. 2 (2020).
20. Arjen Boin, Magnus Ekengren and Mark Rhinard, *Understanding the Creeping Crisis* (Springer Nature, 2021).
21. Committee of Privy Counsellors, 'The Report of the Iraq Inquiry. Executive Summary' (House of Commons, 2016).
22. US Senate Select Committee on Intelligence and US House Permanent Select Committee on Intelligence, 'Joint Inquiry into Intelligence Community Activities before and after the Terrorist Attacks of September 11, 2001: Hearings before the Select Committee on Intelligence, US Senate and the Permanent Select Committee on Intelligence, House of Representatives' (US Government Printing Office, 2004).
23. Richard K Herrmann and Jong Kun Choi, 'From Prediction to Learning: Opening Experts' Minds to Unfolding History', *International Security* 31, no. 4 (2007): 161. See also: Stuart Farson and Mark Phythian, *Commissions of Inquiry and National Security: Comparative Approaches* (Santa Barbara, CA: Praeger, 2010).
24. Farson and Phythian, *Commissions of Inquiry and National Security: Comparative Approaches*, 5.
25. James J Wirtz, 'The Art of the Intelligence Autopsy', *Intelligence and National Security* 29, no. 1 (2014): 1–2.
26. Robert Jervis, *Why Intelligence Fails: Lessons from the Iranian Revolution and the Iraq War*, Cornell Studies in Security Affairs (Ithaca, NY: Cornell University Press, 2010).
27. Paul R Pillar, *Intelligence and Us Foreign Policy: Iraq, 9/11, and Misguided Reform* (New York: Columbia University Press, 2011); Joshua Rovner, *Fixing the Facts: National Security and the Politics of Intelligence* (Ithaca, NY: Cornell University Press, 2011).
28. Richard K. Betts, 'Analysis, War and Decision: Why Intelligence Failures Are Inevitable', *World Politics* 31, no. 1 (1978).
29. Dahl, *Intelligence and Surprise Attack: Failure and Success from Pearl Harbor to 9/11 and Beyond*.
30. Thomas L. Hughes, *The Fate of Facts in a World of Men: Foreign Policy and Intelligence-Making* (New York Foreign Policy Association, 1976); Stephen Marrin, 'At Arm's Length or at the Elbow?: Explaining the Distance between Analysts and Decisionmakers',

International Journal of Intelligence and CounterIntelligence 20, no. 3 (2007); Joshua Rovner, *Fixing the Facts: National Security and the Politics of Intelligence* (Ithaca, NY: Cornell University Press, 2011); Matthew Connelly et al., 'New Evidence and New Methods for Analyzing the Iranian Revolution as an Intelligence Failure', *Intelligence and National Security* (2021).

31. Committee of Privy Counsellors, 'The Report of the Iraq Inquiry. Executive Summary'.

32. Wolfgang Krieger, 'German Intelligence History: A Field in Search of Scholars', *Intelligence & National Security* 19, no. 2 (2004).

33. François Heisbourg, 'A View from France: Not There Yet', in *Zeitenwende – Wendezeiten: Special Edition of the Munich Security Report*, ed. Tobias Bunde et al. (Munich: Munich Security Conference, 2020), 161.

34. Federica Bicchi, 'The EU as a Community of Practice: Foreign Policy Communications in the Coreu Network', *Journal of European Public Policy* 18, no. 8 (2011); Björn Fägersten, 'Bureaucratic Resistance to International Intelligence Cooperation – the Case of Europol', *Intelligence and National Security* 25, no. 4 (2010); Aviva Guttmann, 'Combatting Terror in Europe: Euro-Israeli Counterterrorism Intelligence Cooperation in the Club De Berne (1971–1972)', ibid. 33, no. 2 (2018); Artur Gruszczak, *Intelligence Security in the European Union: Building a Strategic Intelligence Community* (Basingstoke: Palgrave Macmillan, 2016).

35. For instance Alastair Stark, *Public Inquiries, Policy Learning, and the Threat of Future Crises* (Oxford University Press, USA, 2019).

36. Bicchi, 'The EU as a Community of Practice: Foreign Policy Communications in the Coreu Network'; Gruszczak, *Intelligence Security in the European Union: Building a Strategic Intelligence Community*.

37. Eric Stern and Bengt Sundelius, 'Crisis Management Europe: An Integrated Regional Research and Training Program', *International Studies Perspectives* 3, no. 1 (2002): 72; Michael Herman, *Intelligence Power in Peace and War* (Cambridge: Cambridge University Press, 1996), 29.

38. The following timelines are available from the INTEL website (https://www.kcl.ac.uk/eis/research/intel/intel-publications): Catherine Crofts-Gibbons and Nikki Ikani, 'Timeline of Expert Claims and Responses for Ukraine Crisis Involving UK' (2021); Nikki Ikani and Ana Maria Albulescu, 'Timeline of Expert Claims and Responses for Ukraine Crisis Involving Germany and the EU'

(2021); Nikki Ikani, 'Timeline of Expert Claims and Responses for the Arab Uprising Involving UK' (2021); Nikki Ikani and Ana Maria Albulescu, 'Timeline of Expert Claims and Responses for the Arab Uprising Involving Germany and the EU' (2021); Aviva Guttmann and Bahar Karimi, 'Timeline of UK Media and Middle East Experts' Anticipation of the Rise of Isis and UK Government Reactions' (2021); Eva Michaels and Bahar Karimi, 'Overview of Expert Claims and Eu Policy Responses to Isis' Rise to Power in Iraq and Syria' (2021); Eva Michaels, 'Germany's Anticipation of and Response to Isis' Rise to Power: Overview of Open-Source Expert Claims and Policy Responses' (2021).

1 Expectations from Estimative Intelligence and Anticipatory Foreign Policy: A Realistic Appraisal[1]

Nikki Ikani, Christoph O. Meyer, Eva Michaels and Aviva Guttmann

Introduction

What can we realistically expect from estimative intelligence and anticipatory foreign policy? What are appropriate yardsticks to use when retrospectively assessing the performance of governmental and external analysts, policy planners and decision-makers? To what extent and when is being surprised to be expected and excused? When do performance shortcomings point to underlying issues that might be avoided or addressed through learning the right lessons without creating great problems elsewhere? And how can obstacles to lesson learning and remembering in intelligence and foreign policy be overcome? This chapter will try to engage with these questions as it sets out a common conceptual and theoretical framework for the post-mortems analysis and identification of lessons to be learned in this volume.

Even though the intelligence studies literature has engaged with some of these questions, there is no suitable framework to take off the shelf that provides a persuasive normative grounding and one that works for the three European polities at the heart of our study – rather than the frequently studied US context. This chapter draws not only on the relevant literature in the core areas of strategic surprise and post-mortems in intelligence studies and foreign policy, but also considers insights from foresight and forecasting studies, crisis, risks and emergency management, and public administration about the role of experts, expertise and learning. We first develop a normative model of evidence-sensitive anticipatory foreign policy within which we situate intelligence and political receptivity to it. A second section looks at the specific challenges for estimative intelligence when seeking to minimise surprise in foreign affairs. We provide a taxonomy of different degrees and types of surprise and discuss when being surprised might be condonable or expected. Thirdly, we investigate how to identify the most important causes of any performance problems in intelligence-policy nexus. Finally, we look at the specific challenge of identifying and learning the right lessons and how to prioritise among recommendations for change and reform.

Normative Expectations towards Intelligence in Anticipatory Foreign Policy

It is helpful to reflect on whether and to what extent we can learn from the role of experts and expertise in fields beyond foreign policy, such as migration policy or public health.[2] The broadening of the perspective mitigates against the exceptionalism of some of the literature rooted in the US intelligence community. All organisations use expert knowledge not just in a rationalist way to better achieve their policy preferences, but also as a source of legitimation and to justify policies.[3] The degree to which this happens may differ between types of organisations, policy fields and, closely connected, the epistemological status or authoritativeness of knowledge produced in the eyes of decision-makers, epistemic communities and the public. The greater the authoritativeness of expert knowledge, the more influence such expertise should play in decision-making as it potentially improves not only problem-solving capacity, but also enhances legitimacy and builds public support. Furthermore, the authoritativeness of knowledge production has implications for how much discretion we should give to political judgement about whether, when and how to pay attention, prioritise and, ultimately, act upon assessments – or the extent to which experts should be held accountable for any deviations from 'state-of-the art' professional practice.

The highest expectations can be found in normative models of 'evidence-based policymaking' that originated in public health.[4] Here, decision-making draws on knowledge produced through rigorous 'scientific' processes, such as double-blind clinical trials of new drugs and treatments, and on large and cohesive 'epistemic communities'. There is broad consensus on what 'good science' looks like, who is judged competent following what kind of training and what the shared professional norms are. Consequently, politicians who ignore, cherry pick, or even suppress such high-quality expert advice can be deemed reckless, perhaps criminally so, if this leads to the unnecessary loss of life. Yet, even in matters of public health lawmakers cannot always simply 'follow the science' when taking decisions, or delegate such decisions to technocratic arms-length bodies altogether. There will be situations, such as COVID-19 as a newly emergent infectious disease, where uncertainty is initially high, scientists disagree over the interpretation of data, problems cut across scientific disciplines, or when actions considered involve significant externalities beyond public health that require value judgements by democratic representatives. Strikingly, one of the first post-mortems of the UK's handling of the COVID-19 pandemic criticised decision-makers for insufficiently challenging scientific experts and accused the SAGE experts of group-think during the early phase.[5]

In contrast to public health, foreign, security and defence policy is less 'technocratised'. Foreign policies are decided by ministers, not by arms-length agencies, independent officials or scientific committees, and most intelligence communities operate based on a strict separation between analytical judgement and policy recommendations. Intelligence analysts and diplomats come to their profession through very diverse training and professional education routes, many of which vary hugely between countries. Decision-makers in foreign policy cannot always be expected to defer their analytical judgement of the severity of a threat from a foreign country to 'expert' intelligence analysts, but sometimes feel justifiably confident enough to challenge or remake some the analysis presented to them given their insights of meeting foreign leaders personally or their own knowledge of a given country, region or issue themselves. Estimative intelligence remains a particularly challenging area in terms of the authoritativeness of expert knowledge, and previous research shows that government analysts and senior officials remain largely unconvinced about the reliability of forecasts of foreign affairs and violent conflict in particular.[6] Omand cites former US Secretary of State Colin Powell's lecture to CIA analysts: 'I will hold you accountable for what you tell me is a fact. When you tell me what's most likely to happen, then I, as the policymaker, have to make a judgement as to whether I act on that, and I won't hold you accountable for it because that is a judgment; and judgments of this kind are made by policymakers, not by analysts.'[7]

Some scholars working on forecasts relating to political events hope that one day the scientific reliability will approximate those of medicine and public health. For instance, Tetlock's forecasting tournaments show that individuals' forecasting accuracy can be improved through training individuals and groups.[8] The work of Gleditsch and others uses increasingly sophisticated data sets, models and techniques to forecast the probability of the outbreak of instability, civil war and mass atrocities.[9] The accuracy of early warning may be dramatically improved through new information and communication technologies, especially through using computer-aided analytical techniques of large data sets generated in real time from open sources, including social media and other user-generated content.[10] If the 'batting average' of estimative intelligence could be substantially and visibly improved, prevention of violent conflict within and between states could become subject to a more technocratic form of governance, and intelligence would become part of foreign policy as risk management as sketched by Paul Stares.[11] However, the authoritativeness of estimative intelligence is likely to remain limited for three reasons.

Firstly, even achieving reasonably accurate and timely situational awareness by answering the most relevant 'what, when, where and who' questions is very difficult.[12] Answering the 'why question' requires not just a correct assessment of the threat group's true intentions and strategies, but also an understanding of the complex interplay of different types of foreign and transnational actors, including the past motivations and future intentions of the analysts' own most senior consumers. Estimative intelligence requires an even more difficult assessment of what is likely, unlikely or at least possible to happen in the next days, weeks or years. It may help analysts to assume as a starting point that tomorrow's policies resemble those of today, that trends will continue, and transformative events remain rare. Identifying the right comparator and statistical baseline tends to increase forecasters' batting average as Tetlock and others demonstrated. Forecasting accuracy can be further improved by only asking questions that can reasonably be answered and avoiding those that cannot. However, international relations do at times witness periods of accelerated history when unprecedented large-scale events occur within a short space of time, trends culminate and drastically reverse as they reach tipping points, when institutions and political ideologies get transformed and new equilibria are established. Rapid change can come as a surprise even for some of the involved actors in the case of social protests, whereas surprise attacks are the result of strategic and purposeful action. It is the accurate and timely anticipation of these discontinuities, rather than achieving a high forecasting average, that is of the greatest importance to decisions-makers.

The second reason for the limited epistemic status of estimative intelligence lies in the secrecy of some of its most valuable collection methods and the products themselves, even if based on open sources. The need for such secrecy largely explains why governments invest in foreign intelligence as their own dedicated knowledge function rather than relying on outside expertise. If potentially hostile or harm-causing actors knew about the sources, methods and analytical judgements, it would enable them to exclude or kill informants, avoid compromised communication channels, and neutralise or evade any governmental actions designed to thwart their plans. In contrast to terrorist groups or hostile foreign governments, a virus does not seek to keep its intentions secret and it makes no difference whether it knows which methods scientists use to study it or what response governments are planning to combat it. This is why intelligence products are more restricted in their distribution than other knowledge products, even when they are largely based on open sources. An inescapable downside of these restrictions on transparency, public and parliamentary scrutiny and cross-national collaboration is that improvements in the analytical performance of intelligence producers are more difficult to achieve, verify and communicate beyond the narrow circle of the end users.

Finally, there is far less agreement on 'what works' in foreign, security and defence affairs as compared to interventions in other policy areas. This matters because intelligence and particularly diplomatic reporting needs to be policy-relevant even if it does not contain explicit recommendations of what to do (or not do). It may be relatively uncontroversial to expect that all mature and imminent plans for terrorist attacks based on normally reliable evidence should be thwarted, but most emergent threats in foreign affairs are far less straightforward. In fact, even with the benefit of hindsight, it is often not clear what the right decision to high-quality intelligence should have been as alternatives would require the consideration of a wider range of factors as well as some counterfactual reasoning as foreign actors may also react differently to changes in governments' change in position. Furthermore, foreign and security policy requires a range of difficult value judgements, trade-offs and uncertainties about unintended consequences.[13] Sometimes policymakers realise that they do not have any realistic option to stop a crisis from happening or find that the available options are either politically not feasible or come with too high opportunity costs, for instance, about threatening and using military force. Not all crises have only or overwhelmingly negative consequences. Some can offer potential upsides or opportunities. The Arab uprisings toppled some authoritarian, corrupt and human rights violating regimes. Russia's aggression in Ukraine united European leaders around a usually highly divisive issue whilst Ukraine tilted firmly West. Policymakers preserve a substantial degree of discretion to prioritise a particular threat above others and may have good grounds to reject recommended actions. This does not mean that the decision-maker can reject any warning nor that normative judgements of foreign policy choices and learning from mistakes are not possible. However, evaluating these decisions requires a different set of criteria related to good judgement in foreign policy.

Therefore, anticipatory foreign policy and estimative intelligence will require for the foreseeable future a mixture of 'science' through the use of databases, models and theories, 'craft' as analysts acquire knowledge of analytical techniques such as scenario planning, and 'art' as practitioners' individual dispositions, talent and skills matter and benefit from experience.[14] A normative model of evidence-based policy would not be appropriate and we propose instead the following four normative principles for how the intelligence-policy nexus should work in foreign policy: (1) **Well-informed** relates both to the quality of the production process behind estimative intelligence as well as to the receptivity of decision-makers to well-evidenced analysis of future threats and opportunities from authoritative internal and external sources. (2) **Anticipatory** does not mean that all future harm can be easily predicted or prevented, only that governments should aim to live up to their strategic and policy commitments with regard to pre-emptive, proactive, preventive and resilient foreign policy.[15] It means that knowledge producers ought to invest a minimum degree of effort into the investigation of consequential and potentially threatening futures, whilst decision-makers should ringfence a minimum degree of bandwidth to engage with such futures and high-quality warnings as doing so is more cost-effective and less harmful than managing and recovering from crises. (3) **Collaborative** does not deny significant asymmetries between and inevitable tensions within the relationship between civil servants and decision-makers but posits that mutual respect and understanding of one another's distinct roles, duties, requirements and limitations is central to reaching sound analytical judgements about future threats as well as mitigating politicisation pressures. (4) **Reflexive** means that all participants in the policy process need to be committed to regular questioning and learning from their past performance. Clearly, there are limits as to how frequent and resource-intensive such learning processes can be, but a reflexive attitude should be part of the culture of the key involved organisations and an integral part of standard operating procedures of the process itself. This can take the form of formal post-mortems or 'critical case' or 'incident reviews' after events, or more informal and ongoing forms of learning from internal or external critiques of prevailing assumptions, preconceptions and causal beliefs. Willingness to learn is also central to techniques for picking up weak signals from

Table 1.1 Performance expectations for analysts and decision-makers

			Performance Criteria
Knowledge producers			Accuracy
			Timeliness
	Reflexivity		Convincingness
Decision-makers			Due attention and prioritisation
			Openness to inconvenient knowledge claims
			Deference to superior expertise

Source: Revised from Ikani et al., 2020.

'covered' as well as 'uncovered environments and avoiding critical blind spots.[16]

If we break this down even further in Table 1.1 above, we propose that knowledge producers as well as decision-makers can be measured against seven performance indicators. Even though three of these criteria apply primarily to either knowledge producers or decision-makers respectively, it is important to recognise their interdependence. The extent to which decision-makers can be held accountable depends on the convincingness of the intelligence they have received. But equally, intelligence analysts may attribute delays, hedged or unclear warning intelligence to inaccessible, disinterested, hostile or even vindictive decision-makers and the culture they create within an organisation. Reflexivity should be expected from both producers and consumers of intelligence and should ideally involve processes of learning during and after episodes of surprise involving them both given the interdependence referred to above. Practitioners should reflect in regular intervals on which threats and risks need to be monitored by agencies or organisations to avoid weak signals being missed or misinterpreted.

Accuracy

Asking whether knowledge producers reached accurate judgements about threat aspects that mattered is an indispensable and undisputed component of post-mortems involving a degree of surprise. It is necessary to test whether decision-makers should have been surprised about a given threat event if, in fact, they had been provided with (largely) accurate assessments of key aspects of it. Moreover, all knowledge producers ought to aim for maximum accuracy in their analytical judgements as inaccurate threat assessments can lead to costly mistakes. This is in practice far from straightforward: a 'definitive' measure of the accuracy of predictions and forecasts[17] is often illusive as such claims may be expressed in vague, hedged or highly uncertain ways and at various points in time in relation to a given event. Even when assessments are clearly articulated, they may come with variable probability estimates that are hard to pin down for the purpose of judging accuracy. One might argue that the difference between a 5 per cent and a 40 per cent probability for a worst case scenario should matter to policymakers even if both are still not 'likely', but what about smaller differentials? Furthermore, one should be cautious about inferring a good analytical process from accurate assessments or vice versa.[18] Analysts can be right in their conclusions for the wrong reasons as errors of over- and underestimation of risks can cancel each other out or unforeseeable chance events intervene as to influence outcomes. Jervis distinguishes between type 1 errors of inaccurate analytical claims but having followed a sound intelligence process, and type 2 errors where accuracy errors could well have been avoided with better processes of information collection and analysis.[19] Therefore, while assessments of accuracy are necessary and important, they should just be the starting point to consider whether practitioners were performing in line with prevailing professional expectations ('craft') and outside expert insights ('science') in how they gathered and analysed information. To what extent have any shortcomings in this regard affected the accuracy of the analytical judgements? Could any shortcomings be explained or excused by some of the enabling or hindering factors discussed in the next section such as county experts in relevant positions, or the level of difficulty of the diagnostic challenge? For instance, while anticipating surprise attacks could be considered particularly challenging given secrecy and deception, other types of dynamics relating to mass atrocity risks or migration can be assessed in probabilistic terms on a more reliable epistemic basis.

Timeliness of Estimative Intelligence

The accuracy criterion is closely related to the criterion of timeliness of intelligence at the moment when it is brought to the attention of relevant decision-makers. Especially in cases of bottom-up or slow-burning phenomena rather than surprise attacks, it is often easier to arrive at a more accurate and confident assessment of a threat if one waits for more signals and indications from an evolving situation, for instance, human rights violations or public protests exceeding country-contingent 'normal' levels. However, both deliberate waiting as well as unintentional delays can come at a high cost, so it is crucial for the analyst not to be overtaken by events and to provide assessments early enough to maximise options and minimise risks for decision-makers.[20] Some policy instruments such as financial aid targeted at some root causes of conflict, or for example the forging of links with the newly important political actors after the Arab uprisings, require a significant amount of time to take effect. Moreover, some instruments such as the deployment of peacekeepers, election or border monitors require a minimum degree of lead time as many of these assets are not on stand-by but require contributions from member states and the delegation of relevant personnel from their normal line of work. Warning intelligence that arrives too late for such key instruments will have lost some or all of its usefulness to decision-makers. The need for timeliness applies most strongly in cases involving fast-paced developments. Strong liaisons between intelligence and policy departments can enable the former to provide relevant and timely intelligence to inform policy decisions.[21] The greatest challenge here is a rigidity of information processing lines, which can slow down or hinder the formulation of policies that correspond to the new realities on the ground.

Convincingness of Intelligence

One of the less examined aspects of the strategic surprise literature is the need for estimative intelligence in general and warnings in particular to be communicated in a way that is likely to be understood and believed by the decision-makers it is addressed at. It needs to convince them about the probability, impact and relevance of a threat and should significantly increase the chance of being acted upon to prepare, prevent or mitigate. The ability to convince arises from a combination of factors such as clarity, specificity, fear appeal, authoritativeness, and credibility of the source, and, more generally, the degree to which intelligence is successfully tailored to the 'consumer' in terms of content, evidence used, timing of delivery, channel, format and actionability.[22] The literature does recognise that analytical judgements need to be sufficiently clear regarding their meaning and importance. 'The absence of clarity', wrote Handel, may 'strengthen the tendency of some statesmen to become their own intelligence officer'.[23] The intelligence product thus should have an appropriate form and length, which is digestible for senior decision-makers who are notoriously short of time. While in the absence of certainty cautious warnings are still better than no warnings, the ultimate goal is to provide specific, clear and reliable answers to the 'w-questions'. Intelligence analysts should clearly indicate how confident they are in their judgement, what is known and what is unknown, and what the analyst has inferred.[24] They should not 'purchase' greater persuasiveness through exaggerated confidence along the lines of the notorious statement of former CIA Director George Tenet, who told President Bush there was a 'slam dunk case' that dictator Saddam Hussein had unconventional weapons.[25] They should be as specific as possible about the probabilities underlying analytical judgements. We know from past cases such as the Bay of Pigs invasion that decision-makers can easily misinterpret qualitative terms such as 'fair chance' as success being 'likely' rather than odds of 1 in 3.[26] Gaps between assessments and the knowledge on which they are based should continuously be made explicit.[27] Effective communication requires an analyst to have a good understanding of their country's foreign policy and its overall priorities in a given region. This 'common frame' specifies vulnerabilities and prescribes ways of recognising relevant developments.[28] In addition, the most useful intelligence is based on a high awareness of the pre-existing levels of knowledge, worldviews, hot buttons, agendas and information processing habits of key decision-makers. Furthermore, in the case of warning intelligence as a special case of estimative intelligence, research by Dahl indicates that tactical and more actionable warnings are more likely to be listened to and acted upon.[29]

Due Attention and Prioritisation

Post-mortem exercises need to take capacity restrictions of and priority-setting for intelligence analysis as well as the limited bandwidth of foreign policy systems seriously when judging whether decision-makers have paid enough attention to estimative or warning intelligence. As one former UK official said, policymakers today may have more information at their fingertips than at any previous time in history, but they do not have more time for analysing it – quite the contrary.[30] Furthermore, the number of decision-makers and their cognitive capacity to deal with intelligence has not increased and neither has the capacity of states and international organisations to prevent, mitigate or prepare for international threats. The question to ask is whether the government, in collaboration with the intelligence community, sets the right priorities in allocating limited resources and attention to specific countries, regions or to current and emerging threats? It is true that democratically elected governments should have substantial discretion in how they wish to set such priorities. Nevertheless, it is still possible to conclude that governments have been too preoccupied with the management of current problems and crises and failed to ringfence sufficient attention for considering and potentially mobilising against the threats of tomorrow given their commitments to anticipatory and preventive foreign policy. Furthermore, one could conclude that the intelligence communities' analytical resources were spread too thinly to adequately monitor the most severe threats facing the countries. Or alternatively, that disproportionate resources were concentrated on a specific threat even though other threats were similarly or even more severe. For instance, were German decision-makers right to deprioritise Iraq or were UK politicians right to devote so much attention to counterterrorism compared to Russia? Secondly, the question arises whether intelligence services and decision-makers gave enough attention quickly enough to warnings once they had been noticed at a given point in time and prioritised attention and resources for investigating them when compared to other demands.

This will depend also on how well evidenced, communicated and supported any warning intelligence was in a specific case.

Openness to and Interest in Inconvenient Intelligence

The openness to having one's existing beliefs challenged is widely recognised in the literature as a virtue of intelligence analysis in general and estimative intelligence about surprising and potentially threatening futures in particular. The lack of such openness to politically convenient intelligence together with an excessive culture of consensus are also frequently noted vices in post-mortems. As Jervis wrote about the case of Iraq, once the view was established that the country was producing weapons of mass destruction 'there not only were few incentives to challenge it, but each person who held this view undoubtedly drew greater confidence from the fact that it was universally shared'.[31] Intelligence producers therefore need to remain open to complexity and countervailing evidence and remain ready to challenge the conventional wisdom regardless of the social pressure for conformity. Similar biases towards pre-existing beliefs and group consensus can also be found at decision-maker level, but further magnified by politicisation pressures. Yet, we should expect decision-makers, whether as individuals or in groups, to at least seriously consider high-quality and consequential warning intelligence regardless of whether it is highly inconvenient politically. This expectation does not infringe on lawmakers' rights to challenge the evidence and analysis or to robustly interrogate the expert officials. However, we should expect that office holders should refrain from deliberately screening out, discrediting or suppressing intelligence, or the officials who communicate it as we have seen in some cases. They should not succumb to asymmetric receptivity whereby only inconvenient intelligence is challenged or even suppressed whilst convenient assessments get an easy ride or are even actively encouraged. We know from the Chilcot report that the lack of challenge was a problem in the planning for the Iraq invasion.[32] It is inevitable that the intelligence process is affected in terms of focus, pace, resourcing and scrutiny by an issue becoming more salient and contested in the media and the political process – which is commonly understood as politicisation in the literature outside of intelligence studies. However, theses pressure should not lead to undermining the core professional value of analytical objectivity on the part of knowledge producers, whilst decision-makers should not get a free pass for the denial of politically inconvenient advice or a myopic preoccupation with the mediatised threats of today rather than the equally or more severe threats of tomorrow.

Due Deference to Superior Expertise

The expectation that decision-makers should accept intelligence in terms of well-founded and authoritative knowledge claims about a probable future does not interfere with their political prerogative in decision-making about whether to accept such analysis or act on any recommendations that may or may not go with it. Indeed, decision-makers may be considered as experts in their own right as far as questions of political feasibility, public opinion and the weighing up of different options for action are concerned. On occasion some decision-makers may have justified confidence that their own analytical judgements are superior to the advice they are getting, for instance if they themselves have relevant training and experience related to the conflict regions, are able to draw on their own contacts and networks grown over a period of time, or have privileged access to and insights about the thinking of foreign senior decision-makers due to their interactions with them. For instance, the former EU High Representative Javier Solana could draw on extensive knowledge and experience of meeting other leaders as foreign minister and NATO Secretary General. He therefore had some justified confidence into his analytical conclusions, but still regularly sought out and engaged with country experts at relatively junior level to orally discuss and reconsider any assessments, rather than simply defer to the conclusion of any written product. Yet, Solana was arguably the exception that proves the rule given that few politicians in such positions have a comparable track record in foreign affairs. The literature highlights instead the tendency of politicians to overestimate their own knowledge, analytical acumen and judgement,[33] especially when confronted with new threats and countries not regularly covered by quality news media. In such instances, decision-makers should defer to the knowledge claims about alternative futures contained in estimative intelligence produced by authoritative and trustworthy sources with a good track record in their previous assessments. They remain, however, perfectly entitled to reject claims made from a source with known biases or who can be rightly suspected of hidden political biases and motivated by an intent to manipulate. What is not acceptable is any misplaced hubris about one's own knowledge and analytical skills that cannot be justified by training, track record or experience.

Assessing Actors' Performance Before Surprises and their Underlying Causes

As a starting point for post-mortem case studies it is essential to unpack the degree and nature of the surprise. We propose to assess the overall degree of surprise across three dimensions. These are additive to the overall degree but also serve distinct analytical purposes as they each characterise different forms of surprise. The first dimension is the degree of cognitive dissonance caused as a function of the gap between what actors believe to be true in the aftermath of the threat manifestation and their prior beliefs about the threat and potential consequences. The largest scale surprises – Taleb's black swans or the proverbial bolts from the blue – are threats that were not even considered by actors. [34] At the other end of the spectrum are threats that may well have been considered and deemed at least possible, but deemed too unlikely to significantly shift attention, material resources or change policy. In the most extreme case of surprise, actors are likely to feel a sense of cognitive shock and strong pressure to fundamentally transform their threat and risk perceptions, whereas in the mildest version it would entail updating the probability assessments related to the threat. Again, this does not necessarily imply a normative judgement of whether these surprises were or could have been foreseeable as this entails looking at case-specific diagnostic challenges as well as actor-specific capacities and broader political factors, as we discuss in the next section.

The second dimension is closest to the existing writing on strategic surprise in so far as we focus here on the scope of the surprise and draw on the distinction between strategic threat assessment and tactical/operational threat assessment. It is often argued, for instance by Dahl, that strategic intelligence is less difficult than tactical intelligence even though the latter may be more effective for prompting decision-makers to pay attention and act preventively.[35] The question here is how wrong or right actors were across a range of threat-relevant questions: 'who is posing a threat', 'why' and 'under what conditions', 'what are their current and future capabilities', 'what are their concrete plans to do what', 'where and when'.[36] It is relatively easy to identify an actor with hostile intentions, but much more difficult to ascertain when and how such intentions can translate into significant harm (risk assessment). This would also require an accurate assessment of vulnerability of security services or societies to such threats as well as secondary risks that arise from events, such as the immigration of foreign fighters. Even more complicated is the diagnostic challenge for threats that are not emanating from one particular actor, such as a state or terrorist groups, but from bottom-up dynamics of multiple actors, trends and social movements, as was the case with the Arab uprisings. Even if most actors across Europe were not surprised that instability in one North African country could spill over and cause instability in another, they were still surprised about the way it happened, the timing, speed and extent of the spread in the region as well as broader and less immediate consequences for European countries.[37]

Finally, we need to look more closely at the spread of who has been taken by surprise within a political system. While the conventional distinction between analysts and (political) decision-makers is useful, we aim for a more fine-grained assessment for two reasons. Firstly, as mentioned above, foreign policy authority is dispersed in a European context, both at the member state level (for example through coalition governments), and at the European level, where multiple foreign policy institutions co-exist and sometimes overlap. We know for instance that senior decision-makers within EU institutions and the Foreign Affairs Council differed in their level of surprise concerning the events in Georgia in 2008 and Ukraine in 2014.[38] Secondly, many threats are monitored and assessed by multiple parts of the EU machinery and through different techniques, engaging different parts of what might be termed the intelligence community, including diplomats and other officials working on threat-relevant technical issues such as trade, energy and home affairs, especially if threats are not purely military in nature.

It matters whether the sense of surprise was near universal among the most relevant knowledge producers or whether the spread of awareness among either analysts or decision-makers was particularly uneven. Divergences amongst different kinds of analysts or agencies can be expected given differences in sources used, disciplinary backgrounds, analytical methods or informal norms, but could also arise from ways of information-sharing and joint analysis. Another form of an uneven spread in surprise could be seen in divergent perceptions among officials at various hierarchical levels, as senior officials may at times ignore, discount or disbelieve assessments by more junior officials and may thus end up being more or less likely to be surprised by certain threats. Again, this does not mean that those who have been most surprised were necessarily at fault but pinpointing more precisely who was more or less surprised can help to investigate more accurately the potential causes. It helps to arrive at more persuasive judgements, namely whether the observed differences can be partly excused or explained, for instance, by weaker analytical capabilities of an organisation or were rather caused by political signals and administrative cultures hostile to inconvenient analytical judgements.

Once we have accurately ascertained the degree of surprise at the time undistorted by hindsight biases, we need to distinguish between surprises that could or should have been avoided and those that were made substantially more likely by factors that were completely or largely outside of the control of practitioners and organisations. Accountability-focused post-mortems are primarily interested in the correct attribution of blame and (less frequently) praise and thus need to consider systematically factors that should have helped or hindered actor performance at a given moment in time. They need to consider practitioners' formal responsibilities or standards for conduct in office alongside any additional legal criteria for judging gross incompetence, negligence or wrongdoing. Lesson learning-centred reviews such as ours are also interested

Table 1.2 A taxonomy of surprise about security threats

Degree Dimensions	Perfect surprise	Significant surprise	Partial surprise
Dissonance in terms of the recognised gap between event and previous beliefs	Threat not even considered, implies cognitive shock and *belief transformation*	Threat considered, but deemed impossible or very unlikely, implies major *Bayesian belief adaptation*	Threat identified and considered, but considered unlikely, implies slight to moderate *Bayesian belief updating*
Scope in terms of the range of surprising substantive threat characteristics and risks	Threat both strategically and operationally surprising	All the most relevant operational features of the threat are surprising, but strategic notice was available	Some important features of the threat are surprising, strategic notice was available
Spread in terms of who is has been most affected among relevant officials	Entirety of government, analysts and decision-makers	Most analysts and decision-makers	Only some analysts and decision-makers

in factors that either raise or lower expectations of practitioner's performance, but primarily because it might help us to identify the underlying and structural reasons for why performance was lower than could have been expected. Shortcomings in the performance of analysts or leaders are only relevant in so far as they may point to deficiencies in their recruitment, selection, training or oversight or the rules and procedures they were following, not to advance individual critiques or recommend punishments. Indeed, our focus is on improving the foreign policy system as a whole, rather than just looking at one specific part of it, just a specific committee, unit or even specific intelligence agencies. This means also that issues that are outside of the control of practitioners at the time could be addressed in the medium and long term through shifts in resources, better training or changing cultures. As illustrated in Table 1.3 two types of factors can be considered as usually outside of the control of governments and as such common ground for both accountability and lesson learning-focused post-mortems: case-specific diagnostic difficulties and situational factors.

Firstly, the ability of knowledge producers to anticipate certain events is constrained by the *diagnostic difficulty of the case at hand*, which itself is a function of several factors: What is the degree of discontinuity the event poses with the status quo ex ante? Human beings tend to take a linear view of the future, perceiving it as an extrapolation of present trends. And while most future occurrences can indeed be extrapolated from the present, for example in the field of climate change, the most impactful events are often non-linear, black swans or bolts from the blue.[39] The anticipation of such events poses diagnostic challenges to the intelligence analyst as envisioning a multiplicity of futures, their possible consequences, and their threat levels requires often costly out-of-the-box thinking. Efforts to boost 'imagination' through asking 'what if-questions' can help if used sparingly and within a process that ensures impact and follow-up. The massive ripple effects across the Middle East of the self-immolation of Mohamed Bouazizi on 17 December 2010, causing uprisings in multiple Arab countries and even civil war, led to a series of events that required expertise, research as well as imagination to forecast accurately, even though experts had known for years that countries like Tunisia and Egypt were powder kegs.[40] Cognitive simplification – namely making sense of complex patterns by simplifying and filtering them into familiar frames, patterns and stories – exacerbates this difficulty of anticipating large breaks with the status quo.[41] Surprise-sensitive forecasts of emerging threats are very resource-intensive as it requires manpower to distinguish weak signals of change from the noise of masses of routine reporting and data. Another objective diagnostic difficulty arises from the complexity and speed of threat dynamics as well as the difficulties of obtaining information about geographically remote and underdeveloped countries or regions. For instance, one of the most surprising features of the genocide in Rwanda was the sheer speed of the killing combined with the challenge of getting reliable information from remote parts of the country.[42] In the case of Ukraine, it was difficult to gauge the military situation on the ground in Crimea in February and March 2014, or to even identify an unambiguous casus belli.[43] The combination of deception and the spread of false information surrounding the invasion of Crimea meant that the factual

Table 1.3 Factors affecting expectations for intelligence production and use

Factors at play	Lowering expectations	Raising expectations
Case-specific features	• High degree of novelty, namely little to no recent precedence of threat • Unusually fast speed of dynamics on the ground • High degree and novelty of secrecy and deception tactics by hostile actors	• Similar threats have manifested themselves recently or in geographic proximity • Crisis/threat develops at expected or slow pace • Hostile actors are known and have used previous tactics in secrecy and deception before
Situational factors	• High degree of distraction from more salient foreign or domestic threats and risks • Instability of government or senior leadership at the time • High degree of politicisation of foreign policy issues	• Significant/routine bandwidth available given no unusual distractions from other crises • Stability of government or senior leadership at the time • Low degree of politicisation of foreign policy issue/threat

threshold evidence of Russian actions in Crimea had to cross was high.[44] Although deception is as old as warfare itself,[45] Russia's ability to 'merge the overt and the covert' in combination with its so-called 'information operations' underlines how modern threats have changed.[46] This ties into another complicating factor, namely the degree of credibility of both sources and experts when flagging threats, which is affected by previous communications. Georgia faced this problem in 2008, when Western governments' receptivity suffered from Georgian sources' reputation for 'crying wolf'.[47]

Secondly, *situational factors* can create a political environment that greatly impacts both intelligence production and receptivity to it. Power transitions in government or major personnel changes in intelligence production have the potential to distract both decision-makers and analysts. Additionally, decision-makers routinely deal with various crises and issues simultaneously. The Ukraine crisis, for example, played out when EU capitals were already being overwhelmed by the global financial crisis, the eurozone crisis, the aftermath of the Arab uprisings and the rise of ISIS. Such agenda competition may impact receptivity to intelligence. What is more, decision-makers are, like intelligence analysts, human beings who struggle cognitively with entertaining multiple hypotheses and scenarios at the same time.[48] Meanwhile, even though both decision-makers and analysts may to some extent be distracted by either foreign or domestic crises, we should expect a degree of ringfencing of resources for anticipating and responding to upstream problems as discussed above. Moreover, warnings about a certain threat may thus become subject of intense politicisation within the government or between government and opposition. Political conflict and contestation thus can impact receptivity to intelligence, but also the way in which the intelligence is interpreted and used.

Identifying Underlying Causes of Failures and Shortcomings

In the following we will discuss some of main categories of factors that negatively affected performance of intelligence and foreign policy according to the literature and our own research into the three European polities (as listed in Table 1.4).

Information, Research and Expertise Deficiencies

Insufficient information: A key problem for intelligence analysis of any kind concerns the availability of and access to data. Particularly in volatile security contexts it can be very difficult for intelligence collectors to gather confirmed and reliable information. Similarly, in rapidly changing contexts – such as during escalating conflicts – it can be sheer impossible to validate or verify contradictory information. The challenge here is to distinguish between difficulties that are inherent to the case or the diagnostic challenge, those that arise from a lack of resources and collection capacities, and those that arise from inertia and unwillingness to work with the collection tools available and to regularly update and expand their utility, for instance in relation to analysing digital information from social and news media. Comparison with other, similarly well-resourced intelligence agencies working on important threats can help to establish benchmarks of information collection and sound analysis. It may be that a lack of mandate and questionable

Table 1.4 Common underlying causes of performance problems

Type of factors	Type of cause	Manifestations of cause
Primarily among intelligence producers	Information, research and expertise deficiencies	Insufficient resources and prioritisation for information collection from the ground, especially related to important regions, communities or actors
		Insufficient and out-of-date use of information sources, including over-reliance on secret intelligence over open sources from the ground
		Insufficient country experts in the right places and complemented by generalists despite sufficient funding or experts 'in the system'
	Inter- and intra-organisational pathologies	Not enough interaction among staff in functionally dependent but autonomous departments, leading to creation of silos, blind spots and reduced ability to 'connect the dots' between foreign actors and across borders
		Gaps in communication and understanding between HQ and local embassies, delegations and missions
		Inadequate ringfencing of attention due to organisational reforms or competing crises
	Motivational biases	Significant resistance to seeing failures or counterproductive effects of own actions and policies
	Cognitive biases	Resistance to knowledge claims that counter policy preferences in their action-implications
	Professional-cultural biases	Western-statist bias in analysis, which misunderstands real power structures and dynamics in non-Western states and communities cutting across state boundaries
Decision-makers	Intel-politics nexus	Leadership style/hierarchical culture discourages inconvenient truth-telling by civil servants
		Problem of compromised/suspicious warning sources, potentially through self-politicisation/polarization
	Decision-making processes	Lack of clarity about who is responsible for acting (or not acting) on warnings at senior official and political level – no explicit mandate for timely warning
		Too little delegation of decision-making authority creates bottleneck problem and long delays for dealing with upstream problems
		Insufficient attempt to anticipate scenarios and contingencies, especially for high salient cases

prioritisation of threats, countries and actors are the root causes of the collection problem.

Actors on the ground: Having government officials on the ground, like military commanders of field missions, can both be an asset and a liability. Insights from the field are useful because the actors can witness developments first-hand and can talk one on one with stakeholders. This allows intelligence officers to better and in a timelier manner gauge a country's situation, anticipate the next developments and identify risks for their own government. Moreover, we know that evidence from one's own diplomats and analysts in the field is particularly valued by consumers of intelligence and can increase the credibility and convincingness of intelligence, particularly warning intelligence.[49] In contrast, local actors with potentially highly valuable information can appear to Western analysts and decision-makers as politically biased and their warnings are unduly discounted. But there are also risks regarding Western sources of intelligence from the ground. Some, such as mission commanders, can suffer from a loss of analytical sharpness arising from being in the midst of an operation. The associated operational pressures can increase the risk of biases and of producing inaccurate (or wishful thinking) intelligence products. Over time, country experts may become insensitive to weak signals and complacent about their existing information networks rather than updating them regularly. Yet, the more common error is not having any or enough intelligence from country experts on the ground for non-excusable reasons (excusable reasons are budget shortages or the lack of access due to security concerns). This tends to lead to significant information gaps, reliance on unconfirmed reports, and analytical misjudgments.

Under-utilisation of open-sources: The literature as well as our fundings indicate a tendency of intelligence agencies to overlook valuable open-source information, because they favour focusing on and prioritising secret sources instead. This bias is partly understandable because using exclusive information helps intelligence agencies to add value to their analysis compared to what is in the public domain. Furthermore, the material provided by secret sources is generally more easily verifiable by government analysts than that from open sources that will often disguise the identity of their sources to protect them from retribution by repressive state or non-state actors. However, over-reliance on secret sources, particularly from within foreign security services, can create an establishment bias and lead to underestimating bottom-up mobilisation and protests through social media and new communication technologies, as we have seen in the Arab uprisings. High-quality open sources such as quality news media or NGOs with contacts on the ground are by nature more diverse in their own information networks, methods and, above all, analytical perspectives. As such, they can not only help to fill gaps in situational awareness of what is happening in hard-to-reach places or in fast-moving situations, but they may also challenge conventional wisdom and issue warnings. Some NGOs such as the International Crisis Group are well resourced in terms of country experts and sources on the ground, while human rights-focused NGOs collect evidence to a high standard of proof required by courts, and quality news media need to protect themselves against libel and damage to their reputation. Yet, open sources are more variable in the quality of their research and their distinct mandates and perspectives, so they need to be used selectively and with great care to complement as well as challenge information from secret sources.

Country expertise: A frequent cause of poor foreign policy intelligence performance relates to a lack of relevant regional or country-specific expertise. When allocating resources, an organisation cannot be expected to know where the next crisis will erupt, but it can be expected to recruit and allocate country expertise to where it matters most, namely countries and regions of significant importance and/or where ripple or spillover effect due to geographic proximity are greatest. For example, we have seen criticisms, even before the Ukraine crisis, of the UK allowing a substantial decline in Russian speakers and Russia experts in the intelligence–policy interface after the end of the Cold War. Once a crisis emerges, organisations often struggle to provide country desks with extra resources and language-specific expertise, especially if this cannot be re-allocated from other sections. Additional expertise could be brought in through reaching out to external country experts from universities and think tanks, although security vetting and confidentiality requirements can be obstacles to such cooperation. Another way is for intelligence agencies and foreign affairs bureaucracies to employ a good mix of generalists, specialists and 'boundary spanners' that mediate between the two. This would ensure that organisations have a 'surge capacity' that can be mobilised, for instance officers with generalist knowledge of conflict analysis and warning who can familiarise themselves quickly enough with new countries to apply their skills and wider comparative perspectives. Specific diagnostic challenges that can easily slip 'off the radar' of narrow country experts are the recent growth of low-burning, cross-country and internationalised conflicts. Such conflicts that cut across borders without being conventional inter-state wars can be easily missed because of compartmentalised country-specific intelligence analysis as was the cases with ISIS and, for different reasons, with the Arab uprisings.

Intra and Inter-Organisational Pathologies

The literature on strategic surprises has rightly highlighted the problem of functional and epistemic silos within organisations getting in the way of the early detection of weak signals and the sharing of information necessary to 'connect the dots'. This was a key shortcoming identified in the 9/11 Commission report as departments responsible for domestic and foreign security were lacking the incentives and standard operational procedures to regularly communicate and coordinate with each other about such boundary risks and threats. Instead, bureaucratic politics and turf wars between organisations can limit such communication and coordination and effectively lead to governmental blind spots in the monitoring of risk signals from 'uncovered environments'. These could arise either from a confusion over who is responsible for a given risk/threat when there is 'mandate overlap', or on the contrary, an attention deficit as certain risks, threats or countries fall into the 'underlap' between intelligence and law enforcement organisations, for instance the foreign fighter problem in the case of ISIS. Another common pathology is the lack of ringfencing sufficient resources for early detection, preparedness and prevention efforts in foreign affairs bureaucracies as virtually all resources are mobilised to meet politically salient problems and crises. For instance, after the terrorist attacks in London, the UK shifted a vast amount of resources and bureaucratic attention to counter-terrorism, thinning out resources and attention to other threats as discussed in the chapter by Rimmer in this volume. Similarly, the administrative pressures of Brexit may have played a role in why the UK national security advisor recommended the suspension of the Threats, Hazards, Resilience and Contingency Committee (THRCC), which potentially hampered the UK's initial response to COVID-19.[50]

Motivational, Cognitive and Professional-Cultural Biases

A strong theme in the intelligence literature about the causes of strategic surprise is motivational and cognitive biases. A good overview of the role of cognitive biases in forecasting such as confirmation, anchoring and recency biases can be found in Horowitz.[51] In our research we found motivational biases particularly in the challenging tasks of a government analyst to keep a critical eye on one's own country's policies and their potential negative repercussions. For instance, Dina Rezk observed that during the Cold War, UK intelligence was overwhelmingly correct about assessments or predictions about Middle Eastern developments, except when it sought to predict the consequences of US or UK policies in the region.[52] Similarly, Paul Maddrell's collective volume concludes that the intelligence community and policymakers share a common view of the world, a form of 'policy consensus'.[53] The work suggests that intelligence products only rarely deviate from this consensus view and thus rarely reach policymakers. For instance, governments may fail to produce or notice early warnings because it is unthinkable for them that a foreign actor whom they have supported within a relationship of convenience could fail. Yet, a policy consensus does not have to lead to failure if measures are put in place to mitigate or compensate for the motivational biases flowing from it. Examples are specialised warning structures with supportive professional norms, processes that solicit and encourage the articulation of minority views, wildcards and challenges or protections for civil servants and whistle-blowers against pressure or punishment from superiors for inconvenient news and warnings. Motivational biases may be rooted in organisational pathologies such as blame-shifting cultures discussed above.

Knowledge producers can also be vulnerable to Western biases in their situational assessments and developing explanations which misses explanations for change in a threat group's intentions and capabilities and underlying vulnerabilities at the local, national or regional level. Western-trained analysts and diplomats often struggle to appreciate where powers really lie in non-Western, developing states. In some of these states, particularly in Africa, it is not necessarily the Minister or the party leaders who hold the authority, but individual tribal or ethnic leaders, the effective leaders of large businesses or criminal organisations, or local war-lords. The easiest or most visible local interlocutors for Western diplomats are often not the most relevant or influential. Similarly, a country's armed forces may look strong on paper as was the case in Afghanistan before the Taliban takeover, but if the loyalty of soldiers lies with their local tribes or religious communities rather than the nation's central institutions, they may actually be weak when challenged. Sometimes it takes analysts with different disciplinary backgrounds, such as anthropology, to better understand how some countries or actors within them work.

Intelligence-Policy Nexus

Supressing inconvenient truths: Poor performance in foreign policy is often caused by decision-makers' lack of receptivity to information that goes against their own preconceptions. In principle, policymakers agree that the intelligence community should provide them with objective findings so that their policies are based on sound, accurate and pertinent information. All too often, however, policymakers want these 'objective' findings to confirm (and not challenge) their policy. This is called the 'intelligence paradox' and often results in leadership styles or hierarchical cultures that discourage inconvenient truth-telling by civil servants, which can lead to foreign political failures.[54] Also, emotions clearly matter in crises responses. Policymakers often follow their 'gut feelings' about an emerging crisis rather than being led by expert knowledge in their judgements. They can also develop outright scepticism of all expert advice after having been confronted with flawed evidence or biased/ suspicious warnings, rather than to seek input from high-quality knowledge producers. For instance, some policymakers tend to reject expertise by think tanks that produce joint assessments with partner institutions abroad due to a fear of a hidden agenda and biased recommendations. Once-reputable expert sources can also experience gradual politicisation and produce compromised warnings. Analysts also respond to signals of disinterest from decision-makers. For instance, analysts may be hesitant to invest analytical effort in a country low on the list of foreign policy priorities as was the case for Iraq prior to the fall of Mosul for German foreign policy elites.

Decision-Making Processes

It is hard to communicate effectively if it is not clear who the main recipient is and, even worse, if there is a strong sense that nothing will come of any warning, because recipients can easily shift the responsibility for responding to someone else. If everyone is responsible to act, no one is. So, one pathology of warning and response arrangements in foreign policy is a system which obscures the responsibility to deal with any intelligence analysis or warnings once issued – both at the senior official as well as the political level. For instance, one former UK official described the UK intelligence community as being great at 'passing the ball, but no one knows whose responsibility the goal scoring is' when it comes to strategic rather than tactical warnings.[55] The problem of defused responsibility can also affect decision-making by committee with representatives from different ministries and with a lack of sufficiently strong coordination at the heart, as in the German system. Highly centralised and joined-up systems may suffer from a bottleneck problem whereby too many important problems chase too few decision-makers who are unable or unwilling to delegate some authority to respond downwards. The results may be long delays leading to outdated intelligence, lost opportunities to act and a constant focus on current crises rather than future ones. A variation of this problem is an unwillingness of decision-makers to ring-fence at least some time for the most important threats, to look ahead, consider contingencies and alternative scenarios. This may be caused by some governments being driven strongly driven by the media in terms of where they allocate attention, leaving hardly any bandwidth for early detection and prevention of threats.

Lesson Learning from Post-mortems

In line with our expectations of reflexive foreign policy, we would expect both intelligence services as well as decision-makers to be committed to learning from their mistakes in order to improve their performance both during a crisis but more realistically after an episode of strategic surprise when staff have more time to reflect on the strengths and weaknesses of their threat anticipation and response. Learning can and should take place through internal mechanisms such as specific meetings, or dedicated committees and structures focused on and specialised in lesson learning and professional development – as we find frequently in defence ministries. Furthermore, learning lessons after crises may happen not just within government, but also at the level of policy communities and societies through mediatised and public debates. The risk with such diffuse and potentially mediatised learning processes is, however, that lessons learned may be too simplistic or easily misapplied to cases they do not fit with. For instance, is the right lesson from the wars in Afghanistan and Iraq that Western military intervention is always futile and counterproductive, or does it have a role to play in cases such as Syria? Was it right to expect President al-Assad of Syria to fall because of what happened previously to authoritarian leaders in Tunisia, Egypt and Libya? Or was it based on a poor analysis of his power basis and options? And did the fall-out between al-Qaeda and al-Zarqawi over the 'butcher of Falluja's' brutality mean that the use of extreme violence by ISIS/Daesh a couple of years later would be counterproductive too? One of the key potential benefits of setting up official, public or expert inquiries after major strategic surprises is to establish more reliably what, if anything, went wrong in the anticipation of and response to the crisis, and to establish what lessons may be drawn from the events that occurred.[56] Such inquiries may be requested by government or the parliament, a tradition most common in the Westminster tradition, or they may be in the form of academic or non-governmental post-mortem investigations.

In the wake of the Arab uprisings and the Ukraine crisis, formal public inquiries have been conducted in the UK and in France.[57]

In Germany, there have been inquiries made in the Bundestag as well as by think tanks closely affiliated to the government.[58] At the international level, institutions such as the World Bank conducted their own analyses of the events, focusing on the socio-economic drivers of the Arab uprisings for example.[59] Inquiries into the causes of the strategic surprises and the way they have been responded to have equally been conducted by civil society organisations.[60] The United Kingdom research council funded a project on learning lessons from the Arab uprisings.[61] At the European level, there has been no formal public inquiry, but the European Commission has equally funded a research project into the causes of the Arab uprisings.[62] There also have been several academic analyses of the European response to both crises, but they do not engage in the same level of fact-finding and reconstruction, prioritising explanations or criticism of the policy response to the crisis.[63]

While the form of such inquiries and investigations may differ widely, they are rooted by a shared normative expectation that (political) systems need to learn lessons from crisis, particularly in the case of strategic surprises. How did it happen we were caught off guard, and how can we prevent it from happening again? Some public inquiries, particularly those in the field of public health or regarding natural disasters, are deemed a major tool to generate policy change, since they are critical for the public release of important documents and testimonies that over the years have revealed the actions of industry and government.[64] The importance of public inquiries and post-mortem studies for the purpose of drawing lessons from crises is indeed often stressed by politicians. Such studies are deemed capable of 'converting specific knowledge and expertise into recommendations to improve governmental performance'.[65] Since the act of fact-finding and of determining the various processes of cause and effect is already quite time-consuming, academic analyses as well as public inquiries frequently relegate short sections on lessons to be learned to the end of their studies. This leads to several problems for the purpose of lesson learning.

First, the identification of lessons in such studies frequently seems like an afterthought. Studies tend to end with a vague and wide-ranging shopping list of potential recommendations, without clear prioritisation and frequently without guidance on how to implement such recommendations.[66] After the 9/11 inquiry, lauded for its recounting of the facts, critics contended the sections on the identification of lessons were very poor. Falkenrath wrote 'the commission makes no real effort to marshal the empirical evidence so laboriously assembled in the body of its report to support its case for reorganising the intelligence community',[67] while others complained that the lessons themselves were not properly based in the empirical findings preceding them.[68] Indeed, there is a broader sense of scepticism in the case of the US, particularly after the Iraq War, that frequent reorganisations of intelligence and foreign policymaking are doing little to improve performance and are rather futile if not counterproductive reactions to deflect blame after alleged failures of intelligence or security policy. In particular, there is scepticism that any kind of rewriting of organigrams, restructuring of agencies and ministries and creating new roles can offer adequate protection against politicisation pressures in the US political system as a much wider quasi-cultural problem.[69] It is therefore important to correctly identify the root causes of performance problems and not allow pressures for accountability and political blame to get in the way of addressing these, rather than engaging in window dressing.

The lack of attention to the identification and learning of lessons presents problems because such lessons and recommendations are generally at a very high risk of being 'left on the shelf' and often fail to make an impact.[70] This is particularly the case, argues Stark, when the lessons identified do not fit the policy reality on the ground, when they need to be further triaged during policy refinement stages, or when they arrive at the 'street level' without local delivery capacity being considered.[71] Decision-makers thus must be able to understand, react and adapt policies in light of new information, while the implementors of the policy on the ground must be able to do the same.[72] Yet if the inquiry or post-mortem is insufficiently aware of the policy agenda and reality on the ground, the way it is organised and programmed, or when there is insufficient clarity on who should implement the recommendations and how, this becomes very difficult.

There may also be strong political resistance to the recommendations, particularly if the lessons identified do not match the policy preferences of decision-makers.[73] Those in charge of post-mortems may have to weigh short- versus longer-term impacts when framing recommendations that are not just technically and financially feasible, but also politically acceptable. If recommendations conflict too strongly with the aims of government and there is insufficiently strong pressure from within parliament and the public sphere, they are frequently not followed up with.[74] On the other hand, post-mortems may decrease the chances of addressing the root causes of a problem if they succumb to self-censorship on the issue of political feasibility. 'Whereas the establishment of postcrisis inquiries is a recurring pattern, their political impact varies significantly. Some commission reports set off substantive policy changes; others end up in the dustbin. In fact, when it comes to enacting meaningful reform, the latter outcome (the dustbin) appears to be the norm.'[75]

There is a second problem that arises from not paying due attention to the identification and learning of lessons. Even after, through a meticulous reconstruction, one properly identifies what went wrong in a given crisis or strategic surprise, and what lessons can or should be learned, the task of learning those lessons still remains. The act of learning is often mistakenly conflated with the identification of lessons. Yet the mere identification of lessons and potential avenues for improvement in public inquiries or in post-mortems does not mean they actually lead to changed behaviour, particularly at the organisational level. Learning, particularly in those situations, is a deliberate act.

In the vast literature on learning,[76] the object of learning varies. Some refer to acquiring new processes and tools which improve performance. Peter May calls this instrumental policy learning.[77] Others have studied the social dimension of learning.[78] Sabatier defines such learning as 'relatively enduring alterations of thought or behavioural intentions which result from experience and which are concerned with the attainment (or revision) of policy objectives'.[79] Organisational learning modifies the doctrines and conventional wisdom that provide 'institutionalized guideposts for action'.[80] Policy structures, or 'if-then-decision rules', are altered as a result of learning. Thus, lessons learned are the construction of doctrines, knowledge or policy responses to future contingencies. In this, a distinction is made between single-loop learning, learning that occurs 'as long as the learning does not question the fundamental design, goals, and activities of their organization' and double-loop learning, which concerns changing fundamental aspects of the organisation.[81] In the literature on learning from public inquiries, Stark concludes that inquiries are most effective at producing instrumental learning – developing specific policy tools – than at enhancing pre-crisis policy systems/producing major policy change. This resonates with earlier work from Argyris on how organisations tend to permit single-loop learning only.[82] Stark adds that inquiries are effective at producing cognitive organisational learning, in which the coherence between views of different actors is improved, enhancing coordination.[83] The more fundamental forms of social and organisational learning, double-loop learning, are complicated in the case of post-mortems and inquiries since there is an inherent tension in their purpose. An important purpose of such inquiries is accountability: to not just establish what went wrong but also, if possible, who is to blame.[84] Yet this seeking of accountability may lead to blame games, which may be at odds with the more pragmatic purpose of inquiries, which is the learning of rational and procedural lessons. In short, there is an important difference between the identification of lessons, and the learning and institutionalisation of those lessons. The identification of lessons is a first step, while their learning requires an implementation strategy that is tailored to the policy reality on the ground, and which requires auditing and follow-up to ensure the lessons have indeed been implemented.

From the research conducted in this volume as well as the body of literature on successful learning from public inquiries, we can draw several conclusions on how post-crisis investigations identify lessons well, to maximise the chances that the lessons are indeed learned and to reduce vulnerability to future threats. The first step is that such investigations must identify the most important cause(s) of underperformance in the case at hand. As our investigations in the cases in this volume have shown, there are many institutions, scholars and NGOs which have studied investigations into these causes. These should be reviewed and assessed. The causes of such strategic surprise may relate to unavoidable issues, for example the wide uncertainty regarding the COVID-19 disease in the early days of the pandemic, especially regarding whether and how asymptomatic people could spread it. But causes may equally point to issues that may be avoidable in the future, such as the neglect of OSINT by almost all governmental actors in the lead-up to the Arab uprisings. Once these are established, it is possible to assess which of these may be most likely to matter in the mitigation of future threats.

Hereafter, post-mortem or post-crisis inquiries should identify as comprehensively as possible the measures, actions or policy changes which may be suited to remedy or mitigate these causes. It is important that investigations start from abstract and strategic options but work towards more programmatic and operational actions. For each of these actions, the investigator must identify the consequences they may have, both intended and unintended, and whether there are particular risks, displacement issues or trade-offs associated with these changes. This needs to be done in addition to an assessment of how feasible the suggested policy changes are, politically and financially. As stipulated before, when recommendations are unfeasible or conflict with aims of government, they are unlikely to be implemented.[85] Of course, it remains possible that 'politics prejudices learning' and that actors that resist the recommendations use mechanisms to delay, dilute or derail calls for reform, or mobilise bias in ways that lead to recommendations being blocked or ignored.[86] Yet by outlining the recommendations clearly, even those with a higher political cost, it is possible to assess whether they are not followed up in the wake of a crisis due to the lack of political will or for other reasons, which could be mitigated.

Some lessons identified and the recommendations that follow may be implemented quickly with limited fiscal and political costs, whereas others may require a more significant investment. The proposed measures need to be accompanied by a prioritisation of measures to be taken which takes this into account. An example of such a prioritisation would be to draw up a matrix that incorporates the urgency and importance of the suggested recommendations, along with an assessment of their likely implementation costs. In addition, for those lessons with the highest priority, it is important to formulate clearly which actors are supposed to drive the learning process, and who is the addressee of that process. Similarly, it is important to outline the timeframe in which learning is expected to take place, and what the best mechanisms are to ensure the organisations learn but also remember these lessons learned. Organisations can only learn through 'encoding individually learned inferences from experience into organizational routines'.[87]

It is important that these recommendations are specific and that they are tailored as much as possible to the policy reality on the ground. The more specific the recommendations, the likelier their implementation success.[88] This also means that it is impossible to consider beforehand who the actors are with the authority, competences or resources to authorise, lobby for or implement these measures. The literature indeed suggests that issues and actors 'beyond the inquiry room and the corridors of central government' are crucial to successfully implementing any changes and may play a crucial role in avoiding future failure.[89] Recommendations need to be formulated in a way that they are equally relevant to practitioners on the ground and may need to include suggestions regarding their delivery capacity to actually implement the suggestions.

Notes

1. This chapter builds on, substantially revises and expands the theoretical framework developed in Nikki Ikani, Aviva Guttmann and Christoph O Meyer, 'An Analytical Framework for Postmortems of European Foreign Policy: Should Decision-Makers Have Been Surprised?', *Intelligence and National Security* 35, no. 2 (2020).
2. Christina Boswell, *The Political Uses of Expert Knowledge: Immigration Policy and Social Research* (Cambridge: Cambridge University Press, 2009).
3. Christina Boswell, 'The Political Functions of Expert Knowledge: Knowledge and Legitimation in European Union Immigration Policy', Journal of European Public Policy 15, no. 4 (2008).
4. Ian Sanderson, 'Evaluation, Policy Learning and Evidence-Based Policy Making', *Public Administration* 80, no. 1 (2002).

5. House of Commons, 'Coronavirus: Lessons Learnt to Date' (House of Commons: Health and Social Care, and Science and Technology Committees, 2021).

6. Christoph O. Meyer, Chiara De Franco and Florian Otto, *Warning About War: Conflict, Persuasion and Foreign Policy* (Cambridge: Cambridge University Press, 2020).

7. Cited in David Omand, 'Reflections on Intelligence Analysts and Policymakers', *International Journal of Intelligence and CounterIntelligence* 33, no. 3 (2020): 475.

8. Philip Tetlock and Dan Gardner, *Superforecasting: The Art and Science of Prediction* (New York: Random House, 2016).

9. For an excellent overview see Corinne Bara, 'Forecasting Civil War and Political Violence', in *The Politics and Science of Prevision: Governing and Probing the Future*, ed. Andreas Wenger, Ursula Jasper and Myriam Dunn Cavelty (Abingdon: Routledge, 2020).

10. Thomas Chadefaux, 'Early Warning Signals for War in the News', *Journal of Peace Research* 51, no. 1 (2014).

11. Paul B. Stares, *Preventive Engagement: How America Can Avoid War, Stay Strong, and Keep the Peace* (New York: Columbia University Press, 2018).

12. Omand, 'Reflections on Intelligence Analysts and Policymakers', 475.

13. Stephen John Stedman, 'Alchemy for a New World Order: Overselling "Preventive Diplomacy"', *Foreign Affairs* 74, no. 3 (1995); Gerrit S. Kurtz and Christoph O. Meyer, 'Is Conflict Prevention a Science, Craft, or Art? Moving Beyond Technocracy and Wishful Thinking', *Global Affairs* 5, no. 1 (2018).

14. Kurtz and Meyer, 'Is Conflict Prevention a Science, Craft, or Art? Moving Beyond Technocracy and Wishful Thinking'.

15. For example: EU High Representative, 'Shared Vision, Common Action: A Stronger Europe. A Global Strategy for the European Union's Foreign and Security Policy' (Brussels: European Union, 2016); Auswärtiges Amt, 'Grundprinzipien Deutscher Außenpolitik' (2019); UK Ministry of Defence, 'Global Strategic Trends', (2018).

16. Avner Barnea and Avi Meshulach, 'Forecasting for Intelligence Analysis: Scenarios to Abort Strategic Surprise', *International Journal of Intelligence and CounterIntelligence* (2020).

17. Mark M Lowenthal, *Intelligence: From Secrets to Policy* (Thousand Oaks, CA: CQ Press, 2019); John Hollister Hedley, 'Learning from Intelligence Failures', *International Journal of Intelligence and*

CounterIntelligence 18, no. 3 (2005); Richard K. Betts, 'Analysis, War and Decision: Why Intelligence Failures Are Inevitable', *World Politics* 31, no. 1 (1978).

18. Betts, 'Analysis, War, and Decision'; Hedley, 'Learning from Intelligence Failures'.

19. Robert Jervis, *Why Intelligence Fails: Lessons from the Iranian Revolution and the Iraq War*, Cornell Studies in Security Affairs (Ithaca, NY: Cornell University Press, 2010), 2–3.

20. Lowenthal, *Intelligence: From Secrets to Policy*; Loch K. Johnson, 'Sketches for a Theory of Strategic Intelligence', in *Intelligence Theory* (Routledge, 2008), 33–53.

21. Johnson, 'Sketches for a Theory of Strategic Intelligence', 47.

22. Christoph O. Meyer, Chiara De Franco and Florian Otto, *Warning About War: Conflict, Persuasion and Foreign Policy* (Cambridge: Cambridge University Press, 2020), 20–39.

23. Michael Handel, 'The Politics of Intelligence', *Intelligence and National Security* 2, no. 4 (1987): 14.

24. Lowenthal, *Intelligence: From Secrets to Policy*, 215.

25. CNN, 'Woodward: Tenet Told Bush WMD Case a "Slam Dunk"' (2004).

26. Tetlock and Gardner, *Superforecasting: The Art and Science of Prediction*, 55. The authors cite the classic work of Richard E. Neustadt and Ernest R. May, *Thinking in Time: The Uses of History for Decision-Makers* (New York: Free Press, 1986).

27. Peter Gill, 'Sorting the Wood from the Trees. Were 9/11 and Iraq "Intelligence Failures"?', in *Strategic Intelligence: Understanding the Hidden Side of Government*, ed. Loch K. Johnson (Westport, CT: Praeger Security International, 2007), 151–68, 159.

28. Arjen Boin, Paul 't Hart, Eric Stern and Bengt Sundelius, *The Politics of Crisis Management: Public Leadership Under Pressure*, 1st edn (Cambridge: Cambridge University Press, 2005), 22.

29. Erik J Dahl, *Intelligence and Surprise Attack: Failure and Success from Pearl Harbor to 9/11 and Beyond* (Washington, DC: Georgetown University Press, 2013).

30. Interview, 11 June 2021.

31. Robert Jervis, 'Report, Politics and Intelligence Failures: The Case of Iraq', *Journal of Strategic Studies* 29, no. 1 (2006): 21.

32. Chilcot Inquiry, 'Iraq Inquiry': http://www.iraqinquiry.org.uk

33. Paul J. H. Schoemaker, 'Forecasting and Scenario Planning: The Challenges of Uncertainty and Complexity', *Blackwell Handbook of Judgment and Decision Making* (2004): 275–6.

34. Nassim Taleb and Mark Blyth, 'The Black Swan of Cairo: How Suppressing Volatility Makes the World Less Predictable and More Dangerous', *Foreign Affairs* 90, no. 3 (2011).
35. Dahl, *Intelligence and Surprise Attack: Failure and Success from Pearl Harbor to 9/11 and Beyond*.
36. George wrote first about the list of journalistic 'w-questions' to ask about an impending threat, such as where, whether, where, when, what, why. See Alexander L. George, 'Warning and Response: Theory and Practice', in *International Violence: Terrorism, Surprise and Control*, ed. Yair Evron (Jerusalem: Hebrew University, Leonard David Institute, 1979), 16–17.
37. Asef Bayat, 'The Arab Spring and its Surprises', *Development and Change* 44, no. 3 (2013); F. Gregory Gause, 'Why Middle East Studies Missed the Arab Spring: The Myth of Authoritarian Stability', *Foreign Affairs* 90, no. 4 (2011); Jeff Goodwin, 'Why We Were Surprised (Again) by the Arab Spring', *Swiss Political Science Review* 17, no. 4 (2011); Intelligence and Security Commitee, 'Annual Report 2011–2012' (London: UK Stationary Office, 2012).
38. Meyer, De Franco and Otto, *Warning About War: Conflict, Persuasion and Foreign Policy*, chapters 8 and 9.
39. Mark M Lowenthal, 'The Intelligence Time Event Horizon', *International Journal of Intelligence and CounterIntelligence* 22, no. 3 (2009): 373; Nassim Taleb and Mark Blyth, 'The Black Swan of Cairo: How Suppressing Volatility Makes the World Less Predictable and More Dangerous', *Foreign Affairs* 90, no. 3 (2011).
40. Tetlock and Gardner, *Superforecasting: The Art and Science of Prediction*.
41. Schoemaker, 'Forecasting and Scenario Planning: The Challenges of Uncertainty and Complexity', 278.
42. Helen M Hintjens, 'Explaining the 1994 Genocide in Rwanda', *The Journal of Modern African Studies* 37, no. 2 (1999).
43. Roy Allison, 'Russian "Deniable" Intervention in Ukraine: How and Why Russia Broke the Rules', *International Affairs* 90, no. 6 (2014): 1260.
44. Ibid.: 1260.
45. Jon Latimer, *Deception in War* (New York: Abrams, 2003).
46. Lawrence Freedman, *Ukraine and the Art of Strategy* (Oxford: Oxford University Press, 2019).
47. *The Economist*, 'Russia and Georgia Rattle Sabres' (30 April 2008).
48. Schoemaker, 'Forecasting and Scenario Planning: The Challenges of Uncertainty and Complexity', 281.

49. Meyer, De Franco and Otto, *Warning About War: Conflict, Persuasion and Foreign Policy*; Florian Otto and Christoph O. Meyer, 'How to Warn: "Outside-in Warnings" of Western Governments About Violent Conflict and Mass Atrocities', *Media, War & Conflict* 19, no. 2 (2016).

50. Simon Walters, 'Revealed: Boris Johnson Scrapped Cabinet Ministers' Pandemic Team Six Months before Coronavirus Hit Britain' (*Daily Mail*, 12 June 2020).

51. Michael C. Horowitz, 'Future Thinking and Cognitive Distortions: Key Questions That Guide Forecasting Processes', in *The Politics and Science of Prevision: Governing and Probing the Future*, ed. Andreas Wenger, Ursula Jasper and Myriam Dunn Cavelty (Abingdon: Routledge, 2000).

52. Dina Rezk, *Arab World and Western Intelligence: Analysing the Middle East, 1956–1981* (Edinburgh: Edinburgh University Press, 2017), 335–6.

53. Paul Maddrell, *The Image of the Enemy: Intelligence Analysis of Adversaries since 1945* (Washington, DC: Georgetown University Press, 2015).

54. For literature on intelligence failures because of policymakers' preconceptions, see also: Richard K. Betts, *Enemies of Intelligence: Knowledge and Power in American National Security* (New York: Columbia University Press, 2007), 51; Robert Jervis, 'Why Intelligence and Policymakers Clash', *Political Science Quarterly* 125, no. 2 (2010): 186; Joshua Rovner, *Fixing the Facts: National Security and the Politics of Intelligence* (Ithaca, NY: Cornell University Press, 2011); Mark A Jensen, 'Intelligence Failures: What Are They Really and What Do We Do About Them?', *Intelligence and National Security* 27, no. 2 (2012); Roger Jr. Hilsman, 'Intelligence and Policy-Making in Foreign Affairs', *World Politics* 5, no. 1 (1952); Keren Yarhi-Milo, *Knowing the Adversary* (Princeton, NJ: Princeton University Press, 2014), 230; Uri Bar-Joseph, 'The Politicization of Intelligence: A Comparative Study', *International Journal of Intelligence and CounterIntelligence* 26, no. 2 (2013).

55. Paraphrased from interview, 11 June 2021.

56. Adam Burgess, 'The Changing Character of Public Inquiries in the (Risk) Regulatory State', *British Politics* 6, no. 1 (2011).

57. Sénat, 'Rapport D'information No 585 Au Nom De La Commission Des Affaires Étrangères, De La Défense Et Des Forces Armées (1) Sur Le Renforcement De La Fonction D'anticipation Stratégique Depuis Les Livres Blancs De 2008': http://www.senat.fr/rap/r10

-585/r10-5851.pdf; UK Parliament, 'British Foreign Policy and the "Arab Spring", Foreign Affairs Committee – Second Report, House of Commons, 3 July 2012; Sénat, 'Rapport D'information Déposé En Application De L'article 145 Du Règlement Par La Commission Des Affaires Étrangères En Conclusion Des Travaux D'une Mission D'information Constituée Le 4 Mars 2015 (1) Sur La Crise Ukrainienne Et L'avenir Des Relations Entre La Russie Et L'union Européenne Et La France' (Assemblée Nationale Constitution Du 4 Octobre 1958 Quatorzième Législature, 2016); House of Lords, European Union Committee, 'The EU and Russia: Before and Beyond the Crisis in Ukraine' (London: House of Lords, 2015).

58. Susan Stewart, 'The EU, Russia and a Less Common Neighbourhood Lessons Reinforced by the Vilnius Summit' (Berlin: SWP Comment, 2014); *Kleine Anfrage Der Abgeordneten Wolfgang Gehrcke, Dr. Diether Dehm, Annette Groth, Heike Hänsel, Inge Höger, Andrej Hunko, Niema Movassat, Dr. Alexander S. Neu, Alexander Ulrich, Kathrin Vogler Und Der Fraktion Die Linke,* 2014; Muriel Asseburg, 'Proteste, Aufstände Und Regimewandel in Der Arabischen Welt' (Berlin: SWP, 2011).

59. For example: Elena Ianchovichina, *Eruptions of Popular Anger: The Economics of the Arab Spring and its Aftermath,* World Bank Mena Development Report (Washington, DC: World Bank Group, 2018).

60. For example: Iffat Idris, 'Analysis of the Arab Spring' (Birmingham: GSDRC, 2016); International Crisis Group, 'Popular Protest in North Africa and the Middle East' (International Crisis Group, 2011); Kenneth Roth, 'Time to Abandon the Autocrats and Embrace Rights. The International Response to the Arab Spring' (Human Rights Watch, 2012); SIPRI, 'Sipri Yearbook 2015 – the Ukraine Conflict and Its Implications' (2015).

61. Florence Gaub, 'Understanding Instability: Lessons from the "Arab Spring". Report for the "History of British Intelligence and Security" Research Project', in *AHRC Public Policy Series* (Arts and Humanities Research Council, 2012).

62. Cordis, 'Political and Social Transformations in the Arab World': https://cordis.europa.eu/article/id/203777-drivers-behind-the-arab -spring-unveiled

63. Gergana Noutcheva, 'Institutional Governance of European Neighbourhood Policy in the Wake of the Arab Spring', *Journal of European Integration* 37, no. 1 (2015); Tanja Börzel, Assem Dandashly and Thomas Risse, 'Responses to the "Arabellions":

The EU in Comparative Perspective – Introduction', ibid.; Edward Burke, 'Running into the Sand? The EU's Faltering Response to the Arab Revolutions', *Centre for European Reform: Policy Brief* (2013); Richard G. Whitman and Ana E. Juncos, 'The Arab Spring, the Eurozone Crisis and the Neighbourhood: A Region in Flux', *JCMS: Journal of Common Market Studies* 50 (2012).

64. Christoph O. Meyer et al., 'Learning the Right Lessons for the Next Pandemic: How to Design Public Inquiries into the UK Government's Handling of Covid-19' (London: King's College London, 2020), 9.

65. Charles F. Parker and Sander Dekker, 'September 11 and Postcrisis Investigation: Exploring the Role and Impact of the 9/11 Commission', in *Governing after Crisis*, ed. Arjen Boin, Allan McConnell and Paul 't Hart (Cambridge: Cambridge University Press, 2008), 261.

66. Ibid., 264.

67. Richard A. Falkenrath, 'The 9/11 Commission Report: A Review Essay', *International Security* 29, no. 3 (2005): 187.

68. Richard A. Posner, *Preventing Surprise Attacks: Intelligence Reform in the Wake of 9/11* (London: Rowman & Littlefield, 2005), 12.

69. Rovner, *Fixing the Facts: National Security and the Politics of Intelligence*; Paul R Pillar, *Intelligence and US Foreign Policy: Iraq, 9/11, and Misguided Reform* (New York: Columbia University Press, 2011).

70. Alastair Stark, 'Left on the Shelf: Explaining the Failure of Public Inquiry Recommendations', *Public Administration* (2019).

71. Ibid.; Dominic Elliott, 'The Failure of Organizational Learning from Crisis – A Matter of Life and Death?', *Journal of Contingencies and Crisis Management* 17, no. 3 (2009).

72. Chris Argyris and Donald A. Schön, *Organizational Learning*, Addison-Wesley OD Series (Reading, MA: Addison-Wesley, 1978).

73. Claire A. Dunlop, 'Pathologies of Policy Learning: What Are They and How Do They Contribute to Policy Failure?', *Policy & Politics* 45, no. 1 (2017).

74. Sandra L. Resodihardjo, 'Wielding a Double-Edged Sword: The Use of Inquiries at Times of Crisis', *Journal of Contingencies and Crisis Management* 14, no. 4 (2006); Sandra L. Resodihardjo, *Crises, Inquiries and the Politics of Blame* (London: Palgrave Macmillan, 2019).

75. Parker and Dekker, 'September 11 and Postcrisis Investigation: Exploring the Role and Impact of the 9/11 Commission', 255.

76. For a comprehensive overview and analysis of this body of literature, see Claire A. Dunlop, Claudio M. Radaelli and Philipp Trein,

Learning in Public Policy: Analysis, Modes and Outcomes (Cham: Springer International Publishing, 2018), doi:10.1007/978-3-319 -76210-4; Colin J. Bennett and Michael Howlett, 'The Lessons of Learning: Reconciling Theories of Policy Learning and Policy Change', *Policy Sciences* 25, no. 3 (1992).

77. Peter J. May, 'Policy Learning and Failure', *Journal of Public Policy* 12, no. 4 (1992).

78. Peter Hall, 'Policy Paradigms, Social Learning, and the State: The Case of Economic Policymaking in Britain', *Comparative Politics* 25, no. 3 (1993).

79. Paul A. Sabatier, 'An Advocacy Coalition Framework of Policy Change and the Role of Policy-Oriented Learning Therein', *Policy Sciences* 21, no. 2/3 (1988): 133.

80. John Lovell, '"Lessons" of U.S. Military Involvement: Preliminary Conceptualization', in *Foreign Policy Decision Making: Perception, Cognition, and Artificial Intelligence*, ed. Donald A. Sylvan and Steve Chan, New Dimensions in International Studies (New York: Praeger, 1984), 134.

81. Chris Argyris, 'Single-Loop and Double-Loop Models in Research on Decision Making', *Administrative Science Quarterly* 21, no. 3 (1976): 367.

82. Ibid.

83. Alastair Stark, *Public Inquiries, Policy Learning, and the Threat of Future Crises*, 1st edn (Oxford: Oxford University Press, 2018), 10.

84. Arjen Boin, Allan McConnell and Paul 't Hart, *Governing after Crisis: The Politics of Investigation, Accountability and Learning* (Cambridge and New York: Cambridge University Press, 2008).

85. Resodihardjo, 'Wielding a Double-Edged Sword: The Use of Inquiries at Times of Crisis'; Resodihardjo, *Crises, Inquiries and the Politics of Blame*.

86. Alastair Stark, 'Left on the Shelf: Explaining the Failure of Public Inquiry Recommendations', *Public Administration* (2019): 609.

87. Jack S. Levy, 'Learning and Foreign Policy: Sweeping a Conceptual Minefield', *International Organization* 48, no. 2 (1994): 287.

88. Stark, *Public Inquiries, Policy Learning, and the Threat of Future Crises*, 12; Resodihardjo, 'Wielding a Double-Edged Sword: The Use of Inquiries at Times of Crisis'; Resodihardjo, *Crises, Inquiries and the Politics of Blame*.

89. Stark, 'Left on the Shelf: Explaining the Failure of Public Inquiry Recommendations'.

2 Surprise, Revisited: An EU Performance Evaluation of the Arab Uprisings

Nikki Ikani

Introduction

Most actors and commentators across the West were caught by surprise when anti-government protests started in Tunisia and then spread across the Middle East and North Africa in the winter of 2010–11. The events became known as the Arab Spring, the Arab revolutions or, as will be used in this volume, the 'Arab uprisings'.

This sense of surprise when the uprisings started applies to the institutions of the European Union[1] and its major allies in the region – the US, France and the UK, with their dense network of contacts, embassies and intelligence operatives.[2] Nor, as will be discussed below, did any of the big NGOs or mainstream media working and reporting on the Middle East and North Africa emit clear warnings on the prospect of such an event. Even once the protests started in Tunisia in the third week of December 2010, the rapidly growing discontent in both Tunisia and Egypt initially went largely unreported in Western media as well as in reporting from the big NGOs, some of whom were at the time largely focusing on the impasse in Iraq and the Israeli-Palestinian conflict. This volume, amongst others, asks to what extent and when 'being surprised' is to be expected, and when it indicates failures in intelligence collection, analysis, communication or receptivity. In this chapter it will be argued that only after investigating in detail which characteristics of the Arab uprisings were particularly surprising to the European institutions and to what extent, and whether these degrees of surprise were spread evenly across analysists and decision-makers, is it possible to properly explain why the Arab uprisings were so surprising. In keeping with the aims of this volume, this subsequently serves to identify to what extent the surprising nature of the Arab uprisings, and any potential errors made in anticipating this event by the European Union, were excusable given the complexity and diagnostic difficulty of the Arab uprisings, or whether they point to broader structural problems and shortcomings in the European intelligence-policy nexus.

Such an improved understanding of who was surprised, about what, and when, allows for a better evaluation of the EU's performance. From the crisis-ridden past decade we have learnt that major surprises, inside and outside the realm of foreign policy, produce calls for the identification of lessons. After the Arab uprisings, now a decade ago, official 'post-mortem investigations' evaluating the anticipation of the Arab uprisings indeed have been conducted at the national level.[3] Although such systematic and public post-mortems did not take place at the European level, there have been various scholarly accounts of the way the European institutions, in particular the European External Action Service mobilised its response to the Arab uprisings.[4] The approach to post-mortems taken in this edited volume starts from asking more nuanced questions about the degree, scope and spread of surprise in each of our cases than what is found in the literature. It is argued in this chapter that a focus on understanding the nature of the surprise of the uprisings itself renders such scholarly explanations of why the surprise occurred richer, more accurate and more useful for the purpose of learning lessons. For example, if a surprise was a complete bolt from the blue, explanations might point to the lack of scenario studies or culture of forecasting. When a surprise is at least partially expected, by some analysts, scholars might focus on what organisational factors could explain why potential warnings were unsuccessful. The extant literature offers a wide range of potential causes, as shall be discussed below, but would benefit from a more fine-grained identification of the nature of the surprise. This seems especially important since the explanations of the surprising nature of the Arab uprisings that are put forward in the literature are contradictory, and sometimes too vague or sweeping, especially for the purpose of learning lessons.

Extant Assessments of the Surprising Nature of the Arab Uprisings

In the wake of the Arab uprisings, which started in Tunisia in 2010, a variety of studies has been developed in the literature on why the uprisings came as such a surprise. This literature can be divided into a few strands. A first strand identifies a fundamental lack of knowledge as a root cause for this surprise. It argues that commentators and academics greatly overestimated the continuity of the regimes, characterised by authoritarian social contracts of state largesse in exchange for acquiescence, reinforced by policies of deterrence.[5] This is argued to be due to several things. First, there was a dominant focus on a so-called 'Arab exceptionalism' from the waves of democratisation that took place elsewhere in the twentieth century.[6] This produced a fundamental lack of knowledge on how the interlinkage of several factors could together produce such an explosive outcome: the long-standing and growing dissatisfaction with corruption, cronyism and nepotism, the erosion of middle-class incomes, increasing media oppression, and rising food and oil prices across the Middle East and North Africa.

Others focus on more specific epistemological errors producing a lack of knowledge. Goodwin for example argues that insufficient expertise about the role of the armed forces in countries like Egypt and Tunisia, and their willingness to defect from the regimes they were serving, played a crucial role in the West's inability to anticipate the events.[7] Others argue that the emphasis on secret information by intelligence services was a root cause of them missing the warning signs. There was limited knowledge on how smaller scale socio-economic upheaval could be galvanised using mobile phones and novel social media technologies, which greatly facilitated the organisation of activists and the spread of the Arab uprisings from Tunisia to Egypt and other countries in the region.[8] By prioritising secret sources over real-time, open-source data, these and other potential warning signs were missed.[9]

Similarly, there is the argument developed by Kuran after the Iranian Revolution.[10] He argued that it is nearly impossible to predict revolutions, because individuals in oppressed societies are very reluctant to air their opinions in public for fear of repercussions. This makes predicting which uprisings may upend the authoritarian systems, and which may not, nigh impossible for outsiders. Preceding the Arab uprisings there had been multiple labour and union strikes Tunisia and Egypt. In 2008, the Gafsa revolts in a small mining town in Tunisia, for example, had spread rapidly across the region over a period of six months before being violently suppressed.[11] In Egypt, there had been the *Kefaya* ('Enough') movement as well as the April 6 Youth Movement which supported an industrial strike in 2008. Yet, none of these various smaller-scale uprisings and movements accelerated as did the events of 2010–11. Kuran's explanation is that there will always inevitably be a lack of knowledge concerning which revolutionary movements develop a revolutionary bandwagon and which do not, because of this 'individual revolutionary threshold' which is impossible to measure or anticipate.

A second strand of explanations as to why the Arab uprisings were so surprising centralises cognitive psychology. It stipulates that because decision-makers and analysts deal with high volumes of often imperfect information, and need to make sense of them quickly, they tend to rely on shortcuts to arrive at important decisions. Yet, in these short cuts, biases may creep in.[12] An example is confirmation bias, when decision-makers tend to seek information that confirms their pre-existing ideas of a situation. A related issue is cognitive dissonance. This refers to situations when individuals hold certain beliefs or ideas and are faced with evidence that runs counter to these beliefs. Rather than changing their mind, which causes stress, individuals tend to initially try to make these new facts consistent with their prior beliefs. New information may be moulded to fit these old beliefs. Diplomats and intelligence analysts working in the MENA may have picked up signals of rising discontent and anger prior to the Arab uprisings. But during most of the lead-up period of the Arab uprisings, the overwhelming focus was on pursuing business as usual. Focused on signing further Association Agreements with its neighbours, and on cooperating with Arab rulers on issues such as energy supplies to the EU or countering radical terrorism, officials 'explained away' or ignored signals of rising discontent, the argument goes.[13]

Finally, and more specifically for the European Union, most studies in EU foreign policy provided accounts of the way the European institutions, in particular the European External Action Service, mobilised their response to the Arab uprisings.[14] Although the anticipation of the Arab uprisings by these institutions prior to the uprisings is not addressed in this body of literature, this body of literature provides several explanations regarding why the EU was caught by surprise by the events. In the first instance, scholars discuss how the EEAS was only just set up in 2010 after the institutional innovations of the Lisbon Treaty, and only became fully operational seventeen days before the Arab uprisings started. For much of 2010, the EEAS was in a difficult stage of recruitment and transition, which consumed much of the agenda of HR/VP Catherine Ashton and her service.[15] Its first few years were rife with teething problems, as foreign policy portfolios had moved from the European Commission to the EEAS, leading to a host of turf wars.[16]

Whilst the surprising nature of the Arab uprisings to Western actors has thus been explained at length in the literature, two issues remain unresolved. First, as emerges from the above, the explanations differ widely and are occasionally contradictory, for example Kuran's explanation that revolutions are always going to be surprising, versus the explanation that the Arab uprisings could have been foreseen had social media been monitored better or had there been better knowledge of the loyalty to the military regimes. Some of the explanations, moreover, are quite sweeping and vague, offering little opportunity to learn lessons. What were the precise effects of cognitive dissonance or rationalisation on the process of anticipating the Arab uprisings in 2010? What could a closer monitoring of social media have prevented?

Second, throughout these studies, the focus is on explaining this occurrence of surprise. They raise hypotheses on why various global actors, not just the EU, were caught by surprise by the Arab uprisings as they started in Tunisia in December of 2010. This chapter aims to complement this scholarship by focusing on a step it argues should precede such explanations, namely a thorough investigation of the strategic surprise itself: was everyone in the institutions surprised? If not, who was surprised and who was not? And about which parts of the uprisings precisely? Its occurrence in general, or more specific tactical elements such as its exact timing? What was it about the evolution of the threat or development that made it so surprising? And also, how big was the gap between beliefs and expectations before its occurrence and after?

Method

This chapter thus investigates the nature of and the degree of surprise with regard to the Arab uprisings through the application of the analytical framework for conducting post-mortems of EU foreign policy developed in Chapter 1. It does so for a select group of EU institutions preoccupied with the EU's foreign policy towards the MENA region: the European External Action Service (EEAS), its predecessor DG RELEX, the Commission DG focused on (inter alia) the Southern Neighbourhood (DG NEAR) and finally the EU Intelligence Centre (INTCEN), including the EU Military staff's intelligence. The uprisings and political openings enveloped a multitude of countries, which had widely different trajectories after 2011. In some, incumbent regimes were removed, in others they remained in place. In Syria, a full-blown civil war emerged.[17] This study does not aspire to cover all these countries and trajectories. Due to the particular focus of this study on the stage just preceding the Arab uprisings, as well as the very early stages of the Arab uprisings, the geographical scope of this study falls mainly on Tunisia, where the uprisings started in December 2010, and Egypt, where President Hosni Mubarak resigned on 11 February 2011.

The analytical framework developed in Chapter 1 disaggregates the notion of surprise into different kinds and degrees, and equally assumes that surprise may differ significantly among as well between analysts, policy planners and decision-makers. In Chapter 1, surprise is defined as the degree to which an actor recognises that recent or current high-impact events contradict pre-existing assumptions, analytical judgements and expectations. As outlined there, surprise consists of three dimensions: dissonance, scope, and spread. Dissonance refers to the gap between beliefs held before the occurrence of the threat or event, compared to those held after. A perfect surprise occurs when the event was not even considered possible. When the surprise was significant, the threat was considered but estimated very unlikely. A partial surprise consists of a threat which was considered possible, but unlikely. The scope of the surprise refers to which characteristics of the threat were most surprising – its tactical and operational features, the strategic features, or both. The strategic features refer to the long-term and broader assessment of a given threat. Tactical surprise refers to shorter-term, more focused specificities of threat manifestation, prevention and management.[18] Spread, finally, refers to who was taken by surprise: the entirety of government, analysts and decision-makers, some analysts and decision-makers, or most analysts and decision-makers. The empirical part of this chapter maps the dissonance, scope and spread of the surprise regarding the Arab uprisings, mapping for each of these elements whether the surprise was a perfect, significant or partial surprise, and which actors were most affected.

The first step of the research design entailed a reconstruction of the threat evolution in the six months leading up to the Arab uprisings, from June through December of 2010.[19] This reconstruction was built using the best available knowledge today to identify key events, trends and turning points in the period leading up to the Arab uprisings. The main data for this reconstruction came from a Factiva media analysis searching for any warnings by non-governmental actors and high-quality media outlets[20] in the six months leading up to the Arab uprisings. Subsequently I mapped whether, throughout this period, there have been any warnings regarding this threat evolution in the anticipation of the Arab uprisings which may have reached European decision-makers. Meyer, De Franco and Otto define a warning as a communicative act by a persuader (for instance country desk officers or intelligence analysts) intended to raise awareness of an impending threat to values or interests among decision-makers. They are aimed to increase the decision-maker's ability to take mitigating action and include 'knowledge claims' about what is likely to happen, and when. It is 'primarily aimed at influencing a given target's evidential beliefs about a given situation'.[21]

I searched for such warnings emitted or knowledge claims posited by officials working in the European institutions under study here. In addition to archival research on any publicly available documents within these institutions, I interviewed thirty-two policy officials who worked on the MENA region within these institutions during the timeframe under study, including officials in the cabinet of then HR/VP Catherine Ashton, the cabinet of the DG NEAR Commissioner, Heads and Deputy Heads of Delegation and senior officials at the EU delegations in Algeria, Morocco, Tunisia/Libya and Egypt as part of a wider study on learning in EU foreign policy.[22] These were undertaken in two waves in 2015–17 and 2019–20. The interviewees were asked to reconstruct the six months leading up to the Arab uprisings as well as the first phases after the crisis. To avoid ex post rationalisations as much as possible, during the interview the answers and claims of the interviewees were put in the context of a previously created timeline of events and were weighed through corroboration with other interviewees' statements and an assessment of whether written documents supported their assertions. Additionally, to that end, I spoke to at least two officials in every department/institution but the EU Military Staff and presented the interviewees with statements derived from policy documents or responses from other interviewees. I equally conducted a focus group[23] with NGO experts and policy officials working on the MENA in Brussels in 2019. This focus group, which also included member state officials from the UK and Italy working on the region at the time, again was particularly focused on reconstructing the stage just preceding the Arab uprisings as they erupted in Tunisia, as well as the first stages of the uprisings (until the spread to Egypt late January).

Subsequently, I assessed the impact potential warnings may have had at the senior political level. Indicators could be a visible in a shift in attitudes expressed in official statements or in the press, changes in agenda setting, evidence of impact and reaction during committees, summits or in declarations, policies adopted, and action taken.

As identified in Chapter 1, there can be mitigating and aggravating reasons for being caught by surprise. The last section of this chapter therefore discusses the key mitigating factors in the case of the Arab uprisings. I argue that these are case-specific diagnostic challenges, pre-existing relevant capacities for knowledge production and the influence of the prevailing political environment at the time.

Unpacking Surprise: Scope, Dissonance, Spread

Dissonance

From the case study it emerges that the Arab uprisings were not deemed impossible or very unlikely by decision-makers or analysts. One interviewee admits that despite not knowing any of the particulars of when and where: 'we did see [the Arab uprisings] coming. It was unavoidable. Unavoidable because of a lack of dignity. Because of the authoritarian regimes, because of [the age] of the leaders. We knew that all the neighbours were ill. So it was unavoidable.'[24] In the words of another official then working in the cabinet of the DG NEAR Commissioner: 'We always knew that change would come. But we were surprised first by the moment, we were surprised by what triggered it and we were definitely surprised by the kind of avalanche effect that it took.'[25]

Most surprising overall was not the fact that the Arab uprisings took place, but how and when they would, as well as the synergies and potential for spillovers to neighbouring countries the upheaval in Tunisia could engender. Indeed, the scenario of sudden transitions, and even widespread upheavals, had been considered by various institutions occupied with EU policy towards the MENA over the previous years. In an intelligence report produced in 2007 by INTCEN and the EU Military staff intelligence unit called 'Worst Case Scenarios for the Narrower Middle East', a scenario which very much resembled the Arab uprisings had been outlined.[26] The report said that 'social disintegration, or even chaos, are real possibilities in several countries of the region' and that 'most Middle East regimes are politically obsolete. Both the "traditional regimes" (mostly, monarchies) and the remaining representatives of "Arab socialism" have long outlived their usefulness.' The report equally flagged the potential role of social media during such an occurrence, and its potential to facilitate a rapid spread.[27] The existence of this report shows that quite accurate knowledge about the probability of events akin to what became the Arab uprisings had existed in the cobweb of EU institutions. Nonetheless, 'business as usual' continued. As one of the EU ambassadors in the region at the time stated in an interview, the EU external relations leadership did not believe any of the uprisings in the MENA region would gather enough steam to overcome the authoritarian oppression of the ruling regimes: 'I've seen it so many times before. And every time they're able to suppress these [uprisings] and in the end, people don't really revolt. You don't have a real following of the whole population.'[28] EU officials claimed that there even had been more self-immolations in Tunisia in the year prior to Bouazizi's which did not trigger uprisings. Change in the 'apathetic Mediterranean', write Colombo and Tocci, had always gone in the direction of more authoritarian entrenchment, not less.[29] The status quo had always prevailed. In December, after Bouazizi's tragic act, the interviewed officials were expecting the same outcome. During most of the lead-up period scrutinised for this analysis, the EU continued its various 'Association Councils' in order to establish its Euro-Mediterranean agreements with amongst others Morocco, Tunisia, Algeria and Egypt.[30] It was also still actively working on an Action Plan with the Tunisian government three days before the self-immolation of Mohamed Bouazizi in Tunisia on 17 December 2010, which triggered the Arab uprisings.[31] Moreover, the 2007 report was not circulated widely and may well have gotten buried amidst a large number of different reports.[32]

In terms of dissonance, the Arab uprisings were thus only a partial surprise. The fact that the expectations regarding the potential explosiveness of the authoritarian systems in the MENA which existed in several parts of the EEAS, the scrutinised DGs and INTEL were not followed up by policy action has to do with certain mitigating factors, but primarily with the scope and the spread of the surprise, as will be discussed next.

Scope

Pinpointing the scope of the surprise requires us to identify in more detail which characteristics of the Arab uprisings were most surprising. The characteristics of the surprise of the Arab uprisings can be divided into its strategic and operational or tactical features. In terms of the strategic features of the surprise, the long-term assessment of the threat and its likelihood, the Arab uprisings were not a complete surprise. As mentioned previously, expectations regarding the combustibility of the authoritarian regimes did exist, both within the lower ranks of the EEAS and in the Ashton cabinet, as well as in INTCEN. This knowledge was, however, diffuse and scattered around in the European institutions under scrutiny here. It was also frequently tacit. Not specified was how the threat could impact the EU or what action could be taken to better anticipate the events.

To illustrate, there had been a regional meeting of the Heads of Delegation of Egypt, Algeria, Morocco, Tunisia and Libya together with Brussels-based MENA officials in Rabat in 2009, during which a new strategy for the Maghreb and Egypt was on the agenda. During the brainstorming session, it was discussed that the rulers of Egypt, Algeria and Tunisia were seriously ill, and that in Libya there was continuous talk over the succession of Ghadafi. It was established that the medium-term future was highly uncertain.[33] Although according to an EU ambassador present at this meeting the possibility of a revolution was not explicitly raised, there was an explicit discussion about how in five to ten years the political leadership of all the countries they were stationed in (with the probable exception of Morocco) could look substantially different. As they describe:[34]

> [We said] if we talk about a new strategy for the Maghreb, what do we do if we get new governments here? And we looked at each other around the table [. . .] and we said, we wouldn't know what to do. We really don't know. They may disappear. But what will really come? We don't know [. . .] So we made a joke about [how we couldn't even reply to that question]. And that we were just stuck there working on a strategy [projecting] a five to ten years of a vision of what to do in this region [and] we couldn't do anything else but

just fall back on what we knew [and] suppose that this was going to continue.

Yet despite the existence of foreknowledge of the challenges regarding succession and oppression the countries in North Africa faced, both within the European institutions and the member states, almost all short-term operational aspects regarding how the Arab uprisings would manifest and how they could be managed were unknown to the EU and its allies. Particularly surprising tactical features were the fact that the Arab uprisings would start in Tunisia, considered by the interviewed officials as the most stable of the MENA countries; the fact that the military defected from Ben Ali and Mubarak in Tunisia and Egypt; the timing of the uprisings starting in December 2010, the potential consequences of the sequence of events; as well as the probability that the uprisings would spread from Tunisia to other countries in the region. As an official in the Ashton cabinet at the time claims they did foresee an event like the Arab uprisings could happen, [but] 'nobody was in the position to know in advance what would be the trigger. Nobody was in the position to know [the Bouazizi self-immolation] would provoke this in Tunisia.'[35]

Regarding the potential consequences of the uprisings, until very late in the process the EU institutions did not openly share the expectation that the abdication or downfall of Ben Ali in Tunisia was imminent, despite messaging from EUDEL Tunis that 'a point of no return had been reached' at the end of December 2010.[36] To illustrate, on 13 January, when his armed forces refused to use force on its citizens, Ben Ali announced there would be elections in six months and promised not to run for office in 2014. Interviewed EU delegation officials agreed they considered this promise would not quiet down the protests. They briefed Brussels on these findings on 14 January, six hours before Ben Ali eventually stood down. The delegation reported that the atmosphere on the Avenue Bourguiba in Tunis was extremely tense and could escalate fatally, and that the EU should take a stance. This message was relayed live during the Political and Security Committee (PSC) meeting in Brussels which convened that same morning.[37] According to interviewees present both in Brussels and in Tunis at the time of this call, the Delegation warning on the explosive situation in Tunisia was hotly contested in the PSC. French and Italian ambassadors vehemently denied claims that the situation on the Avenue Bourguiba in Tunis was about to escalate. They gave opposite and reassuring messages about the situation in Tunis and the Ben Ali regime.[38] Interviewees at the Tunis Delegation remember being 'shocked' at this strong reaction from two such important EU countries in the region. Later the same day, Ben Ali fled to Saudi Arabia.

The rapid spread of the Arab uprisings from Tunisia to other countries in the region was another major tactical surprise to all interviewees in this study and the focus group. Interviewed officials working on Egypt based in both Brussels and Cairo concede that throughout January, as the protests started to gather force in Egypt, regime change was not anticipated. When asked when they thought a 'tipping point' had been reached, interviewees mention different moments in January.[39] Some officials at the EU delegation in Cairo made an internal, informal bet on 5 February about whether the regime would fall – six days before Mubarak's resignation. Only one delegation official betted that it would.[40] Again, this feature of the surprise was not unique to the EU. The French foreign minister later declared that 'in January, there was nothing in briefings or telegrams to anticipate what is currently going on in the Arab world'.[41]

Upon scrutiny of the forecasts at the time provided in the media, amongst others by the Economist Intelligence Unit or in reports by the International Crisis Group, Human Rights Watch or Amnesty, the spread of the revolutionary movement from Tunisia to other countries in the region was similarly not expected in January of 2011, until well after Ben Ali had fled Tunisia and while the uprisings in Algeria and Egypt were in full force. The Economist Intelligence Unit for example continued to forecast in its briefings that the likely scenario would still be for Mubarak to stand in the 2011 elections until as late as 1 February 2011, days before his resignation and the day he stated he would not stand for re-election.[42]

Spread

Mapping whether the spread of the surprise was universal among the most relevant knowledge producers, or whether it was particularly uneven, is an indispensable first step towards identifying the causes of such surprise, and, potentially, what lessons can be learnt from this. Naturally, some discrepancies in awareness, views and assessment are to be expected, particularly in multilevel institutions such as the EU. Yet an imbalance in who was surprised, for example between analysts and decision-makers, or between different hierarchical levels, may equally point to more problematic issues, such as limited analytical capabilities or organisational culture hostile to dissenting views.[43]

From the research it emerges that the Arab uprisings consisted of a significant surprise to the European Union institutions under scrutiny here, as most but not all analysts and decision-makers were equally affected. This also applies to the realisation of the gravity of the situation and the potential consequences the Arab uprisings would have, which was realised and accepted much sooner in the Delegations than it was accepted in Brussels.

As mentioned in the above, the strategic possibility of upheaval arising in one of more MENA countries was not wholly unexpected to EU officials. There had been the 'Worst Case Scenarios' report on this possibility. The Ashton cabinet member interviewed for this study also reiterated the Arab uprisings had been 'unavoidable'.[44] Similarly, interviewed officials within lower ranks of the EEAS (or DG RELEX prior to December 2010) as well as in the EU delegations raise that they issued occasional warnings up the organisational hierarchy, primarily regarding the worsening socio-economic conditions and human rights standards. They argue there was a very limited receptivity to warnings they made, especially regarding discordant and potentially inconvenient claims.[45] This notion of political inconvenience refers to the fact that for a long time European countries as well as the EU as a whole had cooperated rather closely with the regimes in North Africa and the Middle East, not least because of their focus on counter terrorism. Warning that these regimes might fall, or worse yet suggest the EU should stand with protestors to favour regime change, was quite an 'unpopular' view. Whilst EU delegations in Tunisia, Algeria and Egypt occasionally flagged issues to their Brussels counterparts (such as a growing instability in the Ben Ali government), the view held, especially higher up in the organisation in Brussels, was that the autocratic regimes were fully able to repress such discontent, thereby safeguarding their continuity. 'In Brussels, they were not thinking that there would be major changes' in the region, one interviewee who worked at a North African EU delegation at the time said.[46]

In addition, there existed no 'dissent channels', 'red teams' or other forms of upstream communication to facilitate the bottom-up dissemination of such warnings within EEAS, assert interviewees, except for administrative wrongdoings. Similarly, officials at the EU's Intelligence Centre (INTCEN) in interviews argue that their reporting and their warnings were ignored by their customers in the EEAS, particularly the Ashton cabinet, who they claim discarded reporting which was inconvenient for their policy course.

Table 2.1 summarises the degree and extent to which the European Union institutions were surprised by the Arab uprisings.

Table 2.1 Dissecting the surprising nature of the Arab uprisings

Dimensions	Degree of surprise	Most surprising features
Dissonance	Significant surprise: not deemed impossible nor highly unlikely	• The inability of autocrats to oppress new uprisings as they had done in the past • Military defection in Tunisia and Egypt • The combustibility of the multiple factors and their interrelated nature
Scope	Significant surprise: most tactical features, some strategic features	• Trigger and timing of the events • Spillover uprisings from Tunisia to Egypt and beyond • Pace of uprisings • Role of social media • Beginning of events in 'calm' Tunisia • Ben Ali demise (up until it actually happened) • Mubarak demise (up until a few days prior)
Spread	Significant surprise: most but not all analysts and decision-makers	• Brussels decision-makers and media (late January) most affected • Analysts who were not surprised by strategic occurrence were on tactical features

Source: Based on categories by Ikani, Guttmann and Meyer, 2020.

Performance Problems and Mitigating Factors

After having mapped the dissonance, scope and spread of the surprising nature of the Arab uprisings, it is possible to assess both some underlying performance problems as well as the impact of important mitigating or aggravating factors on the performance of analysts and decision-makers in the institutions under scrutiny. This will be done building upon the six key performance indicators suggested by Ikani et al., 2020.[47] The first performance indicator concerns the accuracy of warnings regarding the most important threat aspects. Were decision-makers provided with accurate assessments of the threats? Another set of important indicators of knowledge production performance concern timeliness and convincingness of the warnings. Although assessing the situation too early carries risks, delaying the sending of assessments negatively affects the possibility for decision-makers to take mitigating action. Hereafter, an important indicator is whether decision-makers give due attention and prioritisation to the analysis, especially if the analyses and warnings already come with a high priority attached to them by the analysts. This requires decision-makers to have an open-mindedness to discordant claims, in other words the willingness to listen to messages which may potentially be inconvenient, politically or otherwise, in order to finally accept the threat analysis or not. In the following, I discuss the three most important mitigating factors impacting the performance studied here.

Diagnostic Difficulty of the Arab Uprisings

This research found that an important mitigating factor affecting the accuracy of the knowledge claims was the high diagnostic difficulty the case of the Arab uprisings presented. The imminent combustibility of the socio-economic situation in many of the countries where the Arab uprisings took place was, as far as sources reveal, unforeseen by not just the European institutions, but similarly by US, UK and French intelligence[48] and the major outlets studied in the open-source analysis for this study.

To keep check on the region, these actors kept track of socio-economic factors primarily. This rendered numbers which seemed quite positive. Expenditure inequality had been either constant or declining in most MENA economies. Except for in Yemen, poverty rates were declining. Only two of the eighteen MENA countries were on the Foreign Policy Failed States Index in 2010.[49]

Yet due to the corruption, nepotism and favouritism, such economic growth could co-exist with rising levels of inequality. The straightforward tracking of socio-economic indicators therefore did not reveal the real problem, which according to a World Bank evaluation study of the Arab uprisings was 'the erosion of middle-class incomes, which either declined or lagged behind incomes of other welfare groups'.[50] The financial crash of 2008 and the subsequent economic crisis had made the elite funnel even more of the limited wealth to their supporting base, leading to growing inequality. Similarly overlooked in policy circles and the media scrutinised was that such increasing inequality across the MENA coincided with the fact that the educated youth expected their lives to be better than previous generations. Their anger was galvanised by the 'decorative' democratic elements, which obscured the enormous democratic deficit and the lack of genuine democratic values. These were insufficiently understood.

As has been argued by Goodwin, an important diagnostic difficulty concerned the limited knowledge of the armed forces in Tunisia and Egypt.[51] Military decisions in these countries to abstain from using force on the protestors on behalf of the incumbent regimes are considered a crucial determining factor in the fall of those regimes.[52] While this view has been challenged by some scholars,[53] interviewees from the European institutions as well as member state policy officials at the MENA delegations partaking in the workshop confirmed that European countries at the time lacked an understanding of the military in Tunisia or Egypt, but also of countries like Algeria, which historically had been rather closely connected to European countries like France. In scholarly circles, Brooks argues, scholarship on Arab militaries was equally minimal, 'a niche and neglected field of study'.[54]

Further aggravating the diagnostic difficulty of this case was the velocity of the Arab uprisings, which escalated within two weeks in Tunisia at the end of December. Moreover, geographically but also in disciplinary terms, the uprisings cut across many areas of expertise, such as the realm of macroeconomics, political and military intelligence on the entrenched regimes in the MENA, but also regarding the impact of social media on the developments.

Capacities for Knowledge Production and Transfer

In addition to the high diagnostic difficulty of the Arab uprisings, there are important organisational factors which may have negatively affected the EU's performance in anticipating the Arab uprisings, particularly concerning the due attention and prioritisation, as well as the openness to discordant claims. As discussed in the above, the recent set-up of the EEAS brought about a host of teething problems and turf battles which are likely to have negatively affected the ability of the EU to monitor the region. Moreover, the Commission, which had previously overseen EU external affairs, was eager not to lose too many of its foreign policy competences. The Commission eventually retained key portfolios with an important budget, such as development aid, energy policy and the European Neighbourhood Policy, which meant that much of what the EU was doing in the MENA countries was not done by the EEAS but by other EU institutions.

Organisational issues are likely have played a role in both the spreading of warnings and their due attention and prioritisation, amongst others of the 2008 'Worst Case Scenarios' report. The report provided a forewarning on events that were very similar to what transpired during the Arab uprising, and did so in a timely manner, namely in 2007. However, the report did not make an impact and, according to interviewees, was largely forgotten by 2010. Arcos and Palacios, the latter the Head of Analysis at INTCEN from 2011 to 2015, provide several explanations for why this happened, among them the fact the report had not been addressed to the member states, but to the European institutions only, which at the time did not have a doctrine or routine process regarding what to do with early warnings.[55] This means that the report, like other documents from the INTCEN production line, landed on everybody's desk, but nobody's desk in particular. Moreover, they argue that the title of 'Worst Case Scenarios' may have created a feeling that the picture painted was not quite likely, or probably, but only the absolute worst case, thereby lowering its prioritisation.

An important factor not mentioned by the authors is that at the time the uprisings started, INTCEN was in an interregnum. The previous head of the EU Intelligence Centre, William Shapcott (who had ordered the report) had resigned in June 2010, just before the death of Khaled Said in Egypt. His successor, Ilkka Salmi, only came to office in February 2011, well after the demise of Ben Ali in Tunisia and just before the fall of the Mubarak regime. Thus, during a crucial time of anticipation, the report's findings and insight could not be brought to the attention to the EU leadership by the head of INTCEN. Moreover, due to a lack of secure reading rooms in EU delegations, EU delegations in the MENA had no access to classified reporting, including the 'Worst Case' report. None of the interviewees outside INTCEN claim to have read the report.

The warnings that were issued, including those mentioned by the interviewees for this research, were thus scattered across institutions and lacked effective and credible communicators. Moreover, it seems that even though issues were flagged, for example regarding the untenable socio-economic conditions in Tunisia, or the issues Mubarak was facing in Egypt in positioning his son Gamal as his successor, they were not quite actionable. As the intelligence studies literature suggests, it is crucial that intelligence reporting is also actionable to decision-makers to accept and to base preventative mitigating measures on.[56] This does not seem to have been the case regarding most warnings prior to December 2010, as the warnings did not indicate more specifically the consequences the threat could have, nor their potential sequence. Once the Arab uprisings started, it emerges from the interviews that the delegations did provide timely and accurate intelligence to Brussels regarding the unrest in Tunisia, the imminent end of Ben Ali's reign and the potential violence that would ensue, but also regarding the escalating situation in Egypt. These warnings were not accepted or prioritised. It is likely that other mitigating factors played an important role here, as will be discussed below.

Political Unwillingness to Accept Discordant Claims

The prevailing political environment is likely to have played a role in producing an unwillingness to accept the discordant claims which did exist in the institutions. Interviewees in EU delegations, the EEAS in Brussels and INTCEN assert that there was a general unwillingness on the part of decision-makers in Brussels to accept politically inconvenient claims, within EEAS and at the member state level. The unwillingness to accept the Tunisia delegations' warnings during the meeting on 14 January, mere hours before Ben Ali's demise, was illustrative of this reluctance. It seems unlikely that the member states in question were indeed unaware that there was a substantial risk of violence in Tunis on that January afternoon. They were, however, unwilling to accept such an assertion announced by the Political and Security Committee as a body.

Even before the Arab uprisings started, member states and the EEAS leadership were hesitant to accept bottom-up dissonant knowledge claims regarding the instability of regimes in Tunisia and Egypt. A few officials within EEAS declared that their warnings about the untenable lack of political pluralism in Tunisia in the years up to the Arab uprisings were very explicit, but that there was 'pressure from various sides' to keep them out of official reporting, including from the member states.[57] These claims cannot easily be traced or confirmed, and since the anonymity of the interviewees is guaranteed, it is difficult to provide more details on the kind of pressure or from which sides exactly. Overall, it emerges from the interviews that in 2010–11 there was very limited openness within the EEAS (and its predecessor DG RELEX) to the occasional timely, accurate and actionable warnings that were made by officials within the institutions and the delegations. The lack of dissent channels, discussed in the above, is likely to have exacerbated this.

This limited openness was, according to the interviewees and focus group participants spoken to in this study, in part due to a political preference not to antagonise interlocutors with whom many EU member states were cooperating closely in the region. A generally held argument in the literature is that bilateral relations between Western powers and authoritarian regimes in MENA are, with a few notable examples, driven by three core objectives: stability, market access and security cooperation on issues such as counterterrorism.[58] In order to achieve these objectives, these countries have historically regularly relied on cooperation with and support for authoritarian regimes. This choice is in part strategic: withdrawing support to authoritarian regimes could start a challenging transition process. Research shows that emerging democracies, often with weak political institutions, are especially likely to go to war.[59] Upheavals or regime collapse, especially in the MENA region, might upend cautious geopolitical stability, often with implications for energy supplies or military bases. This preference for authoritarian stability did not just dissipate as the Arab uprisings started. A good example is the telling off of the European ambassadors to Egypt in December 2010 by Ahmed Aboul Gheit, the foreign minister, after the European Parliament had called for an impartial inquiry into the death in police custody of Khaled Said in Egypt.[60]

Conclusion

This chapter has argued that missing from extant explanations about the 'surprising nature' of the Arab uprisings has been an in-depth investigation of the strategic surprise itself. Such explanations are not complete without more detail on which characteristics of the Arab uprisings were particularly surprising for the EU's institutions and to what extent, and whether experiences of surprise were spread evenly across analysts and decision-makers. This chapter thus complements the extant literature by providing a detailed reconstruction of the way a select group of EU institutions anticipated the Arab uprisings, dissecting the dissonance, scope and spread of the surprise the events presented to the EEAS, DG NEAR and INTCEN based on the analytical framework presented in Chapter 1. Not only does such a detailed investigation of the surprise itself enrich the sometimes contradictory explanations as to why the Arab uprisings were so surprising, but, also, such an improved understanding of who was surprised, about what and when allows for a better evaluation of the EU's performance for the purpose of learning lessons.

The empirical sections of this chapter found that the performance of the European institutions in anticipating the uprisings has been affected by the diagnostic difficulty of the Arab uprisings, as underlined in previous studies. Yet, this has been particularly hampered by the limited capacities for knowledge production and transfer within the institutions, as well as by a political unwillingness within the institutions and likely beyond in accepting discordant knowledge claims. Indeed, it has been shown that foreknowledge regarding the risks of significant upheaval existed within the institutions under scrutiny. However, this was scattered throughout the institutions and across levels of hierarchy, with limited follow-up. This applied in particular to knowledge existing in the EU delegations. In addition to more deep-rooted political resistance to some of the warnings which may have existed, the virtual non-existence of dissent channels and the limited facilitation of bottom-up warnings likely contributed to a limited follow-up. This is where the most important lessons seem to emerge: the EU will always consist of different member states which may have different political preferences, and which may or may not be open to inconvenient or discordant claims. Yet, through the facilitation of some form of bottom-up (anonymous) dissent or criticism through dedicated channels or structures, or by asking 'red teams' to provide alternative perspectives or devil's advocate positions,[61] at least the organisational inhibitions to such bottom-up warnings can be mitigated, and warnings are less likely to be dismissed as easily as occurred in the case of the Arab uprisings. It may also cluster warnings made from scattered positions across institutions, thereby increasing the likelihood they will be investigated. In Chapter 7, Gerhard Conrad discusses how a comprehensive, all-sources form of situational awareness is a crucial next step for the European Union. Such dissent channels could play a structural part in these.

Notes

1. Volker Perthes, 'Europe and the Arab Spring', *Survival* 53, no. 6 (2011).
2. Michael Morell and Bill Harlow, *The Great War of Our Time: The CIA's Fight Against Terrorism – From Al Qa'ida to Isis* (New York: Grand Central Publishing, 2016); Sénat, 'Le Renforcement De La Fonction D'anticipation Stratégique Depuis Les Livres Blancs De 2008' (Commission des Affaires Étrangères, de la Défense et des Forces Armées, 2011); UK Parliament, 'British Foreign Policy and the "Arab Spring"', Second Report of Session 2012–13 (London, 2012).
3. For example: UK Parliament, 'British Foreign Policy and the "Arab Spring"', Second Report of Session 2012–13; Assemblée Nationale, 'Les Printemps Arabes' (Commission Des Affaires Étrangères, 2012).
4. Tanja Börzel, Assem Dandashly and Thomas Risse, 'Responses to the "Arabellions": The EU in Comparative Perspective – Introduction' [in En], *Journal of European Integration* 37, no. 1 (2015); Richard G. Whitman and Ana E. Juncos, 'The Arab Spring, the Eurozone Crisis and the Neighbourhood: A Region in Flux' [in En], *Journal of Common Market Studies* 50 (2012); Susi Dennison, 'The EU and North Africa after the Revolutions: A New Start or "Plus Ça Change"?' [in En], *Mediterranean Politics* 18, no. 1 (2013).
5. F. Gregory Gause, 'Why Middle East Studies Missed the Arab Spring: The Myth of Authoritarian Stability', *Foreign Affairs* 90, no. 4 (2011); Martin Beck, 'The Arab Spring as a Challenge to Political Science', in *The International Politics of the Arab Spring* (2014); Morten Valbjørn, 'Reflections on Self-Reflections – On Framing the Analytical Implications of the Arab Uprisings for the Study of Arab Politics', *Democratization* 22, no. 2 (2015).
6. For example: Larry Diamond, 'Why Are There No Arab Democracies?', *Journal of Democracy* 21, no. 1 (2009).
7. Jeff Goodwin, 'Why We Were Surprised (Again) by the Arab Spring' [in En], *Swiss Political Science Review* 17, no. 4 (2011).
8. Elena Ianchovichina, *Eruptions of Popular Anger: The Economics of the Arab Spring and Its Aftermath*, World Bank MENA Development Report (Washington, DC: World Bank Group, 2018); Philip N. Howard and Muzammil M. Hussain, *Democracy's Fourth Wave?: Digital Media and the Arab Spring*, Oxford Studies in Digital Politics (Oxford and New York: Oxford University Press, 2013).
9. Gadi Wolfsfeld, Elad Segev and Tamir Sheafer, 'Social Media and the

Arab Spring', *The International Journal of Press/Politics* 18, no. 2 (2013); Stephen Tankel, *With Us and Against Us: How America's Partners Help and Hinder the War on Terror* (New York: Columbia University Press, 2018).

10. Timur Kuran, 'The Inevitability of Future Revolutionary Surprises', *American Journal of Sociology* 100, no. 6 (1995).

11. Eric Gobe, 'The Gafsa Mining Basin between Riots and a Social Movement': https://halshs.archives-ouvertes.fr/halshs-00557826/doc ument

12. Kurt Weyland, 'The Arab Spring: Why the Surprising Similarities with the Revolutionary Wave of 1848?', *Perspectives on Politics* 10, no. 4 (2012): 921.

13. Shimon Stein, 'One Year of the Arab Spring: The European Union and the Arab Spring' (Institute for National Security Studies, 2012).

14. Börzel, Dandashly and Risse, 'Responses to the "Arabellions"'; Whitman and Juncos, 'The Arab Spring, the Eurozone Crisis and the Neighbourhood'; Dennison, 'The EU and North Africa after the Revolutions'.

15. Sophie Vanhoonacker and Karolina Pomorska, 'The European External Action Service and Agenda-Setting in European Foreign Policy', *Journal of European Public Policy* 20, no. 9 (2013): 1322; Rosa Balfour and Hanna Ojanen, 'Does the European External Action Service Represent a Model for the Challenges of Global Diplomacy?' (Istituto Affari Internazionali, 2011).

16. Niklas Helwig, 'The High Representative of the Union: The Quest for Leadership in EU Foreign Policy', in *The European External Action Service: European Diplomacy Post-Westphalia*, ed. David Spence and Jozef Bátora (London: Palgrave Macmillan, 2015); Geoffrey Edwards, 'The EU's Foreign Policy and the Search for Effect', *International Relations* 27, no. 3 (2013).

17. For a comparative study of the uprisings, cf. Steven Heydemann, 'Explaining the Arab Uprisings: Transformations in Comparative Perspective', *Mediterranean Politics* 21, no. 1 (2015).

18. Erik J. Dahl, *Intelligence and Surprise Attack: Failure and Success from Pearl Harbor to 9/11 and Beyond* (Washington, DC: Georgetown University Press, 2013).

19. Nikki Ikani and Ana Maria Albulescu, 'Timeline of Expert Claims and Responses for the Arab Uprising Involving Germany and the EU' (2021).

20. NGOs studied: International Crisis Group, Human Rights Watch, Amnesty International. Think tanks studied: ECFR, IFRI, CEPS,

DGAP (English), SWP (English), European Parliament Research service, Carnegie Europe. Media outlets studied: *The New York Times, Financial Times, The Guardian*, Times UK, *The Economist* (including the Economist Intelligence Unit), BBC Monitoring Middle East, BBC Monitoring Media, BBC Monitoring Newsfile and finally, The Telegraph UK. The BBC Monitoring Services monitor and translate local and regional news services in Arabic and French including Al Jazeera.

21. Christoph O. Meyer, Chiara De Franco and Florian Otto, *Warning About War: Conflict, Persuasion and Foreign Policy* (Cambridge: Cambridge University Press, 2020), 28–9.

22. Nikki Ikani, *Crisis and Change in European Union Foreign Policy: A Framework of EU Foreign Policy Change* (Manchester: Manchester University Press, 2021).

23. Three NGO representatives with expertise on the MENA, five policy officials who worked on the region during the Arab uprisings.

24. Interview PO42, EEAS, 1 February 2016.

25. Interview PO50, DG NEAR, 29 June 2017.

26. Single Analysis Capacity, 'Worst Case Scenarios for the Narrower Middle East' (2007), 2, 8.

27. Ibid., 4.

28. Interview PO1, EEAS (Delegation), 20 August 2019.

29. Silvia Colombo and Nathalie Tocci, 'Re-Thinking Western Policies in Light of the Arab Uprising' (Rome: Istituto Affari Internazionali (IAI), 2012), 71.

30. European Council, 'Press Release 3028th Council Meeting General Affairs Brussels'. https://data.consilium.europa.eu/doc/document/ST -12550-2010-INIT/en/pdf

31. European Council, 'Notice of Meeting and Provisional Agenda': https://data.consilium.europa.eu/doc/document/CM-6114-2010 -INIT/en/pdf

32. Rubén Arcos and José-Miguel Palacios, 'The Impact of Intelligence on Decision-Making: The EU and the Arab Spring,' *Intelligence and National Security* 33, no. 5 (2018).

33. Interview PO1.

34. Ibid.

35. Interview PO42.

36. Interview PO1.

37. Political and Security Committee, 'Notice of Meeting and Provisional Agenda 14 January 2011': https://data.consilium.europa.eu/doc /document/CM-1136-2011-REV-1/en/pdf

38. Interview PO1; PO2, EEAS (Delegation), 20 August 2019; PO3, EEAS (Delegation), 4 September 2019; PO53, EEAS (Delegation), 11 July 2017.
39. Interview PO4, EEAS/RELEX, 5 September 2019; PO5, EEAS (Delegation), 9 September 2019; PO18, EEAS (Delegation), 4 December 2019.
40. Interview PO5.
41. Sénat, 'La Fonction "Anticipation Stratégique": Quel Renforcement Depuis Le Livre Blanc?,' (2011).
42. Economist Intelligence Unit, 'Après Ben Ali'.
43. Nikki Ikani, Aviva Guttmann and Christoph O. Meyer, 'An Analytical Framework for Postmortems of European Foreign Policy: Should Decision-Makers Have Been Surprised?', *Intelligence and National Security* 35, no. 2 (2020).
44. Interview PO42.
45. Interview PO1, PO3, PO4, PO53.
46. Interview PO53.
47. Ikani, Guttmann and Meyer, 'An Analytical Framework for Postmortems of European Foreign Policy: Should Decision-Makers Have Been Surprised?'.
48. Michael Morell and Bill Harlow, *The Great War of Our Time: The Cia's Fight against Terrorism--from Al Qa'ida to Isis* (New York: Grand Central Publishing, 2016); Sénat, 'Le Renforcement De La Fonction D'anticipation Stratégique Depuis Les Livres Blancs De 2008' (2011); UK Parliament, 'British Foreign Policy and the "Arab Spring". Second Report of Session 2012–13'.
49. Rebecca Frankel, 'The Failed States Index 2010', Foreign Policy: https://foreignpolicy.com/2010/06/17/the-failed-states-index-2010/
50. Ianchovichina, *Eruptions of Popular Anger: The Economics of the Arab Spring and its Aftermath*, 11.
51. Goodwin, 'Why We Were Surprised (Again) by the Arab Spring'.
52. Risa A. Brooks (2017).
53. Amy Austin Holmes and Kevin Koehler, 'Myths of Military Defection in Egypt and Tunisia', *Mediterranean Politics* 25, no. 1 (2018).
54. Brooks, 3.
55. Arcos and Palacios, 'The Impact of Intelligence on Decision-Making'.
56. James J. Wirtz, 'The Intelligence-Policy Nexus', in *Strategic Intelligence: Understanding the Hidden Side of Government*, ed. Loch K. Johnson (Westport, CT: Praeger Security International, 2007).
57. Interview PO4, PO7, PO8, PO9, all INTCEN, 11 September 2019.

58. Francesco Cavatorta, 'The Failed Liberalisation of Algeria and the International Context: A Legacy of Stable Authoritarianism,' *The Journal of North African Studies* 7, no. 4 (2002); Roberto Roccu and Benedetta Voltolini, 'Framing and Reframing the EU's Engagement with the Mediterranean: Examining the Security-Stability Nexus Before and After the Arab Uprisings', *Mediterranean Politics* 23, no. 1 (2017).

59. Edward D. Mansfield and Jack L. Snyder, *Electing to Fight: Why Emerging Democracies Go to War*, BCSIA Studies in International Security (Cambridge, MA: The MIT Press, 2005).

60. Issandr El Amrani, 'Human Rights: Reluctant to End Repression', *Financial Times* 2010.

61. NATO Development Concepts and Doctrine Centre (DCDC), 'A Guide to Red Teaming': https://www.act.nato.int/images/stories/events/2011/cde/rr_ukdcdc.pdf

3 How Germany and the UK Anticipated ISIS's Rise to Power in Syria and Iraq

Aviva Guttmann and Eva Michaels

Introduction

ISIS's rise to power in Syria and Iraq in 2013–14 was a slow-burning crisis whose effects turned out to have significant implications for European security. The situation escalated while European decision-makers were handling other foreign crises, notably in Ukraine. Many expert observers perceived the Iraqi army's defeat at Mosul and the fall of the city to ISIS in June 2014 as a political-military shock.[1] While this was a key turning point, as has been discussed in the US-centred strategic surprise literature,[2] little attention has been paid to earlier experiences of surprise and to European contexts of estimative intelligence production.

This chapter explores how British and German intelligence communities and external experts anticipated ISIS's expansion in Syria and Iraq and its reach into Europe during an early phase of the crisis (July 2013–June 2014). To answer this, we look at three interconnected sub-questions: what were knowledge producers surprised about as the crisis unfolded, how did they perform, and what were the underlying reasons for performance problems? Both sections of this chapter, on Germany by Eva Michaels and on the UK by Aviva Guttmann, are structured the same way along these questions. The identical structure allows for a cross-actor comparison at the end of this chapter. Throughout, we pay special attention to the conditions under which knowledge producers in both countries operated, by considering factors that hindered or enabled their ability to forecast risk-related developments.[3]

For both countries, we systematically reviewed open-source knowledge claims by selected non-governmental experts about ISIS's activities and structural vulnerabilities that were published between 1 July 2013 and 9 June 2014. Choosing this period allowed for a reconstruction of expert knowledge once ISIS had started activities in Syria and Iraq that were of strategic consequence (for example tightening its grip on Raqqa, expanding its footprint in northern Syria, escalating violent attacks against predominantly Shia targets across Iraq) and before a prominent event (fall of Mosul) occurred. Towards the end of this period, Europe also experienced its first ISIS-inspired terrorist attack by a radicalised returning foreign fighter which highlighted the potential for ISIS to cause serious harm in Europe. Section one focuses on two groups of external experts: journalists reporting for German media organisations (*Frankfurter Allgemeine Zeitung/FAZ, Süddeutsche Zeitung/SZ, Die Welt, Der Spiegel, Die Zeit*) and German think tank analysts (*German Institute for International and Security Affairs/SWP*).[4] In addition, section one draws on four interviews with external experts in Germany, nine interviews with German intelligence analysts, and a workshop with German government and intelligence officials. Section two analyses knowledge claims by journalists reporting for British media organisations (*Financial Times, The Guardian, The Times, The Telegraph*) and researchers at international NGOs (*International Crisis Group/ICG, Human Rights Watch/HRW, Amnesty International/AI*).[5] Section two further draws on workshop findings with members of the UK intelligence community (IC). For both sections, interviews and workshop results have been fully anonymised.

Drawing on the theoretical guidance provided in Chapter 1 and combining different data sets allows us to develop a nuanced understanding of British and German intelligence and expert communities' anticipation of the rise of ISIS as a powerful actor which threatened European interests. Looking at Germany and the UK is intriguing due to the different national contexts shaping the work of intelligence analysts and external experts. While knowledge producers in both countries experienced similar diagnostic difficulties related to the assessment of threats and risks, they had different means at their disposal to overcome them. Their resources were shaped by the respective domestic political environment which varied in terms of national interests in Iraq and Syria (and the Middle East broadly), the intelligence set-up, and the relationships between foreign policymakers and external experts. This was, and still is, reflected in differences in public attention to foreign, security and intelligence issues.[6] Overall, our chapter contributes to knowledge of how terrorist groups emerge and how effectively experts warn about their activities and the underlying conditions that these groups can exploit and exacerbate.

How did the German Intelligence and Expert Communities Anticipate the Emerging Crisis?

What were German Knowledge Producers Surprised About?

The analytical framework of this edited volume, which has been tailored to experiences of surprise about slower-burning, indirect threats and risks, is particularly useful as ISIS's rise to power was far from sudden. For instance, while the fall of Mosul to ISIS was a remarkable development whose ease reportedly even took ISIS by surprise, this did not happen out of the blue.[7] Kurdish officials had warned the Iraqi and US governments as early as January 2014 that ISIS was planning to seize Mosul. US intelligence subsequently anticipated that ISIS would seek to break Mosul's main prison rather than overrun the city.[8] Various warning signals about an ISIS offensive on Mosul were available in expert open sources.[9] However, it proved challenging to assess the actual weakness of the Iraqi security forces and the combined consequences of structural vulnerabilities and ISIS's capability and intent.[10]

These diagnostic challenges were clearly at play in the German context and made it difficult for external experts and intelligence analysts to forecast that ISIS would be able to expand quickly in and around Mosul.[11] But paying additional attention to earlier surprises, or the sum of surprises experts had experienced at this turning point, allows for a more nuanced discussion. As such, this section seeks to find out whether the selected external experts and intelligence analysts[12] were caught by surprise vis-à-vis the following key events:

1. the beginning of ISIS's Anbar campaign with its surge into Fallujah and Ramadi on 31 December 2013
2. ISIS seizing complete control of Raqqa and the road to the Iraqi border in mid-January 2014
3. the ISIS-inspired attack at the Jewish Museum in Brussels on 24 May 2014,
4. the fall of Mosul on 10 June 2014.

Our taxonomy of surprise allows us to distinguish between perfect, significant and partial surprises that knowledge producers and decision-makers may have experienced across three dimensions. We can look at the extent to which threats were considered and deemed likely (dissonance, first dimension) or to which threat characteristics were surprising (scope, second dimension). We can further investigate who was surprised: only some knowledge producers, or most of them, or all of them (spread, third dimension). For the first two dimensions, this includes risk perceptions and the extent to which the consequences of a threat were surprising. Highlighting this is relevant for the case under study: German knowledge producers had agreed early on that ISIS posed a threat, but the risks were harder to assess. Also, the consequences of ISIS's actions were surprising – even more so than the materialisation of the threat. Threats are here conceptualised as a function of ISIS's capability and intent and the extent to which it could exploit structural vulnerabilities in Syria, Iraq and Europe.[13] Risks are understood as a function of the likelihood that ISIS will engage in a specific action and that structural vulnerabilities will deteriorate and of potential consequences.[14]

Interviews with German external experts and intelligence analysts revealed that they were aware of the following structural vulnerabilities: growing rebel infighting in the Syrian civil war, Sunni-Shia tensions in Iraq and the region, ISIS's appeal to radical Islamists in Europe, and, to a certain degree, the weakness of the Iraqi security forces and Iraqi government. They were also aware of ISIS's sophisticated capability and its extreme intent. However, due to their limited ability to identify certain risks related to these vulnerabilities, for instance risks to the stability of Iraq, they struggled to connect some dots.

Intelligence analysts recalled that they found it challenging to fully grasp vulnerabilities which ISIS could exacerbate, such as Sunni grievances in Iraq and eastern Syria and a propensity for violence in Iraqi communities. They experienced tactical surprise about the timing of ISIS's Anbar offensive, that Fallujah was also targeted and how promptly ISIS had been able to exploit Sunni unrest. They were surprised that the coalition of Syrian rebel groups failed to oust ISIS from Raqqa after it had launched a concerted offensive in early January 2014, and after ISIS had suffered losses and lost many of its bases elsewhere in Syria. Intelligence analysts were also surprised that ISIS managed to sustain two major campaigns in Raqqa and Anbar provinces simultaneously. They further experienced surprise about the withdrawal of the Iraqi army from Mosul, the ease with which ISIS captured the city and ISIS's rapid expansion beyond Mosul. The interviews suggest that the spread of the surprise within the German IC was partial for the surge into Anbar province and the capture of Raqqa, and significant for the fall of Mosul. It seems that these three events were all partially surprising for intelligence analysts in terms of scope and dissonance.

The external experts who were interviewed for this study echoed the challenges related to understanding structural vulnerabilities in Syria and Iraq and assessing ISIS's ability to seize and hold territory. Based on their recollections and the analysis of open-source expert claims, it appears that some experienced partial surprise on the dissonance and scope dimension for the first two events (the beginning of ISIS's Anbar campaign and the capture of Raqqa), others experienced significant surprise on these two dimensions for the same events,[15] and most external experts experienced significant surprise on the dissonance and scope dimension when witnessing the fall of Mosul. The latter was, for instance, reflected in the lack of relevant expert claims related to developments in Mosul after ISIS had started its advance on the city on 4 June and prior to its fall on 10 June. On 7 June, *FAZ* reported that at least fifty-nine people had been killed in armed clashes between ISIS and Iraqi security forces in Mosul, in addition to at least thirty-six killed in and around Mosul the previous day.[16] The perusal of open-source expert publications yielded no further results related to the situation in Mosul, including on 8 and 9 June when the fighting intensified.

Looking at the first ISIS-inspired terrorist attack in Europe, which occurred at the Jewish Museum in Brussels, external experts and intelligence analysts experienced partial surprise in scope (the exact location of the attacks had been surprising), but *not* on the dissonance dimension (the threat had been deemed possible and likely).

How did German Knowledge Producers Perform when Confronted with ISIS's Rise to Power?

Surprise is not per se an indicator of performance shortcomings. In order to assess the latter, we turn to the three performance criteria for knowledge producers (accuracy, timeliness and convincingness) while also considering contextual factors (related to diagnostic challenges, pre-existing analytical capabilities and the political environment) which could have hindered or enabled the production of high-quality estimates. Discussing the performance of external experts in a first step, the systematic analysis of open-source knowledge claims shows that most warnings were vague and corresponded to strategic warnings, as is often the case with warnings about war by external experts.[17] The following warnings, presented in chronological order, were found:

- German Muslims were increasingly self-radicalising and susceptible to online propaganda on individual jihad, and radicalised Islamists could commit suicide attacks;[18]
- the Levant was becoming one battle ground,[19] with ISIS being 'the transnational terrorist organisation of the future'[20] and Iraq would fall apart if Syria collapsed;[21]
- Western air strikes against the Syrian regime would strengthen ISIS;[22]
- moderate Syrian rebels would become increasingly radical as they were in dire need of funding and would turn to Saudi Arabia, Qatar and Kuwait;[23] remaining moderate forces would become marginalised;[24]

- weapons delivered to moderate Syrian rebel groups could easily fall into ISIS's hands;[25]
- ISIS would continue to cause more harm in Syria than al-Qaeda in Iraq during the previous decade as it had learned important lessons, such as seizing control of vital areas of public life in its occupied areas;[26]
- the creation of a transnational Islamic state spanning Raqqa and Anbar provinces was imminent, ISIS would seek to expand this to Mosul given its strong presence there,[27] and Raqqa was a taste of things to come;[28]
- Syrian rebel groups and local populations were unable to counter ISIS's rapid expansion in northeastern Syria, and this could contribute to Syria's collapse;[29]
- radicalisation and recruitment of German citizens could happen very rapidly, and returning foreign fighters could launch terrorist attacks in Germany;[30]
- ISIS's cross-border activities were threatening to destabilise the entire region;[31]
- ISIS would be able to provoke regular outbreaks of violence in northeastern Syria and northwestern Iraq;[32]
- the Iraqi army was inherently weak, the Iraqi state had de facto collapsed and would become 'a second Syria' unless it defeated ISIS (a warning provided by Saleh al-Mutlaq, prominent Sunni politician and one of Iraq's three Deputy Prime Ministers.[33])

Most of these would not have qualified as effective warnings according to David Omand, as they did not indicate when harmful events would likely occur and as the consequences of the forecast were only superficially discussed, if at all.[34] Apart from three warnings about the impending establishment of a caliphate spanning Raqqa and Anbar provinces which ISIS would seek to expand to Mosul, Raqqa as a taste of things to come, and the weakness of the Iraqi army, none provided estimates of how the situation would evolve in Anbar and Nineveh provinces or anticipated that ISIS would establish full control of Raqqa and beyond. These three warnings were only formulated in one source (*FAZ* and *Der Spiegel* respectively) and not (re)produced by other experts under study here. Two related findings are noteworthy. First and strikingly, fewer warnings were available after December 2013. Second, some experts had claimed prior to ISIS's full capture of Raqqa in mid-January 2014 that it was on the defensive in Syria,[35] or that its success story was over.[36] These shortcomings notwithstanding, the above warnings were in retrospect largely accurate and produced in a timely manner. Looking at convincingness, external experts often failed to judge the probability and harm of likely future developments, thus struggling to attach relevance to their claims.

Some experts missed opportunities for warnings by misjudging the capability of the Iraqi state and security forces or by drawing unhelpful parallels to earlier escalations of violence. For instance, SWP's Iraq expert Guido Steinberg claimed in August and December 2013 that a new civil war remained an unlikely prospect due to the strength of the Iraqi security forces.[37] After the beginning of ISIS's Anbar campaign in January 2014, Steinberg argued that ISIS would not be able to shake Iraq due to the stability and resources of the government. He also referred to 'Iraq's al-Qaeda groups', rather than distinguishing between ISIS and al-Qaeda, hence missing an opportunity to warn about the threat ISIS posed.[38] Some journalists reached similar conclusions, for instance by arguing in January 2014 that ISIS would not be able to fully capture Fallujah and Ramadi due to the superiority of the Iraqi security forces.[39] Steinberg had also downplayed the risks in December 2013 by arguing that the situation in Iraq had not yet reached the same level of escalation as during the 2005–7 civil war.[40]

Could external experts have been expected to perform better? This question leads to a discussion of the context in which external experts operated. They experienced significant diagnostic difficulties related to ISIS's activities and structural vulnerabilities in Iraq and Syria, while having limited resources at their disposal to overcome them. For instance, most investigative journalists paused their trips to Syria after August 2013, when ISIS had gained more territory in northern Syria.[41] The deteriorating security situation made it difficult for them to draw on their local contacts, including by phone or video call.[42] German media organisations also lacked a presence in Iraq, with some foreign correspondents covering Syria and Iraq from Beirut. Of all the news reports gathered for the open-source database, it appears that only one (!) was written from Iraq.[43] Most interviewees highlighted that Germany lacked genuine Iraq experts during the period under study.

The lack of resources that German media organisations and think tanks experienced, particularly when covering developments in Iraq, had been shaped by the limited interest among German policymakers.[44] The government was not unaware of underlying vulnerabilities in Iraq,[45] but the situation was not high on its priority list. Slightly more attention was paid to Kurdistan where Germany had a consulate and more pronounced economic interests. From May 2014 onwards, a cross-party consensus for stronger support of Kurdistan and the protection of Yazidis emerged in the Bundestag.[46] At the decision-making level, Iraq only became a prominent agenda item after the fall of Mosul and specifically after the Sinjar massacre in early August 2014. Similarly, Germany's Syria policy was vague and aloof during the period under study. It initially sought to bring the al-Assad regime and rebel groups to the negotiating table, followed by Chancellor Angela Merkel's call for a humanitarian corridor in January 2014, followed by a void. Little political attention was paid to 'the war within the war', triggered by increased rebel infighting and ISIS's expansion in Syria. German think tanks and media organisations were, at least partly, tailoring their assessments to this political context.

Whereas international NGOs were unaffected by these political dynamics *and* better resourced to draw on eyewitness accounts and open sources,[47] German non-governmental experts lacked resources for information collection and analysis. They struggled with the speed of dynamics on the ground, the novelty of risk-related developments and the challenge of finding reliable local reports. Overall, news reports prioritised factual information (for example on attacks) over knowledge claims about future harm. Relevance and action claims were also rare.

External experts also experienced diagnostic challenges when gauging the likelihood of ISIS-inspired terrorist attacks in Europe. They provided regular strategic warnings that returning foreign fighters could commit attacks in Germany, or anywhere in Europe.

However, it proved difficult to trace the radicalisation and activities of a rapidly growing number of individuals across Europe. The situation was novel and complex – including a high number of radicalised schoolchildren travelling to Syria, or the situation in Turkey which allowed ISIS recruits easy access into Syria. Overall, external experts could not have been expected to provide tactical warnings about an imminent attack in Brussels. As became known afterwards, the suspect had returned from Syria via Germany two months prior to the attack, German officials had informed French authorities, but French officials had lost the trace due to the sheer number of returning foreign fighters to monitor.[48]

It proves more challenging to evaluate the performance of intelligence analysts due to the lack of access to actual assessments and the challenge of gaining access to those who had monitored the emerging crisis from within the German IC. The interviews allow for a limited evaluation of how intelligence analysts performed. It was easier to get hold of analysts who had been covering Iraq, than Syria or radicalisation/terrorism in Germany. The interviews provided scant insights on the anticipation of an ISIS-inspired terrorist attack in Europe, so this aspect will here be excluded. For all, irrespective of prior knowledge and expertise, ISIS's rise to power was a real puzzle which required in-depth information collection and careful analysis.

Intelligence analysts provided regular strategic warnings about the three developments in Syria and Iraq. The interviews suggest that by December 2013, many analysts had considered it likely that ISIS would launch further coordinated complex attacks in its core conflict zone, including in Nineveh and Anbar provinces, and that it would seek to consolidate its presence in eastern Syria. They had anticipated that ISIS would attempt to expand its territorial control and that it was serious about its intention of establishing a transnational caliphate. However, such a scenario was unprecedented and suggested that ISIS had indeed broken away from al-Qaeda which confronted analysts with a high degree of discontinuity and novelty.

Intelligence analysts faced further diagnostic difficulties, such as the speed of parallel developments across Syria and Iraq, the challenge of access for BND officials in Syria (the situation was better in Iraq, also due to the presence of the German consulate in Erbil and German Embassy in Baghdad), the degree of inter-institutional cooperation required, disinformation by all conflict parties, and uncertainty about the credibility of sources who reported about local conflict dynamics. An example for the last point shall be given. One interviewee mentioned that German journalist Christoph Reuter, who was experienced and well connected and had conducted interviews with ISIS members,[49] was considered too close to the Syrian opposition and hence too biased. This could explain why some of Reuter's warnings, especially those containing action claims,[50] might have been dismissed.

Overall, the diagnostic challenges and structural constraints (related to pre-existing analytical capabilities and the political environment) that intelligence analysts experienced were similar to those of external experts. Interviewees noted the lack of political interest (especially prior to December 2013) and agenda competition (from January 2014). They felt that policymakers faced significant pressures during the first half of 2014 due to the escalation of other crises (for example Ukraine, the Central African Republic), calls to do more to address older conflicts (for example Mali), decisions on six mandate extensions for multinational deployments, and the realisation that the situation in Afghanistan and the global refugee crisis would require significant attention and resources. The state of the German armed forces and procedures for authorising military deployments were also under intense scrutiny during this time.

We also need to consider shortcomings and reflexivity at the individual level. Those intelligence analysts who were interviewed mentioned that they had failed to fully grasp the extent of underlying vulnerabilities in Iraq and Syria and likely consequences, blaming their professional-cultural biases and a lack of resources and expertise. Specifically, they felt in retrospect that they had struggled to comprehend societal dynamics and power structures in Iraq and Syria. By failing to connect certain dots, intelligence analysts had missed out on risks that should have been on their radar. For instance, while they had known that the Iraqi security forces were stronger on paper than in reality, they struggled to assess the actual weakness. The interviewees, who came across as reflective and self-critical, said that they had been aware of some shortcomings at the time, and had tried to compensate for this. In sum, while intelligence analysts and external experts could have performed better when assessing the risks related to structural vulnerabilities in Syria and Iraq, which affected their ability to warn about impending events, they faced significant structural constraints and diagnostic challenges.

Underlying Causes of Performance Problems

To grasp the unique nature of the crisis with the blurring of boundaries between external and internal implications, intelligence producers had to draw on pre-existing knowledge of socio-politico-economic developments in Iraq and Syria, political-religious tensions in the region, Islamist terrorism, and radicalisation in the Middle East and Europe. Yet, analytical resources had been withdrawn, for instance from the military intelligence unit on Iraq after the security situation had temporarily improved prior to 2012. While an augmentation of resources was authorised during the period under study, the procedures (for example for security clearance) were relatively slow, leading to temporary capacity shortfalls.

Some intelligence analysts reflected on the fact that they did not speak Arabic, and that their units lacked Arabic speakers and regional specialists, especially during an early phase of the crisis. They considered this a key limitation when building situational awareness and picking up on weak signals. Intelligence analysts also mentioned that they lacked a 'big picture perspective' of what ISIS could mean in the medium-to-long term and that their tools of analysing the region were not sufficiently dynamic to grasp such a complex development as ISIS's rise to power. This also affected their ability to warn policymakers convincingly. Without going into details for confidentiality reasons, some key units were staffed with entry-level analysts without prior experience of the topic, even at the height of the crisis in June 2014. Intra-crisis learning, which addressed some (but not all) of the structural shortcomings, only occurred at a later stage, after the fall of Mosul. Examples were the merging of analytical units on Syria and Iraq, and the creation of an intra-agency task force on Syria, Iraq and

ISIS. During the period under study, inter-institutional cooperation was limited.

As mentioned, the lack of resources had been shaped by the limited political interest in Iraq and lack of attention to developments within the Syrian civil war. Intelligence analysts expressed frustration about the lack of receptivity among their superiors when flagging up potentially harmful developments in both countries as early as 2012 and 2013. Some mentioned that they found it difficult to challenge conventional wisdom among their superiors; among others the perception that Iraq was a low-intensity conflict and that al-Assad would not stay in power. The limited receptivity among senior members of the German IC was linked to two aspects. First, German intelligence took many clues from US and UK sources (both governmental and non-governmental, among others with a relatively positive narrative on Iraq and its army) from which it did not dare to differ. Second, German intelligence finds it traditionally challenging to make a case at the highest political level, among other reasons due to German foreign policymakers being more attentive to public opinion than expertise about emerging foreign crises. During the period under study, German policymakers were initially distracted by debates about the use of chemical weapons in Syria, a widespread belief in a political solution to the Syrian civil war, and by the federal elections, which led to a gap in leadership at a critical time. These challenges were also highlighted by external experts who mentioned that there was a clear lack of political will to discuss and support any policy measures, such as a no-fly zone over Syria, that experts had suggested. Agenda competition from January 2014 onwards, for instance with the Ukraine crisis and stepped-up contribution in Mali, also affected political receptivity.

How did UK and International Middle East Specialists anticipate ISIS's Rise to Power in Syria and Iraq?

From 2013 onwards, UK Middle East analysts reported about a general deterioration of the political situation in Iraq, about increased infighting among Syrian rebel forces, and about other developments that led to the formation and rise of ISIS. Government stakeholders in the UK, however, failed to recognise the political importance of ISIS and did not foresee the extent of its capacity to appeal to Muslims in Iraq, the region, Europe, and the world. This sub-section distinguishes between five important factors that led to ISIS's rise to power, that can be considered as potential signals, as follows:

- *ISIS becoming a force in the Syrian civil war*: its ability to gain territories in northern Syria, capturing oilfields for its financial sustainability.
- *ISIS becoming a force in Iraq*: the group's increasingly brutal terrorist campaign (coordinated car bombs, shootings and prison breaks) and Maliki's government's poor governance, sectarian divide, alienation of Sunni population, and the army's lack of cohesion. This is also linked to a lack of Western engagement.
- *Cruelty and control of territories*: ISIS's ability to govern territories through a brutal and cruel terror regime. This includes its strict enforcement of Sharia law, kidnappings, crucifixions, forced marriages.
- *Foreign fighters and terrorist repercussions*: with mounting numbers of foreign fighters, ISIS's fight internationalised and the group expanded its reach into Europe.
- *A sophisticated online recruitment machine*: ISIS employed a professional propaganda machine through social media, with which it could reach virtually anywhere around the world.

The categorisation of the rise of ISIS into these five main factors is novel and allows for a more nuanced assessment of what exactly regional specialists had been surprised about with regard to the rise to power of ISIS. Compared to the previous section on Germany, this section places stronger emphasis on experts' anticipation of the risks of Syria returnees and their potential terrorist repercussions. Compared to Germany, the UK was more exposed to this risk due to its large Muslim communities and comparatively large numbers of UK Muslims joining ISIS.

109

What were Middle East Specialists Surprised About?

In terms of degree and type of surprise in the run-up to the escalation of ISIS's rise to power, this section argues that it was a partial surprise for UK and international specialists on the Middle East. This is applicable for each of the factors that led to the rise of ISIS. On the one hand, they were aware of the structural factors and the context in which ISIS emerged, but, on the other hand, Middle East analysts had not expected ISIS to take the shape that it did and were surprised by the global dimension of the threat that it posed. Essentially, specialists were both surprised and not surprised in the sense that they were able to accurately assess strategic risks in the region while failing to gauge ISIS's tactical advances. In what follows, we explain this for each of the five factors that facilitated the rise of ISIS.

ISIS becoming a force in the Syrian civil war: Looking at journalistic and humanitarian accounts related to ISIS in Syria, it becomes clear that UK Middle East specialists were very much aware of ISIS's strength and potential danger.[51] However, with a few exceptions they primarily assessed ISIS as a minor part of the Syrian war.[52] A major focus was put on the international and regional dimension of the war and different external forces supporting various belligerent factions.[53] In this war context, there were too many moving forces and at the time it seemed highly unlikely that ISIS would assert itself as the most dominant rebel group. In this vein, ISIS's capture and control of territories in Syria can be considered as a genuine surprise.

ISIS becoming a force in Iraq: This simultaneousness of being surprised and not surprised about ISIS is most strongly apparent in the case of ISIS in Iraq. On the one hand, specialists knew about Iraq's extremely poor governance and warned about the risks of Sunni insurgencies being fuelled by a sectarian and polarised political environment.[54] The sectarian violence that disrupted large parts of Iraq from mid-2013 was also well documented and received widespread media attention.[55] It was generally expected that an insurgency would gain the support of the local Sunni population.[56] By the same token, specialists had not at all expected the ease and speed with which ISIS was able to gain territory in northern Iraq in June 2014.[57] Blinded by high expectations for a Western-built and -trained army, specialists did not in any way foresee the collapse of the Iraqi army.[58]

Cruelty and control of territories in Syria and Iraq: ISIS's capacity to build the state that it proclaimed was surprising for two main reasons. First, it is rare that a small splinter group would establish itself to the point of introducing government ministries and essentially replacing the central government with a local rule of (Sharia) law.[59] Second, the way ISIS governed was surprising because specialists had not expected the group's open use of extreme violence and cruelty.[60] Where specialists were not surprised, however, was with regard to the effects of ISIS's cruelty on the local population and on the armed forces opposing them. It was clear that this would instil fear and strip the population of any potential to form resistance.[61]

Another element of surprise related to ISIS's extreme violence was that intelligence analysts assumed that publishing such violent acts would horrify the spectators of the videos.[62] Intelligence experts thought showcasing violence would be counterproductive because under al-Zarqawi ISIS did alienate Sunni members of the society – it was one of the mistakes that he made and that helped to bring him down. However, the effect was the opposite, in the region it instilled fear and crumbled opposition but abroad it served as a recruiting attraction for foreigners to join ISIS.[63]

Foreign fighters and terrorist repercussions: In the first months of ISIS's consolidation of power it was not clear to Middle East specialists that the group would eventually become such a massive jihadi magnet for Muslims around the world and that Muslims from Europe and the UK would join ISIS.[64] However, once the flow of foreign fighters and their easy routes via Turkey were known, the threat posed by possible returnees was identified right away.[65] Terrorist attacks like the one in Belgium in May 2014 were in many ways expected and specialists continued to warn about the national security risks of European ISIS fighters.[66]

A sophisticated online recruitment machine: ISIS's capacity to reach its supporters around the words was not surprising per se, given that a lot of its members were young people who grew up with new forms of technology and were familiar with the use of social media. Where Middle East specialists were however taken by surprise was in the professionalism and innovation of ISIS's PR machinery and by the phenomenon of online self-radicalisation.[67] From August 2013 onwards, ISIS carefully crafted videos with impressive filmographic professionalism and managed to reach exactly its intended target audience. Through its online ties around the word, ISIS was then able to convince its supporters to perpetrate terrorist attacks in its name. This was unexpected because Muslim communities have not had members who radicalised in that way before. Even though lone-wolf terrorism had already emerged, ISIS's very professional propaganda and recruitment mechanism via social media was a genuinely surprising turn, which was not foreseen by specialists.

Altogether, one can summarise the various elements as follows: commentators knew about Syrian rebel fragmentation and infighting, but not that ISIS would end up as the most dominant group. Specialists knew about the Iraqi government's widespread corruption, but not that the Iraqi army would thus be so deprived of resources and weak. Experts knew about Iraqi Sunni frustration, but not that so many would join or tolerate ISIS. Specialists knew about ISIS's plans for a caliphate, but not that its cruel regime would last over several months. Specialists knew about ISIS's attraction, but not that Turkey would open the borders and so many foreign fighters would join. Specialists knew that ISIS would use any kind of technology at its disposal, but not that it would lead to self-radicalisation and ISIS-inspired terrorism. Altogether, for Western observers ISIS represented a partial surprise, where most elements were known in advance, but where they developed in an unexpected way.

How did UK and International Knowledge Producers Perform when Confronted with ISIS's Rise to Power?

It was unlikely that ISIS would end up as the most dominant group in Syria: Looking at UK specialists' and international experts' assessments about the rise of ISIS in Syria during the year before the fall of Mosul, as mentioned above, one can say that UK knowledge producers accurately and thoroughly reported about major events in the Syrian civil war. ISIS was a relatively small element of it, up until early 2014. This is understandable, since only after ISIS's rise in Iraq and once it managed to bridge the two areas did it fully crystallise to what extent ISIS had become a force on its own. The cross-national and international dimensions of the war were highlighted numerously though; it was however not clear at the time that ISIS would be the part that was going to eventually bridge the regional elements of the conflict.

Misjudging ISIS's appeal to secular insurgents and Western women: At the time when ISIS came to strength in 2014, Iraqi society was ravaged by deep-seated grievances of the Sunni population towards the governing Shia elites. The rift was so severe that once ISIS gained momentum, it was able to attract insurgents from various backgrounds, no matter its colour. With ISIS's very pronounced religious outlook and radical Islamist self-definition, regional expects had not expected former members of a secular political party, like the Ba'ath, to join an ultra-religious movement like ISIS.[68]

Similarly, via ISIS's global reach, the group was able to appeal to Muslims around the world and give them new meaning in their lives by being part of a caliphate. ISIS could evoke true religious eschatological beliefs that the last battle was coming.[69] While foreign fighters were also motivated to join ISIS by a sense of adventure and a lack of perspective in their professional developments at home, it was surprising for analysts that such a religious fundamentalist ideology would be as appealing to them.[70] Intelligence analysts had not expected that the establishment of a caliphate would become such a massive draw, in particular also to people who grew up in European societies shaped by predominantly secular views.[71]

Relatedly, in 2014 the so-called phenomenon of 'niqab-jihad' appeared, namely Western women leaving their homes for Syria to support ISIS fighters. The main reason for these women to join ISIS was their perception of ISIS jihadists living a 'perfect life'.[72] This was based on the way ISIS members presented themselves on social media, namely as war heroes, religiously devoted, and exemplary Muslims; a life many women admired and wanted to share.[73] Once in situ, women were said to have helped mainly with transferring funds, acquiring equipment, cooking for the men, or simply being their wives.[74] Women leaving Europe to become the wives of ISIS fighters was unexpected in light of radical Islam's well-documented highly misogynistic traits, where women were considered mere sex slaves or birthing machines. With ample reporting about ISIS's regime and its pronounced views about women, the so called 'niqab-jihad' women had thus most likely known (if not necessarily understood) what was awaiting them in Syria. This was of course all the more surprising given that the women were usually born and raised in the West, enjoying the rights attributed to women in a modern-day society. For most analysts it was hard to imagine why anyone would voluntarily give up such freedoms.

The risks of foreign fighters and terrorist repercussions was understood from the beginning: The threat of ISIS foreign fighters and returnees was detected as soon as the phenomenon manifested itself and the security implications for the UK were understood right away. The danger coming from ISIS's foreign fighters thus presented no surprise at all to the UK specialist community. From the beginning, UK media issued clear warnings and concise threat assessments, devised realistic scenarios, and closely followed events in the UK and the region, including Turkey's role as jihadi route facilitator. The actual moment of surprise about ISIS's global reach happened a few months later when in September 2014 the first exclusively online-radicalised ISIS-inspired terrorist attack happened in Melbourne, Australia.[75] It was new because the person had no previous physical contact with ISIS (nor had travelled to the region) and decided to perpetrate the terror act solely on the basis of online self-radicalisation.

Unprecedentedness of online self-radicalisation: An extensive article about ISIS's online presence was written in April 2014 by Fraser Nelson of *The Telegraph*. He stressed how powerless UK authorities were when faced with online recruitment, what he called 'cyber-jihad'. He also stressed how difficult it was for them to detect radicalisation early enough.[76] Josie Ensor, also from *The Telegraph*, emphasised the importance of social media for ISIS's recruitment.[77] Apart from these articles, at that time very little was reported in the media about ISIS's social media propaganda efforts.

Three main reasons can explain why there was only little news about it. First, even though ISIS created its first Twitter account in October 2013, only several months later did ISIS start to massively expand its online capacity. For instance, in April 2014 the group launched a twitter app that was able of sending over 10,000 tweets a day.[78] It is therefore understandable that specialists had only gradually realised the importance of social media for ISIS recruitments. Second, in its global online recruitment and radicalisation tactics, ISIS especially targeted young people. Consequently, it used various social media applications which at the time were mainly known to young people and which might have been less familiar to Middle Eastern specialists from older generations. Furthermore, ISIS obviously used a variety of social media channels (like Snapchat, Kik, Twitter, ASK.fm, Facebook, YouTube, WhatsApp and others); this made it very difficult for journalists to keep the overview and would have led to a sheer infinite amount of data to monitor. Third, the danger of social media links between ISIS and Muslims around the world had only become clear once the phenomenon of ISIS-inspired terrorist attacks started to happen. Namely, attacks that were perpetrated solely based on self-radicaliation and without any physical links between the terrorist perpetrator and ISIS. As mentioned before, this had only started in September 2014.[79] Such a use of online mechanisms for terrorism recruitment had hardly happened before, and the dangers of jihadi online self-radicalisation were not well known before it happened. In terms of discontinuity or uniqueness of a threat, one can argue that ISIS's recruitment capacity via self-radicalisation through social media was unprecedented. Even though lone-wolf terrorism had already emerged, ISIS's very professional propaganda and recruitment mechanism via social media was a genuinely surprising turn and can explain why analysts had not anticipated (or been able to) ISIS as a global terrorism movement. This also explains why UK media had not given that much attention to ISIS's social media strategy.

What were the Main Causes of High and Low Performance?

Looking at ISIS's rise to power as a whole and the shortcomings of the specialist community, there are various underlying reasons that can explain the analysts' performance.

It was unthinkable that a Western-built and -trained army could collapse: Reflecting about the moment of surprise around the fall of Mosul, two aspects are worth mentioning. First, very little attention was given to the army prior to its spectacular collapse in the face of ISIS. Even though it was known that corruption was endemic in Iraq, it was not clear that the army would thus be as deprived of resources. Second, the question arises whether regional analysts ignored reports about possible weaknesses in the army because it was unthinkable that a Western-built and -trained army could fail. In other words, UK specialists fell into the trap of their own propaganda that proclaimed that the Iraqi army was progressing as planned after the successful surge and the transition.[80]

This meant that Iraq could not be allowed to be seen as a failure by the US or the UK, namely because it was highly inconvenient to envisage Iraq falling so easily and needing more Western support. This relates to more general questions of Security Sector Reform and the accuracy of intelligence after a military intervention. An interesting, more general question to ask would thus be: can there be impartial and unbiased intelligence reporting about a security force that was built by the same actor who produced the intelligence?

Underestimating al-Qaeda's adaptability and mutability: After the death of Osama Bin Laden, globally al-Qaeda was in decline. The various al-Qaeda branches refocused more locally and directly addressed grievances against their local government. From al-Qaeda of the Islamic Maghreb (AQIM) to al-Qaeda in the Arabian Peninsula (AQAP), al-Qaeda seemed to be on the defensive and leaders in Europe and the US expected its slow demise.[81]

The error might have been that analysts saw al-Qaeda as one big block and failed to understand that a branch could break off and become a new Jihadi force on its own. The question arises whether Western analysts generally might attribute to such organisations a certain degree of permanence and identity and fail to see them as the expression of underlying discontent or shared set of tribal/religious allegiances and fears that can express themselves in different ways and through different organisational forms. In other words, to understand ISIS or any emerging threat it is crucial to understand the root causes, constituency, networks and coalitions that support it. This is also relevant for assessing ISIS today or any of its new manifestations under a different name.

Lack of understanding of the psychological impact of ISIS videos: Like the public, experts too were shocked to see ISIS's propaganda videos and even more surprised about the popularity of these videos in Muslim online communities around the world. Online, ISIS's extremely violent videos met a group of young men who had been desensitised to violence through computer games and who were attracted to violence as part of manhood adventures. The spread of ISIS violence in these circles can be explained by feelings of revenge against humiliation, a longing for adventure and a desire for a bigger purpose in life. The psychological impact of ISIS's videos on these groups was not well understood at the time.

Conclusion

In this concluding section, we compare the two actors and refer in more depth to the results of two workshops that were held with intelligence and government officials in Germany and the UK in April and June 2021 respectively. Applying the same structure that guided our sections, we first discuss ISIS's rise to power as a surprise for German and British knowledge producers. Second, we look at diagnostic difficulties that they experienced. Third, we evaluate the underlying causes of performance problems in both countries.

What was Surprising for German and UK Knowledge Producers?

Experts in both countries experienced partial surprise about relevant events that marked ISIS's rise to power as a foreign policy crisis. They adequately understood structural vulnerabilities in Syria and Iraq and security risks in the region at the strategic level. When confronted with ISIS's territorial advances in its core conflict zone, especially from December 2013 onwards, knowledge producers experienced tactical surprise. The first ISIS-inspired terrorist attack in Europe was also partially surprising for both actors. While the exact location of the attack was unknown, intelligence communities and external experts in both countries were acutely aware of, and correctly assessed, the risk that radicalised European 'ISIS returnees' posed to European security.

Regarding the fall of Mosul to ISIS, both actors were surprised by the complete withdrawal of the Iraqi army, the ease with which ISIS captured Mosul, and ISIS's rapid expansion beyond the city. UK and German knowledge producers were at least partly aware of the structural vulnerabilities that facilitated the collapse of the Iraqi army, including widespread corruption, low morale and limited military capabilities. Similarly, frustration within Sunni communities was known, and it was expected that ISIS would exploit this. Altogether, the broader regional, long-term developments were well understood, but the speed with which ISIS gained strength and became more destructive was unexpected.

What were Key Diagnostic Difficulties for German and UK Experts?

A major difficulty, which affected Germany more than the UK, was a lack of resources and access, particularly concerning Syria but also Iraqi areas outside of Baghdad and Erbil. It proved challenging to draw on local contacts and find reliable reports, for instance during ISIS's Anbar campaign and prior to the fall of Mosul. Diagnostic difficulties which cut across both countries' expert communities were that the Syrian civil war entailed too many moving parts. The complexity was exacerbated by the speed of parallel developments across Syria and Iraq, while intelligence and expert communities were traditionally organised along country foci. This contributed to limited understandings of certain structural vulnerabilities, such as the actual weakness of Iraqi security forces.

Another diagnostic difficulty revolved around the high degree of discontinuity and novelty with ISIS breaking away from al-Qaeda. Many German and British experts saw al-Qaeda as one big group and failed to understand how ISIS emerged as a different powerful actor. Unlike al-Qaeda, ISIS became a genuinely transnational jihadist organisation with global reach. Additionally, radicalisation happened more rapidly and less visibly than in earlier cases, such as Afghanistan. The situation in Turkey was also novel and diagnostically challenging, with ISIS recruits gaining easy access into Syria.

In terms of threat assessments, we need to distinguish between two aspects. One was the threat stemming from 'ISIS returnees', which was well understood and regularly warned about. The other was the threat stemming from online self-radicalisation by Europeans without prior physical contact with ISIS. This second threat was unprecedented and initially not foreseen by neither German nor UK analysts. It proved difficult to trace the radicalisation and activities of a rapidly growing number of individuals across Europe. Overall, the diagnostic challenges were enormous and affected both British and German intelligence analysts.

What were the Underlying Reasons for Performance Problems in Germany and the UK?

German experts lacked resources during the period under study, which was due to the limited political interest in Iraq and the Middle East broadly prior to the summer of 2014. Senior intelligence officials and policymakers were initially not receptive to expert warnings about the evolving crisis in Syria and Iraq. Among other things, Germany lacked Arabic speakers and regional specialists as well as adequate analytical tools to follow developments in the Middle East which hampered the performance of knowledge producers.

The UK IC also placed Iraq rather low on the foreign political agenda, albeit for different reasons. After the US troop withdrawal in 2011, national narratives in the UK had been shaped by 'Iraq fatigue', based on a desire by policymakers and analysts to distance themselves from Iraq and prevent any scenario that would involve military intervention in the region.[82] A problem experienced by both countries was that structures for efficient inter-institutional cooperation were not yet in place during this early phase of the crisis.

British and German intelligence analysts experienced professional-cultural biases which hindered their performance. British analysts experienced this in the form of a skewed view of the Iraqi forces due to the UK's involvement in the training, equipment and build-up of the Iraqi army. German analysts felt that they had failed to fully comprehend societal dynamics and power structures in Iraq due to 'Western bias'. More reflection upon and compensation for such biases might have improved risk assessments, particularly related to the weakness of the Iraqi army.

Lastly, both countries had to deal with agenda competition during the period under study: the second stage of ISIS's rise to power from January 2014 onwards coincided with the evolving Ukraine crisis, among other international pressures that demanded German and British attention. Prior to that, German and British policymakers had been absorbed by debates about the use of chemical weapons in Syria and potential political solutions to the Syrian civil war, without paying sufficient attention to how ISIS emerged as a powerful player in Syria – among others by benefiting from the demoralisation, decentralisation and fragmentation of Syrian rebel groups.

Comparing experiences of surprise, performance and the underlying causes of performance shortcomings in Germany and the UK, knowledge producers in both countries operated in similar contexts. One major difference was the prior experiences which had shaped national interests in Iraq: while Germany had been demonstrating its political disinterest in Iraq since 2003, the UK had been closely involved, followed by a desire for disengagement after the withdrawal of its remaining forces from Iraq in May 2011. These differences in experience notwithstanding, which clearly shaped analytical lenses, experts in both countries anticipated the emerging crisis quite similarly.

Notes

1. For German and British experts, see, for instance: Tagesschau, 'Baghdad ist auf der Kippe', 12 June 2014; Catherine Philp, 'Islamic insurgents push Baghdad to the brink', *The Times*, 12 June 2014.
2. Eric J. Dahl, 'Not Your Father's Intelligence Failure: Why the Intelligence Community Failed to Anticipate the Rise of ISIS', in *The Future of ISIS: Regional and International Implications*, ed. Faisal Al-Istrabadi and Sumit Ganguly, (Washington, DC: Brookings, 2018), 43; James J. Wirtz, 'When Do You Give It a Name? Theoretical Observations about the ISIS Intelligence Failure', in *The Future of ISIS: Regional and International Implications*, ed. Faisal Al-Istrabadi and Sumit Ganguly, (Washington, DC: Brookings, 2018),

69; Ephraim Kam, 'The Islamic State Surprise: The Intelligence Perspective', *Strategic Assessment* 18, no.3 (2015): 28.

3. This chapter draws on sections of and research undertaken for: Eva Michaels, 'How Surprising was ISIS' Rise to Power for the German Intelligence Community? Reconstructing Estimates of Likelihood Prior to the Fall of Mosul', *Intelligence and National Security*, online first (2021); Aviva Guttmann, 'The Rise of ISIS as a Partial Surprise: An Open-source Analysis on the Threat Evolution and Early Warnings in the UK' (forthcoming with *International Journal of Intelligence and CounterIntelligence*).

4. Outputs by other German think tanks were negligible, for instance by the German Institute for Global and Area Studies (GIGA). Relevant knowledge claims have been compiled in an open-access database: Eva Michaels, 'Germany's Anticipation of and Response to ISIS' Rise to Power: Overview of Open-Source Expert Claims and Policy Responses' (2021). The keyword search (in German) included 'Syrien', 'Irak', 'Islamischer Staat', 'ISIS', 'Al-Qaida/Al-Kaida im Irak'.

5. Relevant knowledge claims have been compiled in an open-access database: Aviva Guttmann and Bahar Karimi, 'Timeline of UK Media and Middle East Experts' Anticipation of the Rise of ISIS and UK Government reactions' (2021). International NGOs specifically shaped policy debates in the UK by writing or being quoted as authoritative sources about the evolving crisis. This claim is based on a perusal of parliamentary and governmental publications and news reports published during this time (see ibid.). The keywords search for the open-source analysis for UK and international experts included 'Islamic State', 'Syria', 'Iraq', 'ISIS', 'Al-Qaeda in Iraq', 'Islamic State of Iraq and al-Sham', 'Islamic State of Iraq and the Levant', 'ISIL' and 'Jabhat al-Nusra'.

6. Christoph O. Meyer and Ana Maria Albulescu, 'Britisches Vorbild: Was die nächste Bundesregierung vom Vereinigten Königreich über kritische Selbstreflexion und außenpolitisches Handeln lernen könnte', *Internationale Politik*, 2021.

7. Hassan Abu Hanieh and Mohammad Abu Rumman, *The 'Islamic State' Organization: The Sunni Crisis and the Struggle of Global Jihadism* (Amman: Friedrich Ebert Stiftung, 2015), 178; Tallha Abdulrazaq and Gareth Stansfield, 'The Enemy Within: ISIS and the Conquest of Mosul', *The Middle East Journal* 70, no. 4 (2016).

8. Martin Smith and Linda Hirsch, 'The Rise of ISIS', Frontline, 2014.

9. For instance: HRW, *Iraq: Wave of Journalist Killings*, 29 November

2013; Anthony H. Cordesman and Sam Khazai, *Iraq in Crisis* (Lanham, MD: Rowman & Littlefield, 2014).

10. For a discussion in the US context, see: Joby Warrick, *Black Flags: The Rise of ISIS* (London: Bantam, 2015).

11. Unless stated differently, the evidence presented in this section is drawn from interviews with external experts (Berlin: 26 August 2019, 4 September 2019, 9 September 2019, 19 September 2019) and intelligence analysts (Berlin: 3 September 2019, 6 September 2019, 18 September 2019, 27 September 2019, 1 October 2019, 4 November 2019, 6 November 2019, 29 November 2019) as well as a workshop with government and intelligence officials on 26 April 2021.

12. The German intelligence community is here understood as including members of the foreign and domestic intelligence agencies, Bundeswehr intelligence analysts, and desk officers in government departments who all produced intelligence on Iraq, Syria, radicalisation and/or terrorism.

13. The conceptualisation of threats has been adapted from: David Strachan-Morris, 'Threat and Risk: What is the Difference and Why Does it Matter?', *Intelligence and National Security* 27, no. 2 (2012). These three components were indeed on the radar of German intelligence analysts when assessing the threat (interviews, Berlin, 3 September 2019).

14. This has been adapted from: Strachan-Morris, 'Threat and Risk', 180.

15. For instance, the following experts had argued in early January 2014 that ISIS was becoming less powerful in Syria and was concentrating its efforts on Iraq, thereby dismissing the idea that ISIS could fully capture Raqqa and strengthen its territorial control in eastern Syria: Alfred Hackensberger, 'Al-Qaida schafft einen Gottesstaat im Niemandsland', *Die Welt*, 5 January 2014; Rainer Hermann and Christoph Ehrhardt, 'Zweifrontenkrieg gegen die Islamisten', *FAZ*, 6 January 2014; Christoph Reuter, 'Signal zum Aufstand', *Der Spiegel*, 12 January 2014.

16. *FAZ*, 'Dschihadisten stürmen Universität', 7 June 2014.

17. Christoph O. Meyer, Chiara De Franco and Florian Otto, *Warning about War: Conflict, Persuasion and Foreign Policy*, (Cambridge: Cambridge University Press, 2020), 265–6.

18. Jörg Diehl and Christoph Sydow, 'Deutscher Salafist ruft zu Selbstmordanschlägen auf', *Der Spiegel*, 1 August 2013.

19. Rainer Herrmann, 'Kampfzone Levante', *FAZ*, 4 August 2013.

20. Wolfgang Bauer, 'Das Syrien-Drama: Assad weiß, wo sie sind', *Die Zeit*, 12 September 2013.
21. Sonja Zekri, 'Abschreckendes Beispiel Irak', *SZ*, 4 September 2013.
22. John Hulsman, 'Schlafwandelnd in Richtung Disaster', *SZ*, 1 September 2013.
23. Markus Bickel, 'Auf sich selbst zurückgeworfen', *FAZ*, 19 September 2013; Sonja Zekri, '50.000 Islamisten sagen sich von Übergangsregierung los', *SZ*, 25 September 2013.
24. Petra Becker, 'Syrian Muslim Brotherhood Still a Crucial Actor', SWP Comment 34, October 2013; Markus Bickel, 'Der Krieg im Bürgerkrieg', *FAZ*, 22 November 2013.
25. Focus (quoting SWP's Heiko Wimmen), 'Waffenlieferungen nach Syrien geraten außer Kontrolle', 16 November 2013.
26. Raniah Salloum, 'Irakische Qaida baut Macht im Norden Syriens aus', *Der Spiegel*, 9 November 2013.
27. Rainer Hermann, 'Ein Afghanistan am Mittelmeer', *FAZ*, 12 December 2013.
28. Christoph Reuter, 'Die schwarze Macht', *Der Spiegel*, 15 December 2013.
29. Ibid.
30. Rüdiger Soldt and Reiner Burger, 'Über die A8 nach Aleppo', *FAZ*, 18 December 2013.
31. Markus Bickel, 'Der Diktator als Staatsmann', *FAZ*, 21 December 2013.
32. Deutsche Welle (quoting SWP's Guido Steinberg), 'Al Qaeda Growing Stronger in Iraq and Syria', 4 January 2014.
33. *FAZ*, 'Im Irak gibt es keinen Staat', 28 April 2014.
34. David Omand, 'Reflections on Intelligence Analysts and Policymakers', *International Journal of Intelligence and Counterintelligence* 33, no. 3 (2020): 477. See also a related in-depth discussion of persuasive warnings in Meyer et al., *Warning about War*, 21–30.
35. Hermann and Ehrhardt, 'Zweifrontenkrieg gegen die Islamisten'; Reuter, 'Signal zum Aufstand'.
36. Hackensberger, 'Al-Qaida schafft einen Gottesstaat im Niemandsland'.
37. Guido Steinberg, 'Der Irak und der syrische Bürgerkrieg', *SWP Aktuell* 46 (2013); Guido Steinberg, 'Irak: im Zangengriff der Konfessionen', *Welt-Sichten*, 5 December 2013.
38. Deutsche Welle (quoting Guido Steinberg), 'Al Qaeda Growing Stronger in Iraq and Syria'.

39. Rudolph Chimelli, 'Drei-Fronten-Krieg gegen den Terror', *SZ*, 7 January 2014.
40. Steinberg, 'Irak: im Zangengriff der Konfessionen'.
41. See also: Christoph O. Meyer, Eric Sangar and Eva Michaels. 'How Do Non-Governmental Organizations Influence Media Coverage of Conflict? The Case of the Syrian Conflict, 2011–2014', *Media, War & Conflict* 11, no. 1 (2018).
42. Interview, Berlin, 4 September 2019.
43. Alfred Hackensberger, 'Die Kurden wollen weg von Bagdad', *Die Welt*, 29 April 2014.
44. This paragraph draws on the political statements in the open-source database (Michaels, 'Germany's Anticipation of and Response to ISIS' Rise to Power') and on six interviews with German policymakers and foreign policy advisors in parliament (Berlin, 27 August 2019, 30 August 2019, 4 September 2019, 5 September 2019, 10 September 2019, 6 November 2019).
45. In a March 2014 report on disarmament, the government briefed the Bundestag about the capability of the Iraqi security forces and identified key challenges (for example capability shortfalls, corruption, infiltration by militant groups, limited loyalty to central government). Deutscher Bundestag, *Unterrichtung durch die Bundesregierung 18/933*, 27 March 2014, 76.
46. Deutscher Bundestag, *Kleine Anfrage 18/1335*, 7 May 2014; Deutscher Bundestag, *Kleine Anfrage 18/1541*, 21 May 2014.
47. They also struggled with the lack of access. Local or semi-local (with headquarters abroad) NGOs filled this gap. Examples are the Syrian Observatory for Human Rights or Raqqa is Being Slaughtered Silently.
48. Michaela Wiegel, 'Ein Fahndungserfolg aus purem Zufall', *FAZ*, 2 June 2014.
49. Christoph Reuter, 'Disneyland für Dschihadisten', *Der Spiegel*, 7 July 2013.
50. Christoph Reuter, 'Der Preis des Zögerns', *Der Spiegel*, 19 August 2012; 'Die schwarze Macht'.
51. Anthony Loyd and Sheer Frenkel, 'Iraqi al-Qaeda joins Syrian rebels in merger that will alarm the West', *The Times*, 10 April 2013; and Anthony Loyd, 'Al-Qaeda sets up Sharia courts in key Syrian city', *The Times*, 3 May 2013.
52. Ruth Sherlock, 'Islamist rebels seize key Syrian helicopter base, boosting hardliners' influence', *The Telegraph*, 5 August 2013; Michael Peel, 'Syrian rebel infighting grows as al-Qaeda kills rival

commander', *Financial Times*, 12 July 2013; Con Coughlin, 'Now Syria's rebels are fighting each other', *The Telegraph*, 19 September 2013; ICG, 'Anything But Politics: The State of Syria's Political Opposition', Report 146, 17 October 2013.

53. ICG, 'Syria's Metastasising Conflicts', Report 143, June 2013; Boris Johnson, 'We've left it too late to save Syria – this conflict can never be won', *The Telegraph*, 16 June 2013; Borzou Daragahi, 'Al-Qaeda affiliated group seizes rebel-controlled Syrian town', *Financial Times*, 19 September 2013; Borzou Daragahi, 'Middle East: Three Nations, One Conflict', *Financial Times*, 27 May 2014.

54. Tom Porteous, 'Sectarianism in the Muslim World is Dividing People who have Lived Together for Centuries', 18 July 2013; *The Telegraph*, 'Iraqis blame government for lack of protection as al-Qaeda claim responsibility for deadly attacks', 12 August 2013; Erin Evers, 'Executions Don't Make Iraq Safe', 11 October 2013; David Blair, 'Al-Qaeda is thriving amid the chaos of Iraq', *The Telegraph*, 24 July 2013. For an unmistakably clear assessment about why Maliki was responsible for the insurgency, see: Sarah Leah Whitson, 'Letter to President Obama regarding the visit of Iraqi Prime Minister Nuri al-Maliki', 29 October 2013; Erin Evers, 'New Weapons Won't Address Iraq's Deeper Problems', 26 December 2013; *Financial Times*, 'Iraq needs a future without Maliki', 30 April 2014.

55. With every mention of another series of terrorist attacks, journalists highlighted the risk of an impending full-out civil war. For early accounts, see: David Blair, 'April Iraq's deadliest month in almost five years', *The Telegraph*, 2 May 2013; for July 2013, see: Hugh Tomlinson, 'Jailbreaks and suicide bombers push Iraq back towards anarchy', *The Times*, 23 July 2013; *Financial Times*, 'Multiple car bombs kill dozens across Iraq', 29 July 2013. For another article mentioning July 2013 as the deadliest months since 2008, see: *The Telegraph*, 'Wave of violence sees at least 47 killed across Iraq', 26 August 2013. For August 2013, see: Hugh Tomlinson, 'Rush-hour suicide bomb attacks kill 71 in Baghdad', *The Times*, 28 August 2013. For September 2013, see: Catherine Philp, 'Dozens killed as wave of bombings hits Baghdad', *The Times*, 30 September 2013. For October, see: Borzou Daragahi, 'Surge in Iraq violence raises fears of return to sectarian civil war', *Financial Times*, 2 October 2013. NGOs too reported especially in July 2013 about the drastic increase of sectarian violence in Iraq, see HRW, 'Iraq: Attacks Amount to Crimes Against Humanity, Authorities Should End Draconian Responses', 11 August 2013; ICG, Crisis Watch, July 2013.

125

56. HRW, 'Iraq: Attacks Amount to Crimes Against Humanity, Authorities Should End Draconian Responses'; ICG, 'Make or Break: Iraq's Sunnis and the State', Report 144, 14 August 2013; HRW, 'Iraq: Harsh Tactics in Advance of Holy Month', 15 November 2013. For an account of local alienation in Sunni areas of Iraq, see: Richard Spencer, 'Five killed in gunfight during raid on home of Iraqi MP', *The Telegraph*, 28 December 2013.

57. Disbelief was felt also because in sheer numbers the Iraqi army was by far the most powerful element compared to the Peshmerga and ISIS: *The Telegraph*, 'Iraqi forces by numbers: who has the biggest army?', 12 June 2014; Geoff Dyer, 'Iraq's under-resourced army no match for Sunni insurgents', *Financial Times*, 11 June 2014; Erika Solomon, 'Islamist insurgents seize Iraqi city of Mosul', *Financial Times*, 10 June 2014; Catherine Philp, 'Citizens flee after Islamist rebels take Iraq's second city', *The Times*, 11 June 2014.

58. Geoff Dyer, 'US alarmed at being dragged into fresh Iraq conflict', *Financial Times*, 10 July 2014; Catherine Philp, 'Every US soldier who has fought there has the same question', *The Times*, 11 July 2014.

59. Richard Spencer, 'Al-Qaeda's Syrian wing takes over the oilfields once belonging to Assad', *The Telegraph*, 18 May 2013; Ruth Sherlock, 'Syria: Al-Qaeda-linked rebels execute regime "militia men" in front of children', *The Telegraph*, 13 September 2013; Alexander Christie-Miller, 'Al-Qaeda strives to build Islamic state in northern Syria', *The Times*, 26 October 2013; Catherine Philp, 'Pay taxes in gold or die, Christians in Syria told', *The Times*, 3 March 2014.

60. Anthony Loyd, 'Boy, 15, is killed in front of parents for "insulting Prophet"', *The Times*, 11 June 2013; Anthony Loyd, 'Boy of 16 is whipped to satisfy the public clamour for "Justice" – The rebel response to crime and disorder is brutality in the name of Sharia', *The Times*, 3 July 2013. In October reports centred on ISIS's use of torture: Alexander Christie-Miller, 'Hanged and beaten, but Syrian activist lived to tell the tale', *The Times*, 23 October 2013; HRW, 'Iraq: Attacks Amount to Crimes Against Humanity, Authorities Should End Draconian Responses'.

61. Richard Spencer, 'Syria: the jihadi town where "brides" are snatched from schools', *The Telegraph*, 29 March 2014; ICG, 'Anything But Politics: The State of Syria's Political Opposition'; Amnesty International, 'Syria: Rule of fear: ISIS abuses in detention in Northern Syria', 19 December 2013.

62. Interview with former UK official, 11 June 2021.

63. Ibid.
64. Anthony Loyd, 'Face to face with the new enemy in Syria', *The Times*, 19 September 2013. For the estimated number of foreign fighters in late October 2013, see: Ruth Sherlock, 'Al-Qaeda recruits entering Syria from Turkey safehouses', *The Telegraph*, 30 October 2013. For the estimated number of UK citizens fighting with ISIS at that time, see: Shiv Malik and Haroon Siddique, 'British family says son has died fighting for Syria jihadists', *The Guardian*, 21 November 2013.
65. Con Coughlin, 'The Syrian civil war is breeding a new generation of terrorist', *The Telegraph*, 3 December 2013. For a good summary of how the danger of ISIS foreign fighters was perceived at the time, see: Roula Khalaf, 'The costs of clandestine talks with Syria's strong-man', *Financial Times*, 17 January 2014.
66. Anthony Loyd, 'Syrian war revitalises al-Qaeda in Iraq', *The Times*, 12 December 2013; Ruth Sherlock, 'Al-Qaeda training British and European "jihadists" in Syria to set up terror cells at home', *The Telegraph*, 19 January 2014; Con Coughlin, 'Syria is now the gravest terrorist threat to Britain', *The Telegraph*, 10 April 2014; Sam Jones, 'Europe's fears of Syria blowback soar in wake of museum attack', *Financial Times*, 4 June 2014.
67. Fraser Nelson, 'Terrorism in the UK: social media is now the biggest jihadi training camp of them all', *The Telegraph*, 25 April 2014.
68. Richard Spencer, 'Iraq crisis Q & A: who or what is ISIS? Is it part of al-Qaeda?', *The Telegraph*, 11 June 2014.
69. William F. McCants, *The Isis Apocalypse: The History, Strategy, and Doomsday Vision of the Islamic State* (New York: Picador/ St. Martin's Press, 2016).
70. Interview with former UK official, 11 June 2021. For further reading about the reasons for foreign fighters to join ISIS, see: Efraim Benmelech and Esteban F. Klor, 'What Explains the Flow of Foreign Fighters to ISIS?', *Terrorism and Political Violence* 32, no. 7 (2020). Their argument suggests that two elements were driving the flow of foreign fighters: ideology and the difficulty of assimilation into homogenous Western countries.
71. Interview with former UK official, 11 June 2021.
72. Tom Coghlan, 'Jihadist groupies flocking to Syria with marriage in mind', *The Times*, 17 February 2014.
73. Ibid.
74. Duncan Gardham, 'Lonely-hearts blog for al-Qaeda fighters', *The Times*, 20 January 2014.

75. The first ISIS attack where the terrorist only had online contact with ISIS was the 23 September 2014 attack by Abdul Numan Haider. For the assessment that this was the first such incident, see Jessica Lewis McFate and Harleen Gambhir, 'ISIS's Global Messaging Strategy Factsheet', *Institute for the Study of War*, December 2014.

76. Nelson, 'Terrorism in the UK'.

77. Josie Ensor, 'British extremist in Syria says "this is no five-star Jihad"', *The Telegraph*, 21 April 2014.

78. Jessica Stern and J. M. Berger, *The State of Terror* (New York: HarperCollins, 2015), 10.

79. Such as the police stabbing on 23 September 2014 carried out by Abdul Numan Haider. See: Hilary Whiteman, 'Lone wolf? Australian police shoot dead teen "terror suspect"', CNN, 25 September 2014.

80. Interview with former UK official, 11 June 2021 and workshop also in June 2021 with members of the UK intelligence community.

81. The White House, Office of the Press Secretary. Remarks by the President at the National Defense University, Washington, DC, 23 May 2013.

82. This was emphasised during the workshop with members of the UK intelligence community in June 2021.

4 The Case of the Ukraine–Russia Undeclared War 2013/2014: Lessons for the EU's Estimative Intelligence[1]

Christoph O. Meyer and Nikki Ikani

Introduction

The annexation of the Crimean Peninsula by Russia in March 2014 was a strategic surprise for the EU of the most negative kind, not least as it was followed by Russia's increasingly direct military interference in eastern Ukraine that sparked open warfare with thousands of people being killed. The events marked a fundamental reassessment for the EU of the threat Russia posed not just to its immediate neighbours, but also to current EU member states with substantial Russian minorities and a history of being occupied or controlled by the Soviet Union. For the wider EU, it removed the already rather minimal basis for cooperative relations with Russia as fundamental international laws and diplomatic norms were broken in the most blatant way and it raised concern over whether the EU's approach to the region was still fit for purpose. When taken together with other Russian coercive and aggressive actions vis-à-vis some EU member states, it signalled for many observers nothing less than an undeclared new 'cold war'.[2] In contrast to the Georgian-Russian seven-day-war of 2008, the Ukraine-Russia conflict of 2014 triggered a number of postmortem studies by governments or parliamentary committees,[3] individual academics,[4] think tanks[5] and, of course, journalists to assess the performance of 'the West', the EU as a whole, or specific EU member states, and what lessons they should take away from this crisis. The overwhelming majority of these reviews focus on decisions and policies vis-à-vis Russia and Ukraine. The question of intelligence is typically treated as part of the wider question of whether 'the West', 'the EU' or particular states should have been surprised by what happened and whether or not these actors bear some responsibility for causing these Russian actions. Those who are more critical of the EU's policies vis-à-vis Ukraine and Russia also tend to claim that Russian military actions should not have come as a surprise.[6] Other scholars[7] claim that the EU at least played a causal role and should shoulder some responsibility for the crisis, while Richard Sakwa is even more critical of EU and NATO.[8] On the other side of the argument, one can find more nuanced and cautious discussions of the predictability of Russian actions,[9] as well as more positive or balanced assessments of the role the EU played before, during and after the crisis.[10]

Our argument speaks to those post-mortem studies interested in the quality of intelligence and diplomatic reporting prior to the events but may also have implications for the burgeoning literature looking at the role of experts, expertise and warning before and during crises affecting the EU in other policy fields.[11] This chapter does not seek to assess whether EU policies towards Ukraine, the other Eastern Partnership countries or Russia were well-designed, but puts into action the theoretical framework developed in Chapter 1 to concentrate on three questions: (1) to ascertain the degree of surprise for analysts and decision-makers by the events leading to the Ukrainian-Russian crisis, (2) to assess the performance of estimative intelligence production and political use given expectation-raising or -lowering factors at play, and finally (3) to go beyond the symptoms to identify the main underlying causes of problems with estimative intelligence and decision-maker receptivity experienced in this case.

Our empirical focus is on those parts of the EU's foreign policy machinery most directly concerned with relations to Ukraine and Russia. The EU's approach to negotiating the Association Agreement (AA) and the Deep and Comprehensive Free Trade Agreement (DCFTA) with Ukraine in Vilnius in the autumn of 2013 was led by the European Commission (DG NEAR) and specifically the Czech Commissioner for Enlargement, Štefan Füle, within a framework provided by the European Neighbourhood Policy of 2004 and the Eastern Partnership of 2009. At the same time, the EU's Foreign Affairs Council composed of national foreign ministers remained the ultimate decision-maker and was responsible for shaping the overall EU strategy vis-à-vis Russia. In-between, the EU's High Representative for Foreign and Security Policy and first Head of the newly created European External Action Service (EEAS), Catherine Ashton, had a legal mandate to ensure that the Commission, EEAS and national ministers arrived at shared definitions and plans for action in EU external affairs, even if her de facto role in this crisis was different. Much of the substantive discussion took place in key committees such as the Political & Security Committee (PSC), the Working Party on Eastern Europe and Central Asia (COEST) or the informal meetings of Ministry of Foreign Affairs (MFA) Political Directors. Intelligence provided to these different decision-makers came from relevant units within the EEAS, such as country desk-officers and the EU's civil and military intelligence assessment hubs, EU-INTCEN and EUMS.INT, the delegations and consulates of the EU in Ukraine and Russia, staff working in relevant directories of the EU Commission such as DG Trade and DG NEAR, and, of course, intelligence shared by EU member states' own services and agencies through various channels, including by their foreign ministers. We are drawing here on twenty-seven interviews with EU officials and member state diplomats and politicians, as well as open-source analysis of NGOs, media and think tanks.

The temporal focus is on the period from summer of 2013 until August 2014, particularly on a series of interconnected events and dynamics which took place during this timeframe without which, we argue, Russian actions nor the threat they posed to the EU can be adequately understood. Over the summer of 2013, Russia intensified its campaign against selected countries aiming to sign an Association Agreement as well as free trade agreements with the EU. This included Russia strong-arming Armenia into not signing the AA with the EU by selling artillery cannons and rocket launchers worth $1 billion to Azerbaijan in June,[12] and imposing trade restrictions against Ukrainian exports in August 2013. This was followed by a series of more or less surprising events, starting with President Yanukovych's short-notice decision not to sign the Association Agreement (AA) at the Eastern Partnership summit in Vilnius on 28–29 November 2013; the Euromaidan protests that erupted subsequently and the violent state reaction to them; the flight of the Ukrainian President on 21 February 2014 seeking eventually refuge in Russia; the initially covert military actions of Russia in Crimea that led to the Ukrainian peninsula's formal annexation on 18 March 2014; and Russia's growing military interference in eastern Ukraine, including the tragic events that led to the downing of the civilian airliner MH17 over Ukraine on 17 July 2014, killing 298 passengers and crew.[13]

Crisis Evolution: Who was Most Surprised about What?

How did this threat manifest itself over this period with the benefit of hindsight? This is not just a question of understanding the degree of surprise over what happened, but also the reasons for why events happened and how these relate to evolving under-standings of EU analysts and decision-makers at the time. The chain of events that led to the Russian intervention in Ukraine had deeper structural roots in a shift in Russian strategy and a dete-rioration in its relations with the West. The underlying structural cause of the conflict can be attributed to Russia's growing sense of victimisation by Western powers and vulnerability to the diffu-sion of Western liberal norms coupled with the widespread view of Ukraine belonging culturally and historically to Russia. The proximate cause turned out to be the complex Ukrainian domes-tic and international dynamics triggered by the country's immi-nent signature of an Association Agreement as well as a Deep and Comprehensive Free Trade Agreement in the autumn of 2013. We argue that the armed conflict in Ukraine was neither inevitable nor easily predictable as some scholars have declared in retrospect.[14] Indeed, the two main reasons that Mearsheimer provides in his 2010 published keynote speech for 'not ruling out' a war between Russian and Ukraine – the expiring Russian lease of Crimea for its navy in 2017 and the 'threat' of NATO membership for Ukraine –

had been pushed far into the distant future through the 2010 treaty extension to 2042 or shelved for the foreseeable future in the case of NATO membership.[15] They were certainly not hot issues at the start of the crisis in summer of 2013.

Ukraine has experienced tensions both domestically as well as with its large neighbour towards the East over its effective political and economic sovereignty since gaining independence in the aftermath of the collapse of the Soviet Union in 1991. These tensions intensified after the 'Orange Revolution' of 2004, which marked the start of numerous and multifaceted attempts by Russia to influence Ukrainian domestic politics in its favour, including the price of its gas exports. Even though Russia had guaranteed Ukrainian territorial integrity and sovereignty in the 1997 inter-state treaty and provided security assurances in the 1994 Budapest memorandum, this sovereignty continued to be disputed by senior Russian leaders and large swathes of Russian public opinion, and was frequently violated in small ways on the ground by the Russian Black Sea Fleet in Sevastopol without much Western media attention.[16] The degree to which Ukrainian statehood was disputed by Russian leaders and territorial sovereignty was not sacrosanct was not fully appreciated in Brussels or Western European capitals more broadly.

However, it was better understood by Ukraine specialists such as Taras Kuzio, who by 2010 was warning in a relatively low-profile think tank report of the growing risk of Russian military interference in Ukraine and was remarkably prescient on the structural and potential proximate causes.[17] At that time, the risk of Russian military interference in Ukraine had risen because of events in 2008 and 2009. After much international controversy, the 2008 NATO Bucharest alliance signalled the agreement 'that these countries will become members of NATO' and signalled support for their applications, although stopping short of granting Ukraine and Georgia membership action plans.[18] The prospect of such a likely expansion into Russia's immediate neighbourhood conveyed in this statement crossed a red line for the Russian leadership, sent conflicting messages to these countries and played an important role in the escalating tensions in Georgia, culminating in the August 2008 Russian-Georgian war over South Ossetia.[19]

In the immediate aftermath of the 2008 war, President Medvedev in an interview announced five new principles to guide Russian foreign policy; among them Russia's definition of regions of 'privileged interests' and 'an unquestionable priority to protect the life and dignity of our citizens, wherever they are'.[20] This so-called *Medvedev doctrine* was little commented upon by West European media at the time, but was noticed and perceived with great unease in the Baltics and many Eastern European capitals. Furthermore, Moscow learnt lessons about capability shortfalls it experienced during the Georgia war and in subsequent years intensified its investment in military and hybrid war capacities. These were developments that were not fully appreciated by most EU and open-source analysts, especially with respect to their scale and speed. While NATO shelved the membership issue for Ukraine and Georgia after the events of 2008, the EU after the initiative of Sweden and Poland aimed to strengthen its relations with six Eastern neighbours, including Ukraine, through the 2009 Eastern Partnership (EaP) initiative. Even though the EaP was not officially targeted against Russia in any way, it would have probably not been launched without changing threat perceptions vis-à-vis Russia after the Georgia war. Russian officials such as Foreign Minister Lavrov and Putin advisor Glazyev criticised the Eastern Partnership, but there were still hopes in Brussels that Russian concerns could be alleviated through better explanations as happened in relation to EU enlargement and the launch of the European neighbourhood policy.[21]

After his second election to the presidency in 2012, Putin adopted a more nationalistic and anti-liberal tone internally to outmanoeuvre some of the opposition forces that had taken to the streets of Moscow in 2011 after the manipulated Duma elections.[22] The regime became more aware of its potential vulnerability to public protests against corruption and authoritarian rule, feeding into a shift towards a more assertive foreign policy, amongst others by launching the Eurasian Economic Union (EEU) as a high-priority institutional initiative to compete with the EU integration project. The participation of Ukraine as a large country with strong cultural and economic connections to Russia was deemed politically essential to the success of this initiative and deemed incompatible with signing the DCFTA with the EU. While the use of Russian carrots and sticks against Ukraine was not new, the summer of 2013 saw a marked intensification of Russian pressure to prevent Ukraine and other neighbouring partnership countries from signing an Association Agreement as well as a free trade agreement with the EU at the Vilnius summit of 28–29 November 2013. Russia started putting significant pressure first on Armenia from May 2013 onwards and then on Ukraine from August 2013 onwards through trade embargoes, threats and other means, whilst domestic Russian voices, parliamentarians and TV anchors increasingly questioned the statehood of Ukraine and deployed harsh rhetoric against supporters of the AA. At the same time, Yanukovych was offered substantial financial incentives by Russia of significant discounts on gas, preferential loans and trade concessions amounting to 17 billion USD overall if he did not sign the AA/DCFTA.[23] Ukraine found itself in dire economic straits at the time, with its currency overvalued and having consumed all its reserves, effectively rendering these 'carrots' as lifelines.[24]

Armenia was the first to yield to this pressure when it announced in September 'to the surprise of everyone, that it would not go ahead with his own Association Agreement' according to a senior EU official.[25] The Armenian decision sparked efforts by senior diplomats in EEAS to instigate discussions about geopolitical risks in relation to Russia with the Commission,[26] but did so without much resolve or success and without explicitly warning of military intervention. Despite growing warning signs, it still came as a significant surprise to most EU leaders and most officials in the European Commission in charge of the negotiations when Yanukovych announced a week before the Vilnius summit on 28/29 November that he would suspend the signature of the AA. The reason is partly that until this point both government and opposition had appeared to be solidly supportive of signing the document after the negotiations had been concluded already in 2012. According to our interviews, the Armenian decision was seen as not directly applicable to Ukraine because the country was much more dependent on Russia for its security, particular in relation to its territorial disputes with Azerbaijan. Yet, some foreign ministers, particularly from Sweden and Poland, were urging their colleagues in the autumn to offer

Ukraine more support against Russian pressure and perhaps institute some 'soft' economic counter-sanctions to deter Russia from its effort and signal European resolve.

The Euromaidan protests in response to the decision were less of a surprise to EEAS officials although their nature, speed and impact were still surprising to most. This was partly because they were not led by the then discredited opposition figures as in the case of the Orange Revolution, but by grassroots activists, NGOs and journalists. Previously, the EU delegation in Kyiv had been much more negative in its reporting about the nature of the Ukrainian regime, and particularly the high degree of corruption, economic mismanagement and political repression than their political masters in Brussels, who were pushing for the Association Agreement to be signed and who concentrated conditionality on politically salient, but arguably fringe issues, such as the release of Julia Timoshenko from prison. Experts on Ukrainian politics argue that the significant failings of the Yanukovych regime would have made it likely that some kind of political unrest would have occurred, even without the government reneging on 21 November 2013 on earlier promises to sign the Association Agreement at the Vilnius summit.[27] In retrospect, it is clear that the European Commission's leadership, and particularly DG NEAR, did neither fully appreciate the degree of public hostility and the fragility of the country, nor the wider geopolitical and security risks at stake. Until late 2013 Ukraine was an issue dealt with by regional and technical specialists in the Commission, EAAS and Council working groups with a strong focus on whether Ukraine had made sufficient progress to meet the Council conditions for signing – following the technocratic logic of the EU enlargement process. For most of 2013, Ukraine was not mentioned on the formal agendas of the EU's Political Security Committee, whilst the ministerial-level Foreign Affairs Council was strongly preoccupied with other issues, especially the Syria conflict. Ukraine appears on the agendas of the Political and Security Committee only from 10 December onwards after the Euromaidan had started.

At the height of the domestic crisis, the leaders of EU states brokered an agreement with representatives of the Euromaidan, Yanukovych and Russia, which foresaw a national unity government and early general elections in September 2014. However, when uniformed snipers from the Ukrainian interior ministry police unit *Berkut* killed eighty-eight protesters in Kyiv on 20–21 February 2014, Yanukovych's remaining support in and outside parliament crumbled and he decided to flee first to the east of Ukraine and then to Russia.[28] Again, this event was not widely anticipated by EU observers and, according to interviewees, also came as an unwelcome surprise to Putin himself. According to some of our interviewees, Russia's relative acquiescence to Ukraine negotiating the AA with the EU was dependent on Ukraine being headed by 'their man' Yanukovych. This trust may have weakened, but his departure must have been a watershed moment for the Kremlin. While definitive and reliable evidence is outstanding, our desk research and practitioner interviews suggest that Putin had asked to update pre-existing plans for taking over Crimea many weeks prior to this event – even if planning may not have been as advanced and detailed and still involved an element of experimentation and improvisation according to a RAND study.[29] We believe that some basic plans for Crimea were in place in the run-up to the Vilnius summit, but consider it unlikely that these plans would have been put into action if the Ukrainian President had signed the AA in November as was widely expected. While definitive evidence from deliberations in the Kremlin is missing, we argue that it was the combination of the prospect of Ukraine turning to the EU and the West by signing the AA, together with the domestic political impact of losing a Russia-friendly regime to yet another colour revolution, that tipped the Kremlin to consider such an extreme and high-risk option.

In the run-up to Vilnius, the EU delegation in Kyiv and Moscow and the EEAS were planning for some Russian push-back and retaliation, including a gas cut-off, but did not discuss a military intervention in let alone annexation of Crimea. According to interviewees, for Russia to deploy regular military forces to annex the territory of a sovereign country was not considered a serious possibility even among many EU officials with substantial experience of dealing with Russia. The reason given for why it appeared unimaginable was that it would have constituted such a radical departure from the norms that had guided diplomacy and security relations, particularly in Europe, for such a long time. EU officials cited the agreement under international law, especially the Budapest memorandum, in this context. Indeed, this might tally with the result of a survey of international relations experts at the height of the crisis (24 February 2014), where only 14 per cent of 905 experts foresaw a Russian military intervention.[30] While Russia experts did somewhat better than the average, many such experts, including from countries such as Poland, admitted their surprise to us in interviews. Meanwhile, a Russian official had told the *Financial Times* on 20 February: 'If Ukraine breaks apart, it will trigger a war. They will lose Crimea first [because] we will go in and protect [it], just as we did in Georgia.'[31] Yet Russia experts such as the Carnegie Moscow Centre's Director Dimitri Trenin invoked as late as 23 February 2014 – when the operation was probably already under way – a number of economic and stability related reasons for why Russia would not seek to break up Ukraine through military force.[32] The Crimea operation was no doubt a high risk move for Russia given the substantial military presence of Ukrainian troops in Crimea as well as the potential reaction from the EU and the US. However, Putin could have reasonably assumed based on previous history that the EU would struggle to find the necessary unanimity needed for painful sanctions.

The Crimea operation, whilst indicating substantial Russian planning and efficiency in execution, turned out to be easier than Putin could have reasonably anticipated. In just two weeks, Russian special forces and the military intelligence directorate (GRU) operating without any insignia – known as the 'little green men' – managed to overthrow local Ukrainian authorities in Crimea with significant support from a small group of Ukrainian *Berkut* elite police forces, local powerbrokers and pro-Russia politicians.[33] They were significantly helped in their efforts by actions and communications from Ukrainian authorities, as an extensive analysis of RAND concluded.[34] This contributed to some Ukrainian officers in Crimea not being motivated to fight back and defecting when put under pressure. Moreover, Ukrainian forces lacked important capabilities and, importantly, were not given clear instructions from Kyiv to fight back as the US and other Western diplomats urged restraint. A referendum about the peninsula joining Russia was organised for 16 March in violation of the Ukrainian constitution and against all international standards, with the Russian Duma formalising the annexation on 18 March 2014 after the expected result.[35]

As far as the Foreign Affairs Council is concerned, we must conclude that the majority of ministers did not accept any suggestion that Russia could respond in extraordinary ways and might even violate Ukrainian sovereignty by force. The sense of frustration on the part of Poland over this disbelief was no secret and was mentioned by two other interview partners in the EEAS. As the crisis escalated, the readiness to accept Polish claims and those of a later EU delegation in Moscow changed gradually, even though disbelief that Russian troops were on the ground in Crimea continued well into March amongst some senior diplomats from countries such as Spain, Greece, Cyprus and Italy, as well as at the very top of the EU hierarchy. Even when shown pictures of the 'little green men', some national diplomats in Moscow as well as in Brussels, including the EEAS Managing Director for Europe and Central Asia, still refused to believe that Russia would send soldiers into a sovereign country. The last doubters came around only a few weeks later when the Russian Parliament annexed Crimea and medals were awarded on 25 March by the Ministry of Defence for actions relating to 'the return of Crimea 20.02.14–18.03.14'.[36] Acceptance of some elements of these warnings was higher in some parts of the EEAS than in the European Commission, where most career officials struggled to understand how Russia could possibly interpret the AA/DCFTA as a threat. As regards the Czech Enlargement Commissioner Füle, interviewed officials attribute to him a very strong personal commitment to get the Association Agreement signed at almost any cost as his political legacy in the last year of his tenure. It is therefore likely that Füle accepted that there was a possibility of Russian unhappiness and some economic and diplomatic reaction but did not consider these inherently harmful nor a reason to reconsider his push to get the AA signed.

What happened next in Donbas came as less of a surprise to the EU. Putin's victory speech on 18 March after the referendum vote talked about parts of eastern and southern Ukraine as historically belonging to Russia within an overall narrative of *NovoRossya*.[37]

Table 4.1 Overview of the nature of surprise

Events	What type of surprise to decision-makers	What type of surprise to knowledge producers
U-turn of President at Vilnius	Significant surprise	Partial surprise
Euromaidan	Partial surprise	Partial surprise
Yanukovych fleeing the country	Significant surprise	Partial surprise
Military intervention in and annexation of Crime	Perfect surprise for most, but some divergence	Significant to perfect surprise
Russian support and eventual intervention in Donbas region	Partial surprise	Partial surprise

Russian-backed separatists in the Donbas region tried initially to gain similar levels of support as those experienced in Crimea, but these efforts largely failed. The initially relatively limited deployment of Russian special forces and regular troops indicated that Putin did not follow the same game plan as in Crimea, and outright annexation was not, at least initially, the intended objective rather achieving federalisation of the ground through relying on well-supported local separatist forces.[38] A more likely goal seems to have been to create an internal conflict in eastern Ukraine as a thorn in the flesh for the country, effectively putting a halt to all NATO efforts. In contrast to what happened in Crimea, the Ukrainian state started to defend its political control over the Donbas from spring onwards through increasingly effective military means; first against the Russia-backed separatists and from July–August 2014 against 3,000–5,000 regular Russian troops drafted in by Putin from across the border to prevent a probable military defeat of the separatists.[39] Some EU intelligence services were worried that Russia might go further in the conflict and annex of larger parts of Ukraine to create *NovoRossya* stretching from eastern to southwestern Ukraine or even 'taking Kyiv'.[40] Rather than a false positive warning one could argue that a more determined than expected Ukrainian military fightback and stricter Western sanctions after MH17 have forestalled this possibility for the time being.

Assessing Performance, Including Mitigating and Exacerbating Reasons

We know from the previous section who was surprised about what and to what extent. However, being surprised is not an indication of performance problems per se as explained in Chapter 1. Could the EU's varying intelligence have been expected to deliver more accurate, timely and convincing intelligence assessment about the key events we have looked at, most notably the invasion and annexation of Crimea as the tactical dimension of surprise? And were the EU's different decision-makers sufficiently attentive, open-minded and, ultimately, accepting of high-quality estimative intelligence at least with regards to its knowledge claims?

If we start with the crucial case of Crimea, we observe that very few outside observers, including Russia specialists, forecast, let alone predicted, the annexation of Crimea as a Russian tactic. Given the absence of an inquiry, we do not know what precisely US intelligence knew about Russian plans for the invasion nor how well they substantiated and communicated any warnings. In response to criticism from Senator John McCain of Ukraine being an 'intelligence failure', the US Director of National Intelligence Clapper claimed '[w]e tracked (the situation in Ukraine) pretty carefully and portrayed what the possibilities were and certainly portrayed the difficulties we'd have, because of the movements of Russian troops and provided anticipatory warning of their incursion into Crimea'.[41] However, it is striking that none of our European interviews recalled receiving any warning from the US and claimed that their counterparts did not know any better, including UK ministers as part of the Five Eyes intelligence alliance. Our interviews also indicate that NATO, which in contrast to the EU was supposed to specialise in anticipating Russian threats, was by all accounts similarly blindsided by the events.[42] The diagnostic difficulties involved in this case were indeed formidable: a distinct departure from previous patterns established since the end of the Cold War, a significant rupture of a core principle of international law that Russia has often endorsed itself to attack Western liberal interventionism, as well as specific treaties protecting Ukraine's independence and territorial integrity signed by Russia itself in the 1990s. There are those, such as former Polish Prime Minister Sikorksi, who argue that the 'seven-day war' of 2008 between Georgia and Russia should have been a clear warning sign that Russia was ready to invade a sovereign country. This is not, however, how this crisis was perceived in most of Western Europe: the dominant interpretation was that the Georgian leadership under Saakashvili bore substantial responsibility for the war by aggressively wanting to reassert full control over the separatist provinces of Abkhazia and South Ossetia, but, more importantly, by falling for Russian provocations and starting the military offensive on South Ossetia first.[43] Lessons that could have been learnt from the episode were further diluted by the quick settlement of the crisis, and the signalling for more cooperative relations with Russia under the new President Medvedev. Furthermore, high-level political attention, willingness to learn and budgetary resources to implement any lessons were negatively affected by the escalating financial crisis, including the significant cuts to defence and security spending.

Furthermore, the way in which President Putin and his small and informal inner circle of advisors work made it particularly difficult for outside observers to know the true intentions of the Russian leadership. They managed to keep their planning secret – as surprise was important for its success – even after it was put into action, and this secrecy was coupled with disinformation through various 'spokespeople and experts', public and private denials, and of course public propaganda measures. Some senior Russian officials such as Lavrov were kept deliberately out of the picture to provide deniability. One of the few warning signals of what might happen came in September 2013 from Putin's advisor, Sergey Glazyev, 'on the sidelines of the discussion' to a *Guardian* reporter: 'We don't want to use any kind of blackmail', said Glazyev. 'But legally, signing this agreement about association with EU, the Ukrainian government violates the treaty on strategic partnership and friendship with Russia.' Should this happen, he said, Russia could possibly intervene if pro-Russian regions of the country appealed directly to Moscow: 'Signing this treaty will lead to political and social unrest [. . .] The living standard will decline dramatically . . . there will be chaos.'[44]

EU officials when asked about this article said they did not recollect it and it could count as a classical weak signal that was ignored at the time. The reason is easy to understand. Over many years, most analysts and indeed EU leaders have become desensitised to rhetoric from Moscow that was often considered to be over the top, outlandish and designed primarily for internal purposes. According to former Polish Foreign Minister Sikorski

> [. . .] the difference between Carl [Bildt] and me and a couple of other colleagues and the rest was that we thought that when Putin says he will do something, we should believe it, and other colleagues said 'nah, that's just propaganda for internal consumption, he can't possibly mean that'. [It is] in the eye of the beholder whether you take a hostile Putin speech as a warning or as an irrelevance. . . .[45]

In the specific case of Glazyev, he is known to have Ukrainian origins and radical views and could thus be easily discounted as somewhat of a fringe figure, prone to propagandistic hyperbole. Indeed, some European diplomats were explicitly assured by Foreign Minister Lavrov and his deputy not to worry too much about 'these Glazyevs [. . .] we are serious people, we are not paranoid' and that they would calm down the 'hotheads'.[46] These reassurances were even more credible given Russia's recent reputational investment in the Sochi Winter Olympics.

The Crimea operation itself seemed very high risk, not just in terms of its operational success on the ground but also in terms of potential Western reactions. We consider it likely that the decision to act in this way was a highly contingent one, namely that the final decision was only taken after Yanukovych was irrevocably 'lost' to Russia as a guarantor of Russian interest in Ukraine. This in turn created further diagnostic difficulties of understanding what happened in Ukraine itself as similarly important as appreciating the full extent of the underlying Russian hostility to the EU's Eastern Partnership and the broader approach of NATO and the US to these countries. It is far from clear, for instance, whether Russia would have taken the same action if Yanukovych had resisted Russian pressure and signed on the dotted line at Vilnius as was widely expected in Western capitals.

The EU could hardly be expected to live up to higher standards than the intelligence services of its constituent members, the US or NATO. On the contrary, the Brussels-based institutions were highly dependent on intelligence assessment from their members as they lacked sophisticated HUMINT or SIGNINT related to Russia for lack of an appropriate legal basis. The existing intelligence assessment structures such as INCENT and EUMS.INT have not yet evolved into providers of all-source authoritative intelligence with credibility for all EU actors, as will be discussed in more detail in the following chapter. Dealing with security and defence aspects was still relatively new to an organisation specialising for decades in market integration and socio-economic regulation and policymaking until the European Security and Defence Policy was created in 1999. Furthermore, the European Commission was in charge of the neighbourhood policy and trade policy even if the Council remained the ultimate decision-maker, and it lacked sufficient expertise of geopolitics and security matters generally, and Russia's foreign and security policy specifically. As such, EU officials were overly reliant on what they learned from their direct meetings with Russia's leaders and from official communications. Both in public hearings and in our interviews, EU officials pointed out that Russia had given little warning both in private and public about the strength of its opposition to the Association Agreement with Ukraine in particular. Negotiations of the Agreement had evolved without any significant public controversy since 2007.[47]

One could argue that the Commission's leadership, including the Commissioner of DG NEAR and the Commission President, could have been more receptive to attempts from within the EEAS to more carefully consider the geopolitics of the relationship with Ukraine. However, the EEAS was an extremely young body created in 2010; substantially understaffed and with little of its own resources, buffeted by recent crises, with a high turnover and many new staff, and lacking a highly esteemed and experienced leadership at the very top. HP/VP Ashton lacked the expertise, networks, confidence and credibility of her predecessor Solana, even though she had in theory more legal authority. She also suffered from the structural overload of her triple-hatted role (Commission VP/Head of EEAS/Chair of FAC) and the badly thought-out role of the EEAS. So, if anything, we should lower expectations towards the EU Commission and the EEAS regarding anticipating the strategic surprise of Crimea in a timely fashion.

The situation is somewhat different regarding the central decision-making organ in EU foreign policy, namely the Foreign Affairs Council. We have heard that the Polish and Swedish foreign ministers had warned their peers that Russia was exercising extreme pressure on Ukraine and that the EU needed to back up the country to prevent such pressure from escalating further. It is fair to argue that a number of European member states which generally saw Russia as more of a threat to their national interests and sovereignty have indeed been accurate and timely in picking up the distinct assertive and ethno-nationalist shift in Russian foreign policy post-2008 and particularly 2012, and thus have been broadly correct in giving 'strategic notice' of Russia as a growing threat. The Polish Foreign Minister claimed that he had also given more tactical warning about military action in Crimea and pointed to evidence of his comments on WikiLeaks made after the Georgia conflict to substantiate this.[48] We have been unable to verify the content of other specific, early and tactical oral warnings from other sources. The most likely explanation for this mismatch in recollection was that any warnings from the Polish and the Swedish side suffered from the problem of convincingness among other officials and their peers. Both Sikorski and Bildt had been known as publicly outspoken Russia hawks for a number of years and may have suffered in a similar way from cry-wolf or warning fatigue syndrome as we have argued in the case of many public pronouncements by Kremlin sources above.

More generally, the EU foreign policy machinery is always afflicted by all knowledge claims being subject to 'national flag' discounting, or what Kuus has called the 'pens down syndrome', which implies that experienced officials stop taking notes once they hear another member state official talking about national hot-button issues, whether it is the French about terrorism and stability in Africa, or the Poles about Russia.[49] Instead of listening to their peers for the distinct sensitivity and knowledge they may bring, their assessments are not fully engaged with cognitively, and are even substantially discounted because of their familiarity and attributed national biases. Vice versa, one can argue that neither Bildt nor Sikorski fully realised the extent to which their advocacy was compromised and could have taken more steps to enhance the convincingness of their warnings, including making them more actionable and specific, or seeking to convince other, less compromised countries to deliver their message with more credibility first. More problematically, our interviews indicate substantial problems with being open-minded and accepting of high-quality intelligence among some senior diplomats from countries such as Spain, Greece, Cyprus and Italy, as mentioned above. So even if the absence of a high-quality timely warning may be excused, the lack of receptivity on the part of some member state officials and EU senior officials to crisis warnings and current intelligence was not excusable by mitigating factors.

While the diagnostic difficulty relating to the Crimea operation was undoubtedly high, the same cannot be said about anticipating the U-turn of Yanukovych on signing the Association Agreement, the likelihood of protests and the fragility of the regime to such protests. EU Commission services, particularly in DG NEAR, and the EU delegation in Kyiv were tasked to look at some of the key issues that were the root cause of citizens' dissatisfaction with the regime. Furthermore, the EEAS could have been expected to look at the situation in Ukraine from a broader foreign and security perspective. Our research indicates that the current intelligence from EUDEL Kyiv especially was quite nuanced and detailed, even if the stability of the regime and mobilisation potential of protestors was underestimated by paying too much attention to opposition figures from previous protests rather than monitoring more social media and new social movements. Many of the EU's professional observers in Ukraine did see the significant deficiencies of the regime and the corruption and were sceptical whether the progress that had been made was sufficient to meet the Council conclusions. Another product more closely approximating a warning about the situation in Ukraine from within the Brussels system was a short report by a Ukrainian specialist within the EU's Intelligence Analysis Centre, INTCEN. According to two different interviewees as well as one media article in the *New York Times*, it contained an assessment that Yanukovych might not sign and that the non-signature could lead to protests and instability.[50] However, the precise wording and emphasis in the document again remains unclear, and it did not appear to contain any warnings about Russian military actions. Moreover, INTCEN publishes roughly 500 reports each year, so the significance of any single report should not be overstated.

Yet, our research does provide substantial ground for criticising the EU Commission and particularly DG NEAR under Czech Commissioner Stefan Füle for a lack of open-mindedness to discordant evidence about Ukraine more narrowly, or, to put it more bluntly, wishful thinking about the degree of progress the Yanukovych regime had made. Füle was not receptive to evidence that could have meant postponing the signature at the Vilnius summit signature and disappointing expectations in Ukraine and within the EU, particularly by some Eastern European countries pushing very hard for an agreement. It is unclear whether and to what extend Füle was aware of warnings of Russian hostility to the deal and how far it might go to scupper it. In retrospect, the EU Commission's leadership clearly failed to spot early enough that it was being played by Yanukovych to extract more concessions from Russia during a time of severe domestic economic distress, and that non-signature was a significant possibility despite some political reporting to this effect from the ground and from within the EEAS. If they had heeded more of the reports from their own sources in Kyiv or the analysis coming from EEAS, the EU would have been less surprised about the protests in Ukraine, or indeed the fragility of the President's hold on power.

Key Underlying Causes of Performance Problems

We have argued above that with regard to the Russian invasion of Crimea, it would be difficult to accuse the EU of performance problems in early or timely tactical warning given the degree of diagnostic difficulty posed by this case, given the evidence that most other better-equipped and more-specialised actors did not appear to do any better, and indeed given the resource limits and structural limitations of the EU intelligence and foreign policy machinery. The EU collectively, and specific bodies within it, may still learn lessons to improve their analytical accuracy by taking various steps that would mitigate at least some of the root causes of surprise. One dimension would be the intelligence collection side. If the EU wanted to improve not only its strategic warning, but also its tactical warning above other actors, it would require significant changes to what kind of intelligence EU institutions can gather to penetrate the planning and decision-making of the Russian President and the government's inner circle, in particular HUMINT and SIGINT. The most ambitious option would be a change in the 'national security' exclusion of the EU Treaties to provide the EU with the authority for a dedicated intelligence function; a substantial increase in resources to build up such capacities and create a leak-proof infrastructure involving member states. The next Treaty revision might also address the structural flaws of asymmetric actorness in EU foreign affairs visible in the conduct of trade and neighbourhood policy on the one hand and CFSP on the other hand.[51] Abolishing the unanimity requirements in foreign affairs might also help to drive demand and better resources for higher-quality intelligence tailored to the needs of the EU decision-makers.

More realistically, the EU could seek to create a centre or unit within the EEAS tasked exclusively with the assessment of the military and hybrid threat that Russia poses, rather than one that just focus on the narrower challenge of tackling Russian disinformation and propaganda. One could, for instance, create a special Russia security analysis and warning centre within the EEAS that could draw on a range of different open sources as well as assessed intelligence from trustworthy analysts seconded by member states. Member states themselves would not only need to substantially improve their own collection capabilities vis-à-vis Russia, but also to change some of their attitudes towards sharing with each other – or at least with a trusted group of states – key insights gleaned from precious and sensitive sources and techniques. Any high-significance intelligence originating from member states, such as warnings about impending military action, would be inevitably faced by significant scepticism from those peers who fear being manipulated for national political ends and who tend to trust their own national intelligence services and diplomatic reporting more. Member states will therefore need to be highly conscious about these biases and build trust and credibility over time through sharing intelligence on less politically salient issues. The same problem of trust arises for more intensified cooperation and intelligence sharing with NATO as a body more specialised and resourceful on the Russia threat. The EU would benefit from creating a dedicated warning doctrine and officers for warning just as the US has, or used to have before the officers for warning were disbanded and the function integrated into everyone's job on the National Intelligence Council.

The EU institutions could have done better in terms of understanding the strategic shift in Russian foreign policy, particularly after 2012, if they had listened more to the assessments and warnings coming from of some of their own member states. There was too much political discounting of such warnings and too little effort to focus on using diversity in perspectives and competing knowledge claims productively to pinpoint, challenge and, if necessary, revise key assumptions about the behaviour of Russia. However, the national flagging of intelligence and the pens down syndrome are quasi-structural features of the EU foreign policy process – debiasing officials would need to be part of a cultural change agenda to 'listen better' to each other, recognise one's own biases in information collection and analysis, particularly on a salient case such as Russia, and to build trust that intelligence can be shared without being leaked by those parties interested in scuppering a political consensus on action, sometimes called the 'Trojan horses' of Russia among EU member states.[52] An easier proposition would be for the EU institutions to invest more in recruiting and cultivating country expertise for the region, which could have helped to anticipate the fall of Yanukovych as we witnessed in the prescient INTCEN report authored by a Ukraine specialist. Moreover, giving the reports from EU delegations more attention and weight in EU foreign policy would have helped to anticipate the protests and their likely impact, thus helping to connect the dots of dynamics and calculations in both Kyiv and Moscow – a lesson also raised in Chapter 2 on the Arab uprisings.[53] This could also be achieved by giving member states' ambassadors the option of endorsing such reports and thus create a kind of consensus report from the ground up. There was also a problem in not tasking EU delegations in neighbouring countries to analyse problems with a cross-border dimension together, rather than send their own reports independently, with spillovers and interdependencies between neighbouring countries being ignored.

We can also see some motivated biases related to bureaucratic cultures and dominant worldviews at play. For instance, our interviews indicate that some parts of the EEAS had a better understanding of the geopolitical risks involved in the EaP process compared to the Commission. However, the latter was in the lead in negotiations with Ukraine over the AA and DCFTA, particularly DG Trade and DG NEAR. The literature has highlighted extensively how the EU neighbourhood policy has been built on the template of the EU enlargement process and how the technocratic rigidity inherent in the process was not adequate for giving strong enough incentives for EaP countries to change towards the norms required, especially not if facing pressure from Russia.[54] This technocratic template was not sufficiently sensitive to the geopolitical and security risks faced by specific countries. This also meant that managing the ENP/EaP required expertise in law, economics and public administration, but did not require expertise on security and defence risks. Some of this expertise and more diverse worldviews could have been provided by staff in the EEAS and by member state officials on Council committee working groups. However, the EEAS was not well equipped in terms of its leadership at the time, its resources and expertise to make its distinct voice heard. Some of these inter-institutional pathologies and flaws are hard to overcome if the 'original sins' committed in the creation of the EEAS are not addressed.[55]

Several academic post-mortems, especially those coming from (neo-)realist scholars such as Mearsheimer, contend that Crimea was ultimately attributable to 'liberal bias' in the EU and the West more generally. It is true and perhaps not surprising that officials working in the Commission in particular, but also in other parts of the Brussels, especially in the European Parliament, tend to see foreign policy more as being based on 'rule of law', 'multilateralism' and creating 'win-win' situations where everyone gains compared to the views held in some foreign ministries inside and particularly outside of Europe. Indeed, there is plenty of literature that explores Russia and the EU having different views of international politics. However, the EU's normative beliefs and worldviews are far from unique and are shared by many other democratic countries, diplomats and experts. It is not unreasonable to suspect that officials working for an institution that is underpinned by liberal values and in charge of the EaP process believed much of their own rhetoric that the Association Agreements would economically benefit not just the countries concerned but potentially also their neighbours such as Russa. However, we argue that 'EU liberal bias' is neither a sufficient nor a necessary explanation for not issuing accurate warnings about Russian military action in Crimea or the Donbas sooner given our previous discussion of the chain of events that led to the Russian action and the fact that many other actors and organisations did not do any better. Indeed, Eric Voeten analysed data from the TRIP research project survey from February 2014 and suggests that those international relations experts who self-identified as liberals and constructivists were somewhat less likely to see the possibility of military intervention than Russia experts and those without a clear theoretical or ideational affiliation.[56] However, the difference was not huge, and still only a small percentage accurately predicted such action.

Therefore, the EU institutions do not just need to increase their self-awareness with regard to key assumptions they hold about international politics and the behaviour of foreign states; rather, the knowledge producers, not just those with intelligence in the job title, need to take psychological factors, and in particular motivational biases as a source of threat misperception, more seriously and take mitigating action against it. However, we know that debiasing at the individual level through training measures is difficult and its success is limited. In other words, even if one is aware of one's own biases, it is hard to avoid falling prey to them. A better strategy against such biases is to build robust challenge of underlying assumptions into the diverse membership of analytical teams, particularly those that work on highly salient and politicised topics such as Russia. The EU should not just seek experts with relevant country expertise on Russia and neighbouring countries or sectoral expertise related to energy and trade, but should take bureaucratic and national biases seriously. This entails bringing together teams from different institutions and with different national backgrounds, particularly countries with high and low threat perceptions vis-à-vis Russia. Furthermore, the Commission and EEAS could create a channel for officials to express their dissent with dominant assumptions and create dedicated opportunities to assess wild-card scenarios in estimative intelligence. Better protecting officials, particularly those seconded to the EEAS from member states, from negative career repercussions would also benefit officials being more open to speaking 'inconvenient truths'. Training intelligence consumers such as leading politicians and officials in dealing with such reports and recognising that some kinds of top-down and high-pressure leadership have inadvertent consequences for the quality of analysis received might help to prevent salient political agendas to crowd out discordant political reporting, as we have seen with regard to assessing the nature of the Yanukovych regime and the run-up to the Vilnius summit in parts of the Commission.

In the longer term, a more joined-up and better-informed EU role in foreign affairs would require the EEAS as an agency to be merged into the EU Commission, a scenario that member states, then including the UK, explicitly sought to avoid when drafting the Lisbon Treaty. In the meantime, the European Commission under President von der Leyen instituted some changes in the internal functioning of the institution to increase attention on foreign policy issues and improve coordination between internal and external action. It is doubtful whether these changes, on their own, will create a more geopolitical Commission and mitigate the problem of policymaking in silos.

Conclusion

In comparison to other cases in this book, this case involves a highly surprised actor and an analytically very difficult chain of events. Our post-mortem of how the EU handled the intelligence side of the evolving Ukrainian-Russian crisis confirms some parts of the published analysis. For instance, it agrees that a particular challenge was the joined-up analysis of the interplay between what happened in Ukraine's domestic politics and what happened in the Kremlin, the familiar challenge of 'connecting the dots' as the House of Lord report puts it. This also means that we disagree with those who argue, sometimes with the benefit of hindsight, that such military action in Crimea and Donbas was, if not inevitable or highly likely, at least a strong possibility. This substantially underplays the diagnostic challenges involved in accurately understanding what was happening on the ground, and, more crucially, in penetrating the highly secretive inner circle of Russian President Putin and his military leaders in order to issue timely, accurate and convincing warnings. It also underestimates the degree to which signals from Russia over the years have been ambiguous, cacophonic and dishonest, and that it was far from obvious that taking such high risks was in the best interest of Putin, let alone the Russian state more broadly. We are thus more forgiving of the intelligence performance of the EU in relation to Russia's military actions in Crimea. What is far more problematic is that the EU should have had a better understanding of what was happening in Ukrainian domestic politics, and we have noted some significant problems with open-mindedness and receptivity among some of the EU's leadership, both in the Commission and the Council.

Most extant post-mortems fail to understand differences within the EU in terms of knowledge production, receptivity and impact of intelligence. We found significant differences in how the strategic threat of Russia was seen within Brussels and, especially, among member states, and these can, partly, account for different levels of receptivity to warnings within and across institutions as well as between member states. The EU might have increased its chance of being less surprised sooner by taking more seriously the role of bureaucratic and national biases in the analytical process, and might have designed ways of using those biases constructively for identifying and challenging unspoken assumptions. It would have also helped to set up more systemic surprise-sensitive forecasting exercises ahead of major decisions such as the signature of the Association Agreement with Ukraine.

Whether this would have made a difference to the EU's diplomacy and member state actions before or during the crisis is another matter. Interviewees say that even with perfect warnings and receptivity to warnings the EU would not have lent military support to Ukraine, and most thought that the prospect of agreeing sanctions on Russia in late 2013 in response to the pressure on Ukraine would have been very low. However, the EU might have signalled its resolve to punish Russia for any violation of Ukrainian sovereignty sooner by outlining and signalling the possibility of a tough sanction package.[57] It could have also used its influence with Ukrainian authorities to avoid some of the mistakes that helped Russia substantially in carrying out its action in Crimea, whilst confirming that Ukraine would stand by or even extend the guarantees regarding the Russian naval base in Sevastopol. Conversely, of course, the EU could have stepped back from pushing for a signature at Vilnius and consulted Russia more closely about the Association Agreement and its compatibility with the Eurasian Economic Union. Better intelligence would have enabled politicians to consider the value choices and trade-offs posed by each of these options.

Notes

1. This chapter draws on a small amount of material contained in and research undertaken for chapter 9 in Christoph O. Meyer, Chiara De Franco and Florian Otto, *Warning About War: Conflict, Persuasion and Foreign Policy* (Cambridge: Cambridge University Press, 2020). The chapter is partially based on research undertaken as part of the FORESIGHT project funded by the European Research Council (Grant 202022). The author gratefully acknowledges research assistance from Katherine Crofts-Gibbons and Ana Albulescu. The usual caveat applies on the authors' responsibility or any mistakes.
2. As seen from the West, the Russian threat is multifaceted and comprises assassinations and kidnapping of foreign critics and intelligence operatives, cyber-attacks against public authorities in the Baltics, Germany, the UK and the US, funding and supporting authoritarian and nationalist parties in France and Hungary, as well as propaganda activities through open and less open methods. For a discussion see Andrew Wilson, *Ukraine Crisis: What It Means for the West* (New Haven, CT and London: Yale University Press, 2014),

117, 25; Roy Allison, 'Russian "Deniable" Intervention in Ukraine: How and Why Russia Broke the Rules', *International Affairs* 90, no. 6 (2014). Matthew Kroenig, 'Facing Reality: Getting Nato Ready for a New Cold War', *Survival* 57, no. 1 (2015).

3. For instance, House of Lords, European Union Committee, 'The EU and Russia: Before and Beyond the Crisis in Ukraine' (London: House of Lords, 2015); Sénat, 'Les Relations Avec La Russie: Comment Sortir De L'impasse?' (Paris: French Senate, 2015).

4. Hiski Haukkala, 'A Perfect Storm; or What Went Wrong and What Went Right for the EU in Ukraine', *Europe-Asia Studies* 68, no. 4 (2016); John J. Mearsheimer, 'Why the Ukraine Crisis is the West's Fault: The Liberal Delusions that Provoked Putin', *Foreign Affairs* 93, no. 5 (2014).

5. Michael Kofman et al., 'Lessons from Russia's Operations in Crimea and Eastern Ukraine' (Santa Monica, CA: RAND Corporation, 2017).

6. Mearsheimer, 'Why the Ukraine Crisis is the West's Fault: The Liberal Delusions that Provoked Putin'.

7. Neil MacFarlane and Anand Menon, 'The EU and Ukraine', *Survival* 56, no. 3 (2014).

8. Richard Sakwa, *Frontline Ukraine: Crisis in the Borderlands* (London: I. B. Tauris, 2016); Richard Sakwa, 'The Death of Europe: Continental Fates after Ukraine', *International Affairs* 91, no. 3 (2015).

9. Haukkala, 'A Perfect Storm; or What Went Wrong and What Went Right for the EU in Ukraine'.

10. Ireneusz Pawel Karolewski and Mai'a K. Davis Cross, 'The EU's Power in the Russia–Ukraine Crisis: Enabled or Constrained?', *JCMS: Journal of Common Market Studies* 55, no. 1 (2017); Tuomas Forsberg and Hiski Haukkala, *The European Union and Russia* (Basingstoke: Palgrave, 2016); Nikki Ikani, 'Change and Continuity in the European Neighbourhood Policy: The Ukraine Crisis as a Critical Juncture', *Geopolitics* 24, no. 1 (2019).

11. Marianne Riddervold, Jarle Trondal and Akasemi Newsome, eds, *The Palgrave Handbook of EU Crises* (Basingstoke: Palgrave Macmillan, 2021); Mark Rhinard, 'The Crisisification of Policy-Making in the European Union', *JCMS: Journal of Common Market Studies* 57, no. 3 (2019).

12. Reuters, 'Russia Starts Delivering $1 Billion Arms Package to Azerbaijan': http://www.reuters.com/article/2013/06/18/us-russia-azerbaijan-arms-idUSBRE95H0KM20130618

13. Russia has denied any responsibility in this event despite overwhelming evidence provided, including the Dutch Safety Board investigation report, see Sanneke Kuipers, Ellen Verolme and Erwin Muller, 'Lessons from the Mh-17 Transboundary Disaster Investigation', *Journal of Contingencies and Crisis Management* 28, no. 4 (2020).

14. Hubert Zimmermann, 'Neorealism', in *The Palgrave Handbook of Eu Crisis*, ed. Marianne Riddervold, Jarle Trondal and Akasemi Newsome (Basingstoke: Palgrave, 2020), 104. One line of argument is that the West should have left Ukraine as a 'buffer-state' within the Russian sphere of influence, see: Mearsheimer, 'Why the Ukraine Crisis is the West's Fault: The Liberal Delusions That Provoked Putin'; Lawrence Freedman, 'Ukraine and the Art of Crisis Management', *Survival* 56, no. 3 (2014).

15. See for a similar argument Kimberly Marten, 'Putin's Choices: Explaining Russian Foreign Policy and Intervention in Ukraine', *The Washington Quarterly* 38, no. 2 (2015).

16. Some observers accept the Russian argument that Crimea has long belonged to Russia such as Sakwa, *Frontline Ukraine: Crisis in the Borderlands*; Rajan Menon and Eugene B. Rumer, *Conflict in Ukraine: The Unwinding of the Post-Cold War Order* (Cambridge, MA: The MIT Press, 2015). Forceful challenges to this viewpoint come from Taras Kuzio, 'The Crimea: Europe's Next Flashpoint?', in *The Jamestown Foundation Report* (Washington, DC: The Jamestown Foundation, 2010); Wilson, *Ukraine Crisis: What It Means for the West*; Taras Kuzio, *Putin's War against Ukraine: Revolution, Nationalism, and Crime* (Toronto: CreateSpace, 2017).

17. Kuzio, 'The Crimea: Europe's Next Flashpoint?'.

18. NATO Bucharest Summit Declaration, 3 April 2008: https://www.nato.int/cps/en/natolive/official_texts_8443.htm.

19. Meyer, De Franco and Otto, *Warning About War: Conflict, Persuasion and Foreign Policy*, 219–20.

20. Paul Reynolds, 'New Russian World Order: The Five Principles' (2008): http://news.bbc.co.uk/1/hi/world/europe/7591610.stm

21. Forsberg and Haukkala, *The European Union and Russia*.

22. Elias Götz, 'Putin, the State, and War: The Causes of Russia's near Abroad Assertion Revisited', *International Studies Review* 18, no. 4 (2016); ibid.

23. Forsberg and Haukkala, *The European Union and Russia*, 36.

24. Mark Adomanis, 'Confused About What's Happening in Ukraine?', *Forbes*, 2013.

25. Interview 30 June 2017.

26. Ibid.
27. Kuzio, *Putin's War against Ukraine: Revolution, Nationalism, and Crime*.
28. Some estimates from Ukrainian prosecutors of $32 billion lack credibility according to Wilson, but Yanukovych did leave with two helicopters and a significant amount of money abroad (Wilson, *Ukraine Crisis: What It Means for the West*, 93).
29. Kofman et al., 'Lessons from Russia's Operations in Crimea and Eastern Ukraine'.
30. Eric Voeten, 'Who Predicted Russia's Military Intervention?', *The Washington Post*, 12 March 2014.
31. Kathrin Hille and Roman Olearchy, 'Russia Rattles Sabre over Fate of Crimea': https://www.ft.com/content/84909a9e-9a55-11e3-8e06 -00144feab7de
32. Dimitri Trenin, 'Why Russia Won't Interfere', *The New York Times*, 23 Feburary 2014.
33. Kuzio, *Putin's War against Ukraine: Revolution, Nationalism, and Crime*, 240–1; Wilson, *Ukraine Crisis: What It Means for the West*, 108–11.
34. Kofman et al., 'Lessons from Russia's Operations in Crimea and Eastern Ukraine'.
35. Forsberg and Haukkala, *The European Union and Russia*, 37; Wilson, *Ukraine Crisis: What It Means for the West*, 108–13.
36. Critics of Russia saw the dates on the medal as inadvertent confirmation that Russia was engaged in a coup at a time when Yanukovych was still legitimate President of Ukraine and had not yet called for 'help' from the Russian state.
37. Vladimir Putin, 'Address by President of the Russian Federation', news release, 2014.
38. Kofman et al., 'Lessons from Russia's Operations in Crimea and Eastern Ukraine'.
39. Wilson, *Ukraine Crisis: What It Means for the West*.
40. Andrew Roth, 'Putin Tells European Official That He Could "Take Kiev in Two Weeks"', *The New York Times*, 2 September 2009. Until archives are open such accounts need to be approached with due caution of course.
41. James Clapper, 'Dni Clapper: Ukraine Intelligence "Not a Failure by Any Stretch"', news release, 10 March 2014: https://www.dni .gov/index.php/newsroom/speeches-interviews/speeches-interviews -2014/item/1027-dni-clapper-ukraine-intelligence-not-a-failure-by -any-stretch

42. Interview, August 2017.
43. Tagliavini report, 'Independent International Fact-Finding Mission on the Conflict in Georgia (IIFFMCG)' (Brussels: Council of the European Union, 2009).
44. *Guardian* article of 22 September 2013 by Shaun Walker, titled 'Ukraine's EU Trade Deal Will be Catastrophic', cited in Forsberg and Haukkala, *The European Union and Russia*, 36.
45. Interview, 18 August 2017.
46. Interview, 16 November 2017.
47. Rilka Dragneva and Kataryna Wolczuk, 'The EU-Ukraine Association Agreement and the Challenges of Inter-Regionalism', *Review of Central and East European Law* 39 (2014): 217; Gunnar Wiegand and Evelina Schulz, 'The EU and its Eastern Partnership: Political Association and Economic Integration in a Rough Neighbourhood', in *Trade Policy between Law, Diplomacy and Scholarship: Liber Amicorum in Memoriam Horst G. Krenzler*, ed. Christoph Herrmann, Bruno Simma and Rudolf Streinz (London: Springer, 2015).
48. He is quoted in two diplomatic cables on the WikiLeaks database as warning senior US diplomats after the Georgian war that Crimea may be next, although he described it in one of the cables as 'low-probability': https://wikileaks.org/plusd/cables/09WARSAW1164_a.html
49. Merje Kuus, *Geopolitics and Expertise: Knowledge and Authority in European Diplomacy* (Chichester: Wiley Blackwell, 2013).
50. The content of the report, but not the report itself, was made available to a *New York Times* journalist, see Andrew Higgins, 'Ukraine Upheaval Highlights E.U.'S Past Miscalculations and Future Dangers', *The New York Times*, 20 March 2014.
51. Thomas Gehring, Kevin Urbanski and Sebastian Oberthür, 'The European Union as an Inadvertent Great Power: EU Actorness and the Ukraine Crisis', *Journal of Common Market Studies* 55, no. 4 (2017).
52. Mitchell A. Orenstein and R. Daniel Kelemen, 'Trojan Horses in EU Foreign Policy', *JCMS: Journal of Common Market Studies* 55, no. 1 (2017).
53. On this matter, see also: House of Lords, 'The EU and Russia: Before and Beyond the Crisis in Ukraine'.
54. Nikki Ikani, *Crisis and Change in European Union Foreign Policy: A Framework of EU Foreign Policy Change* (Manchester: Manchester University Press, 2021).
55. Task Force EEAS 2.0, 'From Self-Doubt to Self-Assurance: The

European External Action Service as the Indispensable Support for a Geopolitical EU', ed. Pierre Vimont, Christophe Hillion and Steven Blockmans (Brussels: CEPS, SIEPS, FES, 2021).

56. Daniel Malaniak, Susan Peterson and Ryan Powers, 'Trip Snap Poll I: Nine Questions on Current Global Issues for International Relations Scholars' (2014); Voeten, 'Who Predicted Russia's Military Intervention?'.

57. Interview with UK senior official, 6 April 2020.

5 The Case of the UK: Intelligence Assessment, Priorities and Knowing that you are Being Warned

Paul Rimmer

Introduction

The purpose of this chapter is to identify lessons arising from the UK's experience of the three case histories examined in this book. Drawing on the framework set out in Chapter 1, it especially highlights the intelligence/policy interface from the perspective of a former senior intelligence practitioner. Focusing on the UK's key intelligence assessment bodies, the Joint Intelligence Committee and Defence Intelligence, it argues that only Crimea can really be characterised as a case where there was a failure to warn. Even that is against an environment where the policy community in the UK was focused on better relations with Russia and the UK's intelligence capacity was directed at counterterrorism in Syria and Afghanistan. Overall, it concludes that surprises are more likely in areas which are a low priority for intelligence collection and assessment – and can never be completely avoided. The provision of effective warnings requires long-term and detailed understanding of a region or issue. Early warning needs to be treated as a specific discipline, with products that clearly stand out as such to the customer. Also, as highlighted by numerous studies, and as in Chapter 1, this chapter stresses the importance of open-source information to build a picture that should not rely on secret sources alone.

Few UK intelligence assessments, or extracts from them, relating to these case histories have been released into the public domain. This chapter therefore draws heavily on reports on the events and the UK intelligence community (IC) and wider government's reaction to them by the Parliamentary Intelligence and Security and Foreign Affairs Committees, as well as the British government's response to those reports. It also reflects the author's personal experience as Chief of the Assessments Staff from 2009–12, preparing papers for the Joint Intelligence Committee, and attending meetings of the National Security Council and its sub-committee during the Libya crisis, NSC(L). Finally, in early 2021, the author was able to interview a number of Defence Intelligence and Cabinet Office analysts who were in the relevant posts at the time. Unfortunately, time and COVID-19 restraints meant that policy staff were not able to be interviewed. This, combined with a lack of access to classified intelligence reports produced at the time and an understanding of the policy response to them, is a key limitation to this work. The perspective of this chapter is, accordingly, very much one from the point of view of the UK intelligence assessment community.

Structures for Intelligence Analysis and the Intelligence/Policy Interface in the UK

The Joint Intelligence Committee (JIC) is the senior body for intelligence assessment in the UK. Meeting weekly on a Wednesday afternoon, it comprises senior (2*–4*) representatives of the intelligence agencies, defence intelligence and policy departments, such as the Foreign, Commonwealth and Development Office (FCDO), Ministry of Defence (MOD) and Home Office, plus others depending on the issues under discussion. Founded in 1936 as a sub-committee of the Committee of Imperial Defence, the peacetime defence planning body, in 1957 it moved to the Cabinet Office, where today the Assessments Staff in the Joint Intelligence Organisation (JIO) prepares draft intelligence assessments for the committee to consider. The JIC's role includes the following:

1. 'to assess events and situations relating to external affairs, defence, terrorism, major international criminal activity, scientific, technical

and international economic matters and other transnational issues, drawing on secret intelligence, diplomatic reporting and open source material (. . .)

2. to monitor and give early warning of the development of direct and indirect threats and opportunities in those fields to British interests or policies and to the international community as a whole.[1]

The Chair of the JIC is a Permanent Secretary-level (4*) member of the Cabinet Office with a background in national security. In accordance with a recommendation of the 2004 Butler Report on Intelligence on Weapons of Mass Destruction, the JIC Chair is also 'someone with experience of dealing with Ministers in a very senior role, and who is demonstrably beyond influence, and thus probably in his last post'.[2] Crucially, the JIC Chair 'is specifically charged with ensuring that the Committee's monitoring and warning role is discharged effectively'.[3]

Prior to 2010, the JIC's assessments were generally drafted in response to requests from individual departments to inform policymaking, with the traditional national security departments, such as Defence and the Foreign Office, its most engaged and demanding customers. It also supported the work of Cabinet Committees and sub-committees on specific topics, although they tended to meet on an ad hoc and irregular basis. But the creation of a National Security Council (NSC) by Prime Minister David Cameron's coalition government in that year gave the JIC added impetus and focus. Also meeting weekly, the NSC was the natural docking point for strategic-level intelligence assessments on a regular and formal basis. The ideal customer then, but with inevitable limitations about the number of issues and their priority that could be considered each week. Realistically, only one or two topics can be addressed at an NSC meeting, so it cannot maintain a constant global overview.

Nevertheless, the creation of the NSC meant that a process now existed for cross-departmental consideration of important foreign policy and national security issues, drawing on the most sensitive intelligence available, and bringing that analysis to the attention of the Prime Minister and relevant Cabinet Ministers alongside advice from policy departments and recommendations for action.

When examined against the 'Factors Affecting Expectations for Intelligence Production and Use' in Table 1.3 of Chapter 1, this gives the UK JIC/NSC system a positive context within which intelligence assessments are considered at a strategic level. The focus that a weekly NSC meeting chaired by the Prime Minister gives is important, but, whilst priorities are essential to drive work, they are also limiting in terms of the effort that is likely to be applied to lower priority issues. This can be where the JIC Chair's specific early warning responsibility can be important – the ability to, metaphorically, tap the Prime Minister on the shoulder and say 'you haven't asked me about this, but I think you should know. . .'.

But the JIC is not the only source of intelligence assessments in the UK. The Assessments Staff, which takes the lead in drafting papers for the JIC to discuss, brings in analysts from across government to consider drafts (and to help with drafting) at meetings known as Current Intelligence Groups (CIGs.) Here, drafts are discussed and redrafted in detail before being brought to the senior members of the JIC itself. But the Assessments Staff itself is relatively small, at just a few dozen personnel, most on secondment from other parts of the national security community. The Assessments Staff, therefore, critically relies on deep expertise from other parts of the IC, such as the Joint Terrorism Analysis Centre for terrorism, and Defence Intelligence (DI). Often overlooked in popular examination of the UK IC – which tends to focus on the intelligence agencies, the Security Service (or MI5), the Secret Intelligence Service (MI6) and GCHQ – DI (as well as being responsible for military intelligence collection) actually comprises the largest all-source intelligence assessment body in Whitehall, with over 400 military and civilian staff. In its remit to support defence planning and military operations, DI holds a body of expertise ranging from Russian military doctrine to the technical specifications of weapon systems from around the world. It is the first port of call for detailed knowledge of issues that are a priority for the Ministry of Defence, such as military capabilities, and chemical, biological and nuclear warfare. DI also maintains an early warning capability.

Whilst nominally having the ability to look at anywhere in the world, DI's focus is driven by defence priorities and interests and it cannot afford to expend effort on low priority countries of little or no interest to defence – indeed, it would be criticised for doing so. Nevertheless, DI can respond to a developing crisis in a formerly low-priority country or region that suddenly attracts the interest of decision-makers in government by using its trained all-source analysts to draw initially on open-source information as well as on support from close allies who may have a greater interest in that particular issue (for example Australia or New Zealand for the Pacific, or the US for South America). That can be developed over time, including through acquisition of secret intelligence, as a crisis develops and continues. The important caveat to that ability, however, is that deep subject matter experts cannot be generated overnight.

The UK's parliamentary oversight body, the Intelligence and Security Committee (ISC), itself recognised this in its Annual Report 2012–13,[4] noting concern:

> that Defence Intelligence's intelligence collection capabilities, which have been built up slowly and at considerable cost to support the [Afghanistan] campaign, may be easy prey for a department looking to make financial savings. We urge the Government to ensure that these vital capabilities are preserved and to give consideration as to how they can be redeployed when not required in support of combat operations.

It also noted that it had:

> repeatedly warned of the risks of cutting resources – in particular to Defence Intelligence – to the UK's ability to provide the necessary level of global coverage. Whilst we recognise that burden-sharing arrangements with allies may offset some of the impact, there must continue to be a critical mass that can respond to unexpected events without this being at the expense of coverage of other key areas. We are concerned that shifting resources in response to emerging events is 'robbing Peter to pay Paul': we must maintain the ability to respond to more than one crisis at a time.

These warnings came on the back of previous cuts in Defence Intelligence's resources. As part of MOD's Head Office, it comprised a disproportionate chunk of that area's budget compared with the other finance and policy staff principally located in MOD's Main Building in Whitehall. It was, therefore, easy prey whenever the Head Office budget had to find savings. But in December 2011, Defence Intelligence became a part of the newly created Joint Forces Command (JFC – renamed Strategic Command in December 2019), which was created following a recommendation of the 2011 Levene Review[5] into the structure and management of defence. JFC/Strategic Command was established to 'provide the foundation and supporting framework for successful operations by ensuring joint capabilities like medical services, training, intelligence, information systems and cyber operations, are developed and managed (. . .) [and] also provide the command and control for overseas defence operations'.[6] DI thus became recognised as an essential enabler alongside other strategic assets, rather than as an over-large part of the Defence Head Office bureaucracy.

In terms of the UK government's overall assessment capability, therefore, it is important to recognise that the JIC is the principal body for providing the NSC and key national security Cabinet Ministers with all-source intelligence assessments that are agreed across Whitehall. Whilst its papers depend on input and argument from the collection agencies, FCDO and other experts around Whitehall, Defence Intelligence is a key component of the assessment machinery, providing much of the underlying long-term and technical deep analytical expertise that goes into JIC papers – and therefore on to the National Security Council. Although both the JIC and DI work to priorities under the broad umbrella of the NSC, DI's priorities are (as noted above) defined by the Ministry of Defence, of which it is an integral part, which might not quite align with those for other departments such as the Foreign, Commonwealth and Development Office. Its early warning responsibilities are also, therefore, aligned to defence priorities.

The Importance of Priorities and the Relationship Between the Intelligence and Policy Communities

As already emphasised, and as highlighted in the 'Resources' section of Table 1.3 in Chapter 1, when it comes to intelligence collection and assessment, prioritisation is everything. No UK intelligence organisation has sufficient resources to maintain a detailed global overview – even the US, with its massive capability compared with its allies, cannot do that. It is, therefore, essential that effort is driven by customers' requirements. Most obviously, intelligence is needed to support military planning and deployments, to pursue terrorist organisations and prevent terrorist attacks and to understand potential adversaries' intentions and capabilities as well as potential areas of unrest where the UK has significant interests. But deep and detailed understanding does not come easily, it requires time and the accumulation of expert knowledge. When a crisis breaks out in an area otherwise given a low (or no) priority, intelligence bodies can draw on open-source information, connections and allies for feeds, as well as the broad analytical experience of its staff. But that is inevitably a 'sticking plaster' solution that helps them to get by. It should come as no surprise that crises occur without warning when effort and attention is consciously directed elsewhere and also that politicians can be distracted by events which, perhaps, a dispassionate observer may not consider to be a priority for the UK. As noted in Chapter 1, there can be a tension between what customers want (or think they want) and what they need (or what the intelligence assessment community thinks they need.) The risk, of course, is that intelligence collectors and analysts become experts in areas that might be deemed to be a high priority but which in fact turn out to be irrelevant in the face of real-world events.

From 2003, intelligence assessments in support of military operations in Iraq and Afghanistan inevitably dominated DI's work, with subsequent operations in Libya, Syria and Mali broadening the demand. In addition, DI retained its position as Whitehall's centre of expertise on foreign weapon systems (supporting UK decisions on its own acquisition and defensive/offensive measures) and on chemical, biological and nuclear weapons and ballistic missiles, their development and proliferation. It also maintained an early warning capability for a few significant issues, such as the threat from Argentina to the Falkland Islands. Inevitably, effort on Russia had reduced, but by the time of the Russian intervention in Crimea in early 2014 there was a recognition that DI's Russia effort needed to be considerably increased and that long-term effort on China also needed building up.[7]

After 9/11 and intensified by the terrorist bombings in London in 2005, however, counterterrorism sucked up a significant proportion of the effort of the UK IC and particularly the focus of the collection agencies, MI6 and GCHQ, as well as MI5. Whilst relatively small-scale terrorist attacks in the UK do not threaten our way of life in the way that an attack from Russia (or, indeed, a global pandemic) could, try telling that to a Home Secretary or Prime Minister faced with deaths on the streets of London. The UK's Intelligence and Security Committee of Parliament illuminated this tension across the broader UK IC in its Report on Russia, published in July 2020:

> (. . .) by 2006, operational effort was being directed to the fight against international terrorism: in 2006/07, MI5 devoted 92% of its effort to counterterrorism work, with SIS and GCHQ at 33%. The remaining resource was thinly spread across a number of areas – Hostile State Activity being just one, and Russia being just one of the hostile states. This is understandable: the threat from international terrorism at that time – just a year after the 2005 terror attacks which claimed the lives of 52 people – had to be the primary focus.[8]

With counterterrorism so utterly dominating the efforts of the intelligence agencies in the early years of the twenty-first century, it is not surprising that other issues and countries did not get the detailed attention that, arguably, would have aided the identification and early warning of the issues considered in this book.

The Arab Uprisings

Turning first to the Arab uprisings, pressures within the Arab world, including autocratic governments and poor employment prospects, were long recognised. This was acknowledged in the UK Foreign Affairs Select Committee Report on the Arab uprisings, published in July 2012:[9] 'Many of the factors . . . had been recognized in successive United Nations Development Programme (UNDP) reports on Arab Human Development from 2002 onwards.'

Nevertheless, the report notes that: '. . . almost all of those who provided evidence to the Committee agreed that the scale and success of the protests took most people by surprise, including close observers of the region and even those who participated in the uprisings'. The FCO itself argued that:

> While we were aware of the fundamental underlying frustrations of people in the region, and were orientating our policies to address them, we did not predict that a spark in Tunisia in December 2010 would trigger such an outpouring of protest. No other international player, academic analyst, or opposition group within the region foresaw this either.

Defence Intelligence regional analysts also recognised that the region was a pressure cooker and that some form of crisis was a case of 'when, not if'. But they felt strongly that no one could have predicted the specific spark and its consequences.[10]

The problem, therefore, lay in trying to predict when those long-recognised pressures would boil over. It was, of course, by no means certain that they would, given the ability of the region's rulers to contain and buy off unrest to date. George Joffé echoes the views of UK analysts and the predicament facing forecasters: 'They may well know and even expect that certain types of paradigm shifts are going to take place in international relations but they cannot identify both the precise moment when they will occur, nor can they recognize the catalyzing event that makes such a shift possible.' As he goes on to say:

events at the start of 2011 in North Africa seem to fall within this category of unpredictability; most observers knew that change of some kind was inevitable but nobody knew when it would happen, nor were they aware of the events that would spark the process off. Most striking of all, few observers realized the vulnerability of the autocracies that existed there and the fragility they would demonstrate when challenged.[11]

It was by no means evident at the end of 2010 that the self-immolation of a young street vendor in Tunisia would be the spark to such dramatic regional events.

The Select Committee Report, however, does not let the FCO off so easily: 'Whereas the world of Whitehall was fairly blind to the imminence of change, if you talked to civil society types in Egypt in 2010, they were telling you that things were getting close to blowing point, and it was the same with good, astute investigative journalists.'[12] The report goes on to criticise what it had described in a previous report as shortcomings in basic diplomatic technique, namely shortfalls in staff at Embassies focusing on internal political problems and with a good local feel, including language skills and travelling outside the capital. Overall, the Select Committee concluded that

> the decline in staff numbers in post in the MENA [Middle East and North Africa] region may have contributed to a lower information gathering capacity but it cannot be conclusively drawn that such a decline had affected the FCO's ability to predict the Arab uprisings. Nevertheless, it is reasonable to believe that had there been more emphasis on political reporting and larger political teams in post, this would have improved the FCO's information gathering before the uprisings, and its ability to respond once they had begun.[13]

The Parliamentary Intelligence and Security Committee (ISC) took a slightly different tack in its Annual Report of 2011–12.[14] Like the FCO, the intelligence Agencies defended their performance, with the Chief of SIS saying 'there were no sort of secrets there which could have told us they were going to happen, because all the organisations that hold the secrets had no clue it was going to happen, and they were as caught by surprise as much as anyone'.[15]

Defence Intelligence similarly noted that whereas it had assessed regimes such as that in Egypt as 'unsustainable', as a result of the 'demographics, the economic situation and a whole range of other factors' they were unable 'to predict the spark which would cause it all'.[16]

The ISC concluded overall that it was 'understandable that the intelligence community was taken by surprise, as indeed were the governments in the countries affected'. But, like the Foreign Affairs Select Committee, it did query whether the Agencies' lack of anticipation of the events betrayed broader shortcomings in understanding the region. It then went a step further and, having earlier praised the prioritisation set by the NSC, recommended that these events showed 'the need for the intelligence and security Agencies to maintain a global coverage, in addition to the strategic priorities set by the National Security Council and the Joint Intelligence Committee'.[17] In other words, the Agencies should configure themselves to respond to the government's articulated priorities, but also 'maintain a global coverage'. It is, therefore, not surprising to see that the government's response pushed back firmly on this point:

> It is not possible to have intelligence resources everywhere at all times. The Agencies rightly focus effort on the Priorities for Intelligence Coverage (formerly the R&P [Resources & Priorities]), set annually by the NSC and JIC, prioritising those countries where secret intelligence can add greatest value on issues of concern to the UK. The challenge for the Agencies is to respond to that prioritisation while retaining flexible capabilities that can be deployed globally in response to new or changing requirements, such as the Arab uprisings, with support from allies where necessary.[18]

As noted above, and as described in Chapter 2, there is a broad acceptance that, whilst the underlying pressures in the Arab world were long known, the timing, rapid spread and impact of the sequential uprisings caught both intelligence and policy officials by surprise. In this case, therefore, it does not appear to be the case that there was a dysfunctional relationship between those two communities. The IC was not in a position to provide early warning because of the nature of the events, which were often spontaneous and not centrally organised – and therefore not amenable to whatever intelligence collection was devoted to them. Combined with the region being a relatively low priority for intelligence collection and analysis, surprise was baked in. Detailed figures for the percentage of effort devoted to intelligence collection and analysis of specific countries and themes are redacted from the UK ISC's reports, but what is left in gives a sense of the situation – and the efforts to rectify the position once the revolts got underway:[19]

> Events in January 2011 resulted in a rapid reversal in SIS's and GCHQ's plans to reduce their focus on the region and their allocation of resources ... SIS ... had to respond from a near-standing start. They had allocated [figure redacted] % of their resources to the Arab Nations target in 2010/11 and acknowledged that 'when the upheavals took place around the Arab world ... our coverage of individual Arab countries had been falling for some time'.

The then National Security Adviser, Sir Peter Ricketts commented:

> Given the level of collection of intelligence material, the Agencies would not have been able to predict in January this year [2011] that in March, they would suddenly be asked to turn on a very high level of collection. I pay tribute to the agility that they showed in being able to do that.

SIS's Chief noted that the Agency was 'able, because of our global network, because of our partnerships in the region and because of a ... stable of agents, we were able to turn that around quite quickly'.

The Foreign Secretary, William Hague, praised GCHQ's response:

> ... their ability to turn the antennae in the right direction was quite remarkable and the volume of material produced by GCHQ on Libya was colossal: up to the point of an entire full red box every day for me to read of GCHQ reports on Libya.

Defence Intelligence was also praised for its contribution, particularly in support of the Libya campaign in which it 'played a key, nearly central, role'.

Overall, therefore, the impression is of an IC that, whilst taken by surprise and with limited capabilities, was able to recover and play a valuable role in supporting subsequent policy and operational decision-making. Indeed, when the National Security Adviser was commissioned to write a lessons-learned paper on the Libya campaign,[20] its focus was almost wholly on organisational and operational matters. In respect of the IC, it gave a positive impression of its interface with those needing to make policy and operational decisions:

> real time military, intelligence and diplomatic assessment including from theatre gave Ministers an understanding of the detailed context in which to take strategic decisions, as well as to identify areas where further action was needed.[21]

This was delivered at meetings of a National Security Council sub-committee, NSC(L), specifically established to manage the Libya crisis, supported by a group of officials (NSC(L)(O)), both of which at times met daily.[22] What is clear is that, as is often the case in crises, when rapid decisions are required, the NSC(L) arrangement created the environment in which there was a demand and a need for tailored intelligence collection and joined-up assessment (bringing together expertise from across Whitehall) to support those decisions. This is summarised in two important paragraphs in the lessons-learned paper:

> The intelligence picture was briefed to Ministers at NSC(L) by the Chairman of the JIC or an alternate . . . The Joint Intelligence Organisation (JIO) in the Cabinet Office . . . produced daily written intelligence summaries and situation reports in addition to formal assessments, drawing on inputs from Defence Intelligence, FCO Research Analysts and the intelligence Agencies.
>
> Real-time military, intelligence and diplomatic assessment of the situation, including from theatre, gave Ministers as clear an understanding as possible of the detailed context in which to take strategic decisions as well as identify areas where further action or advice was required (. . .) The role of the Chief of Defence Intelligence in providing assessment of the military situation was important in bringing HMG's wider intelligence assessment capability to bear.[23]

Importantly, this gives due attention to the importance of intelligence assessment in supporting decision-making, rather than focusing simply on intelligence collection, which, whilst essential, is only part of the story.

ISIS

Discussion of early warning in the context of the rise of ISIS is rather more complex than the other two case studies examined here. By 2013, a conflict was already underway in Syria, and another had been underway for ten years in Iraq. Concern about the domination of the insurgency groups in Iraq by Sunni jihadi groups had been voiced by the UK IC for several years. A July 2006 JIC paper said:

> We judge al-Qaida in Iraq (AQ-I) is the largest single insurgent network and although its leadership retains a strong foreign element, a large majority of its fighters are Iraqi. Their motivation is mixed: some are Islamist extremists inspired by the AQ agenda, others are simply hired hands attracted by the money. Some are drawn in by the opportunity to take on Shia militias: the jihadists' media effort stresses their role as defenders of the Sunni.[24]

A March 2007 JIC paper[25] built on this assessment with the following: 'A number of Sunni groups are involved in sectarian attacks, but we judge AQ-I is in the vanguard . . . Its strategic main effort is the prosecution of a sectarian campaign designed to drag Iraq into civil war.' It continues: 'We judge AQ-I will try to expand its sectarian campaign wherever it can: suicide bombings in Kirkuk have risen sharply since October [2006] when AQ-I declared the establishment of the notional "Islamic State of Iraq" (including Kirkuk).'

However, as covered in Chapter 3, a combination of the Sunni 'Awakening' and an increasingly successful effort by US and Iraqi forces to kill AQ-I leaders significantly diminished the organisation's power, although it continued to exist and to operate at a reduced level. In the spring of 2010, US and Iraqi forces 'either picked up or killed 34 out of the top 42 al-Qaeda in Iraq leaders', and by June of 2010 the organization had 'lost connection with [AQ's senior leadership] in Pakistan and Afghanistan'.[26]

Nevertheless, despite the 'defeat' of AQ-I, ISIS became prominent around July 2013, when it launched its 'Soldier's Harvest' campaign to diminish Iraqi security forces and capture territory, through taking partial control of Fallujah in late December 2013 and Mosul in June 2014. To what extent was this a surprise to the intelligence – and by extension the policy and operational – community in the UK?

It has been argued that, with AQ-I essentially defeated by 2011, the US military drawdown in Iraq that followed meant that intelligence access was inevitably diminished.[27] Lacking detailed tactical intelligence, the IC was able only to provide higher-level strategic intelligence, which warned of the threat in broad terms, but without the granular detail to fill out the picture. Given the UK's close relationship with and heavy reliance on the US for intelligence inputs, gaps in the US intelligence picture were inevitably mirrored in the UK. There is also a sense that UK Agencies were focused on the terrorist threat to the UK and UK interests and not on the, admittedly large-scale and horrific, killings inside Iraq and Syria, which were seen as internal matters and not the priority for the UK policy community.[28]

Official UK government reporting on this topic is lacking, with the ISC reports from the end of 2013 to 2016 remarkably thin in content. However, the ISC's Annual Report 2015–16[29] indicates that SIS effort on ISIS was probably a relatively small part of its overall and regional and counterterrorism work:

1. Key specific geographical requirements and tasks in line with those set out in the National Security Strategy and the Strategic Defence and Security Review 2015, including in Russia, the Middle East and Asia: 19% (. . .)
2. Other operational activities (including prosperity, counterterrorism, counter-proliferation, cyber and access, and foreign materials): 21%.[30]

Where the ISC does focus its reporting is on the threat to the UK, acknowledging in its 2016–17 report that:

Daesh (also referred to as the Islamic State of Iraq and the Levant/ISIL/ISIS) poses the greatest threat to the UK and its interests around the world. The 'core' Daesh organisation, operating out of Syria and Iraq, has continued to prove its capability to direct large-scale coordinated attacks in Western countries and the Middle East.[31]

At least one factor in the UK IC's assessment of ISIS, therefore, is that its ability to make assessments of ISIS was weakened by a lack of priority for intelligence collection and assessment on its impact in the region. This was compounded by a focus of effort and resources on the direct terrorist threat more narrowly and on the UK's interests.

The lack of published material on the UK intelligence assessment community's views at the time is an obstacle to making a confident judgement, but it would be surprising if it did not reasonably closely align with that of its US counterparts. One such US perspective, from former CIA Deputy Director Mike Morell in a CBS News interview in June 2014,[32] may offer a clue. He argues that the rapid rise of ISIS was not lost on the IC:

[ISIS predecessor] al Qaeda in Iraq was essentially defeated when the U.S. military left at the end of 2011, and the intelligence community monitored the growth of al Qaeda post-2011 in great detail with intelligence reporting, with analysis. We made very clear that this group is becoming more and more dangerous.

His fellow interviewee, House Intelligence Committee Chairman Mike Rogers, defended the work of intelligence organisations, saying the rise of ISIS was 'a policy failure' because the Obama administration failed to take action against the rise of Sunni militants operating across the border in Syria:

Our argument at the time was if we don't do something to disrupt their growth in eastern Syria, we are going to be in serious trouble. We watched them grow, then we watched them launch an attack from eastern Syria, a safe haven in to Iraq.

Intelligence was there. We didn't do anything in Syria, we didn't do anything when they took Fallujah, we didn't do anything when they took Mosul, they got into Tikrit, and said, 'Hey, this is a problem.' Well, no kidding.

This perspective – that failure to recognise the significance of the rise of ISIS was a policy, not an intelligence failure – is echoed elsewhere. Simpkins argues that

> in 2014, the Obama administration was not receptive to the strategic intelligence regarding the ISIS threat in Iraq. This was mainly due to the Obama administration's reluctance to get drawn back into Iraq after pledging and ultimately getting U.S. troops out of Iraq. Further, at the time, the Obama administration was focused on the Syrian civil war and al-Qaeda in Afghanistan, which caused the administration to be blind to the ISIS threat.[33]

Simpkins also reflects in this case on the relevance of Dahl's analysis that 'strategic-level intelligence and warnings are surprisingly easy to acquire and are often readily available before major attacks, but they are unlikely to be acted upon by decision makers, and in any case too general to be useful'.[34] Ultimately, even though the IC raised warnings about ISIS, the inadequacy of the collected intelligence resulted in an underestimation of the will and capability of ISIS and an overestimation of the will and capability of the Iraqi army. It is also worth bearing in mind that the UK intelligence assessment community does not analyse the policies of its close allies, such as the US – a responsibility which falls to the policy community, such as the FCDO.

UK Defence Intelligence analysts involved at the time have highlighted the risks taken when operations draw down, with a corresponding reduction in collection and assessment effort limiting the IC's ability to monitor a situation which may not have been completely resolved (as in this case).[35] UK customers' attention was also focused on other priorities, including Syria (where al-Assad's regime, rather than ISIS, was seen as the enemy), the UK withdrawal from Helmand in Afghanistan, and the need to understand Iran's nuclear programme during negotiations to agree what became the Joint Comprehensive Plan of Action (JCPoA.) All these issues meant that policymakers' attention was occupied elsewhere. Even with a reduced effort, however, DI was producing monthly updates on the level of violence in Iraq that attracted attention. But it lacked the deep, granular detail that would have contributed to real understanding, for example of ISIS's relationships and leverage on the tribes. Neither the UK nor the US had the collection or analytical horsepower to gain deep insights into the human dimension of what was happening to properly understand how far ISIS had infiltrated Iraqi society. Nor did the UK have a sufficient relationship with the Iraqis to help fill its gaps.

It was only with the capture of Mosul and direct threat to Baghdad that the ISIS problem gained sufficient attention and resources to effectively understand it. As ever, the UK community responded very effectively when in crisis mode. DI called on analysts with previous Iraq experience, and an initial study was produced on Iraqi tribes (in part to help understand how they had been seduced by ISIS). Syria analysts were brought in to provide insights into how the group had developed and gained valuable battlefield experience there. Analysts were also seconded into a cross-government group hosted in the FCO. The UK's direct involvement following the massacre of Yazidis at Sinjar in August 2014 inevitably raised the priority and demand for intelligence analysis.[36]

Crimea

As noted above, the ISC said in its July 2020 Russia Report that the intelligence agencies' effort on hostile state activity, including Russia, was 'thinly spread'. In fact, it had been expressing concern for many years about the impact that the focus on counterterrorism was having on other issues. In its Annual Report 2001–2, the Committee raised a concern that, as resources were being transferred to counterterrorism, coverage of other areas had become increasingly thin: 'These reductions are causing intelligence gaps to develop, which may mean that over time unacceptable risks will arise in terms of safeguarding national security.'[37] Similarly, its Annual Report 2002–3 said: 'The Committee believes that, with the focus on current crises, the Agencies' long-term capacity to provide warnings is being eroded. This situation needs to be addressed and managed by Ministers and the JIC.'[38]

So, as the ISC put it, did the UK government take its eye off the ball? Its Russia Report acknowledges that, following the dissolution of the Soviet Union, the West hoped to make Russia at least a partner. Despite setbacks, including the murder of Alexander Litvinenko in 2006, the government still tried for a reset, including through Prime Minister David Cameron's visit to Moscow in 2011. In a speech during that visit,[39] he acknowledged the difficulties, but also spoke of 'working together to develop a modern and ambitious partnership which will help both our countries achieve a more prosperous and secure future'. Whilst some in government may have felt that it was an aberration, the murder of Litvinenko had, however, undermined that thesis and illustrated the threat Russia posed. The ISC's conclusion – that the UK IC had indeed taken its eye off the ball – was contested by the Agencies and DI. MI5 defended its reprioritisation to meet the terrorist threat, DI acknowledged that 'our coverage of Russia undoubtedly suffered as a consequence of that prioritisation, which was necessary for the conduct of military operations'. SIS's perspective was that 'the appetite for work against the Russian threat has sort of waxed and waned', while for GCHQ 'some of the kind of hardcore capabilities that were necessary to keep in the business we maintained and then, really, as the reviews and the discussion around what happened in Crimea really brought minds more to the fore again on Russia'.[40]

Nevertheless, whilst acknowledging 'the very considerable pressures on the Agencies since 9/11, and that they have a finite amount of resource, which they must focus on operational priorities', the Committee concludes that 'reacting to the here and now is inherently inefficient and – in our opinion – until recently, the Government had badly underestimated the Russian threat and the response it required'.[41] The Committee does, however, then pile into the policy departments (namely the FCO, MOD and Home Office in particular), suggesting that they are ultimately at fault for not addressing the issue sufficiently and therefore for not appropriately prioritising Russia for the IC to respond to:

> Accepting the counterterrorism pressures on the operational organisations, there is nevertheless a question over the approach taken by the policy departments. We have previously discussed the extent to which economic policy dictated the opening up of the UK to Russian

investment. This indicates a failure of the security policy departments to engage with this issue – to the extent that the UK now faces a threat from Russia within its own borders. What appears to have been a somewhat laissez-faire policy approach is less easy to forgive than the response of the busy Agencies. We welcome the fact that this has now been recognised and appears to be changing.[42]

The ISC's overall conclusion, therefore, seems to be that whilst it felt the IC should have put more effort into Russia in the early 2000s, the major fault lay principally with policy departments (particularly FCO and MOD) in not articulating Russia as a sufficient priority compared with counterterrorism. Certainly, the view of intelligence analysts was that the government focus and priority was on developing a positive relationship with Russia. Against that backdrop, it was difficult to argue against the diversion of staff in DI's Russia team to meet the more urgent and current needs for more analysis on the Middle East, especially Syria.[43]

There was a general feeling amongst DI analysts that the period prior to the annexation of Crimea was a difficult one in which to get acceptance in the policy community of intelligence assessments that were negative about Russia's intentions.[44] Russia was perceived to have moved on from the chaos of the Yeltsin years and NATO and the EU were pursuing relationships with Georgia and Ukraine despite awareness of Russian unhappiness. Russian success in its conflict with Georgia was in spite of military deficiencies and poor performance, and events there were not seen as necessarily indicative of future actions. A depleted Russia team was unable to study the country and its military in depth, still less to provide an effective warning function. For the IC, there was also a gap in understanding the West's own policies (which, of course, it does not analyse) and their impact or likely impact on Russia.

The Euromaidan protests from November 2013 sparked Defence Intelligence analysis but focused on the domestic situation and internal stability in Ukraine as the priority. There were simply not enough analysts to take a broader look, including at Russian military capability, in any depth. Warning about Russian intentions towards Crimea was also complicated by deception and denial, the fact that there was already a Russian presence there and, as the crisis developed, by some Ukrainian forces changing sides. DI analysts assess that Western reluctance to accept what was happening – that, for example, the 'little green men' were Russian forces – gave Russia two to three days' advantage.

Ultimately, there was a warning failure, but it was on the back of depleted resources focused on the region because of other, higher, priorities elsewhere (the Middle East) and perhaps also a persistence in the desire by the policy community to look for a positive outcome. The ISC also concluded that Russia's centralised system and ability to act on what it saw as a key issue of national interest without the complexities involved in consulting allies was also a factor in the speed with which the crisis unrolled:

> It is not clear to the Committee whether HMG and our allies have yet found an effective way to respond to the pace of Russian decision-making. This has severely undermined the West's ability to respond effectively to Russian aggressions in the past – for example, the annexation of Crimea in 2014.[45]

Conclusion, Lessons Learned and the Future

The effective provision of early warning (or perhaps just warning, as by definition it has to be early to be of value) is a fundamental issue for the IC. As noted above, it is explicitly referred to in the terms of reference for the Chair of the JIC. There is always a concern in the IC that a crisis might erupt without warning. Or worse, that it subsequently comes to light that the IC possessed information which might have provided due warning if only it had been recognised as such or communicated in such a way that the policy or operational readership had recognised it as a warning and been able to respond. In terms of the performance criteria set out in Table 1.4 of Chapter 1, listing 'Non-excusable performance problems', these would fall under the 'Information, research and expertise deficiencies' and 'Intra-organisational pathologies' causes. Every surprise – whether the attack on Pearl Harbor, 9/11 or the three case studies in this book – is meticulously examined to identify errors and lessons. Intelligence providers and analysts work under the constant burden that, in such an event, their words will be crawled over to determine whether they missed or underplayed what was unfolding and whether their customers could clearly understand what they were being told. That, of course, brings with it a risk of creating structural incentives to under- or over-warn or to hedge assessments to avoid post-mortem blame. This can be where strong leadership to ensure rigorous analysis and to protect the analyst becomes particularly important.

Ultimately, therefore, I would argue that the provision of warning can be broken down into three elements:

1. Is information available that could contribute to a warning assessment?
2. Is the issue of sufficient priority to warrant attention and analysis?
3. Is the warning conveyed in a manner that makes it clear to customers that they are being warned, so that they are in a position to consider a response?

A positive outcome in all three would place the analysis, and the response to it, in the right-hand column ('Raising expectations') of Table 1.3 in Chapter 1. As this book makes clear, the diagnostic challenge for these three case histories it examines is quite different. The Arab uprisings were a series of popular revolts building on a combination of common factors that had been brewing for years, but with no clear sense of when (or indeed, if) they would boil over. ISIS was a non-governmental military/terrorist organisation that evolved from its predecessor, AQ-I, and which thrived in the context of existing conflicts in Syria and Iraq. By contrast, the annexation of Crimea was a conscious political decision by a state, backed up by military force. So, the circumstances and requirements in each case were quite different too. In the case of the Arab uprisings, at least, there is no real sense that they represented an intelligence failure, in that clear information was available that could have provided specific early warning. Nevertheless, there are lessons to be taken on the use of open-source and diplomatic reporting that apply more widely. In the case of ISIS, there appears to have been a combination of a lack of detailed, insightful intelligence and a simple lack of priority in focus on events within Syria and Iraq, including the impact of US policies, compared with the external threat to the UK. By contrast, the lack of warning of the risk of the Russian annexation of Crimea looks more convincingly like a failure. But a failure on whose part? The IC, from whom such a warning would have been expected to come, but which had been denuded of analytical resources and told to focus on other, higher, priorities for collection and assessment? Or the policy community, still clinging to a desire to have a political and economic relationship with Russia, the time for which had passed?

Certainly, within the UK assessment community there does not seem to have been a view that there was a single set of lessons to learn from these events. But they did all contribute to and reinforce the growing recognition that open-source information had a significant and growing part to play in building the overall intelligence picture. In itself, this is nothing new and was, indeed, one of the key conclusions in the Franks Report on the Argentinian invasion of the Falkland Islands in 1982:

> The aim should be to ensure that the assessments staff are able to take fully into account both relevant diplomatic and political developments and foreign press treatment of sensitive foreign policy issues ... We consider that the assessment machinery should be reviewed ... [including] the arrangements for bringing to the Joint Intelligence Organisation's attention information other than intelligence reports.[46]

But, increasingly, there has been a recognition in recent years that modern tailored news feeds, web scraping tools and computer-aided analysis should be able to do much more to assist the analyst. Whilst steps have been taken to improve exploitation of open-source information, with the creation of dedicated teams of specialists in exploiting open sources, broader education of analysts and use of specialist tools, there is more to do. This was acknowledged in the March 2021 Defence Command Paper 'Defence in a Competitive Age',[47] which highlighted that 'Understanding and assessment will be increasingly important to effective decision-making and action' and stated that 'We will need to invest in the capabilities that enable us to obtain and exploit information at speed to give us advantage over our rivals.'[48] It concluded, in the case of Defence Intelligence, that 'Open source intelligence, automation and AI provide potentially game-changing ways to understand and counter these new challenges.'[49]

Techniques such as 'crowdsourcing' are also being explored for their ability to provide insights that aid forecasting.[50] In 2020, the Professional Head of Intelligence Assessment in the Cabinet Office initiated an open-source crowdforecasting exercise, known as Cosmic Bazaar, to give analysts from across government (not just the IC) the opportunity to develop their open-source analysis and forecasting skills. The platform is universally accessible from government IT systems for practical and inclusiveness reasons, and it has attracted some 1,300 analysts from forty-five organisations and departments. Its first year has been one of experimentation and learning – crowdsourcing forecasts in this way demands questions with a deadline that can be objectively measured, for example: 'will an official announcement of a ceasefire come into force by the end of April?' But it has helped analysts to develop their open-source tradecraft skills, opened up sharing of resources and sites and has been participated in with enthusiasm.[51]

But where does this leave the JIC's (and the JIC Chair's personal) responsibility for early warning? As a committee, the JIC's strength is in providing strategic intelligence assessments that have broad agreement across government and thus are a valuable underpinning for National Security Council discussions. It can provide a similar function in a crisis too. It also does a degree of horizon scanning, with its annual consideration of 'Countries at Risk of Instability' (CRI). This exercise examines countries around the globe, focusing in particular on their resilience in the face of threats, ranging from political and economic to climate-related or broader societal risks (or a combination thereof). Whilst countries move up and down the list, it is really more an opportunity to examine trends and to assist the allocation of government overseas expenditure than an early warning trigger.[52]

Future options for the way that the JIC deals with warning might be to more explicitly factor in early warning within the JIC's work programme and perhaps more clearly differentiate between the early warning roles of the JIO, as an assessment body, and the

JIC, as a strategic cross-HMG committee. But another (or parallel) approach could be to clarify and formalise across government the roles and responsibilities for early warning between the JIO and other assessment bodies, such as JTAC for terrorism and DI – particularly, in the case of the latter, for military threats.

This echoes a sense in Defence Intelligence by 2014 that early warning as a specific discipline and methodology, delivering tailored products clearly identified as warnings, needed to be revived. During the Cold War, early warning was more or less limited to warning of a Warsaw Pact attack on NATO. Since study of the Soviet Union and Warsaw Pact occupied the vast majority of DI's effort at that time, early warning was a natural extension of this broader work. In the 1990s, DI developed an online classified dashboard which contained basic information about individual countries, their political and military situation etc., and which purported to provide an early warning function. But it suffered from being piecemeal and from uneven updating and, whilst an easily accessible Wikipedia-style reference tool, it did not appear to customers to be clearly an early warning device, and it gradually fell into abeyance before being suspended in 2015.

There were occasions and events where DI felt it was providing early warning and could point to it in documents – but often the key material was buried in long reports, which were not readily accessible to all but the most determined reader.[53] As noted above, there is a risk that analysts may do this in order to avoid the reputational risk that can come with 'crying wolf', particularly in the wake of the Iraq WMD experience. By late 2014, however, there was a recognition – including as a result of Crimea in particular – that early warning needed to be reinstituted as a distinct discipline, drawing on NATO and US tools and methodology, with a 'warning manager' appointed to focus on that specific responsibility. Informally referred to as 'getting left of the bang', the project gained that full-time manager in April 2015, subsequently with support.[54] A key issue was to get buy-in from the relevant analytical teams that would need to provide the inputs and regular monitoring. But some obvious, perennial warning problems, such as the threat of a Russian attack on NATO and another Argentinian attack on the Falkland Islands, which were clear necessities for DI to monitor, helped the analysts to understand the need. Despite requiring some initial work to collate the relevant material, decide the questions that needed answering and the corresponding watchcon levels (which some regarded as yet another burden on already busy teams), analysts soon realised that day-to-day monitoring could relatively easily become part of their daily work without much overhead and indeed gave them a useful product for raising awareness of their concerns. These warning problems were then supplemented by others in response to customer demand, or on the recommendation of analysts. This aligns with Cynthia Grabo's thinking that warning is a specialised function that requires dedicated processes and people – the latter with a personal skillset that gives them confidence to speak up and ask difficult questions. She also stresses the need for those people not to be subsumed into current intelligence and day-to-day crises reporting.[55] A number of factors helped Defence Intelligence to get traction with this set of arrangements:

1. Warning problems could be established relatively quickly and flexibly, without the need for a bureaucratic approval approvals process by seniors.
2. They moved away from just being about unlikely but high-impact events (such as a Russian attack on NATO), to include issues with more immediate 'operational' value, such as the risk of chemical weapons use in Syria.
3. This entailed close engagement with customers.
4. This included a visually distinct 'look' and handling – warning products were clearly different from regular intelligence assessments, with watchcon levels that indicated a change had occurred that merited consideration of some response.

Together, this enabled Defence Intelligence to create some seventeen warning problems quickly (the actual number of problems maintained at any time changes, or they can be adjusted, depending on the requirement or events), with the full-time warning manager relentlessly following up with analytical teams to check that they were updated on a regular basis. Admittedly, to begin with, Defence Intelligence was ahead of its customers in setting up problems, but closer engagement drew customers in and improved their sense of ownership. Those operationally relevant problems, especially related to Syria given its priority at the time, made a real difference in customer engagement. That could, admittedly, range from a report being read 'with interest' to some more tangible reaction. A sign of success was when customers started using warning language back to Defence Intelligence, paid attention to the watchcon levels and made decisions on the back of them.[56]

Having a formal process also enabled DI to play a more engaged role with allies in this field. Amongst the Five Eyes nations (UK, US, Australia, Canada and New Zealand), discussion of early warning takes place under the umbrella of the US Defense Warning Network,[57] with the ambition to 'follow the sun' and hand off live problems from one to the other during respective working days or to overnight watches. Similarly, NATO has an Intelligence Warning System (NIWS), described as 'the Alliance's collaborative means of providing long term crisis anticipation to the North Atlantic Council'.[58] Whilst contributions are inevitably patchy, it is nevertheless a forum for participants to exchange lessons and methods.

In conclusion, early warning remains (as one would hope) a lively topic in UK government intelligence assessment circles. Of the three case studies in this book, Crimea probably provided the most stimulus for the topic, as a specific time-bound event most evidently not predicted, although the issue of avoiding surprise is constantly on analysts' minds. Overall, the key takeaways for the UK community appear to be:

1. Surprises are more likely in areas which are a low priority for intelligence collection and assessment.
2. To be able to provide warning, an analyst needs a baseline of what is 'normal' and this requires a long-term effort to develop a deep understanding of the actor(s) involved, their military forces, how they deploy, and so on.
3. Open-source information plays a key role in contributing to understanding, whether for high- or low-priority countries or issues. But it can also be particularly valuable in filling the gap for those low-priority countries where intelligence

resources are not tasked or are limited. Assessment bodies therefore need to continue to invest in open-source tools, training, techniques (such as crowdsourcing) and the means to integrate open-source information with highly classified intelligence.

4. Surprises can never be completely avoided. It is, therefore, incumbent on the IC to be able to react promptly to the ensuing changed situation.

5. Finally, early warning works best when treated as a specific discipline in its own right, with a methodology and distinct products that stand out to the policy or operational customer.

Notes

1. HMG, 'Joint Intelligence Committee'.
2. UK Parliament, 'Review of Intelligence on Weapons of Mass Destruction', Report of a Committee of Privy Counsellors, HC898 (London: The Stationery Office, 2004).
3. HMG, 'Joint Intelligence Committee'.
4. Intelligence and Security Committee of Parliament, 'Annual Report 2012–2013' (2013), recommendation H.
5. HMG, 'Defence Reform' (2011). Part 9 explains the need for a JFC.
6. HMG, 'Joint Forces Command is Now Called Strategic Command'.
7. Personal knowledge and discussions with DI analysts, April 2021.
8. Intelligence and Security Committee of Parliament, 'Russia' (2020), para. 72.
9. UK Parliament, 'British Foreign Policy and the "Arab Spring"', Foreign Affairs Committee – Second Report, House of Commons (2012).
10. Interviews with DI analysts, March 2021.
11. George Joffé, 'The Arab Spring in North Africa: Origins and Prospects', The Journal of North African Studies 16, no. 4 (2011).
12. UK Parliament, 'British Foreign Policy and the "Arab Spring"', para. 14.
13. Ibid., para. 20.
14. Intelligence and Security Committee of Parliament, 'Annual Report 2011–2012' (2012), para. 40ff.
15. Ibid., para. 39.

16. Ibid.
17. Ibid., recommendation B.
18. HMG, 'Government Response to the Intelligence and Security Committee's Annual Report 2011–2012' (2012), under recommendation C.
19. Intelligence and Security Committee of Parliament, 'Annual Report 2011–2012'.
20. HMG, 'Libya Crisis: National Security Adviser's Review of Central Coordination and Lessons Learned' (2011).
21. Ibid., 3.
22. Ibid., 3. Between 20 March and 25 October 2011, NSC(L) met sixty-two times, with thirty-two of those meetings chaired by the Prime Minister.
23. Ibid., paras 16–17.
24. Joint Intelligence Committee, 'Iraq, Insurgency, Sectarianism and Violence' (2006).
25. Joint Intelligence Committee, 'Iraq: How Important is Al Qaida in Iraq' (2007).
26. US Department of Defense, 'News Briefing with Gen. Odierno from the Pentagon' (2010).
27. See, for example: Brian Keith Simpkins, 'How Intelligence Failures Contributed to ISIS Territorial Gain in Iraq' (American Military University, 2017).
28. Interviews with DI analysts, March 2021.
29. Intelligence and Security Committee of Parliament, 'Annual Report 2015–2016' (2016).
30. Ibid., 13.
31. Intelligence and Security Committee of Parliament, 'Annual Report 2016–2017' (2017), para. 20.
32. Rebecca Kaplan, 'Rise of ISIS Poses Fresh Challenges for U.S. Intelligence Community', CBS News, 27 June 2014.
33. Ibid.
34. Eric Dahl, *Intelligence and Surprise Attack: Failure and Success from Pearl Harbor to 9/11 and Beyond*, (Washington, DC: Georgetown University Press, 2013), 22.
35. Discussion with DI analysts, March 2021.
36. Discussion with DI analysts, March 2021.
37. Intelligence and Security Committee of Parliament, 'Annual Report 2001–2002' (2002), para. 79.
38. Intelligence and Security Committee of Parliament, 'Annual Report 2002–2003' (2003), para. 67.

39. HMG, 'PM's Speech in Moscow', 12 September 2011.
40. Intelligence and Security Committee of Parliament, 'Russia', para. 73.
41. Ibid., para. 74.
42. Ibid., para. 75.
43. Discussion with DI analysts, April 2021.
44. Discussion with DI analysts, April 2021.
45. Intelligence and Security Committee of Parliament, 'Russia', para. 96.
46. Oliver Franks and Privy Council, 'Falkland Islands Review: Report of a Committee of Privy Counsellors' (London: Her Majesty's Stationery Office, 1983), paras 317, 319.
47. UK Ministry of Defence, 'Defence in a Competitive Age' (2021).
48. Ibid., 12–13.
49. Ibid., 65.
50. See, for example: Perry World House, 'Keeping Score: A New Approach to Geopolitical Forecasting' (2021).
51. Ibid., 19, and conversations with JIO staff, April 2021.
52. Personal experience and discussion with JIO staff, April 2021.
53. Personal recollection and discussions with DI analysts, March 2021.
54. Ibid.
55. Cynthia Grabo, *Handbook of Warning Intelligence: Assessing the Threat to National Security* (vol. no. 12). (Lanham, MD: Scarecrow Press, 2010).
56. Personal recollection and discussions with DI analysts, March 2021.
57. US Department of Defense, 'Directive 3115.16', dated 5 December 2013, updated 10 August 2020.
58. NATO, 'NATO Nations Discuss Warning Intelligence Reform' (2019).

6 'We Never Plan for the Worst Case': Considering the Case of Germany*

Ulrich Schlie and Andreas Lutsch

Introduction

Events related to the Arab uprisings, ISIS's rise to power and Russia's aggression against parts of Ukraine in 2014 posed complex, though distinct challenges for the Federal Republic of Germany. How well were German leaders and officials informed about nascent as well as short-term developments beforehand and once these crises erupted? The widely shared appearance of sharp discontinuity in the way related historical processes unfolded raises questions about the degree to which decision makers and officials in government were taken by surprise. Just like a realistic question cannot be framed based on a surprise/no-surprise dichotomy, it

* This article was finished in April 2021. In the meantime, Putin's aggression against Ukraine has turned the world upside down. More than many other states, Germany gave the impression of being surprised and overtaken by events. Germany's all but complete underestimation of the aggressive potential of Putin's Russia, its athropic strategic approach, and failed diplomacy stirred up an international debate on German security and foreign policies which is still ongoing. It appears that the wide-spread miscalculation of Russian behaviour was partly a result of wishful, if not naïve, thinking, neglect of history, and sheer absence of a strategic debate deserving that name. The transformative events of 2022 underline the urgent necessity for adaptations with regard to military strategy, diplomacy and intelligence as is argued below. The issue of a National Security Council was discussed in the 2021 Bundestag election campaign but not taken up by the new coalition government.

will not be possible, also under ideal circumstances with access to pertinent government files and documents, to justify a flat answer to the question of the degree of surprise (see Chapter 1).

Thus, when considering the case of Germany, we are wise to appreciate humility as an analytic virtue and when we try to understand how little we can ascertain about relevant processes based on documentation which is hitherto available in the public domain. Moreover, we must be cognizant of the fact that we would need to study the knowledge and beliefs of leaders and officials when seeking to examine how well informed or surprised government officials were in each of the three cases. This will remain difficult even when the archival record permits deeper insight into government thinking at the time. We do not wish to obscure the point that the question of how much German leaders and officials were surprised cannot now or in the next two or three decades be examined with a reasonable level of confidence based on publicly available sources. This also holds true for scholarship which seeks to reconstruct analytical judgements of intelligence analysts as well as leadership receptivity to secret intelligence products. By definition, those products are secret and mean to inform the perspectives of a selected, and at times very small, number of political and military leaders and civil servants.

It is obvious that questions related to 'good governance' raise formidable difficulties when they ask about lessons learned, not learned, or yet to be learned by the German government considering the cases under study here. Approximation to the analysis of those questions is not excluded, though. Attempting to learn based on an imperfect data set is also much better than not trying to learn at all. This is what our chapter seeks to contribute.

The first section of our chapter raises issues which should inform potential post-mortem analyses of non-linearity or crisis anticipation performance of the German government. The second section focuses on central aspects of that performance with an eye to the Ukraine crisis of 2013–14. Section three discusses the discrepancies between audibility of calls for strategic far-sightedness in German foreign and security policy and discernible change in the practice of that policy during the twenty-first century. The fourth section lays out key aspects of how structures of Germany's assessment system were adapted in the years following the Arab uprisings, ISIS's rise to power and Russia's aggression against Ukraine in 2014. As such, this chapter pays specific attention to the locus of estimative strategic intelligence within assessment capacities. Finally, the chapter offers a brief conclusion by pointing to overdue changes in Germany's approach to security policy that revolves around the need to become more strategic and serious about the possibility of surprise, including surprise related to existential threats.

Specific Considerations and Guiding Questions in Search of Lessons

Considering the outbreak of the Arab uprisings, ISIS's rise to power and Russia's aggression against Ukraine in 2014, analysts and scholars may retrospectively examine either in government or based on then-declassified government records whether and which specific efforts were made by the German government in the 2010s to identify, assess and potentially learn from positive and deficient aspects in anticipatory assessment regarding those cases and, potentially, additional ones. Specific considerations and guiding questions building on the theoretical framework in Chapter 1 of this volume should inform any such endeavour, with prejudicing what the available evidence may indicate in the future. An overarching point is that lesson learning needs to be attempted with both humility and precision.

To begin with, to the extent efforts were made within the German government to think about 'lessons', an important aspect to notice is that recording 'lessons' is profoundly different 'from actually learning from experience'.[1] Identifying what went wrong or what seemed to have worked rather well in those three cases will not be free from hindsight knowledge (which is not necessarily hindsight bias) despite recognition of analytical problems which this perspective poses. Also, it will be not per se be a recipe for better anticipation or avoiding surprise in the future, no matter how rigorous the analysis is done and no matter whether it will be formally mandated, say, by cabinet, a minister, or the head of an agency. In fact, even before a government will be able to learn something from any such analysis, suppose production of the latter was indeed completed, non-trivial questions are bound to arise about how to make use of such analytical results. Also, how important is publicness?[2] Who is supposed to receive unconstrained access to the results which the analysis presents? Will parliamentary committees, including oversight communities, receive copies? Should only some in government be allowed to read or be briefed about key judgements or just excerpts? And what would each of those and other variants imply? These sorts of questions are particularly relevant when secret intelligence becomes an object of retrospective investigation.[3] In other words, retrospective analysis for the purpose of learning rather than recording may well be important. But even the management of a single and, ideally, objectively candid analysis can raise issues which can erect barriers to more systematic learning.

Moreover, to the extent that the German government made efforts to think about 'lessons', relevant actors in government who are tasked to identify lessons may have understood the meaning of learning lessons about anticipatory assessment differently than others. Even when confusion can be mitigated by precisely defining who should learn which lessons, this possibility remains considering different outlooks, analytic requirements, depths of insight, and responsibilities, say, of development aid officials, diplomats, military officers, strategic intelligence analysts and top-level decision-makers. One would also want to develop an understanding where and on which levels in government discussions about lessons took place and how much sustained attention of, or even interaction with, top-level leaders could be secured during the process. Considering the vast differences between the three cases addressed in this book – the Arab uprisings, ISIS's rise to power and Russia's aggression against Ukraine in 2014 – and considering the complexities inherent in each of those cases, it seems reasonable to expect differences in the ways differently concerned actors shaped a potential intra-governmental discourse on 'lessons'. For example, even the meaning of the word 'crisis' may well remain ambiguous and, by extension, the meanings of composita like 'crisis early detection', 'crisis management', 'crisis prevention', 'crisis reaction', and so on. In short, analysts and scholars with an interest in carving out 'lessons' from the recent past will be well-advised to be very specific about the exact object of analysis and to consider that any attempt of thinking about general 'lessons' requires prior and rigorous consideration of 'lessons' to be drawn from experiences in individual cases such as Russia's aggression against Ukraine in 2014.

In addition, and bearing in mind that the approach of this book is broad, one would have to be very precise when tailoring key questions to be investigated. This may mean limiting their scope, to begin with: should 'lessons' be learned about past government practices of anticipatory assessments? Or would this be too broadly defined? Should the search only and precisely concern the ways in which secret intelligence shaped anticipatory assessments? If so, is this about foreign and/or defence intelligence? Are we examining strategic estimates and/or estimates included in current intelligence? Or, to name yet another alternative, should 'lessons' be learned only about how Germany's warning system functioned in each of those and, potentially, in other cases?

Suppose secret intelligence input to the broader process of anticipatory assessment in government was to be made the subject of inquiry. Even then there will be different categories of specific questions which may be of concern. For example, even if questions concerning the quantity and quality of intelligence collection were to be left aside, important as they are, one would want to consider the quality of the analytic process which culminated in estimates of where developments in the Maghreb region and greater Middle East, Syria and Iraq, and Ukraine were headed, what the nature of changes was, how fast changes unfolded, and so on. One would also want to be very careful about judgements which touch on the issue of competence of individuals who made estimates.

One would also want to be fair enough to acknowledge that no universally accepted method exists allowing estimators to anticipate when non-linearities occur, while, on the other hand, most conflicts have a degree of shape or structure that allows prior exploration or even explanation of conditions which can with a certain (to be specified) likelihood give rise to non-linearities.[4] Especially, the concept of 'prediction' in the sense of forecasting as a form of historical prognosis is often referred to in a careless way to insinuate that intelligence analysts, in particular, can or should be expected to deliver 'predictions'.[5] In fact, they cannot – at least unless forecasting methods are applied. But even when such demanding methods are applied, inherent limitations of intelligence cannot be overcome. Intelligence can 'help reduce uncertainty'[6] or, conversely, appreciate uncertainty, that is, 'disturb prevailing policy and decrease rather than increase' the certainty of judgement.[7] Often, intelligence accomplishes both at the same time.

In line with this understanding, an interesting expectation arises regarding the case of the Ukraine crisis, for example. Even in the absence of strategic consensus in Germany on how to analyse and estimate Russia's national security decision-making, long before the Euromaidan protests and at least since the Georgia War in 2008, the scope of Russia's categoric aversion to a Western-bound Ukraine may have been rather well understood at least by observers working in all-source environments while decision-makers may have resisted the notion that the case of Ukraine amounted to a zero-sum geostrategic conflict also involving the US as an extra-regional great power. In other words, expecting largely warranted 'a priori strategic assumptions' may well be realistic at least with regards to analysts in all-source environments committed to understanding the world how it is and not how it should be. Moreover, it would also appear realistic to expect that, as the crisis unfolded, various 'tactical' indications of Russian military actions could not remain hidden to defence intelligence structures in various countries.[8]

Because expecting 'predictions' from intelligence analysts, or anticipatory analysis more generally, about complex political, social and military phenomena in other countries would mean expecting too much, retrospective analysis of estimative performance should be cautious or even avoid attempts to measure how well estimators 'predicted' what happened. The more interesting issue would be to try to understand the shape of mindsets which framed the thinking of analysts and provided a basis for their best estimates as well as the contours of the information basis that was available to them at the time.[9]

What's more, one would have to avoid the fundamental errors of conflating 'incorrect answers with deficient if not incompetent ways of thinking', on the one hand, and of 'equat[ing] reasonable, well-grounded inferences with those that proved to be correct', on the other.[10] All of the mentioned points, of course, relate to a central difficulty involved in any effort to retrospectively focus

on the secret intelligence input to the broader process of anticipatory assessment in government: 'In judging the performance of
any intelligence organization we need first to come to a realistic
understanding of the limits to intelligence.'[11]

Perhaps even more difficult to assess would be the additional
question of what difference it would have made if decision-makers
(in this case: German decision-makers) were – hypothetically – less
surprised or, hence, better informed. Would this have enabled them
to make decisions which would have made a difference before the
potential occurrence of non-linear events such as the Arab uprisings, ISIS's rise to power and Russia's aggression against Ukraine
in 2014? An intuitive answer may be some form of yes, but this
may be misleading. Besides the issue of leadership receptivity to
anticipatory assessments, including secret intelligence assessments,
and the issue of availability of levers to influence other states'
behaviours within the constraints of the international environment, one may actually expect insensitivity of leaders to most early
detection, early warning or even crisis anticipation information as
long as national interests are judged not to be at stake if and when
estimated changes materialise.[12] In fact, top-level decision-makers
may even not always value better anticipatory assessments regarding issues which do affect national interests and they may hence
prefer to count on their own abilities to contribute to crisis management if a crisis materialises – despite the problem that crises
can be hectic, stressful, unusual and complex 'episodes of threat,
uncertainty, and urgency'.[13] Moreover, decision-makers may not
unequivocally value better anticipatory assessments even in more
important cases, because the more accurate assessments are, the
more they can increase potentially unwelcome political pressures
to act with measures which may be costly, unpopular, difficult to
legitimise or contested in terms of their adequacy and effectiveness
to prevent, mitigate or manage problems.[14] Anticipatory assessments may hence tend to constrain freedom of manoeuvre before
and also when a non-linearity occurs. This can make assessments
unwelcome, especially when they illuminate how little a government may be able or resolved to shape the course of certain foreign
events at distant places by measures of preventive or reactive crisis
management.[15]

The Ukraine Crisis and Germany's Anticipation Performance

'We EU representatives are always a little naïve, and believe that our mission will turn out all right because we are fighting for the right values. We never plan for the worst case.' These are the words that a senior official with the European Commission was quoted as saying in *Der Spiegel* in 2014, looking back on Ukraine.[16] Although the quote goes back to a high EU diplomat, it might have come from a senior civil servant from the German government who bluntly addresses strategic planning deficits in the German system. Against this background, the experience of the Ukraine crisis is intrinsically linked to the still ongoing debate on how to reorganise German security policy. With the decision not to sign the EU Association Agreement in November 2013, the events of the spring of 2014 that would lead to the Russian annexation of Crimea and the crisis in eastern Ukraine took their course. Most of this came as a strategic surprise to German diplomacy. This was not because Ukraine was neglected as a topic. It was rather due to a natural focus on Russia which can be explained, inter alia, by a durable framing of 'Ostpolitik' and the remembrance of the Soviet Union's approval for Germany's reunification. The resulting under-appreciation of the Ukraine question in German diplomacy was comparable to tendencies within the European Union where that question was not given the appropriate strategic weight. The NATO Ukraine Commission played only a subordinate role in the overall diplomatic structure of the Alliance. The lack of attention paid to Ukraine by politicians and the media in Germany became a problem precisely at the moment when the geo-economic penetration of Europe by German companies was taking shape – for example through the transport of Russian gas directly to Germany on the seabed via the Baltic Sea pipeline Nord Stream I, the longest underwater pipeline in the world, one of Europe's biggest infrastructure projects.

Attention to geostrategic drivers for Russian foreign economic policy in Eastern Europe was generally absent from political and strategic discussions at top levels in Berlin. At the same time, from the very outset the Nord Stream project was designed by Russia to undermine the position of Ukraine as a dominant transit state for the transport of Russian gas to Europe, and the Russian parallel project South Stream – a second underwater pipe on the bed of the Black Sea – prompted yet another shift of power in Eastern Europe which increased risks to the architecture of trans-European security.[17]

Aside from the underestimation of the strategic significance of Ukraine, serious errors in European diplomacy contributed to significant hesitations along the journey to the as-yet unsigned EU Association Agreement. Legal experts and translators took almost a year to write the finished version of the agreement text. Political and diplomatic misjudgements of the active players were all the more serious as a result. In particular, EU negotiation leader Stefan Füle did not pay sufficient attention to the personality of the then Ukrainian Prime Minister Yanukovych and his relationship with Russia, just as the geopolitical arguments and motivation of the Russian administration under the leadership of President Putin were underestimated. Even when Füle's visit to Kyiv on 21 November 2013 was cancelled at short notice by the Ukrainians, this did not lead to deeper reflection in Brussels and Berlin about a possibly changing strategic situation.

In Berlin, all political attention was at this point focused on the negotiations to establish a new coalition government. The acceptance speech of the new Foreign Minister Frank-Walter Steinmeier in the *Auswärtiges Amt* on 17 December 2013 can be seen as a cautious step back, and as preparation for a fundamental change of course in German foreign policy towards Ukraine.[18] Steinmeier had already held this post from 2005 until 2009 under Chancellor Angela Merkel. He was generally seen as one of the most insightful advocates of a Russo-German rapprochement. However, in his acceptance speech, he expressed clear criticism of Russia's instrumentalisation of the economic situation of Ukraine and the non-signature of the EU Association Agreement. Still, it was not clear enough to Western services and diplomatic missions at this point to what extent the diplomatic crisis would further intensify over the coming weeks.

When, at the 50th Munich Security Conference on 31 January 2014, Federal President Joachim Gauck delivered an eloquent statement with coalition-wide support on Germany's willingness to assume greater responsibility in the world, it was by no means clear that Ukraine would become the next test case in that regard.[19]

In mid-February 2014, there were further dramatic developments in events in Ukraine. In a parliamentary session that was broadcast on television, Victor Yanukovych was stripped of his office, and parliament elected the former vice head of government Aleksandr Turchnikov as President with a large majority. In the early hours of 19 February 2014, thousands of people had demonstrated in the Maidan square for early presidential elections and a new constitution as well as Yanukovych's compact with the parliamentary opposition. There were protests all over the country. The United States demanded an immediate withdrawal of security forces from the Maidan. EU Commission President Barroso, on the other hand, was only prompted under the pressure of events to announce targeted measures by the European Union. The Russian occupation of Crimea occurred gradually through camouflaged individual movements. Added to this was the fact that some 60,000 members of the Ukrainian combat forces had gone over to the new pro-Russian government. This 'strategic surprise' was only gradually revealed in the various telephone calls that Federal Chancellor Merkel had with President Putin. Because of these events, personnel resources were pooled both in the German Embassy in Kyiv and in the headquarters of the Foreign Office and the Defence Ministry in Berlin, so that the accelerating developments could be grasped as promptly as possible by intense monitoring.

At the NATO Defence Ministry Council meeting on 26 February 2014 there were disputes within the Alliance about whether Ukraine should even be an issue on the agenda. This judgement was also connected with the impetus of the strategic surprise and the inadequate diplomatic analysis that underlay it. In the end, as a result of the speed of developments, Ukraine was discussed with German involvement.

In late February 2014, the critical situation came to a peak. In several places on the Black Sea peninsula of Crimea, at two airports, outside the regional parliament in Simferopol and near the port city of Sevastopol, there were sightings of men in the uniforms of the pro-Russian combat unit Berkut, who were undertaking targeted action on behalf of the Russians. At this point they had already taken power with the help of outside influence, when the Ukrainian government was announcing that its own security forces still had complete control on the Crimean Peninsula. The ISES paper on the further response to Ukraine argued for the early involvement of the new Ukrainian government and a revival of the NATO-Ukraine Commission with the aim of supporting democratic reforms, the democratic control of the security sector, defence reforms and practical military cooperation.

The various efforts by diplomats – including a joint trip by the High Commissioner for National Minorities of the OSZE, Astrid Thors, and the Swiss OSZE special envoy to Kyiv, Tim Guldimann, as well as discussions held by Federal Minister Steinmeier with the Russian Foreign Minister Sergei Lavrov in Geneva – helped to establish an overview of the situation. And their purpose was to help the European states reach a unified position on the Crimean question.

At the European Council meeting of 6 March 2014, an agreement on sanctions was reached.[20] The agreement in the political judgement altered nothing about the fact that in the crucial phase between October 2013 and February 2014 most mechanisms of a far-sighted strategic analysis had failed. In some European capitals, including Berlin, internal developments in Ukraine had been misunderstood in terms of their effects on the political calculations of the Kremlin and Putin's geopolitical ambitions. Had national security planning been strategically oriented, and the diplomatic initiatives of the German Foreign Office been tempered in terms of security policy, some of the misjudgements could have been avoided, and the political and strategic deficits that were clearly present in Brussels could have been mitigated.

Against this background, it may come as a surprise that in the assessment of the foreign policy of the Merkel era the 2014 Ukraine crisis is commonly seen as a phase of great visibility and diplomatic activity. Above all, this has to do with the role that the Chancellor played in international crisis management during the crucial phase of the conflict, with her important telephone calls to President Putin and the American President Obama. This has been sufficiently appreciated in retrospective academic treatments of the period, and it has been perceived as a particularly active moment for and as a highlight of German diplomacy.[21] An awareness of deficits in the structures of German foreign and security policy continued to increase in the Federal Government, the Bundestag, and the public in 2013–14. This realisation was spurred not least by scholarly contributions made in the wake of the discussion about Germany's international role at the Munich Security Conference, which was held at the time when the Ukraine crisis was unfolding. The Ukraine crisis of 2013–14, more so than the Comprehensive Approach discussion in the Afghanistan War (especially since 2006), the Libya crisis and the dramatic Syrian civil war, drew attention to the fact that a comprehensive overview of the security policy situation is necessary for successful government action. It was, above all, the diplomatic leadership of Chancellor Angela Merkel that led to a link between the events of the Ukraine crisis, Germany's international responsibility and the paradigm shift in contemporary history.

Strategic Far-Sightedness: Discrepancies between Audibility and Practice

The perhaps over-hasty identification by Heinrich August Winkler of the Ukraine crisis as a 'parting of the ways in the international system'[22] is indicative of the emphasis given to the Ukraine crisis. From the contemporary perspective within the German government, the crisis was placed in a line that began with Putin's speech at the Munich Security Conference in 2007, that became visible in the Russian opposition against the attempts in 2008 to bring Ukraine and Georgia into NATO, and that became more salient in the Russo-Georgian War of 2008 which resulted in Russia's official recognition of Abkhazia and South Ossetia as independent states.

In retrospect, during this phase, calls for strategic far-sightedness in German foreign and security policy became distinctly more audible. The Foreign Office and the Federal Defence Ministry in particular, in terms of the responsibilities within their respective departments, set in motion internal measures for the creation of crisis structures.

Overall, the demand for new structures to deliver strategic planning, analysis and coordination is one of the major recurring themes in German foreign and security policy.[23] The experiences of the Ukraine crisis may have reinforced this. It has led above all to the recognition of the political necessity of a consistent overall strategic approach. This again, however, is not a new recognition. It was given fresh impetus in the context of the Ukraine crisis, although no crucial breakthrough has occurred since then. It is remarkable that despite a more clearly articulated demand for crisis-proof structures and far-sighted security policy, no progress has been made in the discussion about a strengthening of the Federal Security Council, including a joint Situation Centre for the Federal Government. Consequently, Germany is lagging far behind almost all of its partners in the coordination of foreign and security policy. In this regard it compares very badly, particularly in comparison with the US, France and the UK.

Disdain for strategic policy documents, and the unwillingness to engage with the strategic principles of such countries as France or the UK in terms of their consequences for political action in Germany, is also reflected in the absence of debates on the subject in the German Bundestag. Pertinent parliamentary debate was not planned, let alone a vote on the subject. Involvement of individual parliamentarians in the production of documents did not take place, as is customary in France, for example, within the context of the French White Paper process. Added to this is the fact that in Germany – unlike the US, the UK or France which are nuclear powers with global interests – a strategic culture remains relatively undeveloped in which also security policy documents are an essential element in the definition and communication of national security objectives. This 'strategic special case' may on the one hand be a feature of foreign policy debate in Germany. However, it also causes problems when it comes to thinking about reference points associated with the publication of documents on security policy. Changes in strategic culture cannot be achieved without the involvement of the German Parliament. Joint sessions between the Defence Committee and the Foreign Affairs Committee, an annual debate about the Chancellor's State of the Nation message, and strategically deployed joint conferences, for example between the Bundestag and the Assemblée Nationale, could provide important impulses here.

In terms of inter-ministerial thinking and coordination, too, Germany is failing to keep pace with developments in countries such as Canada, Switzerland or Norway, if we compare it for example with the state of Afghanistan coordination in Canada after 2006 or inter-ministerial processes within the Swiss Federation. These obvious deficits cannot be explained only in terms of the inherent constraints of coalition governments, in which the leadership positions in specialist departments devoted to foreign affairs, defence or development are assigned to different parties. That structure surely incentivises those leaders to preserve their departmental competencies and to insist on joint leadership. But, in addition, these constraints can be explained against the background of party politics in Germany which have led to a tendency of giving more and more political weight to coalition committees composed of key players from ministries, parliamentary groups and party presidents. Other reasons stem from more deep-rooted factors in the political culture, the relative unimportance of foreign and security policy issues to the career paths of the deputies representing the different party groups in the Bundestag, insufficient pressure from the expert public, and not least a lack of insight into the demands of inter-departmental actions between senior officials from the various ministries.

The decision made in the Bundestag on 28 April 2014 by the executive committees of the CDU/CSU and SPD groups devoted to crisis and conflict resolution only exposed in general terms Germany's responsibility for a just world order and reaffirmed its commitment to 'mastering global challenges [. . .] in a coordinated deployment of all instruments of foreign, security, defence and development policy'.[24] The small degree to which the experiences of the Ukraine crisis were used to effect operational changes became visible also in the results of the review process undertaken by Minister Steinmeier in 2014.[25] The review process was supposed to open up a fundamental survey of German foreign policy and a broad public debate. But it led to no considerable organisational consequences for the conduct of German foreign and security policy such as, to provide an example, a strategic guidance to recalibrate the role of Germany's foreign missions. A concrete example is the establishment of a department for crisis prevention, stabilisation, conflict resolution and humanitarian aid in the German Foreign Office that is intended to somehow bundle instruments, funds and competencies of German foreign policy in the field.

The 2016 White Paper process launched by Defence Minister von der Leyen[26] at around the same time – which was first intended as a process to involve the participatory contribution of the German public in the discussion of fundamental questions of German foreign and security policy beyond the tighter circles of the specialist public to a previously unknown degree – did not mention any strategic surprises sparked by the Ukraine crisis. Consequently, the two processes did not lead to any structural changes in the sphere of foreign and security policy and had no lasting impact on the narrower debate. In particular, Minister Steinmeier's review process in the Foreign Office squandered the opportunity to pave the way for an inter-ministerial understanding of threats and risk to security as well as attempts to cope with them. The regularly recurring problems that arise in the context of discussions on White Papers, to formulate a cross-coalition consensus on security policy, once again emphasise the necessity that a broadening of cross-party convictions concerning security policy and the willingness to draw operational conclusions from them, are among the most urgent desiderata of German security policy, which suffers from a deficit between the conceptual demand of 'networked security'[27] and its practical application.

A detailed consideration of inter-ministerial structures regarding security policy and the coordinating function of the Federal Chancellery reveals the existing deficits which have become much more visible as the result of contemporary geopolitical developments. With the Federal Security Council (under its new rules of procedure of 13 August 2015),[28] there is already a government cabinet committee that has an advisory function particularly in the field of defence policy. It contributes to the preparation of relevant political decisions of the Federal Chancellor or the Federal Government. It is also backed by an inter-ministerial secretariat with liaison officials and liaison officers under the direction of a managerial official. The Federal Security Council was established in October 1955 by the Second Adenauer cabinet under the name Federal Defence Committee. The presidency was held between 1964 and 1966 by Heinrich Krone as Minister for the Federal Defence Council, who between 1961 and 1964 had already coordinated the Council's agenda as Minister for Special Affairs. Beyond questions of arms export policy, the Federal Security Council now has no coordinating or strategically guiding function.[29] However, an overall strategic approach would require an effective joint situation centre, joint instruments for planning and analysis, inter-departmental project teams and a constant exchange on all levels. This would be consistent with a networked approach, the growing significance of a coordinated process between states, particularly with Germany's strategic partners, the development of a joint security policy within the European Union, integrated structures within NATO and the transatlantic security partnership with the US in an age of rapidly accelerating globalisation, re-emergence of great power competition and an increasing US geostrategic focus on the Western Pacific region.

An understanding of the importance of crisis prevention has been growing within the Federal Government since 2014. The German Foreign Office's Crisis Reaction Centre helps to ensure that there can be swift reactions to crises around the clock. A crisis prevention database collects information for global crisis developments. The Foreign Office runs the Federal Government's Crisis Staff regarding all foreign situations and maintains close connections with them. But there have been no further institutional steps towards reform. Despite numerous announcements concerning the establishment of a National Security Council, there have not been even any minor attempts to develop the organisation of the Federal Security Council. In response to a critical written request by Alexander Graf Lambsdorff, Grigorios Aggelidis, Renata Alt, other deputies and the FDP parliamentary group relating to concrete results of the attempts by Minister Kramp-Karrenbauer to establish a National Security Council pursuant to a speech she gave on 7 November 2019 at the University of the German Federal Armed Forces, the Federal Government stated in a letter from the Federal Defence Ministry from 13 January 2020: the Federal Defence Ministry had

> taken a long-term view and prospectively outlined that a future Federal government could strive for a further development of the Federal Security Council with the goal of planning, deciding and acting even more far-sightedly, quickly and precisely in policy areas such as diplomacy, the military, economy and action, internal security and development cooperation.[30]

At the same time, knowledgeable observers from abroad, such as Julianne Smith, now the Ambassador of the US to NATO, recommended – in a clear analysis of the internal political situations and the pronounced egoism of departments within Germany – that they should follow the examples of Japan (2013) and the United Kingdom (2010) and develop a new approach towards the structure of security policy.[31] The internal political debate around the Federal Security Council is characterised by spurious constitutional arguments and alarmist scenarios whereby the introduction of a National Security Council might involve a change in the political system. The debate in the Bundestag about the proposal by CDU deputy Schockenhoff from 2008, for example, revealed a phalanx of rejections ranging from the FDP via the SPD, Alliance 90/The Greens all the way to Die Linke, based on a familiar canon of well-trodden arguments on the subject.[32]

In the literature, concerns about democracy are repeatedly voiced in connection with the establishment of a National Security Council. Critics argue that the upgrading of the Federal Security Council to a National Security Council '[would] shift the existing distribution of competences between the Federal Government and the Länder in favour of the Federal Government', and 'given the lack of Parliamentary checks, would lead to a perpetuation of the democratic deficit that we have already noted'.[33]

This is an unwarranted overstatement. The creation of a National Security Council would be in accordance with constitutional guidelines, with existing principles of democratic legitimisation and federalism, and with the administrative orders of the Office of the Federal Chancellor. Just as in France and the UK, such a structure would also be in line with intelligence oversight practices of the Federal Chancellor's office, parliament, courts and other federal German entities. When it comes to secret intelligence, Germany's briefing culture is not comparable to the US, for example, where the head of government also systematically receives information inputs directly from the intelligence community, including current intelligence tailored to their needs as well as strategic intelligence products. In Germany, the chiefs of federal intelligence services meet once a week with State Secretaries from pertinent ministries in a session which is chaired by the head of the Federal Chancellor's office.[34] The Foreign Minister can derive his – still relatively strong – position within the foreign and security planning and decision-making process from his departmental responsibility alone. The Foreign Minister only assumes a coordinating role, and an extremely limited one, in the context of the usual departmental coordination within the Federal Government. In the field of politics at the European level over the last few years he has had to surrender several responsibilities to other departments. This also explains why the Foreign Office has clung so stubbornly to the departmental responsibility for security policy assigned to it. It is only in the preparation of Bundestag mandates in connection with deployments of the German armed forces abroad that there is shared responsibility between the Foreign Office and the Federal Defence Ministry. Cross-departmental task forces could be a reasonable solution to the problem. But they were only practised – successfully – in the context of the collapse of the former Yugoslavia in the 1990s when officials from the Foreign Office and members of the Federal Defence Ministry worked together in a special Bosnia task force. Considering increasing strategic uncertainties regarding the next decades, organisational changes aiming at a whole of government approach and enabling strategic debates are even more urgent.

It would be especially important to connect assessment capacities for situational awareness, explanation and estimation on the comprehensive basis of reports from the embassies, the federal intelligence services, the armed forces, and the disarmament and arms control organisations. Establishing a centralised situation centre as a secretariat under the auspices of the Federal Security Council (perhaps based on the British model, with at least 200 posts) would have to go hand in hand with establishing a leadership centre with the task of providing a daily establishment of the situation, political assessment and proposals for action. Such a Security Council, to be led by a secretary of state or a distinct Federal Minister of Security, would support decision-making of the Cabinet as a whole. Political safeguards – creating a corresponding committee of the German Bundestag – should follow. A national political and military planning and leadership component would also require long-term education and training of the leadership staff.[35]

Adaptation of security policy decision-making structures neither calls for a change to the constitution nor requires any kind of incisive legislation. Above all, the departmental principle is not in conflict with stronger coordination in strategic analysis and planning under the auspices of the Federal Chancellor's office. On the contrary, as long as security policy, threat and risk analysis, strategic planning and the deployment of resources affect core areas of different departments, an intensive coordination should be expected to be a necessary consequence of departmental thinking as understood in functional terms. In the field of the 'security constitution', some military deployments require a decision by the whole cabinet.[36] The German constitution aims, with competence guidelines and a system of checks and balances, to achieve 'functional appropriateness'.[37]

Germany's Anticipatory Assessment Capacities and the Stature of Intelligence

To the extent that it is publicly discernable, the evolution of Germany's anticipatory assessment capacities may at first glance appear to be caused by or correlated with potential intragovernmental efforts to explicitly learn lessons from the recent past, including lessons concerning the performance of anticipatory assessments related to the Arab uprisings, ISIS's rise to power and Russia's aggression against Ukraine in 2014. As the previous section highlighted, it is important to note that incisive change in the architecture of Germany's national security system remained absent despite the cumulative turbulences due to surprises related to the Arab uprisings, ISIS and Ukraine.

Just like Germany does not yet have a kind of National Security Council, there is no entity in Germany comparable to organisations such as the Office of the Director of National Intelligence (ODNI) or the National Intelligence Council (NIC) in the US or the Joint Intelligence Organisation (JIO) and the Joint Intelligence Committee (JIC) in the UK. As argued above, a comparable kind of organisation in Germany might serve as situation and assessment centre for a reformed Bundessicherheitsrat. If established, it should not be constrained to current intelligence but should also represent the locus for most authoritative, all-source fusion, inter-disciplinary (political, military, etc.), integrated and hence inter-departmentally coordinated strategic intelligence production, to inform and 'speak truth to power'[38] to the highest levels of government concerning foreign and security policy matters which are most pressing from a strategic perspective geared towards national interests. Recommendations focusing on intelligence assessment have been made by intelligence experts at least since the mid-1990s based on arguments on how to better prepare Germany for an era of increased international complexity, power diffusion, fragile and failed states close to the EU, transnational threats like terrorism, and renewed relevance of inter-state conflict, including great power competition and its fundamental implications for the future of the European and transatlantic security order.[39]

In comparison to such a potential quantum leap forward, the pattern of discernable change in Germany's anticipatory assessment capacities since the 2010s reveals the evolution of an ancillary inter-ministerial approach to increase the coherence of horizon scanning and crisis early detection assessment capacities in Germany (*Krisenfrüherkennung*/KFE). The Foreign Office, the Ministry for Economic Cooperation and Development and the Ministry of Defence established units to conduct KFE assessments to monitor political, economic, societal and military potentials for crises developments in other countries and regions of interest. Directed by the Foreign Office, an inter-departmental 'Horizon Scanning working group' (*Arbeitsgruppe* KFE) consisting of analysts from these ministries as well as from the Ministry of the Interior, the Chancellery and Germany's foreign intelligence service, the Bundesnachrichtendienst (BND) is regularly convened to jointly evaluate potentials of crises. This group also prepares a specific analytic product (*KFE-Kurzanalyse*). Results of the group's work are regularly reported to a body consisting of heads of departments at least from involved ministries.[40] Products are hence received well below the level of decision-makers and thus tend to be far away from their immediate focus of attention.

These activities to adapt Germany's anticipatory assessment capacities were embedded in an increasingly active specialist discourse on methods and potential practices of strategic foresight. This discourse was often elusive and usually connected to broader debates about Germany foreign and security policy and the over-hyped assertion of 'Germany's new responsibility'. At times, calls for better crisis early detection capacities were prematurely associated with the outcome of an improved capacity to think and act strategically.[41] This evades the problem of how to organise anticipatory assessment capacities in government to which top policymakers pay attention. A feature in this discourse appears to be an underdeveloped, if existing at all, understanding and appreciation of the specific benefits that secret intelligence may bring to the table. Several contributions tend to convey the impression that the meaning of crisis early detection is more or less synonymous with secret intelligence support to policymaking or that the former necessarily involves the latter.[42] Hence, the mentioned increase in horizon scanning and crisis early detection activities tends to suggest greater reliance on secret intelligence input to German decision-making.

But considering the configuration of the inter-agency approach to horizon scanning and crisis early detection, this development cannot be equated with a more prominent stature of secret intelligence support to German foreign and security policy decision-making which, from a strategic perspective, would have to be at the centre of attention. The exact ways in which the BND contributes with its unique, all-source assessments to these activities under Foreign Office direction are not publicly known.[43] As a matter of principle, the BND retains a monopoly within the German system considering that it 'collects and evaluates the information required to gain knowledge about foreign countries that are of importance to the Federal Republic of Germany in terms of foreign and security policy'.[44]

An additional difficulty is that concepts like early detection of non-linearities or crises (based on monitoring of indicators), on the one hand, and strategic intelligence estimates, on the other, appear to have been used interchangeably most of the time within the public discourse in Germany. In fact, they relate to methodologically specific analytic product categories.[45] Current intelligence relates to yet another category. Even a cursory glance at topics which intelligence analysts examined in bodies like the NIC in the US or the JIC in Britain reveals that strategic estimates rarely, if ever, offered indications and warning intelligence, but rigorous and all-source-based appraisals of the most fundamental, in fact often vital, life-and-death-type of issues which those nations faced, for example:[46]

1. the evolution of military balances, particularly nuclear balances and vitally important regional military balances;
2. political-military strategies of great power and other competitors to succeed under peacetime, cold war, crisis, and limited war conditions, with particular emphasis on their willingness to threaten the use and to use force to achieve political objectives;
3. strategic intentions of competitors and enemies; and
4. the prospects and consequences of the proliferation of weapons of mass destruction.

Despite public audibility of calls for better strategic foresight, Germany's public discourse needs to rediscover the core of the strategic approach, namely, to take 'account of the part played by force or threat of force in the international system',[47] that is, the part of power and force to coerce, deter and compel. It appears to be imperative to prioritise the most consequential problem areas, namely first and foremost catastrophic risks due to outcomes of the evolution of inter-state relations such as, for example, diplomacy backed by threats, diplomacy backed by force and force backed by diplomacy[48] under changing technological but nuclear conditions. The related choice would also demand working against the tendency, which may all too easily creep into horizon scanning activities, 'to confuse the unfamiliar with the improbable': 'The contingency we have not considered seriously looks strange; what looks strange is thought improbable; what is improbable need not be considered seriously.'[49]

Assuming a National Security Council were to be formed, including a pertinent situation and assessment centre, secret intelligence, particularly including strategic intelligence estimates, would be critical and the stature of intelligence would grow. That would be a novel development in Germany. Ideally, strategic intelligence support could, in turn, form the basis for additional layers of integrated strategic analysis which would have to receive the attention of top-level leaders.[50] Such a development would be unheard of in the Federal Republic of Germany – at least considering what the historical record shows thus far.

Conclusion

It is to be hoped that the profound experiences with international crises since the 2010s, with the COVID-19 pandemic and with catastrophes due to climate-dependent weather extremes will raise awareness in Germany for the necessities of better crisis preparedness, of a more efficient coordination of the instruments required for security policy, and, in the end, of a deeper understanding of security policy which is appropriate for its actual strategic significance and for dealing with structural changes in international relations. In Germany, the need for a more consistent strategic overall approach will grow in the years to come. This need will become a problem for German foreign and security policy to the extent that it will not be possible to achieve structural and mental adaptations to the changing reality. Or is a truly painful, or even existential, crisis necessary before Germany will want to learn this lesson? The most recent debate of August 2021 about misguided assessments, alleged intelligence failures, lack of cooperation and of political responsibility which resulted in a belated decision to evacuate the German embassy in Afghanistan also has to be seen exactly against this background. Changes in the field of strategy and in relations between public administration and the public require structures for German foreign and security policy which will lead to a real change in awareness. This requirement refers to structural and organisational questions within the Federal Government, the relationship between the armed forces and political bodies, the stature of intelligence within the German national security system, and the sphere of parliament and foreign policy. It also refers particularly to the role that a long-term strategic orientation of politics involves towards present and future challenges. In addition, it requires an ability to define and impose one's own interests, to link the various fields together, and to create budgetary conditions under which more interrelated security instruments can be equipped with the funds they need to fulfil their new tasks. More than ever since the end of the Cold War era, one of the requirements of political action in a world shaped by increasing uncertainties is the willingness and ability to be prepared for strategic surprises, including potential surprises related to existential threats.

Notes

1. Lani Kass and J. Philipp London, 'Surprise, Deception, Denial and Warning', *Orbis* 57, no. 1 (2013): 71. See also Chapter 1.
2. On publicness and lesson learning, see: Stuart Farson and Mark Phythian, eds, *Commissions of Inquiry and National Security. Comparative Approaches* (Santa Barbara, CA: Praeger, 2010).
3. For an example of how the top-secret post-mortem report on US intelligence and the Iranian Revolution of 1979, a report written by an independent observer with a security clearance, Professor Robert Jervis, was received by CIA leaders, see: Robert Jervis, *Why Intelligence Fails: Lessons from the Iranian Revolution and the Iraq War* (Ithaca, NY: Cornell University Press, 2010), 116.
4. For this point, see: Charles F. Doran, 'Why Forecasts Fail: The Limits and Potential of Forecasting in International Relations and Economics', *International Studies Review* 1, no. 2 (1999).
5. On 'historical' as opposed to 'scientific predictions', see: Bertrand de Jouvenel, *L'Art de la conjecture* (Monaco: Editions du Rocher, 1964).

6. Bowman H. Miller, 'U.S. Strategic Intelligence Forecasting and the Perils of Prediction', *International Journal of Intelligence and CounterIntelligence* 27, no. 4 (2014): 699; Thomas Fingar, *Reducing Uncertainty: Intelligence Analysis and National Security* (Stanford, CA: Stanford University Press, 2011).

7. Robert Jervis, 'Book Reviews', *Political Science Quarterly* 127, no. 1 (2012): 145. Intelligence 'often tells those in charge that their ideas may not be right and that several possibilities are plausible (. . .) When the world is uncertain, and the information available is even more so, intelligence must strive to reflect this.'

8. On the methodological hypothesis that these two aspects, namely the monitoring of 'tactical indicators' and the use of 'strategic assumptions' in estimates, represent core criteria for success or failure in understanding the potential for strategic surprise attacks, see: Abraham Ben-Zvi, 'Hindsight and Foresight: A Conceptual Framework for the Analysis of Surprise Attacks', *World Politics* 27, no. 3 (1976).

9. On the importance of 'mindsets' in intelligence analysis see, inter alia: Richards J. Heuer and Randolph H. Pherson, *Structured Analytic Techniques for Intelligence Analysis* (Thousand Oaks, CA et al.: CQ Press, 2021), 183f.

10. Jervis, *Why Intelligence Fails*, 124.

11. Percy Cradock, *Know Your Enemy: How the Joint Intelligence Committee Saw the World* (London: John Murray, 2002), 290.

12. Jervis, *Why Intelligence Fails*, 179.

13. Stephen B. Dyson and Paul 't Hart, 'Crisis Management', in *The Oxford Handbook of Political Psychology*, ed. Leonie Huddy, David O. Sears and Jack S. Levy (Oxford and New York: Oxford University Press, 2013), 395–422, 395.

14. For the differentiation between better and more effective anticipation, see: Lars Brozus, *Fahren auf Sicht. Effektive Früherkennung in der politischen Praxis* (Berlin: SWP, 2018). For a critique of German passivity vis-à-vis the Syrian civil war despite apparently sufficient situational awareness, together with the counterfactual argument that even better anticipatory assessments would not have prompted a more resolved policy approach of chancellor Merkel: Sönke Neitzel and Bastian Matteo Scianna, *Blutige Enthaltung. Deutschlands Rolle im Syrienkrieg* (Freiburg: Herder, 2021), 113.

15. Paul R. Pillar, 'Predictive Intelligence: Policy Support or Spectator Sport', *SAIS Review* 27, no. 1 (2008).

16. Nikolaus Blome et al. 'Bis jenseits der Grenze', *Spiegel*, November 2014: 87.

17. See also: Nikki Ikani, 'Change and Continuity in the European Neighbourhood Policy: The Ukraine Crisis as a Critical Juncture', *Geopolitics* 24, no. 1 (2019); Nicholas Wright, 'No Longer the Elephant Outside the Room: Why the Ukraine Crisis Reflects a Deeper Shift Towards German Leadership of European Foreign Policy', *German Politics* 27, no. 4 (2018); Wolfgang Seibel, 'Arduous Learning on New Uncertainties? The Emergence of German Diplomacy in the Ukrainian Crisis', *Global Policy* 6, S1 (2015); Benjamin Teutmeyer, 'Die Rolle der NATO in der Ukraine-Krise', *Zeitschrift für Außen- und Sicherheitspolitik* 7 (2014); Mark Webber and James Sperling, 'NATO and the Ukrainian Crisis: Collective Securitisation', *European Journal of International Security* 2, no. 1 (2016); International Staff and Office of Secretary General, 'NATO Restricted Engaging the New Ukraine', 25 February 2014, Document PO (2014) 0101.

18. Federal Foreign Office, speech by Dr Frank-Walter Steinmeier, Federal Minister for Foreign Affairs, at the handover ceremony on 17 December 2013.

19. Office of the Federal President, 'Germany's Role in the World: Reflections on Responsibility, Norms and Alliances', speech by Federal President Joachim Gauck at the opening of the Munich Security Conference on 31 January 2014.

20. European Council, 'Press Release 3028th Council Meeting General Affairs European Council. "Statement of the Heads of State or Government on Ukraine." 6 March 2014. Brussels'.

21. See, for example: Kai Oppermann, 'Deutsche Außenpolitik während der dritten Amtszeit Angela Merkels', in *Zwischen Stillstand, Politikwandel und Krisenmanagement. Eine Bilanz der Regierung Merkel 2013–2017*, ed. Reimut Zohlnhöfer and Thomas Saalfeld (Wiesbaden: Springer VS, 2019).

22. Heinrich August Winkler, *Die Geschichte des Westens, Band 4: Die Zeit der Gegenwart* (München: C. H. Beck, 2016), 11.

23. Ulrich Schlie, 'Deutsche Sicherheitspolitik nach 1990: Auf der Suche nach einer Strategie', *Zeitschrift für Strategische Analysen* 4, no. 3 (2020); Ulrich Schlie, 'Warum Deutschland künftig mehr denn je auf einen gesamtstrategischen Ansatz in der Außen- und Sicherheitspolitik angewiesen ist', in *Das Weißbuch 2016 und die Herausforderungen von Strategiebildung*, ed. Daniel Jacobi and Gunther Hellmann (Wiesbaden: Springer VS, 2019); Cord Meier-Klodt, *Einsatzbereit in*

der Krise? Entscheidungsstrukturen der deutschen Sicherheitspolitik auf dem Prüfstand (Berlin: SWP, 2002).

24. Beschluss der Geschäftsführenden Vorstände der CDU/CSU-Fraktion im Deutschen Bundestag und der SPD-Bundestagsfraktion, 'Deutsche Außenpolitik als Beitrag zur Lösung von Krisen und Konflikten', 28 April 2014.

25. Auswärtiges Amt, 'Review 2014: Aussenpolitik weiter denken', 25 February 2015.

26. Bundesregierung, *Weissbuch zur Sicherheitspolitik und Zukunft der Bundeswehr*, 13 July 2016.

27. The concept of 'networked security' comes from the 2006 White Paper. See also: Schlie, 'Warum Deutschland künftig mehr denn je auf einen gesamtstrategischen Ansatz in der Außen- und Sicherheitspolitik angewiesen ist'; Schlie, 'Deutsche Sicherheitspolitik'; Klaus Naumann, 'Die Gewährleistung kohärenter Außenpolitik – Wie "vernetzt" man "Sicherheit"?', *Zeitschrift für Außen- und Sicherheitspolitik* 8 (2015); Andreas Wittkowsky, Wanda Hummel and Tobias Pietz, '"Vernetzte Sicherheit": Intentionen, Kontroversen und eine Agenda für die Praxis', *Zeitschrift für Außen- und Sicherheitspolitik* 5 (2012).

28. Deutscher Bundestag, Unterrichtung durch die Bundesregierung, 'Neufassung der Geschäftsordnung des Bundessicherheitsrates', 18, Wahlperiode, 18-5773, 13 August 2015.

29. See also: Kai Zähle, 'Der Bundessicherheitsrat', *Der Staat* 44, no. 3 (2005); Volker Busse, 'Organisation der Bundesregierung und Organisationsentscheidungen der Bundeskanzler in ihrer historischen Entwicklung und im Spannungsfeld zwischen Exekutive und Legislative', *Der Staat* 45, no. 2 (2006); Gerold Lehnguth and Klaus Vogelgesang, 'Die Organisationserlasse der Bundeskanzler seit Bestehen der Bundesrepublik Deutschland im Lichte der politischen Entwicklungen', *Archiv des öffentlichen Rechts* 113, no. 4 (1988): 536ff.

30. Deutscher Bundestag, Antwort der Bundesregierung auf die kleine Anfrage der Abgeordneten Alexander Graf-Lambsdorff, Grigorios Aggelidis, Renata Alt, weiterer Abgeordneter und der Fraktion der FDP – Drucksache 15990 – 'Schaffung eines Nationalen Sicherheitsrates', 19, Wahlperiode, 19-16508, 15 January 2020, 2.

31. Julianne Smith, 'Eine Frage der Staatskunst. Deutschland sollte erneut über einen Nationalen Sicherheitsrat nachdenken', *Internationale Politik* January/February (2019).

32. See also: Andreas Schockenhoff, 'Die Debatte ist eröffnet . . . und

Streit erwünscht: Warum Deutschland eine Sicherheitsstrategie braucht', *Internationale Politik* 5 (2008): 89–95.

33. Ines-Jacqueline Werkner, 'Die Verflechtung innerer und äußerer Sicherheit. Aktuelle Tendenzen in Deutschland im Lichte europäischer Entwicklungen', *Zeitschrift für Außen- und Sicherheitspolitik* 4 (2011): 73.

34. Wolfgang Krieger, *Die deutschen Geheimdienste* (München: C. H. Beck, 2021), 115.

35. These reflections are based on a memorandum written by Hans-Georg Wieck in 1990 (private papers Ulrich Schlie).

36. BVerfGE 115, 118 Rn. 113.

37. BVerfGE 150, 1 Rn. 197.

38. On US experiences see: Robert Hutchings and Gregory F. Treverton, eds, *Truth to Power. A History of the U.S. National Intelligence Council* (Oxford: Oxford University Press, 2019). On British experiences, see: Michael S. Goodman, *The Official History of the Joint Intelligence Committee. Volume I: From the Approach of the Second World War to the Suez Crisis* (London: Routledge, 2015).

39. Harald Nielsen, 'The German Analysis and Assessment System', *Intelligence and National Security* 19, no. 4 (1995); Gerhard Conrad, 'Warum wir einen Nationalen Sicherheitsrat brauchen', *Die Welt*, 26 November 2019.

40. Deutscher Bundestag Wissenschaftliche Dienste, *Sachstand: Strukturen der Krisenfrüherkennung in der deutschen Außen- und Sicherheitspolitik. WD 2 – 3000 – 070/20* (Berlin, 2020). See also: Federal Government, *Guidelines on Preventing Crises, Resolving Conflicts, Building Peace* (Berlin, 2017); Federal Government, *Operations Manual: Interministerial Approach to Preventing Crises, Resolving Conflicts and Building Peace* (Berlin, 2019).

41. Oliver Gnad, 'Wie strategiefähig ist deutsche Politik? Vorausschauende Regierungsführung als Grundlage zukunftsrobuster Entscheidungen', in *Internationale Sicherheit im 21. Jahrhundert. Deutschlands internationale Verantwortung*, ed. James Bindenagel, Matthias Herdegen and Karl Kaiser (Bonn: Bonn University Press, 2016).

42. Brozus, *Fahren auf Sicht*; Florian Roth and Michel Herzog, 'Strategische Früherkennung – Instrumente, Möglichkeiten und Grenzen', *Zeitschrift für Außen- und Sicherheitspolitik* 9 (2016).

43. For a progress report see: Deutscher Bundestag, 'Antwort der Bundesregierung auf die Große Anfrage der (. . .) Fraktion der FDP', Drucksache 19/13251, 4 September 2019; Deutscher Bundestag, 'Vernetztes Handeln in der Außen-, Sicherheits- und

Entwicklungspolitik stärken', Drucksache 19/8058, 27 February 2019.

44. Unofficial translation of §1 sec. 2, *Gesetz über den Bundesnachrichtendienst*. See also: Christian Bareinske, 'Auslandsaufklärung', in *Handbuch des Rechts der Nachrichtendienste*, ed. Jan-Henrik Dietrich and Sven-R. Eiffler (Stuttgart: Boorberg, 2017); Christoph Gusy, 'Gesetz über den Bundesnachrichtendienst (BND-Gesetz – BNDG)', in *Sicherheitsrecht des Bundes*, ed. Wolf-Rüdiger Schenke, Kurt Graulich and Josef Ruthig (München: C. H. Beck, 2014).

45. See: Harold P. Ford, *Estimative Intelligence: The Purposes and Problems of National Intelligence Estimates* (Lanham, MD: University Press of America, 1993); Thomas Fingar, *Reducing Uncertainty: Intelligence Analysis and National Security* (Stanford, CA: Stanford University Press, 2011).

46. On the methodology of indications and warning intelligence see: Cynthia Grabo, with Jan Goldman, *Handbook on Warning Intelligence. Complete and Declassified Edition* (Lanham, MD, et al.: Rowman & Littlefield, 2015). See also: David Omand, *How Spies Think. Ten Lessons in Intelligence* (London: Penguin, 2020).

47. Michael Howard, 'The Strategic Approach to International Relations', repr. in *The Causes of Wars and other Essays* (Cambridge, MA: Harvard University Press, 1983), 36.

48. On a related foundational understanding of the meaning of 'crisis' and crisis-related anticipation, preparation, prevention and reaction: Klaus Naumann, 'Die Gewährleistung kohärenter Außenpolitik – Wie "vernetzt" man "Sicherheit"?', *Zeitschrift für Außen- und Sicherheitspolitik* 8 (2015).

49. Foreword by Thomas S. Schelling, in Roberta Wohlstetter, *Pearl Harbor. Warning and Decision* (Stanford, CA: Stanford University Press, 1962), vii.

50. For a dated but good example of how an integrated strategic analysis process may look like based on all-source, top-level strategic intelligence estimates which will be separately considered from the viewpoint of what they imply for defence and foreign policy see: 'Report on Implications for U.S. Foreign and Defense Policy of Recent Intelligence Estimates', dated 23 August 1962, presented to President John F. Kennedy by a 'Special Inter-Departmental Committee'. Its members were the US Secretary of State, Secretary of Defense, the Director of Central Intelligence and the Chairman of the Joint Chiefs of Staff. In this instance, the basis for this integrated strategic analysis

was National Intelligence Estimate 11-8-62, 'Soviet Capabilities for Long Range Attack', dated 6 July 1962. The analysis of implications was conducted by three working groups: one concerning implications for defence policy was chaired by the U.S. Assistant Secretary of Defense for International Security Affairs (Paul H. Nitze), a second working group concerning implications for foreign policy was chaired by the Special Assistant to the Secretary of State (Charles Bohlen) and a third group concerning intelligence on Soviet strategy was chaired by the Assistant Director for National Estimates, CIA (Sherman Kent). See: Raymond L. Garthoff, *Intelligence Assessment and Policymaking: A Decision Point in the Kennedy Administration* (Washington, DC: The Brookings Institution, 1984).

7 Lessons Learned and Still to be Learned: The Case of the European Union

Gerhard Conrad

> Joint analysis and assessment provide the critical underpinning for common strategy ... The EU (...) lacks a sufficiently robust process for joint analysis, assessment, and planning that brings together the relevant civilian and military actors. Such a process must also cover more than just crisis response.[1]

In late December 2012, diplomats and experts convened at Wilton Park, the secluded sixteenth-century home in the English countryside run by the British Foreign and Commonwealth Office, to share insights and assessments on how the newly built European External Action Service (EEAS) had already met expectations and where there was room for improvement. Already at that early stage, Wilton Park made the point in demanding joint analysis and assessment as core prerequisite for qualified EU decision-making. In view of Nikki Ikani's and Christoph Meyer's findings on the Arab uprisings and Ukrainian crisis, it is of interest to discuss whether lessons have been learned or are overdue to be learned by European institutions and member states in order to achieve the kind of strategic autonomy as a global actor that has been invoked by numerous Council Conclusions and the EU Global Strategy.[2]

Major Post-mortem based Findings and Lessons

Nikki Ikani's insightful analysis of the situational awareness inside the emerging EEAS and the dynamics of the Arab uprisings shows that anticipation of possible disruptive events in the Middle East and North Africa had been available in principle though not subject to stringent and comprehensive analysis and without being put in structural and organisational contexts that would have enabled decision-makers to take due note in time.[3] Ikani's conclusion already provides a significant starting point and outline for defining lessons to be learned from the collective underperformance in situational awareness and foresight:

> It has been found that foreknowledge regarding the risks of significant upheaval existed within the institutions under scrutiny, yet was scattered throughout the institutions and across levels of hierarchy, with limited follow-up. It has been identified that the performance of the European institutions has been affected by the diagnostic difficulty of the Arab Uprisings, as underlined in previous studies, yet has been particularly hampered by the limited capacities for knowledge production and transfer within the institutions, as well as by a political unwillingness within the institutions and likely beyond in accepting discordant knowledge claims. The virtual non-existence of dissent channels and the limited facilitation of bottom-up warnings has likely contributed to this.[4]

Based on his extensive post-mortem on the Ukrainian crisis which occurred at a time when the initial formative period of the EEAS had come – or should have come – to an end, Christoph Meyer was able to put forward a wide range of lessons that should be – or should have been – learned by the EU, its institutions and member states:[5]

1. The intelligence collection side. If the EU wanted to improve not only its strategic but also its tactical warning capability, it would require significant changes in what kind of intelligence EU institutions can gather to penetrate planning and decision-making of the Russian President and its inner circle, in particular HUMINT and SIGINT.
2. A change in the 'national security' exclusion of the EU Treaties (Article 4 II) would be the most ambitious option to provide the EU with the authority for a dedicated intelligence function, and a substantial increase in resources to

build up such capacities and create a leak-proof infrastructure involving member states.

3. Addressing the structural flaws of asymmetric actorness in EU foreign affairs, also visible in the conduct of trade and neighbourhood policy on the one hand and CFSP on the other hand, during the next Treaty revision.

4. Abolishing the unanimity requirements in foreign affairs might also help to drive demand and better resources for higher-quality intelligence tailored to the needs of the EU decision-makers.

5. Seeking to create a centre or unit within the EEAS tasked exclusively with the assessment of the military and hybrid threat that Russia poses, rather than one that just focuses on the narrower challenge of tackling Russian disinformation and propaganda.

6. Increasing the self-awareness of the EU institutions with regard to key assumptions they hold about international politics and the behaviour of foreign states. A working strategy against such biases is to build robust challenge of underlying assumptions into the diverse membership of analytical teams.

7. The EU should take bureaucratic and national biases seriously. This entails bringing together teams from different institutions and with different national backgrounds, particularly countries with high and low threat perceptions vis-à-vis Russia.

8. Furthermore, the Commission and EEAS could create channels for officials to express their dissent with dominant assumptions and create dedicated opportunities to assess wild-card scenarios in estimative intelligence.

9. A more joined-up and better-informed EU role in foreign affairs would require for the EAAS as an agency to be merged into the EU Commission, a scenario that member states, then including the UK, explicitly sought to avoid when drafting the Lisbon Treaty. Increased attention in the Commission to foreign policy issues will have to be fostered and coordination improved between internal and external action to mitigate the problem of policy silos.

10. Overcoming the differences within the EU in terms of knowledge production, receptivity and impact of intelligence. The EU does not have a single decision-maker in foreign affairs and not a single source of authoritative and consensus intelligence.

The basic task of this chapter will be to relate these findings to the respective organisational structures and reform processes that the EEAS has undergone so far. The aim will be first to provide additional background and detail to reported deficiencies, then to comment on efforts already made until 2019 with regard to their relevance for the use of estimative intelligence in decision-making, and finally to propose steps for making the EU fit for purpose as a geopolitical actor.

Further Background and Detail on identified Flaws and Deficiencies

The Wilton Park conference referred indirectly to the unsettled situation of an EEAS that had just been created by a Council Decision on 26 July 2010. It was reached under major time pressure, conflicting aims of member states and European Institutions as well as under significant political and financial constraints.[6] Organisational disruptions and strains were caused by merging considerable parts of the Council Secretariat with sizeable elements of the Commission based RELEX-directorates while adding to that a substantial percentage of member states' diplomats. Emerging EEAS structures and their relations with the Commission and the Council had to be redefined, re-activated and stabilised for much of the novel service's formative period.[7]

In addition, the period between the appointment of Lady Ashton as High Representative (HR) on 19 November 2009 and the establishment of the EEAS in January 2011 was a time of transformation of pre-Lisbon CSFP and CSDP Council structures and procedures[8] into a new format that had to be built under fire from inside and outside the European Union. The new HR had to run CFSP and CSDP with structures in full transition, if not erosion, for more than a year. Far-reaching transformation of that kind impairs corporate identity, intercultural leadership and promotes silo thinking that exists anyway in complex multinational organisations. The emerging EEAS was not an exception to that rule,[9] and so were the Council structures for producing and disseminating estimative intelligence.

In the times of HR Javier Solana (1999–2009), situational awareness for CFSP and CSDP decision-making was produced essentially in two orbits, diplomacy represented in the Policy Planning and Early Warning Unit[10] and intelligence assessment provided by the Intelligence Directorate of the European Military Staff (EUMS.INT)[11] and the civilian intelligence capacity of the EU Joint Situation Centre (EU SITCEN).[12] All these entities had ultimately been created by Solana and were intended to directly support him in his function as High Representative for the Foreign and Security Policy of the European Union.[13]

In 2007, SITCEN and EUMS.INT were put by Solana into a functional framework called Single Intelligence Analysis Capacity (SIAC). The fused civil and military SIAC products were submitted to him and – according to his discretion – to the Policy Unit in the Council Secretariat and the Political and Security Committee (PSC) of the member states that in turn prepared the proceedings of the Council of Foreign and Defence Ministers of the Union.[14] The heads of SITCEN and the Policy Unit, William Shapcott (since its inception in 2002) and Christoph Heusgen (since 1999; to be succeeded by Helga Schmid in 2006), together with the DG of EUMS, were directly reporting to Solana and advising him on situational affairs and on matters of CSFP and CSDP.[15]

Upon Solana's departure in November 2009, and in view of the emerging post-Lisbon structures, Lady Ashton created a new managerial set-up, with key functions staffed by Commission officials, and hence alien to the CFSP and CSDP Council structures, and even more so to the intelligence dimension of SITCEN.[16] To make things worse, SITCEN lost its experienced director when it would have needed him most, just at the very start of the transition process[17] while numbers of EEAS management just had to be put in place in the course of late summer and autumn, only weeks prior to the unfolding events.[18]

These organisational upheavals alone would have been instrumental in preventing SIAC's far-sighted 2007 'Worst Case Scenario' for the Middle East from having any tangible effect on situational awareness in 2010, as Nikki Ikani rightly mentions.[19] Beyond that, however, this example is indicative for general elements of an intelligence failure caused by flaws in tradecraft and processes that should be overcome if estimative intelligence is meant to play a significant role in EU decision-making. As pointed out by Arcos and Palacios, the paper itself was a decent piece of estimative intelligence based on a wide range of contributions, some even provided by Commission services, that had been fused and analysed by SITCEN and EUMS.INT. The assessment was classified as confidential and hence strictly limited in distribution due to its sources and political sensitivity. Apart from Solana, the paper was distributed only to his cabinet, the European Special Representative (EUSR) for the Middle East (Peace Process), the Policy Unit as well as SITCEN, EUMS.INT and very few recipients in the Commission as respective contributors.[20] As a piece of predictive intelligence without defined time lines and prospects, it is however highly unlikely (and in that point also acknowledged by Arcos and Palacios) that it ever transcended the quality of a meritorious food-for-thought paper. No explicit trigger for action, not even a call for further systematic scrutiny, follow-up research and analysis, could be taken from its conclusions. Significantly, Shapcott did not mention it either in his thoughtful analysis on warning procedures in the EU.[21] Intelligence analysis is not supposed to engage in policy recommendations.[22] It should, however, provide clear-cut comments on its relevance and implications, especially in case of results questioning conventional wisdom. Here, announcing sustained further scrutiny, intelligence collection and assessment would have been very well placed, including a proposal to introduce the issue to the Early Warning System (EWS) of the Council already in place for years.[23] However, as the paper was not part of the agreed SIAC Working Programme that had to be commissioned by the Council presidency, it was not eligible and probably never intended to be introduced into that mechanism.[24] Being labelled as 'worst case scenario', only further diminished its actionability.

Intelligence studies as well as professional experience clearly indicate that 'unwelcome' analysis that is not further promoted by a sustained analytical follow-up process is a lost cause.[25]

No such follow-up analysis and reporting inside the EU structures is known, despite at least some external critical voices.[26] The 2007 'Worst Case Scenario' was hence doomed to remain a solitaire that could not even be unearthed at the outset of the crisis in December 2010 and be put forward with the personal authority of SITCEN's founding director who had already left in June.

Furthermore, SITCEN had also been weakened during its integration into the EEAS. By losing its former Situation Room-based capacity of Open-Source Collection and Analysis that became allocated to a newly built Managing Directorate 'Crisis Reaction and Operations Centre (CROC)',[27] the potential for comparing OSINT findings on the developing crisis with secret estimative intelligence provided by member states' services was largely diminished.[28]

This again did not go well with that fact, that according to the conventional interpretation of Article 4(2) of the Treaties, both, SITCEN/INTCEN as well as EUMS.INT were (and still are) neither mandated nor equipped with means for secret intelligence collection. Secret intelligence has always been provided on a strictly voluntary basis by member states' services exclusively to the mandated structures, i.e. INTCEN and EUMS.INT.[29] This weakness may however be reduced, if and when a broad variety of civil and military, internal and external services engage in supporting INTCEN and/or EUMS.INT on issues of common interest. Different data, perspectives and assessments on the same subject may significantly widen the basis for SIAC analysis and even mitigate risks of bias and selective perception. For that, however, staff need to be adequately qualified, authorised and equipped with additional open sources for independent assessment. Under such circumstances, INTCEN and EUMS.INT need not to be (in fact must not be) restricted to merely patching together pieces of intelligence from pre-existing national reports of various backgrounds and outlook. The 2007 'Worst Case Scenario' was obviously an example of that kind that was, however, not further supported by intelligence contributions from member states' services in 2010/11, not least since national services had not been aware of the impending events themselves.[30]

The inconsistencies and flaws of the emerging EEAS structures and processes were further detrimental to any impact of SITCEN/INTCEN on decision-making. Despite being still directly allocated to the HR/VP by Council Decision 427/2010, thereby maintaining its formal status from Council times, the vacancy in leadership until early 2011, combined with limited receptivity and understanding of the emerging leadership including the HR on the function and proper use of estimative strategic intelligence in contrast to current crisis related intelligence,[31] clearly limited practical options for directly bringing intelligence analysis to bear on the top management.[32]

Added to this was a pervasive lack of infrastructure for the secure and timely handling of classified information. Within the Council Secretariat and hence in SITCEN, the Policy Unit and EUMS such structures and procedures had been developed and put in place in the respective premises at *Kortenberg* and *Lipsius* as early as 2001/2002.[33] The new EEAS Headquarters at Rond Point Schuman[34] and most of the Commission building at Berlaymont lacked this kind of security. Distributing confidential SIAC analysis, storing it and working with it was hence at best cumbersome, if not impossible. In the absence of enforceable regulations demanding the regular and systematic use of estimative intelligence in policy decision-making at desk levels and beyond, classified SIAC products too often did not make it out of secure central registries to their recipients. Widespread silo mentality separating the predominantly diplomatic policy units from CSDP and especially intelligence-related former Council entities (also manifest in the local separation between Kortenberg and Schuman) as well as lack of effective oversight and coordination between the various units of different backgrounds and leanings only added to these structural dysfunctionalities.[35] Given all that, accidental warnings in delegation reporting and political desk analysis in headquarters could not stand any structural chance of being processed properly, as already pointed out in Ikani's post-mortem.[36]

Without a dedicated institutional and procedural framework which enables the systematic establishment and update of all-sources-based situational awareness and strategic foresight, single warnings cannot be properly processed and upgraded to authoritative estimative intelligence.[37] As single reports, opinions, situational snapshots, they do not have relevance, especially if they produce dissonance with established opinion. That inconvenient delegation reporting on the crisis in Tunisia was vividly rejected by interested member states' representatives in the PSC even hours before the regime collapsed is a significant confirmation of that general rule.[38]

In addition, this latter case clearly shows that single-source material should not have a place in multilateral political decision-making fora without prior proper comment and assessment by the mandated and qualified structures. Otherwise, it nearly inevitably becomes a matter of political discussion or even haggling among member states' delegations following national predispositions without an established and checked factual framework. Under such circumstances, the chance for decision-making on a pro-fessionally established situational picture (*Lagebild*) that at least reduces uncertainty while discussing and analysing more or less likely courses of event[39] is lost. The general cognitive and psycho-logical risks of analysis well known in political science, psychology and intelligence studies[40] still persist as human factors as well in these processes. But it is only such a rigorous intellectual analytical exercise with peer reviews and cross-checks that can at least reduce the risk of seriously flawed situational awareness. Structures and processes of that kind would provide a professional framework for adequately considering and handling dissenting assessments and opinions as rightly demanded by Ikani and Meyer.[41]

Taken together, these observations finally reveal a major general systemic weakness in the set-up of decision-making in the emerging EEAS and generally in EU institutions, the absence of a clear-cut conceptual and factual separation between establishing situational awareness and policy decision-making. Prior to 2010, SITCEN and EUMS.INT provided their reporting and assessment as Council entities directly to the Secretary General and High Representative who in turn tasked the Secretariat's Policy Unit with developing policy proposals and recommendations to the PSC and Council. Solana had deliberately dismissed early attempts of his policymakers to put the emerging intelligence analysis cell under their control. Policy Unit and SITCEN remained separate entities directly linked to his authority and guidance. Hence, Shapcott was able to state for his tenure that situational awareness and policy functions were (more or less) separate.[42] However, these were rather personal support functions for the HR[43] who decided how to make proper use of them, including the presentation of SITCEN reporting in the PSC through its Director.[44] The presence of the Director SITCEN in the PSCE however was not universally considered as an accepted standing procedure, and therefore ceased after Solana's tenure and by some accounts as early as 2007 during the German presidency.[45] It remains to be seen then, to what extent, if at all, lessons have been learned from a widely perceived early underperformance in making use of estimative intelligence in situational awareness and decision-making.

Lessons Learned Regarding Structures and Procedures?

There is no doubt that, from the very outset, efforts were made to identify deficiencies in the newly created EEAS and to better structure and streamline the service. Article 13(3) of Council Decision 427/2010 EU on the creation of the EEAS already stipulated a first evaluation of the service, its establishment, structure and performance by mid-2013.[46] Based on these findings, reforms were implemented by autumn 2015,[47] followed by further steps in 2016 and again in March 2019 towards the end of Federica Mogherini's mandate as HR/Vice President.[48] Numerous analyses have also identified inconsistencies and weaknesses already underlying the 2010 Council Decision and in consequence also its implementation.[49]

A recent fairly comprehensive stocktaking exercise has been the work of a Task Force EEAS 2.0 on the occasion of the service's tenth anniversary. Its report and recommendations address core issues raised in Meyer's chapter, especially concerning asymmetric actorness, institutional self-awareness and the need for a more joined-up and better-informed EU role in foreign affairs. Its findings were submitted to member states and EU Institutions in early 2021 and are currently under discussion.[50]

While discussion and action on political decision-making, inter-institutional relations and member states' dynamics with regard to the EEAS have traditionally been paramount, and particularly in the fields of CSDP-related early warning/early action, crisis prevention, management and response, it will be important to understand whether lessons have also been learned with regard to the role and function of estimative intelligence in decision-making.[51]

The Early Warning System (EWS)

Conflict Prevention, Early Warning and Early Reaction (EW-ER) have been core issues from the outset in CFSP, and particularly ESDP/CSDP. Already the Policy Planning and Early Warning Unit (PU) of the Council Secretariat and the European Military Staff (EUMS) were explicitly mandated in that sense by the Amsterdam Treaty of 1997 and by Council Decision 2001/80/CFSP.[52] The Intelligence Directorate of the EUMS (EUMS.INT) was tasked mainly for that purpose, based on the contributions of member states in defence intelligence products, while the PU was meant to work on the basis of diplomatic correspondence shared by member states' ministries of foreign affairs (MFAs). After 2002, the Joint Situation Centre (SITCEN) with its newly created civilian intelligence analysis capacity joined in what was already then called the Council Early Warning System (EWS).

The main product of that EWS was a biannually updated confidential Watchlist, containing states to be monitored closely by the EU. Establishing the Watchlist was originally a main task of the PU, and hence started not from a situational but a rather unsuitable operational perspective. Over time, the reviewing process also involved SITCEN, the EUMS and some Commission agencies. Countries were listed and annotated with concise analytical statements on risks and threats for their stability and categorised according to levels of imminence and urgency. A draft version of the Watchlist was sent to the Political and Security Committee (PSC) for endorsement before being finalised. The Watchlist was shared with the SG/HR, the PSC, individual member states, Commission agencies and relevant Council working groups.[53] The obvious core flaw of the system, however, was that member states with conflict-ing national interests and perceptions were involved in authorising the list already in its formative analytical phase. It was hence easy for observers to note that 'the Council has difficulties in prioritis-ing between different situations on the verge of crisis and deciding upon if and how to respond'.[54] A similar observation was that 'the Council's foreign policy tools are mostly used for the implemen-tation of reactive, rather than preventive, strategies. EU decision-makers tend to have a focus on existing crises. Consequently, the Council does not constitute a very conducive environment for those advocating the establishment of preventive mechanisms or early action.'[55] Political predisposition, even the taboo of not working on 'allies, partners and friends' in the European Neighbourhood, was hence decisive in undermining proper and independent esti-mative intelligence from the outset,[56] a limitation that could be observed in the run-up to the Ukraine crisis also.[57]

A second initiative was started shortly after the establishment of the EEAS in 2011, based on specific Council conclusions on Conflict Prevention.[58] EEAS and Commission services put in place the EU Early Warning System (EWS) as part of their broader activ-ities in the field of security policy. The procedures and methodol-ogy of the system were tested in two regional pilot studies in 2012 and 2013 before the system was rolled out in September 2014 cov-ering all non-EU countries.[59] The EWS was designed as a key com-ponent of the EU's Comprehensive Approach to External Conflict and Crises (2013),[60] while the Joint Staff Working Document (SWD 2016)[61] described it as a deliverable of the 2015 Action Plan for the Comprehensive Approach and 'a tool for EU decision-makers to manage risk factors and prioritise resources accordingly'.[62]

As before, however, the role of estimative intelligence remains limited if not haphazard. The process starts with country-related risk-scanning, with specific attention to human security. The findings are then complemented with intelligence-based analysis from the SIAC, which focuses on risks to the EU and its member states. The results are then brought together with the latest qual-itative situation analysis available from open sources and inter-nal assessments. Taken together, these different sources provide a first global compilation of conflict risk and its implications for the EU. The result of this rather opaque process involving a wide range of policymaking but not dedicated assessment capabilities is then presented to the EEAS and Commission services as a starting point for political prioritisation, action, and, later on, assessment and follow-up. Apart from the first modest and inconclusive step in terms of stringent analysis of facts and situational awareness, the process is again purely political and operational, with strong inputs from EU institutions, delegations and member states with their specific national foreign policy priorities and judgements on the feasibility and appropriateness of early action, or inaction. The wording and structure of the Staff Working Document shows again that the fundamental phase of building situational awareness by a stringent process of establishing and assessing facts had been simply glossed over. No mention is made of who exactly is supposed to engage in that exercise, even less with what kind of qualification, in what organisational and methodological framework, configuration and process. Professional assessment would require highly specialised scrutiny of information, establishing of facts, figures and causalities in separation from policymaking structures, ultimately resulting in coherent and stringent estimative intelligence that would then – and only then – have to be introduced as starting point for political decision-making processes. Already this first glimpse reconfirms that the core deficiency in understanding the production of estimative intelligence and its proper use in decision-making, as identified by Ikani and Meyer, has not been overcome.

The EEAS Crisis Reaction System (CRS) and the Integrated Political Crisis Response (IPCR)

Crisis reaction and crisis response have been and still are one of the main fields of European ambition in becoming a viable global actor of strategic relevance.[63] By its nature, crisis-related situational awareness has to be highly dynamic in the timely detection, identification, follow-up and assessment of disruptive events. It implies special requirements for anticipatory and real-time tactical intelligence collection and assessment which in turn have specific consequences for the respective capabilities to be created for that purpose.[64]

Estimative intelligence in turn is strategic and, if success-ful, would have provided the basic situational understanding to decision-makers, at the latest shortly prior to or at least at the outset of a crisis, as well as constituted the starting point for direct-ing further tactical intelligence collection and assessment.

Crisis reaction and response is hence a different category that – in the case of CFSP/CSDP – involves the specialised directorates of the Civil Planning and Conduct Capability (CPCC) and the Military Planning and Conduct Capability (MPCC) of the EEAS. The question of how to organise intelligence collection, produc-tion and dissemination in this context involves specific tactical J2 (intelligence) capabilities that are already envisaged, at least in principle, for the MPPC,[65] whereas similar tactical field intelli-gence collection and assessment capabilities for the CPCC seem to rest still somehow with INTCEN and EUMS.INT.[66]

Already that sketchy overview shows the urgency for further action in that domain also. Since this study is on early warning and estimative strategic intelligence, further elaboration and discussion are beyond the scope of this chapter.[67]

Intelligence Structures: The EEAS Intelligence Support Architecture (ISA)

The results of the post-mortems on the Arab uprisings and Ukrainian crisis are unequivocal: even the best estimative intel-ligence can only make a difference if it is properly managed in its production and – at least as important – in its timely dissemi-nation in an actionable form to the relevant recipients.[68] For the EEAS, as a new structure which is highly distinct from the Council Secretariat, the Intelligence Support Architecture (ISA),[69] was meant to provide that kind of framework.

Being conceptualised by INTCEN and EUMS.INT, the ISA was signed by the High Representative in 2012. It envisaged Prioritised Intelligence Requirements (PIR) for SIAC that were to be defined on senior EEAS management level. An Intelligence Steering Board (ISB) led by the HR/VP and an Intelligence Working Group (IWG) on managerial level were intended to organise that process.[70] The

ISA, however, never really materialised, essentially due to a vicious circle of limited interest and lacking understanding in wide parts of the EEAS. This was complemented by occasional SIAC weaknesses in timeliness, topical relevance and actionability of its output.

After years of benign neglect, a slow comeback based on increased customer awareness of timely and relevant SIAC reporting and assessment culminated in an updated and upgraded ISA issued by HR/VP Mogherini in late 2019. Since then, support of EEAS decision-making by SIAC estimative intelligence has become (again) a leadership issue; SIAC is (again) directly attached to the HR/VP and has an advisory function on situational awareness and questions of intelligence support by member states. By increased timeliness and relevance of its output and institutional outreach, SIAC has managed a stronger though still not mandatory regular integration into the decision-making processes of the EEAS and also beyond in many cases of Commission-led internal security. A significant indication for that development could be noted in 2020, when member states united in the Foreign Affairs Council asked for SIAC to prepare a 360° Threat Assessment in preparation of the Strategic Compass for the EEAS.[71]

SIAC could hence be on the verge of becoming a function that would regularly support a wide range of EU activities if that emerging trend can be formalised and stabilised by a system of inter-institutional Terms of Reference between EEAS, Commission and Council, defining agreed regular procedures and competences.

At the same time, adequate coordination among member states in their support to SIAC needs to be developed as well. The case was explicitly made in general though unequivocal terms by the EEAS in its Implementation Plan on Security and Defence as early as in November 2016.[72] Since then, it has been repeated by various Council Conclusions and Joint Action Plans on the security implications of the global strategy, especially in the fields of countering hybrid and cyber threats.[73]

Numerous proposals by scholars on how to arrange for such a consolidated inter-governmental procedure of intelligence support – mainly invoking the option of an Enhanced Cooperation (ENCO) according to Article 328 of the Treaty on the Functioning of the European Union (TFEU) and hence without involving national prerogatives according to Article 4(2) of the Treaties – were made already in 2017, 2018 and again in 2019.[74]

EU INTCEN, EUMS.INT and SATCEN as main Intelligence Actors

Any kind of institutional and inter-institutional organisational reform will however remain meaningless if estimative intelligence fails to be of high quality, topically relevant, actionable and timely. As the post-mortems have convincingly demonstrated, creating and updating situational awareness and strategic foresight for decision-makers is a challenging and delicate process of its own. It becomes flawed from the outset if it is compromised by operational wishful thinking and predisposed unchecked perceptions. It is not by accident that the mantra 'speaking truth to power' has become a core principle of professional ethics for the US intelligence community.[75]

Intelligence studies are clear in that the processes of collection and analysis proper are also influenced by cognitive, psychological and intellectual human factors.[76] After all, intelligence production essentially shares many intellectual and cognitive specificities with social sciences. Hence, it is already a challenge and not without the risk of failure to achieve results that can be qualified as true, that are as close to factual reality as possible. It is all the more important to safeguard collection and situational analysis from additional external influence driven by politically motivated interest, bias and cognitive flaws.

Much effort has been put in from the outset by SITCEN and EUMS.INT to meet these core demands. As already mentioned, Solana created the Single Intelligence Analysis Capacity (SIAC) in 2007, bringing together the military and civilian capabilities of EUMS.INT and INTCEN. Earlier, in 2004/2005, he had been able to add capabilities of EU security services to SITCEN for providing assessments on all aspects of the terrorist threat to Europe, thus creating a fusion capacity between internal and external intelligence. In addition, the Satellite Centre of the European Union (SATCEN) in Torrejón/Spain has over time become a major and

235

regular contributor of imagery and geospatial intelligence to SIAC. After years of neglect, OSINT has been upgraded recently, though this project seems still to be subject to further development in numbers, technical infrastructure and skills.

A specific example of all-sources estimative intelligence of major potential significance for future developments is the Hybrid Fusion Cell (HFC) at INTCEN.[77] Created in 2016 in compliance with specific Council demands reacting to the Ukrainian crisis, it is an inspiring case of a lesson learned. The HFC is a cross-institutional cooperative format, collecting information and expertise inside the EEAS and the Commission, and beyond that from all member states on the levels of intelligence services, ministries and administration. As part of SIAC, the HFC draws comprehensively on civil and military intelligence and expertise available in both directorates. Though still a small fusion cell and not a major fusion centre, it already shows the potential to become the role model for a larger framework of a comprehensive approach in creating all-sources estimative intelligence.[78] For that, member states will however have to engage adequately with expert staff and timely contributions, EU institutions will have to support in terms of budget, infrastructure and expertise, and all sides will have to coordinate a wider range of expert training to staff, not least by involving member states' services as well as the various Centres of Excellence (CoE) on Hybrid and Cyber, the Joint Research Centre (JRC) of the Commission and national academia.[79]

Building up, maintaining and further developing highly qualified human resources as key for success in producing and using estimative intelligence is yet another lesson to be learned by member states as well as by EU Institutions, and particularly within the EEAS and its intelligence structures. Being conscious of the heterogeneity of their staff in terms of nationality, administrative and professional background, topical and methodological expertise, the management of INTCEN and EUMS.INT has engaged in sustained efforts to establish common ground in tradecraft, not least by arranging training courses in intelligence assessment provided by British academia (Intelligence Studies) and at an advanced stage by member states' intelligence services and their academies. Though being essential, these courses cannot compensate for a potential lack of expertise in regional or topical subject matters, that is the core requirement of target knowledge.[80] The national selection processes for staff to be seconded to INTCEN or EUMS.INT need to adequately address this core prerequisite for competent intelligence production. Specific job-related qualifications cannot be left to chance. Starting to build up expertise on the job practically from scratch is a widespread though risky habit known in national administrations as well. Such instant expertise, however, leads to low-quality analysis, mainly depending on pre-existing and – due to insufficient own awareness and capabilities – unscrutinised results that are patched together following superficial deliberations of plausibility and common sense. Mainstream convictions, (mis)perceptions and cultural bias will rarely be challenged by accommodating that kind of analytical middle ground.

As the post-mortems have clearly shown, it is this lack of a structured methodology in processing but not suppressing dissonance and in striving for the best possible professional understanding that is a major reason for underperformance in situational awareness and anticipation. Sustained efforts in ensuring specific qualification of staff are hence a must for qualified intelligence support to responsible decision-making.

Conclusion: Further Professionalising Production and Use of Estimative Intelligence

As should have become abundantly clear, authoritative, timely and actionable estimative intelligence is of vital importance for responsible decision-making, especially in light of increasingly complex and dynamic political, economic, military and security challenges. For EU member states, institutions and the EEAS this should mean:

1. Drawing a clear conceptual and organisational line between creating estimative intelligence in an extended SIAC framework on the one side and policymaking in the respective regional and thematic directorates in the EEAS and the Commission on the other.

2. Placing strict emphasis on topical relevance, timeliness and the intellectual commitment to clear judgement and foresight in order to create actionable intelligence for decision-makers.

3. Organising a regular structured outreach of SIAC into EEAS decision-making, as well as ensuring an enhanced role of SIAC and its output in the Commission.

4. Based on these initial steps, an EU-wide unified structure for creating independent situational awareness with SIAC at its core – but equipped with a strong capacity for collecting and analysing EU delegation reporting as well as Commission expertise, OSINT/ SOCMINT, IMINT and GEOINT – could be envisaged.[81]

5. Promoting a higher level of member states' voluntary commitment to support SIAC in implementation of various Council resolutions. Inter-governmental coordination of support with expert staff and finished intelligence should be organised, in consultation with the HR/VP and SIAC, ultimately within the framework of 'Enhanced Cooperation' according to Article 328 TFEU.[82]

6. Ensuring high-professional SIAC standards in tradecraft and topical expertise in view of the need of experts with the ability and willingness to reach to independent actionable conclusions on facts, reasons, backgrounds, implications and prospects.

The essential basis for that however is a valid political perception among member states and EU institutions that independent all-sources estimative intelligence really matters, and that situational awareness and strategic foresight are neither marginal nor discretionary add-ons but a prerequisite for responsible decision-making. Elements of these ideas can already be found in the recommendations of the Task Force EEAS 2.0.[83] It is now a question of political will and leadership to move ahead.

Notes

1. Daniel Keohane and Robert Grant, 'From Comprehensive Approach to Comprehensive Action: Enhancing the Effectiveness of the EU's Contribution to Peace and Security', Conference Report, Wilton Park, December 2012, p. 2.
2. For an overview of this discussion, see: Barbara Lippert, Nicolai von Ondarza and Volker Perthes, eds, 'European Strategic Autonomy. Actors, Issues, Conflicts of Interests', German Institute for International and Security Affairs, SWP Research Paper 4, March 2019.
3. See Chapter 2 in this volume.
4. Ibid.
5. See Chapter 4 in this volume.
6. See: Maxime Lefebvre and Christophe Hillion, 'The European External Action Service: Towards a Common Diplomacy?', *European Issue* no. 184, 25 October 2010; European Institute, 'The European External Action Services Comes of Age', December 2013. For a good overview over the early uncertainties of the formative period, see: Antonio Missiroli, 'The EU Foreign Service: Under Construction', RSCAS Policy Paper 2010/04; Steven Blockmans and Christoph Hillion, eds, 'EEAS 2.0. A Legal Commentary on Council Decision 2010/427/EU Establishing the Organisation and Functioning of the European External Action Service', CEPS, 7 February 2013.
7. The EEAS was launched on 1 December 2010 and became operational a month later when entire administrative entities were transferred from the General Secretariat of the Council, the European Commission's DG RELEX and parts of DG DEV. In numerical terms this means that on 1 January 2011 2,805 agents (of which 1,084 local) were transferred from the Commission (establishment plan figures: 585 administrator (AD) posts from DG RELEX, 93 from DG DEV and 436 from the Delegations) and 675 posts were transferred to the EEAS from the Council Secretariat (establishment plan figures: 411). One hundred and eighteen new posts were created in the period 2011–13 to establish the management structures in headquarters and to add staff in EU delegations to perform the new tasks under the Lisbon Treaty.
8. Upon the entry into force of the Treaty of Lisbon in 2009, the European Security and Defence Policy (ESDP) was renamed Common Security and Defence Policy (CSDP). See also: Sven Biscop,

'From ESDP to CSDP: Time for Some Strategy', *La revue géopolitique*, January 2010.

9. See: David Spence, 'The Early Days of the European External Action Service: A Practitioner's View', *The Hague Journal of Diplomacy*, no. 7 (2012): 119–21; Thomas E. Henökl, 'The European External Action Service: Torn Apart Between Several Principals or Acting as a Smart "Double-agent"?', *Journal of Contemporary European Research* 10, no. 4 (2014); Loes Debuysere and Steven Blockmans, 'Europe's Coherence Gap in External Crisis and Conflict Management. The EU's Integrated Approach between Political Rhetoric and Institutional Practice', Bertelsmann Stiftung, November 2019; Petru Dumitriu, Knowledge Management in the United Nations System, Joint Inspection Unit, 2016; Sukai Prom-Jackson and Eileen A. Cronin, 'United Nations Review of Change Management in UN System Organizations', 2019.

10. Florian Güssgen, 'Of Swiss Army Knives and Diplomacy. A Review of the Union's Diplomatic Capabilities', Jean Monnet Working Papers in Comparative and International Politics, April 2001; Simon Duke, 'Under the Authority of the High Representative', in *The High Representative for the EU Foreign and Security Policy – Review and Prospects*, ed. Gisela Müller-Brandeck-Borquet and Caroline Rüger (Baden-Baden: Nomos, 2011), 42–5.

11. Duke, 'Under the Authority of the High Representative', 50–1.

12. Ibid., 45–50.

13. See: Hylke Dijkstra, 'The Council Secretariat's Role in the Common Foreign and Security Policy', *European Foreign Affairs Review* 13, no. 2 (2008); Duke, 'Under the Authority of the High Representative', 42–51.

14. Duke, 'Under the Authority of the High Representative', 47.

15. The outreach by even those prominent members of Solana's entourage to the HR/SG himself was again fairly irregular if not limited by his restless and often informal ways of management, see: Hylke Dijkstra, 'Solana and his Civil Servants: An Overview of Political-Administrative Relations', in *The High Representative for the EU Foreign and Security Policy – Review and Prospects*, ed. Gisela Müller-Brandeck-Borquet and Caroline Rüger (Baden-Baden: Nomos, 2011), 76–81.

16. See for the Cabinet of Catherine Ashton: https://eeas.europa.eu/archives/ashton/team/index_en.htm. For the members of her Corporate Board, see: Martin Schmid, 'The HR/VP and the Organisation of the EEAS' Senior Management', in *The EU's External Action*

Service: Potentials for a One Voice Foreign Policy, ed. Doris Dialer, Heinrich Neisser and Anja Opitz (Innsbruck: Innsbruck University Press, 2014), 81–96. For the first set-up of Managing Directors and their respective backgrounds, see: Toby Vogel, 'Ashton Names Team to Advise on EEAS. Senior Officials will Help Set Up External Service as MEPs are Left Out of Preparatory Team', *Politico*, 21 January 2010. For an insightful analysis about the background and structure of Ashton's entourage and top management, see also: Sandra Lesteven, *La mise en place du service européen pour l'action extérieur*, *Cahier Thucydide* no. 11 (2011).

17. Significantly, Shapcott was not part of Ashton's preparatory group set up in January 2010 while Helga Schmid as head of the competing Policy Unit was. Hence, intelligence had lost its voice from the outset in the transition process.

18. See: Blockmans, 'The European External Action Service One Year On: First Signs of Strengths and Weaknesses', CEPS, January 2012, 9–10. Ilkka Salmi, successor of Shapcott, took over as late as January 2011, not without sceptical comments as to his future position under Ashton, see Andrew Rettmann, 'Ashton Picks Finn to be EU "spy-master"', Atlantic Council, 20 December 2010. For a discussion of the process, see: Andrew Rettmann, 'Competition Heating up for EU Intelligence Chief Job', *EU Observer*, 14 September 2010. Also, the first Managing Director for the Middle East, North Africa and the Southern Neighbourhood, former Commission DDG RELEX Hugues Mingarelli, started late, again without a specific track record in Council-based CFSP or CSDP matters or confidential intelligence analysis.

19. See Chapter 2 in this volume, and Ruben Arcos and José Miguel Palacios, 'The Impact of Intelligence on Decision-Making: The EU and the Arab Spring', *Intelligence and National Security* 33, no. 5 (2018).

20. See Arcos and Palacios, 'The Impact of Intelligence on Decision-Making', 8, 18.

21. William Shapcott, 'Do They Listen? Communicating Warnings: A Practitioners Perspective', in *Forecasting, Warning, and Responding to Transnational Risks*, ed. Chiara De Franco and Christoph O. Meyer (Basingstoke: Palgrave Macmillan, 2011), 123–5. This happened possibly not least because it failed to meet the conditions outlined by himself (ibid., 121–123).

22. Arcos and Palacios, 'The Impact of Intelligence on Decision-Making', 9–10.

23. See: Shapcott, 'Do They Listen?', and the section on p. 230–2 on Early Warning System.
24. Arcos and Palacios, 'The Impact of Intelligence on Decision-Making', 7–8.
25. See: Cynthia M. Grabo, *Anticipating Surprise: Analysis for Strategic Warning*, Joint Military Intelligence College's Center for Strategic Intelligence Research, Washington 2002. For further development, see: Hélène Lavoix, 'Communication of Strategic Foresight and Early Warning', *Red Team Analysis*, 3 March 2021; 'Revisiting Timeliness for Strategic Foresight and Warning and Risk Management', *Red Team Analysis*, 1 October 2018.
26. See for example Eberhard Kienle, 'Ambiguities and Misconceptions: European Policies towards Political Reform in the Southern Mediterranean', in *Europe and the Middle East. Perspectives on Major Policy Issues*, ed. Al Siyassa Al Dawliya (Cairo: Al Ahram Commercial Press, 2010), 11–16.
27. Jochen Rehrl, ed., *Handbook for Decision Makers. The Common Security and Defence Policy of the European Union*, (Vienna, 2014), 38; José-Miguel Palacios, 'EU Intelligence: On the Road to a European Intelligence Agency?', in *Intelligence Law and Policies in Europe: A Handbook*, ed. Jan-Hendrik Dietrich and Satish Sule (Munich: C. H. Beck, 2019), 214.
28. Becoming only part of a largely unspecific General and External Relations Division; see John M. Nomikos, 'European Union Intelligence Analysis Centre (INTCEN): Next Stop to an Agency?', *Journal of Mediterranean and Balkan Intelligence* 4, no. 2 (2014): 7–8; Chris Jones, 'Secrecy Reigns at the EU's Intelligence Analysis Centre', *Statewatch* 22, no. 4 (2013).
29. Gerhard Conrad, 'Europäische Nachrichtendienstkooperation – Entwicklungen, Erwartungen und Perspektiven', in *Reform der Nachrichtendienste zwischen Vergesetzlichung und Internationalisierung*, ed. Jan-Hendrik Dietrich et al. (Tübingen: Mohr Siebeck, 2019), 162–3; Palacios, 'EU Intelligence', 215; Gerhard Conrad, 'Situational Awareness for EU Decision-making: The Next Decade', *European Foreign Affairs Review* 26, no. 1 (2021): 56–7.
30. See Chapters 5 and 6 in this volume.
31. There has been a persistent misperception of INTCEN and EUMS .INT as having merely a function in crisis response and management, mainly derived from Article 4(3) of Council Decision 427/2010 where SITCEN is mentioned together with – but not as part of – the crisis management and planning directorate.

32. See the section on the Intelligence Support Architecture (ISA) on p. 233–5.
33. Duke, 'Under the Authority of the High Representative', 59–61; Conrad, 'Situational Awareness for EU Decision-making', 67–9.
34. See: Blockmans, 'The European External Action Service One Year On', 11 n. 35.
35. See: Jolyon Howorth, 'Catherine Ashton's Five-Year Term: A Difficult Assessment', *Les Cahiers Européens de Sciences Po*, no. 3 (2014): 9–10; Blockmans, 'The European External Action Service One Year On', 11.
36. See Chapter 2 in this volume.
37. See: Shapcott, 'Do They Listen?', 118–19. He points to the respective flaws in preparing intelligence-based substantive warning.
38. See Chapter 2 in this volume.
39. Bjorn Gunnar M. Isaksen and Ken R. McNaught, 'Uncertainty Handling in Estimative Intelligence – Challenges and Requirements from Both Analyst and Consumer Perspectives', *Journal of Risk Research* 22, no. 5 (2019): 643–57. See also Chapter 4 in this volume.
40. See: Martha Whitesmith, *Cognitive Bias in Intelligence Analysis: Testing the Analysis of Competing Hypotheses Method* (Edinburgh: Edinburgh University Press, 2020). On the systemic conflict between estimative intelligence and customer bias or prejudice see: Robert Jervis, 'Why Intelligence and Policymakers Clash', *Political Science Quarterly* 125, no. 2 (2010): 185–204, and *Why Intelligence Fails: Lessons from the Iranian Revolution and the Iraq War* (Ithaca, NY: Cornell University Press, 2010).
41. See Chapters 1, 2 and 4 in this volume.
42. Shapcott, 'Do They Listen?', 124.
43. On Solana's very personalised style of management and decision-making see: Dijkstra, 'Solana and his Civil Servants', 16.
44. On how Solana developed SITCEN's role in supporting policymaking, see: Per M. Norheim-Martinsen, *The European Union and Military Force: Governance and Strategy* (Cambridge: Cambridge University Press), 96–9.
45. This was perceived as deciding the rivalry between the German-led Policy Unit and SITCEN in favour of the former.
46. See: Council conclusions on the EEAS Review, General Affairs Council meeting Brussels, 17 December 2013 (https://www.consilium.europa.eu/uedocs/cms_data/docs/pressdata/EN/genaff/140141.pdf); European Parliament recommendation to the High

Representative of the Union for Foreign Affairs and Security Policy and Vice President of the European Commission, to the Council and to the Commission of 13 June 2013 on the 2013 review of the organisation and the functioning of the EEAS (https://www.europarl.europa.eu/doceo/document/TA-7-2013-0278_EN.html).

47. High Representative Federica Mogherini announces adoption of a modified organisational chart of the EEAS, Bruxelles, 28 July 2015 (https://eeas.europa.eu/headquarters/headquarters-homepage/6076_en).

48. See sections on Intelligence Structures and on INTCEN on pp. 223–7.

49. See: Steven Blockmans and Christoph Hillion, eds, EEAS 2.0; Steven Blockmans and Ramses A. Wessel, 'The EEAS at Ten: Reason for a Celebration?', *European Foreign Affairs Review* 26, no. 1 (2021): 5–12.

50. Christophe Hillion and Steven Blockmans, 'From Self-Doubt to Self-Assurance', Report by the Task Force EEAS 2.0. January 2021.

51. See also Conrad, 'Situational Awareness for EU Decision-making', 63–70.

52. Jort Hemmer, and Rosan Smits, 'The Early Warning and Conflict Prevention Capability of the Council of the European Union: A Mapping of the Pre-Lisbon Period', Clingendael, March 2010, 9–10; Shapcott, 'Do They Listen?', 119.

53. Hemmer and Smits, 'The Early Warning and Conflict Prevention Capability of the Council of the European Union', 9–10; Artur Gruszczak, *Intelligence Security in the European Union. Building a Strategic Intelligence Community* (Basingstoke: Palgrave Macmillan, 2016), 129–30.

54. Hemmer and Smits, 'The Early Warning and Conflict Prevention Capability of the Council of the European Union', 13.

55. Ibid.

56. See also the necessarily cautious but indicative remarks of Shapcott, 'Do They Listen?', 118–22, on the limitations and inhibiting factors for warning during his watch. On the general problem of conflicting interests in Council structures, see: Marcus Kaim and Ronja Kempin, 'A European Security Council. Added Value for EU Foreign and Security Policy?', SWP Comment no. 2, January 2019; Lisa Musiol, 'Better Early than Sorry: How the EU Can Use its Early Warning Capacities to their Full Potential', International Crisis Group, 22 October 2019. See also: Maciej Stepka, 'EU Crisis Management and Conflict Prevention: Identifying Institutional Constraints for Early Warning Analysis Utilization', *Politeja* no. 49 (2017): 127–42.

57. See Chapter 4 in this volume.

58. Council conclusions on conflict prevention 3101st Foreign Affairs Council meeting Luxembourg, 20 June 2011, Doc. 11820/11 (https://www.consilium.europa.eu/uedocs/cms_data/docs/pressdata /EN/foraff/ 122911.pdf). See also: Rehrl, *Handbook for Decision Makers*, 37.

59. Council of the European Union, 'EU Conflict Early Warning System: Objectives, Process and Guidance for Implementation', Joint Staff Working Document, August 2017, 282; Jochen Rehrl and Galia Glume, eds, *Handbook on CSDP Missions and Operations* (Vienna, 2015), 37–9.

60. Doc. 9644/14, JOIN (2013) 30, 11 December 2013.

61. SWD (2015) 85, 10 April 2015.

62. Jochen Rehrl and Galia Glume, eds, *Handbook on CSDP Missions and Operations*, Vienna 2015, 37.

63. See an early assessment outlining the general principles and ambitions: International Crisis Group, 'EU Crisis Response Capability – Institutions and Processes for Conflict Prevention and Management', Report No. 2, 26 June 2001: https://www.crisisgroup.org/europe -central-asia/eu-crisis-response-capability-institutions-and-processes -conflict-prevention-and-management

64. Gruszczak, *Intelligence Security in the European Union*, 125–33.

65. See: Christian Rauwolf, 'Intelligence in EU-led Military Missions and Operations', in *Intelligence Law and Policies in Europe: A Handbook*, ed. Jan-Hendrik Dietrich and Satish Sule (Munich: C. H. Beck, 2019), 162; Council Decision (EU) 2017/971 of 8 June 2017 determining the planning and conduct arrangements for EU non-executive military CSDP missions (https://eur-lex.europa.eu /legal-content/EN/TXT/?uri=celex%3A32017D0971); details in: EU Concept for Military Command and Control, EEAS(2019) 468, 23 April 2019, 19–21 (https://data.consilium.europa.eu/doc/docu ment/ST-8798-2019-INIT/en/pdf).

66. It is telling that the EEAS factsheet does not mention situational awareness and assessment at all. EEAS: The Civilian Planning and Conduct Capability (CPCC), 2021: https://eeas.europa.eu /topics/military-and-civilian-missions-and-operations_en/5438/The %20Civilian%20Planning%20and%20Conduct%20Capability %20(CPCC). INTCEN and EUMS.INT are tasked with providing strategic intelligence in the mission planning and assessment processes, however, by virtue of lacking capabilities already, not on an operational/tactical level.

67. For a critical review of recent reform in this field see: Debuysere and Blockmans, 'Europe's Coherence Gap in External Crisis and Conflict Management', no. 9.
68. See: Shapcott, 'Do They Listen?', 120–1.
69. Rehrl and Glume, *Handbook on CSDP Missions and Operations*, 41–2.
70. Terri Beswick, 'EU Early Warning and Early Response Capacity for Conflict Prevention in the Post Lisbon Era', Clingendael, January 2012, 8.
71. See: Dick Zandee, Adája Stoetman and Bob Deen, 'The EU's Strategic Compass for Security and Defence. Squaring Ambition with Reality', Clingendael Report, 31 May 2021; Jana Puglierin, 'Direction of force: The EU's Strategic Compass', ECFR, 1 April 2021; Niklas Nováky, 'The Strategic Compass. Charting a New Course for the EU's Security and Defence Policy', Marten's Centre, December 2020.
72. Council of the European Union, 'Implementation Plan on Security and Defence', 14392/16, 14 November 2016, paragraphs 8 and 33.
73. Conrad, 'Situational Awareness for EU Decision-making', 60–1.
74. Pia Seyfried, 'A European Intelligence Service? Potentials and Limits of Intelligence Cooperation at EU Level', BAKS Working Paper 20/2017; Raphael Bossong, 'Intelligence Support for EU Security Policy: Options for Enhancing the Flow of Information and Political Oversight', SWP Comment 2018/C 51, 3 December 2018; Conrad, 'Europäische Nachrichtendienstkooperation', 173–7.
75. Office of the Director of National Intelligence, Principles of Professional Ethics for the Intelligence Community: https://www.dni.gov/index.php/how-we-work/ethics
76. See Chapters 2 and 4 in this volume. See also: Whitesmith, *Cognitive Bias in Intelligence Analysis*; and Jervis, 'Why Intelligence and Policymakers Clash', and *Why Intelligence Fails*.
77. Conrad, 'Situational Awareness for EU Decision-making', 60–1.
78. The argument for a comprehensive all-sources approach to intelligence analysis as a basic requirement for adequate situational awareness and strategic foresight has been authoritatively made by David Omand, 'Means and Methods of Modern Intelligence and their Wider Implications', in *Intelligence Law and Policies in Europe: A Handbook*, ed. Jan-Hendrik Dietrich and Satish Sule (Munich: C. H. Beck, 2019), 38–63.
79. Conrad, 'Situational Awareness for EU Decision-making', 64–5.
80. On the wide range of requirements for qualified intelligence analysis, see as an insider perspective: David T. Moore, 'Species of

Competencies for Intelligence Analysis', *American Intelligence Journal* 23 (2005): 29–43.

81. For more detail, see: Conrad, 'Situational Awareness for EU Decision-making', 63–7. Regarding the requirements of modern intelligence processes, see: Omand, 'Means and Methods of Modern Intelligence and their Wider Implications', 55–62. 'Professional analysis as a necessary basis for situational awareness and foresight in support of responsible decision-making is not limited to proper intelligence production and compartmentalised in these structures. It should rather be an essential, though always independent, part of national governmental as well as European institutional bodies.'

82. Conrad, 'Europäische Nachrichtendienstkooperation', 173–7.

83. Hillion and Blockmans, 'From Self-Doubt to Self-Assurance' (no. 50).

8 Which Lessons to Learn from an Era of Surprise? Key Findings and Implications from the Dual Comparison

Christoph O. Meyer, Aviva Guttmann and Nikki Ikani

Introduction

The core premise of this book was that we can learn more about estimative intelligence and the prospects for anticipatory foreign policy through a double comparison of cases and actors rather than single actor case studies. What are the distinctive features of each of these cases so that we can avoid misapplying potential lessons learned to future crises that may only superficially look similar? Or is it possible to discern also common and potentially novel challenges across all three of these quite different cases? Might such challenges constitute more enduring characteristics of future threats and opportunities in foreign affairs? To what extent are these characteristics novel, quasi-structural features of contemporary security threats that together constitute an era of surprise alluded to in the title of the book? Or conversely, are most of the diagnostic challenges in these recent cases well known from previous case studies and enquiries going back to the Cold War era, with the real problem being the inability to remember and update previous lessons? Which aspects of intelligence production and use are the most challenging for all three polities at the heart of our study? And what does this tell us about the most important lessons yet to be learned, the failures of previous attempts to reform and internalise lessons, or indeed the nature of common new challenges facing the three polities? Alternatively, can we discern significant differences between these three polities in how they handled some of the challenges in estimative intelligence production and use? If so, are any weaknesses and strengths identified unique to these polities given the way they organise, resource and target their intelligence and foreign policy? Or could practitioners in Brussels, Berlin and London benefit from learning innovative lessons from each other or mitigate each other's weaknesses through closer collaboration?

This chapter seeks to answer these questions by drawing on the evidence and arguments presented throughout this volume and in closely related publications of the underlying INTEL research project, including the case timelines based on open sources. It builds on the theoretical discussion in Chapter 1, in which we have outlined the normative model of anticipatory foreign policy, the taxonomy of surprise, the overview of performance criteria together with mitigating or aggravating factors, and the discussion of underlying problems and challenges of organisational learning. This chapter is structured into three sections: the first section is organised around the three cases – the Arab uprisings, ISIS's rise to power, and the Ukraine crisis – in order to discern which aspect made each of them particularly challenging to track, explain and forecast, and to analyse commonalities and differences in the nature and level of surprise experienced by our three actors. The second section then directs the focus to the comparative performance of the three polities mentioned above, bearing in mind the prevailing conditions at the time. Can we discern substantial differences in performance and the underlying causes of it across these three actors? What are their relative strengths and weaknesses? The third section then turns to the challenge of identifying and learning the right lessons from these cases as well as from each other. Which lessons have these actors already learned after the close succession of crises between 2010 and 2014? And which lessons are yet to be correctly identified or learned in a lasting way? Finally, we discuss the implications for future research in intelligence studies and foreign policy arising from our key findings and arguments.

What Made these Cases Challenging to Estimative Intelligence and Created Surprise?

We found that the severity of the diagnostic challenges presented by each case could much better explain the scope and scale of surprise experienced by analysts and decision-makers than the structural features or capacities of the three polities. In other words, the variability in surprise between cases was significantly higher than those between the three polities. This could not necessarily be expected given that the UK intelligence community is better resourced and the intelligence-policy system is generally judged to be more capable than in Germany and far more than in the EU according to the literature.[1] Yet these supposed advantages did not help UK intelligence producers and consumers to be substantially less surprised than those of either Germany or the EU. Our desk research indicates that even the US as the most ambitious and well-resourced Western intelligence and foreign policy community did not fare that much better with respect to the cases of surprise experienced. The only exception in relative terms was the EU as the, on average, most surprised actor across all cases. But this might have been expected given the upheaval of establishing the new External Action Service at the time and the EU's distinct comparative disadvantage in terms of mandate, decision-making structures, and means of intelligence collection. We will return to these differences, relative strengths and weaknesses and the lessons these polities could learn from each other in sections 3 and 4. In the following we shall explore why these three cases generated divergent rather than uniform levels of surprise.

The main explanation is the degree of novelty of the events that transpired compared to previous patterns of behaviour and recent cases involving neighbouring or otherwise similar states. Our least surprising case, ISIS's rise to power had significant precedence in so far as Western actors had experienced in Iraq and Afghanistan that insurgent guerrilla movements could capitalise on resentment and grievances against non-Muslim foreigners and against other religious or ethnic communities in the country when given

Table 8.1 Overview of degrees of surprise and key causes across cases

Dimension	Arab uprisings	ISIS's rise to power	Ukraine/Russia
Nature of surprise across three actors	Significant surprise in terms of dissonance, scope and spread	Partial surprise in terms of dissonance and scope, some differences in spread	Complete surprise in terms of dissonance, but divergence in terms of scope and spread
Collection challenge	Significant reliance on traditional HUMINT (too) closely related to incumbent regimes, focus on mainstream parties instead of growing opposition	Lack of presence on the ground, particularly Syria; collection focus elsewhere (al-Qaeda) and limited own resources to monitor threat and US dependence	Lack of intelligence from Putin's inner circle, source selection biases in terms of opposition actors rather than grassroots actors driving the Euromaidan
Analytical challenge	Understanding of impact of social media on eruption and spread of popular movements; understanding of role of security/armed forces; break from previous patterns of oppression	Understanding the interplay between events in Iraq/Syria; uncritical reporting on Iraqi army; gauging ISIS tactics and degree/source of support	Conflicting signals about Russian intentions regarding Ukraine; dynamic interplay between events in Kyiv and Moscow; novelty of annexation
Receptivity challenge	Prioritisation of warnings affected by political considerations arising from relations with regimes and belief that previous patterns of stability would continue	Discordant policy agenda and Iraq fatigue (UK); deferral to the US and UK; considered initially low geographic and threat priority	EU strong policy commitments and geopolitical blind spots; UK/Germany deferral to EU and constructive relations with Russia

the ideological, material and political opportunity. Professional observers from inside and outside of government were generally aware of the sectarian tensions created by the al-Maliki government in Iraq, particularly between 2010–14. Equally it could be expected from previous and recent cases that instability and escalating civil war from 2011 would create opportunities for jihadist groups. The emergence of ISIS as the most dominant group, the speed and extent of their military successes, and their strategy of building a caliphate did come as a surprise as documented in Chapter 3, but, overall, this case is best described as a partial and more tactical surprise rather than a strategic surprise given what Western analysts had learned about the region since 2003.

In comparison, one of the main reasons why the Arab uprisings were considered more surprising related to the significant discontinuity presented by the speed of the regional contagion of instability that challenged many of the authoritarian governments in the region within the space of a few months – rather than whether specific rulers managed to stay in power or not. Western analysts may have expected some of these regimes, such as Egypt under Mubarak, to be more vulnerable to a rising build-up of resentment even if the timing of such a challenge was uncertain. However, there had been a long period of authoritarian stability in which regional rulers supported by their security forces and the army had managed to quell or appease previous protests. This expectation was not unreasonable as the survival of a number of regimes demonstrates, such as Bouteflika's power in Algeria, the continued rule of Mohammed VI of Morocco, or the bloody crackdown on the 2011 uprisings in Bahrain. The key surprising feature remains the forcefulness of the protests for more democracy and justice happening either at the same time or in close succession in the region, facilitated by and in some cases supported by elements or large parts of the security apparatus. Given these novel features in relation to recent history of the region, the Arab uprisings and particularly their tactical features did come as a significant surprise to most of the experts and decision-makers.

Finally, Russia's formal annexation of Crimea into its own territory was made possible through a surprise-enabled military operation vis-à-vis both Kyiv and Western capitals. To use special forces and regular troops to annex the territory of a sovereign country was a stark departure from fundamental principles of international law and treaties guaranteeing Ukrainian sovereignty that Russia itself had signed. It differed from Russian behaviour in other so-called frozen conflicts as well as its incursion into Georgian territory in 2008 or indeed previous ways in which Russia tried to pressure Ukraine through threatening hikes in the costs of gas or imposing trade restrictions. However, the Ukraine/Russia case also demonstrates that there is some scope for interpreting the degree of historical precedence of continuity and discontinuity differently.

252

In the eyes of some Eastern European states, the Russo-Georgian War of 2008 had created a clear historical precedent of Russia being prepared to act in a far more aggressive way than previously to assert control over Western-leaning countries in its neighbourhood and even to threaten their territorial sovereignty. Similarly, we have learned that already in 2008 the UK intelligence community considered Crimea as a potential next target. However, this did not enable the production of better intelligence nor avoid surprise among leaders.

What were the underlying and cross-cutting causes of surprise? In the case of the Arab uprisings it is widely acknowledged by the interviewees that they did not fully appreciate the depth of resentment and grievances felt in the countries that we selected for this study. These were related to rising inequality, rampant corruption and loss of job opportunities. As argued in Chapter 2, this was not necessarily apparent from standard socio-economic indicators and analysts had little previous understanding of who would lead any protest movements. The same is true for the Euromaidan protests that erupted after President Yanukovych's U-turn over signing the association agreement with the EU. European observers had failed to appreciate how narrow the power basis of Yanukovych among local elites had become, the extent of public dissatisfaction with corruption and the important role of grassroots actors rather than those discredited opposition actors behind the Orange Revolution. Without these protests and their fall-out, President Yanukovych would not have fled the country and Russia would probably not have intervened in the way it did as we argue in Chapter 4. So even in the case of a military threat that might be seen as a conventional challenge to intelligence, grassroots protests played a key causal role. ISIS's rise to power is somewhat different insofar as it was partially caused by the public protests in Syria as part of the Arab uprisings as well as the deep resentment, grievances and fears of Sunnis and former Ba'athists. While it was not a surprise that the policies of the al-Maliki government would alienate many Sunnis, the depth of the resentment and fear was not well understood. A major reason for surprise was related to the low prioritisation of Iraq in the foreign political agenda-setting at the time. This resulted in a lack of sources and resources on the ground and a limited degree of receptivity for warnings related to ISIS's rise to power. Another cause of surprise was that structures for efficient inter-institutional cooperation were not yet in place, which contrasted with the cross-border operation and threat posed by ISIS.

One of the reasons why diplomats and intelligence analysts struggled to accurately and timely identify the growth and likely impact of the currents of popular discontent is undetected or unaddressed source biases. Western analysts had not sufficiently updated their networks of contacts and informants to include younger activists and civil society actors and organisations. Instead, they tended to rely on their relations to local establishment actors in MENA countries with a substantial focus on counterterrorism. These sources were prone to over-optimism in what they told Western analysts about their ability to detect and control extremist movements, but they were also themselves genuinely surprised by the developments on 'the street'. Interviewees said that this also affected regional powers such as France and Italy which had cultivated contacts to the security apparatus and were therefore hearing even more optimistic versions of what those actors were (erroneously) telling their leaders. A former UK official drew comparisons to similar lessons identified, but apparently forgotten, from Sir Anthony Parson's post-mortem for the FCO concerning the fall of the Shah when the UK Embassy in Tehran had allowed itself to get too close to the regime to the detriment of opposition and street-level sources. In the case of correctly assessing ISIS's growing strength and Iraqi army vulnerabilities, Western analysts were again too reliant on over-optimistic reports from their allies in government. They lacked the ability to verify, challenge and complement such intelligence as a result of limited access to non-elite or establishment sources on the ground. With the mounting civil war in Syria for instance, most embassies had been evacuated, Western news media had problems reporting from the ground, and informants could not be met due to the high-risk environment. Similarly, many EU member states struggled to gain reliable information about what was happening in Crimea and the Donbas at the height of tensions and actual fighting, whilst others, such as Poland, benefited in intelligence terms from its 2011 decision to open a new consulate in Sevastopol.

A second reason for the difficulties in correctly assessing the popular sentiment that might motivate support of protests and armed insurgency was the limitations in terms of processing and analysing open sources from both old (legacy) and new (social) media platforms and correctly gauging their likely impact. These were underutilised not only as an important source of information about shifting social, political and military dynamics that might have compensated somewhat for the lack of direct access to sources on the ground. More fundamentally, it was underestimated how communication technologies and media would cumulatively affect political mobilisation and conflict dynamics. The growth in the ownership of mobile phones and social media use and reach enabled young protesters to organise and mobilise on a scale that would have been impossible only five years earlier. This outflanked government censors and the security apparatus, as evidenced, for instance, in the role of social media in building the We Are All Khaled Said movement that kick-started events in Egypt. This change was complemented by the important role of Qatar-government financed Al Jazeera and other Arabic-speaking media in making visible and giving legitimacy to the protests and their successful impact in Tunisia across the region in a way that would have been inconceivable ten years earlier.

Similarly, ISIS's success in terms of its psychological warfare designed to weaken enemies' willingness to fight would have been far less effective without social media platforms and amplification via traditional media, some of it even encouraged by Western actors and sources in the mistaken assumption that portrayals of extreme violence would backfire on ISIS. Furthermore, ISIS used various web-based communication channels to recruit new members, such as Snapchat, Kik, Twitter, ASK.fm, Facebook, YouTube, WhatsApp and others, and to showcase the 'success story' of the caliphate and the lifestyle of a foreign fighter. Similarly, the success of the Euromaidan protests three years later was substantially facilitated by grassroots activists and bloggers using new communication technology such as encrypted messaging applications. Intelligence agencies could not have been expected to immediately curtail ISIS's online reach (since this would have needed the involvement of private companies), but they realised rather late how social media provided jihadi recruitment and radicalisation with a new dimension and effectiveness. These social media channels were typically used by younger generations. Many older intelligence analysts were less familiar with them and could not understand the impact of the content, particularly acts of extreme violence previously seen as counterproductive, on some young people. Furthermore, technical tools and analytical methods which could make sense of a new large body of data were still under development and not yet broadly in use in 2010/2011.[2] While some countries such as the UK were further ahead in paying attention to the role of social media in the case of ISIS, Western analysts struggled to fully understand these technology-enabled protest movements and underestimated the susceptibility of their own citizens to them.

A third common diagnostic difficulty was related to the challenge of understanding and projecting the impact of the interplay and dynamics between neighbouring countries. This played a role in all three of our cases even if not all three polities were affected equally. In the case of the Arab uprisings, the speed and degree of regional contagion was greatly facilitated by the reach of legacy and new media in the common language of Arabic. In the case of ISIS, some analysts and diplomats, particularly in Germany and the EU, struggled to understand how insurgent groups used the civil war in Syria to regroup and rebuild and moved with ease across borders until their military successes prompted their declaration of a caliphate spanning territory across Iraq and Syria. The extent of the interconnections between both conflicts and the permeability of the traditional borders were under-appreciated until after ISIS's rapid expansion in the summer of 2014, which prompted, for instance, Germany to form a taskforce covering both countries. In the case of Ukraine, what analysts struggled to fully appreciate was how the success of the Euromaidan and the potential departure of Yanukovych were likely to be perceived in Moscow. This means that delegations and embassies in Moscow were not asked to explore specifically what Russia's reaction might be to developments in Ukraine, whilst analysts based in Kyiv were not specifically asked how decisions and dynamics might impact on Russian interests. A common cause of these diagnostic difficulties is insufficient and sluggish mechanisms for joining up country expertise, regional analysis and policy development. Too often, intelligence analysis as well as diplomatic reporting follows the boundaries created by international law, policies and organigrams. In Germany, the UK and the EU there are 'country desks' which are in charge of reporting separately about specific countries. These country experts are the core contact points which link embassy or intelligence reporting about a specific country. This country reporting typically happens disconnected from reporting about neighbouring countries, which in turn is tied to another country desk. Some intelligence agencies additionally have thematic foci, for instance in the form of a counterterrorism unit which looks at various regions from a specific angle. However, this is the exception rather than the rule and we found little inter-institutional cooperation between country experts and thematic units.

The problem of too much analysis happening within country silos and thus creating blind spots for some political, ethnic and strategic actions that cross these borders is not just an artefact of international law and a convenient category for the structuring of organisations and expertise. It is also a symptom of a fourth root cause of diagnostic difficulties seen in our cases, namely Western biases in political thought about the workings and role of political and security institutions. It might be thought of as a form of institutional mirror-imaging. The latter term is well known as a cognitive trap of intelligence analysis whereby analysts make up gaps in evidence about an adversary's plans and intentions by assuming that the adversary might think the same way they do: 'What would I do in this situation?' is maybe a useful question to ask oneself when applied to someone operating with a similar socialisation and worldview, but it tends to lead analysts astray when this is not the case. Most Western analysts are socialised in their political thinking and training to give a certain meaning and significance to constitutions, rule of law, ministers or the army and to analyse their performance and capacities in a certain way. The silent, often implicit or intuitive assumption that institutions in foreign countries work at least roughly similarly to those in Western states can lead to significant errors in current and estimative intelligence. This failure to understand where power lies and how it works can easily lead to a misconstrued assessment of the stability of government, the power dynamics between actors, who is taking the most consequential decisions, and which foreign source should be considered as authoritative and trustworthy. In many developing countries, key institutions such as ministries, the judiciary and the armed forces play quite different roles within a political system than in Western democracies and are frequently shaped or bypassed by tribal, ethnic and religious loyalties. It might not actually be the Prime Minister or President who holds power but tribal or religious leaders, warlords, heads of secret police services, elite military formations, militias or criminal syndicates.

For instance, the failure to properly appreciate the power dynamics and fears between the majority Pashtun and other ethnic minorities is one of the root causes for why the Western-supported government and armed forces in Afghanistan failed to command sufficient support. In Syria, many analysts misjudged the ethnic power base of President al-Assad, its pervasiveness and viability in state structures, and why keeping him in power was seen as an issue of survival for Alawites and other minority groups in the country. In the case of Ukraine, the role of oligarchs and their alliances with Russian speakers or ethnic Russians was similarly important to understand the main power-brokers in Crimea and the Donbas and why local authorities, parliaments and stationed armed forces gave up control so easily in response to the Russian-orchestrated coup. Similarly, in Western democracies civilian control of the military is a given, and militaries can rely on obedience, loyalty and shared national identity among soldiers. Their effectiveness can be assessed in terms of the number of soldiers, their level of training and skills and of course the weapon systems at their disposal. In stark contrast, the Iraqi army turned out to be strong on paper and according to its Western trainers but much weaker in reality when confronted with a real test of its resolve to fight ISIS. We saw the same dynamic of national armies folding against a numerically supposedly weaker force after the withdrawal of US forces from Afghanistan in 2021 even if some of the contributing factors, such as the impact of the withdrawal of US logistical support, were different. In the case of the Arab uprisings, the issue was not so much the weakness of the armed forces, but that they were a political actor in their own right – a state within the state – who under some conditions were ready to shift their loyalties away from regimes as we have seen in Egypt first with President Mubarak and then, less surprisingly, with President Morsi. In all three cases, Western analysts have misjudged, albeit to varying degrees, the capacities, roles and likely stance of the regular armed forces when faced with mass protests comprising their own sons and daughters. This contrasts with the role of special forces that are directly linked to power elites.

Furthermore, in all three cases estimative intelligence was affected by resourcing priorities set by political masters and which, by their nature, are largely if not completely outside of the control of organisations and units charged with producing intelligence. This is not the same as to lament the politicisation of the analytical process familiar from the US context, but to point to two overlapping ways in which political decisions and discourses have affected the gathering, analysis and communication of estimative intelligence in our cases. Prior to the manifestation of the threat none of the crises, with the possible exception of the Russian attack on Ukraine, was deemed a high collection and analysis priority for our three polities. Most crises occurred in countries considered to be a medium priority, and the type of threat event had not been singled out in functional and resourcing terms for in-depth monitoring and regular reporting. This is not to say that more resources would necessarily have made a difference to the surprise experienced, but more eyes on the ground could have increased the granularity, timeliness and potentially the actionability of intelligence and diplomatic reporting, particularly in the cases of ISIS and Ukraine. For instance, since 2001 and particularly 2004 UK decision-makers had shifted an extraordinary amount of analytical resources to counterterrorism with the net effect of substantially reducing the capabilities for the analysis of Russia before the Ukraine crisis, as critics cited by Rimmer in Chapter 6 argue. Similarly, Germany did not consider Iraq nor indeed Syria of direct strategic importance and, unsurprisingly, lacked country and area expertise of the region. Germany was also slow to respond to requests from the intelligence community for more resources in 2012 and 2013 given growing risk indications. The EU had tried to establish the External Action Service on the cheap during a

259

period of post-financial crisis austerity, creating a service with too few personnel in relation to the money it was spending, and too few country and security experts. It was partly as a result of this lack of expertise and adequate structures and procedures where they could have mattered most – in DG NEAR, DG Trade and an emerging EEAS – that the EU ended up being the most surprised polity in the Arab uprisings and the Ukraine case.

Finally, in subtle ways governments' policy agendas and informal signals shift the focus of intelligence producers towards certain risks and away from others. Knowledge producers, even if they are not working on policy themselves, are highly aware of what the policy and current political agenda is, which kinds of assessment are in demand and likely welcome, and which, conversely, are more likely to be either ignored or resisted. In the case of UK intelligence attention to Iraq and Syria at the time, there was a strong interest in al-Qaeda and the risks of terrorist attacks at home, not in state instability, mass atrocity risks, and their secondary effects. There was a sense of Iraq fatigue amongst foreign policy communities generating a strong desire for the US military withdrawal from Iraq to be a success. This in turn depended on the stability of the al-Maliki government and for the training of the Iraqi national army to be a success. And indeed, American reports made regularly available to UK analysts showed that everything was going to plan with the training and gave little indication that the army was far from cohesive. This led one former UK official to say that 'we believed our [US and UK] own propaganda'. In such a political environment, and given the reliance on the heavily engaged US, it would require a lot of autonomy, motivation and potentially even courage from British intelligence analysts and their superiors to invest time in following up on some of the open-source reporting that raised doubts about the combat readiness of the Iraqi army. It would have required challenging US reports and questioning the effectiveness of its training efforts through a far less committed and more junior ally.

In the case of the EU, the leadership was interested in assessments related to the desired outcome of the Ukrainian leadership being ready to sign the AA and member states feeling that the country had fulfilled the European Council's conditions for moving forward – rather than engaging in contingency planning for a range of negative scenarios such as non-signature, instability and Russian military aggression, especially at a time of seeking Russian money and cooperation in Syria. In the case of the Arab uprisings, forecasts of authoritarian instability were also considered as highly inconvenient at the time given the beneficial relations that some member states had with regimes in the region, not least as a consequence of the post 9/11 'war against terrorism'. For Germany, Iraq appeared to be a problem for the US and the UK primarily, and it was unclear which kind of threats would be relevant to German interests and citizens. It is hard to show that these political signals about what was welcome and unwelcome were causally decisive to the degree of surprise, but they did create varying distraction and friction for knowledge producers. While UK and German interviewees stressed that they did not change assessments to suit political priorities and were not too afraid to speak 'truth to power', there were more instances of EU officials, typically mid-ranking ones, who said they encountered some push-back from superiors against the reporting or from member states in the system, including attempts to remove 'client-states' from watchlists. We also came across indications that superiors, not just in the EU but also in Germany, did not reflect the expert consensus in their own house when they advised ministers or went public with their assessment.

How the UK, Germany and the EU Handled Estimative Intelligence

In Chapter 1 we identified some of the most common underlying causes that affected performance across all three polities in the collection, analysis, communication and political processing of estimative intelligence. Based on the empirical findings from across the volume we can now look more closely at differences in performance between the three polities and their underlying causes. This actor-focused comparison may point to areas where closer collaboration could help to mitigate their distinctive weaknesses or where learning from each other could help to spread their relative strengths. In the following we will discuss each polity separately but will also draw comparisons to the other two polities

Table 8.2 Distinctive strengths and weaknesses for warning-response for each polity

	Strengths	Weaknesses
United Kingdom	• Strong coordination and prioritisation structures (NSC/NSA) for intelligence requirements, crises and strategies • Well-resourced cross-governmental structure for all-source intelligence assessment via JIO and JIC • Strong learning culture to drive improvements through internal as well as external post-mortems	• Politically salient threats can lead to over-prioritisation of intelligence collection efforts • Written culture and orientation towards a consensus product can hamper the impactful articulation of minority views • Lack of clear accountability for acting on warnings at working and departmental level
Germany	• Strong political commitment to conflict and crisis prevention • Good capacities for structural prevention through development and peacebuilding • Strong area expertise inside and particularly outside of government (academia, NGOs) for warning	• Insufficient political and media attention to intelligence/security threats • Cultural, parliamentary and organisational obstacles to setting up and learning from post-mortems • Weak structures for prioritisation of intelligence requirements across key government ministries
European Union	• Collection capacities through country and thematic experts, delegations, GEOINT and (in principle) broad intelligence support by member states' services • Alternative hypotheses and potential for warning for free through multinational experts and divergent receptivity • Drive to learn from crises through investment in early warning and response system and hybrid fusion cell	• Country silos reinforced by institutional policy silos creates geographical and security blind spots • Nationality-conditioned receptivity problems to inconvenient and warning intelligence, exacerbated by lack of protection for seconded EEAS officials • Limitations in resources, processes, structures, mandate and unanimity requirement hinder definition of intel priorities and rank threats

to highlight some of their most distinctive strengths and weaknesses (see Table 8.2 for results).

The UK: Strong Joined Intelligence Production but Prioritisation Problems

In relative terms, the UK was handling warning-response problems posed by the three cases slightly better than the other two polities, although not to the extent that one might have expected given the state's reputation in intelligence and foreign policy, its significant collection and analysis capacities and privileged relations with the US as the world's best-funded intelligence community. One might argue that the UK had little scope to distinguish itself in the case of the Arab uprisings as these were diagnostically a very difficult if not impossible challenge for estimative and warning intelligence, as argued by Ikani and Rimmer in this volume. However, the UK was only a little bit better than Germany and the EU in understanding and anticipating ISIS's rise to power and did not perform significantly better in terms of anticipating or making sense of Russian actions in Ukraine compared to the other two actors. The findings related to these two cases jar with the evidence from interviews that the UK has substantial strengths in its institutional set-up, its culture, collection and analytical capacities. In many ways the EU has tried to replicate key aspects of the British model, such as the JIC and the assessments staff, in the formative stage of creating and developing SITCEN/INTCEN under its first British director William Shapcott. But also, many German practitioners and experts invoke the British model as one to learn from if not to emulate, as the chapter by Schlie and Lutsch underlines. A key strength of the UK system is the learning and accountability culture surrounding intelligence and defence, including post-mortems conducted through reviews led either by specialised committees of the House of Commons and the House of Lords, or inquiries led by eminent experts such as the Nicoll, Franks, Butler or Chilcot reports. The Butler report in particular led to a number of significant changes to improve assessment, including the development of analytical capability through the creation of the Professional Head of Intelligence Assessment. These inquiries can draw on wide expertise from academia and think tanks and substantial interest from the news media, particularly in the rare form of public hearings, as was the case with the Iraq inquiry. The UK learning culture is thus strongly linked to the external environment, which provides an incentive for both parliamentarians as well as journalists to specialise in this area – a marked contrast to the EU and Germany.[3]

Another strength of the UK system is its flexibility and ability to work, often informally, across departmental boundaries. This is particularly an asset when it comes to emerging crises, when the intelligence community and government needs to draw quickly on staff from across and sometimes outside of the system to improve its ability to keep track of an escalating threat. Officials seconded to or working on papers for the JIC are often reminded that they are not there to act as representatives let alone lobbyists for their host ministry, even if such guidance does not eliminate such influence altogether as we have seen in the Treasury's interest in economically profitable relations with particular countries such as China. The involvement of the same individual senior officials in the production of JIC papers who are responsible for policy decisions that the assessments are intended to inform may raise eyebrows from a US perspective. It does, however, increase the chance that intelligence assessments remain policy-relevant without necessarily overstepping the sensitive line to policymaking policed by the JIC chair. Indeed, one of the strengths of the UK system is the management of the relationship between officials and decision-makers, which offers officials plenty of opportunities for interactions with more senior customers up the chain, providing them with a good sense of where policymaking is and how consumers 'tick'. After the 2004 Butler Review, safeguards have been strengthened to ensure the integrity and independence of intelligence assessment and promote vigorous internal discussion and challenge to avoid intelligence being politically instrumentalised and altered. One element of this safeguard is the JIC's strong orientation towards finding a consensus about analytical judgements among officials and expressing this on paper rather than through oral briefings, thus reducing the risks of decision-makers cherry-picking divergent intelligence assessments from various producers. This seems to explain why we have not come across any clear cases of politicisation of the analytical process in the UK such as overt pressure to change assessments or senior officials overruling the professional view of their in-house experts to suit political agendas – in contrast to some of this happening in the EU and Germany.

However, a potential weakness of the UK system for estimative and warning intelligence is its dependence on the integrity, credibility and motivation of a small number of senior officials such as the JIC Chair and the newly created National Security

Advisor as the secretary of the National Security Council. This is particularly true after the 2010 creation of the National Security Council helped to establish clearer priorities in terms of on what issues intelligence assessment was required. As Rimmer writes: 'whilst priorities are essential to drive work, they are also limiting in terms of the effort that is likely to be applied to lower priority issues. This can be where the JIC Chair's specific early warning responsibility can be important – the ability to, metaphorically, tap the Prime Minister on the shoulder and say "you haven't asked me about this, but I think you should know . . .".' The UK system does not have the US equivalent of officers specialised on warning (a role controversially abolished under US President Obama) nor a committee that only does conflict warning as we are seeing in the EU and Germany. The risk with the UK set-up is therefore that too little official attention is available for the analysis of the threats of tomorrow compared to the demands of current crises, operations and the political priorities. Rimmer cites the criticism of the Intelligence and Security Committee that the UK may have devoted a disproportionate amount to the threat of terrorism, leaving resources for monitoring or detecting other threats too stretched. Furthermore, the UK's close cooperative relations with the US as part of the Five Eyes agreements create incentives for specialisation and deferring to the more senior and well-resourced partner. This can turn into a problem in situations when US intelligence turns out to be skewed by political imperatives, as was the case in the over-optimistic assessments of the US-trained Iraqi army prior to 2014. The UK intelligence community was not resourced to provide the granularity needed for actionable estimative intelligence and tactical warning about insurgent groups in Iraq and the effectiveness of Iraqi army that might have contradicted or complemented US assessments.

While the British system excels in working well under crisis conditions with strong coordination facilitated by coordination mechanisms such as COBR, it does not provide enough clarity about who leads on warnings and preventive action. As one former UK official said 'when we get warning information, we are all very good at Whitehall in passing the ball to each other, but no one thinks it is their job to score'. The issue of accountability for warning, prioritising warning and acting on warning – or indeed deciding not to do so – is one of wicked problems of warning-response, not least because the risk is high of creating asymmetric incentives for or against warning. If officials worry about negative career implications for missing a crisis, they may tend to over-warn, whereas if they feel apathy or even hostility from their clients to early warning they may not warn at all or only too late when a crisis is already in the media. Similarly, decision-makers in the UK may feel incentivised to share the responsibility and blame for handling warnings with others on a committee which can create a bias against acting early as most warnings are initially expressing a minority view. The awareness that British media may well cover intelligence, warning or policy failures extensively and the strong possibility of post-mortem inquiries in the British system may create pendulum swings in the political climate that help or hinder warnings and receptivity to them. One former official opined that the pendulum had swung too far against warning: 'Arguably we have been more criticised over the last couple of decades for giving unnecessary warnings [. . .] There was a long shadow over the system still [because of the failure to find WMD in Iraq], that your confidence level has to be very high before you are flashing red-lights and I think this is a problem.'[4]

The EU: Strong Country Expertise, but Policy Blind Spots and Receptivity Problems

A puzzling contrast emerges between the EU's capacity to produce often highly accurate and timely strategic and warning intelligence and prescient reporting from delegations on the ground, and the limited receptivity to and impact of such assessments. While one should not give too much weight to a single prescient analysis from INTCEN such as the paper predicting an Arab uprising-type event in 2007 as a 'worst case scenario',[5] there was at least another such report that correctly anticipated the probability of Yanukovych's U-turn before Vilnius followed by public protests.[6] It shows the EU has some strengths in providing expert analysis regarding the stability of key countries in its neighbourhood. Even though it lacked the ability to send or recruit spies or intercept signal intelligence, these shortfalls were not fatal in either of the three countries and did not account for major differences in the EU being surprised when compared to the UK or Germany. Indeed, few member states can compete with the broad network of EU delegations across the world, sometimes reinforced further by civilian and military missions, and the combined capacities of the European Commission and the External Action Service in terms of technical expertise in areas of relevance to external affairs, such as energy, transport, the environment, immigration, digital space and more. On top of this, the EU can draw through its seconded officers on at least some of the analysis by member states and can use informal channels to gain further information beyond what is shared on paper. However, during the period of investigation between 2010–14 many of the assets could not be used fully because of the upheaval and shortages created in the process of setting up and bedding down the External Action Service under its first double-hatted High Representative/Vice President as Conrad writes. The EU's greatest asset is the diversity of officials who bring not only significant in-depth country or thematic expertise to their roles but also diverse worldviews and perspectives rooted in their national training and socialisation. The benefits can be illustrated by a mid-level official from a Baltic country warning about Russian action in Georgia a short time before it happened[7] or the Foreign Ministers of Poland and Sweden warning their colleagues about Russia's intensions as Meyer and Ikani write here. Given its multinational nature, the EU system produces 'alternative hypotheses for free', namely without the need to set up red-cells and devil's advocates. It also provides a degree of protection against group-think and politicisation in the intelligence production process and promotes greater objectivity. The first British Head of SITCEN wondered if the UK's Iraq dossier would have 'got past first base if it had to be prepared jointly with a couple of other European services'.[8]

Yet, even high-quality intelligence often struggled to get noticed and fully accepted by the senior decision-makers of EU institutions and particularly those of member states. One might argue that the shortcomings in receptivity are simply because the EU's own products do not matter greatly in political debates in Brussels and national capitals. However, this is not necessarily true given the accounts we have heard of warnings or inconvenient reporting from EU delegations being met with a rather hostile rejection, even including requests from superiors in Brussels to alter them. As Conrad alludes to and our own interviews confirmed, the annual EU country-watchlist suffered at times from influential member states putting pressure on officials to remove certain 'client-states' from the list. It should be noted that this kind of behaviour is not unique to the EU, but rather is a typical feature of consensus-based international organisations such as the United Nations and the OSCE.[9] What could be an asset for intelligence production if used well in a specialised professional framework independent from political interference, namely diverse national viewpoints, becomes too often a liability in creating either low receptivity to or highly asymmetric estimative intelligence. It underlines that estimative intelligence in general and warnings are strongly influenced by the rules, incentives and dynamics governing foreign policymaking. This means that as long as unanimity requirements in CFSP continue, EU intelligence production and use will be influenced and hampered by national advocacy.

The EU's production of estimative intelligence also suffered from some unique institutional challenges, namely the split of policies between the European Commission, and within it particularly the Directorates General of Trade, Neighbourhood and Enlargement Relations (DG NEAR), and the European External Action Service (EEAS). The perennial challenge of working across country silos was made worse by policy silos as the European Neighbourhood Policy was operated by different players according to different rules and with different technical expertise (in DG NEAR and DG Trade) than the Common Foreign and Security Policy via the European External Action Service. There is plenty of literature on the teething problems and continuing pathologies of the EEAS, but from the perspective of estimative intelligence one key problem is the lack of safeguards for seconded national officials in the EEAS. They might face a dilemma if their assessment or warning conflicts with national policy agendas or worldviews. As a consequence, they might fear negative career repercussions at home. The second problem is continuing challenges to make the EU's external action more security-sensitive (or geopolitical) when those parts of the EU with the authority and the budgets lack the technical background, training, incentives and personnel resources to think about and act against security threats. Finally, the EU remains dependent on member states for the sharing of finished intelligence as it lacks autonomous collection capacities and legal authority in sensitive areas. This sharing is limited in terms of classification levels because of suspicions particularly among some net-contributor states that the Brussels information infrastructure is vulnerable to penetration by hostile powers or at risk of leaking by some member states. As a result, intelligence is often shared least and regarded with most suspicion by peers when it would be most valuable. Moreover, the EU sometimes struggles to get the personnel with the right skillset and training for intelligence analysis necessary to build a highly respected EU brand of analysis and estimative intelligence, as Conrad writes. It remains dependent on member states wanting the EU to succeed and investing accordingly in it through seconding personnel and sharing valuable intelligence. This problem is mirrored when it comes to the appointment of its top leadership. This has become apparent in member states' appointment of Catherine Ashton as the EU's first double-hatted High Representative. For all of her merits, she had neither the expertise, the networks nor the political backing of her predecessor Javier Solana. The fact that the EU eventually ended up on the sidelines in all three crises is an indication that the EU's main problem was neither the collection nor the analysis, but institutional pathologies and nationally conditioned resistance to inconvenient judgements.

Germany: Long-term Orientation to Prevention, but Weak Prioritisation and Coordination

Germany's performance in estimative intelligence and receptivity in the three cases was not substantially different in quality than either the EU or the UK. In the one case where it was lagging behind the UK, namely ISIS's rise to power, one might argue that this happened in a region not considered a strategic priority by the government. This priority setting could be criticised as short-sighted, not just in retrospect as some officials tried in vain for a long time to raise attention and resources for these countries. Only after the milestone successes of ISIS did the German government set up a taskforce to work across the two countries and surge resources related to it. In the case of Ukraine, Schlie and Lutsch argue in this volume that the German government had allowed the country to be 'pushed from the focus to the periphery of German diplomacy. In the European Union, the Ukraine question was not given the weight that it deserved despite its strategic importance.' While Germany did not perform any worse in anticipating the threat from Russia than either the EU or the UK, one might have had higher expectations of the country given its resources and interests in Ukraine and particularly in Russia. Even if the Ukraine/Russia crisis happened at an unfortunate moment for Germany given that it was in the middle of governmental change, Schlie and Lutsch alongside other German commentators argue that long-standing shortcomings of German intelligence and foreign policy structures were revealed by these crises. These commentators criticise the German intelligence and foreign policymaking system as not fit for the purpose of high-quality foresight, crisis preparedness and strategy-making.

One can identify three interlocking problems in the case of Germany. The first is the lack of sufficiently strong mechanisms for prioritising intelligence resources based on a strategic assessment of current and future threats. As Schlie and Lutsch write, Germany lacks the equivalent of a National Security Council as in the UK or the United States, a JIO/JIC as in the UK or a NIC/DNI as in the US. The structures for the production of authoritative all-source intelligence in which all the major agencies and perhaps even policy ministries, as in the UK, are involved do not exist. This leaves the burden on the BND with the monopoly for foreign secret intelligence and the Foreign Office for coordination. Yet, the practice of coalition government means that the Foreign Ministry and the Defence Ministry are often held by ministers from different parties and the cherished constitutional principle of *Ressortautonomie* makes cross-ministerial coordination more difficult than in Westminster systems where the Prime Minister can more easily appoint and dismiss ministers. Even relatively moderate attempts to strengthen coordination structures, such as beefing up the Federal Security Council, have often encountered substantial cross-party political resistance in the German Bundestag. This is not just because of partisan interests in raising the profile of the Foreign Ministry typically held by smaller parties, but also because of resistance against any 'centralisation' in the Federal Republic's political discourse for decades.

However, the deeper second problem is the prevalence of a substantial unease in German strategic and political culture with security and defence matters in parliamentary debates as well as in public discourse. While peace and development studies communities are well-institutionalised, -resourced and politically supported, security and defence policy communities in Germany feel that their calls for better coordination and resources often fail to get a lot of traction in parliament and news media discourse. There is still a strong societal resistance against 'militarism' and suspicions about the role and importance of intelligence. There is also deep reluctance to systemically consider the implications of a more hostile environment, where many state and non-state actors do not share the German view that military force has no political use or should only be considered as a last resort. German politicians feel, rightly or wrongly, the punishment of voters who are risk averse and often do not feel that foreign conflicts affect them. This view has started to change since 2015 but is still often used by politicians as a smokescreen to shy away from substantive debates about what needs to change. This environment creates political disincentives to regularly listen to strategic warnings and to wait for action until a crisis is visible for all to see. It can also lead on occasion to a politicisation of intelligence. This was the case with Foreign Minister Westerwelle's call for President al-Assad to go. While this was publicly backed by the Director of the BND when he argued that al-Assad's departure was inevitable within months, there are indications that some experts in his own house arrived at a different assessment.[10]

A third related weakness of the German system is the lack of a strong learning culture after crises or major policy failures generally, but particularly those in external affairs.[11] A number of efforts have been made since 2014 to strengthen early detection of crises, horizon-scanning and coordination structures. However, Schlie and Lutsch argue that the fundamental problems remain largely unresolved and that reforms have only been superficial. The learning exercises were led from the top of ministries rather than independent experts or authoritative figures with access to official documents or with public hearings of witnesses, as we frequently see in the UK.[12] Germany also lacks a freedom of information law as in the UK, so regular access to government documents generally is more difficult for news media, researchers, think tanks and NGOs than in the UK. As a result of the deficient learning mechanism and lack of media scrutiny, the German government tends to gloss over mistakes that were made. Instead, it focuses on those lessons that are relatively easy to implement by spending a little more and restructuring units within ministries, rather than tackling more fundamental problems with inter-ministerial structures, priority setting and strategy. This is made possible by the lack of parliamentarians who specialise in foreign and security affairs and who make it part of their political mission to improve German capacities and structures. Hence, while there are plenty of calls for Germany to learn from the UK and other experienced players, to work more closely with the EU in the framework of 'networked security' as Schlie and Lutsch write, it may take major attention-focusing events to prompt the kind of soul-searching and systematic review that would bring about the changes that are needed.

This is not to say that Germany does not have some strengths in estimative intelligence, warning and anticipatory policy. It embraced conflict prevention as a priority in foreign affairs earlier than others back in the early 2000s, and since 2014 and 2017 it has tried to learn lessons to that effect. It further invested substantial efforts into early detection, response and structural prevention of crises, whilst investing more into the German intelligence apparatus and the BND in particular. Germany has a strong network of peace research and area studies institutes that can complement the analysis of emerging crises. Relatively high-quality German language news coverage provides valuable information from some hard-to-reach countries. As a result, Germany is well-equipped for spotting what one might call crises of instability and structural prevention of violent conflict abroad, but it often struggles when preventive action requires difficult and potentially publicly visible political choices, such as selling arms to conflict parties, deploying troops, or more robust forms of diplomacy and statecraft. The positive flipside of lacking a UK culture of intensive media scrutiny related to intelligence and foreign policy is the creation of political space for preventive foreign policy in countries that are not strategic priorities. However, that quickly reaches limits, when, for instance, a country such as Russia is involved.

Learning to Learn from an Era of Surprise

What lessons should practitioners in Berlin, Brussels and London learn from the three major surprises between 2010 and 2014? Chapters 5–7 and the preceding section already contain some specific lessons, many of which are tailored to the specific institutional set-up, strategic culture, ambitions, vulnerabilities and capacities of each of the three polities. In the following, we will concentrate on identifying some of the overarching lessons that emerge from the analysis of the three cases discussed above, especially those that may have broader applicability to future threats.

The first lessons must be the crucial self-reflection that many Western analysts and decision-makers had settled into the post-Cold War 'normal' in Europe's neighbourhood, where instability may happen in some countries but regional order was shaped by a set of norms and rules. They were slow to recognise how structural changes created a higher degree of instability and a possibility of ruptures to create threats that Europeans were ill-equipped to manage. In retrospect, it becomes clearer that the 'era or surprise' cannot be reduced to one single novel feature, but the unexpected and rapid interplay of three factors, often cutting across national borders: (1) the growth in resentment of particularly younger people with corrupt, authoritarian and repressive governments in Europe's wider neighbourhood; (2) the huge potential of new communication technologies together with new media to mobilise, recruit, but also to intimidate and influence; and finally (3) the willingness and capacity of revisionist state and non-state actors to revive old or embrace new bold strategies that broke with fundamental norms and international law supported by Western powers. The operational lesson is to improve collection and analytical capacities related to these phenomena and to do so in a

273

way that does justice to their interconnectedness, rather than replicating or creating new methodological, policy or country silos. It requires closing the growing mismatch in the abundance of information and the analytical capacity to provide forward-looking assessment. Reform efforts should not just concentrate on better tools for the analysis of large amounts of data, but also look at the age profile and specific professional skills of analysts, broadening language skills and diversifying socio-economic and disciplinary backgrounds. Furthermore, intelligence services need to intensify their efforts and find new ways of accurately identifying, penetrating and analysing the decision-making structures and channels of state and non-state actors. This is particularly salient given the shortcomings of secret intelligence to discern the strategies and tactics of either Russia or ISIS.

Even more fundamentally, the era of surprise brings to the fore a central problem of estimative and warning intelligence: the tension between the challenges of identifying and understanding the patterns of normal behaviour of key actors and institutions and those associated with recognising growing indications or trends of political and social systems reaching potential tipping points that might create instability and paths towards a 'new normal'. It can be hard for country experts steeped in knowledge of history to overcome 'pattern bias' as the tendency to search for evidence which confirms pre-existing theories, particularly if their 'baseline of the normal' is defined in too broad and vague terms, so that underlying assumptions cannot be tested and genuinely novel developments are spotted too late. Improvements would also require at an organisational level a recognition that the goal of being alerted to the most severe, but possibly rare and unprecedented, threats in practice conflicts with achieving a 'high batting average' across forecasting cases favoured by 'superforecasters'.[13] Striking the right balance between false negatives and positives, between warning too soon and creating warning fatigue and warning too late, is a difficult and inescapable challenge as noted by scholars of strategic surprise such as Betts,[14] and has been found to be a distinct difficulty in the US intelligence production process.[15] Decades ago this prompted Grabo to argue that warning is a specialised function that should not be left to analysts preoccupied with serving the immediate needs of policymakers in current intelligence. This lesson was forgotten by the Obama administration, which abolished officers for warning in the National Intelligence Council.[16] Scholars specialising in foresight and future studies highlight the differences in approach between probabilistic and surprise-sensitive forecasting.[17] The latter requires specific techniques for suspending disbelief and premature cognitive closure in group discussions, drawing out hidden and implicit assumptions underlying interpretations, and constructing consequential, plausible and coherent scenarios of the future with the involvement of decision-makers.[18] This requires investments in the organisational structure. It involves systematically asking 'what if-questions' and considering what kind of indications one would expect to see if significant changes towards a radically different future were afoot.[19] Such indications would then need to be further monitored and analysed so that the mid- and long-term warnings can be transformed into concrete and actionable situational awareness for policymakers.

One can conceive of different methods of doing this, for example through new quantitative tools of gathering and analysing event data that can pick up, for instance, growing instances of human rights violations or protests in unusual locations that go beyond previous fluctuations at such specific locales. Yet, opportunities for 'big data' gathering and analyses should not be fetishised but juxtaposed by and combined with more intuitive and individual-based deep country or area expertise rooted in a sound specific knowledge of history, civilization, culture and language. Oftentimes events may appear unusual or unlikely against a recent history of five to ten years but may be far less surprising when set against events and experiences over a longer timeframe of decades that may still exist or resonate strongly in the memories of specific communities. Country experts need to keep their ears to the ground through either living in the region or regularly travelling there. To avoid conservative bias of country experts and interpretative blind spots shared by certain area studies communities, country experts need to be systematically challenged by junior experts and those with different training backgrounds who may be more inclined to see events as novel, or acquire different networks of sources, or employ different analytical lenses.

However, improving the accuracy of surprise-sensitive forecasting alone is unlikely to prevent decision-makers being surprised because it does not address the substantial receptivity challenges that warning sources need to overcome. Our earlier research has shown that a combination of factors need to come together for warnings to be listened to, prioritised and more likely to be heeded.[20] Warning is an exceptional and most difficult mode of intelligence-politics interaction as it expects 'producers' to provide 'consumers' with a 'product' that usually they did not request, whose central claims they do not like to believe, and which would be highly inconvenient and possibly unwelcome in its implications if accepted. In order to be heard, warnings need to stand out from the rest of the intelligence briefings and be recognised as such. They usually need to be articulated loudly and persistently enough, ideally orally or through multiple and rarely used channels, and originate from sources that are deemed highly authoritative and credible in the eyes of the decision-maker. Effective warning takes analysts to the edge of persuasion because they need to explicitly debunk some of the assumptions and worldviews that consumers may cling to.

Even more challenging, the best strategic warning needs to be specific and granular enough to be actionable. It should try to spell out when and in what way precisely a threat to the interests of political leaders, the state or the public may materialise. If being precise about the timing and scale of such threats is difficult, as we have seen to varying degrees in our three cases, warning intelligence should try to spell out wht kind of realistic preparatory, preventive or mitigating action, including closer monitoring of precursors, could be taken immediately to enhance preparedness, speed up reaction time and reduce the probability of undesirable futures. Estimative and warning intelligence would ideally come with the identification and explanation of factors inducive for Russia to change its posture and policy towards Ukraine or circumstances under which the loyalty of Ukrainian security forces to the state would be strengthened, how Sunni resentment in Iraq could decrease and how non-jihadist rebel groups in Syria could gain strength, or about how democratic transitions in MENA countries could develop in a more peaceful, less polarising and more inclusive direction. This intelligence could help policymakers and their operational advisors to advance specific unilateral or multilateral policies of risk prevention or mitigation.

For estimative intelligence to better support anticipatory foreign policy, not only analysts but also professional communities, ministries and senior decision-makers need to become better at listening and learning from their own successes and mistakes. In Chapter 1 we identified several forms discussed in the literature of how lesson learning takes place, particularly instrumental policy learning, organisational learning and social learning. Instrumental learning concerns lesson drawing from experience, generally aimed at adapting a policy with the aim of increasing its effectiveness. It concerns 'new understandings about the viability of policy interventions or implementation designs' and is focused on policy instruments.[21] The objects of such learning are policy programmes, instruments or tools. This volume has identified a number of such instrumental policy lessons. Chapter 2 on the Arab uprisings for example suggested that European institutions could improve the communication of and receptivity to 'upstream' communications of warnings from within the EEAS and Delegations. Chapter 4 suggested some instrumental learning possibilities, such as the improvement of collection capabilities on Russian intentions and policies, or the creation of a unit within the European External Action Service tasked with the assessment of the military and hybrid threat Russia poses in its entirety. The chapter also suggested improving cross-cutting, thematic or regional analyses to overcome the tendency for reporting in country silos that all three actors struggled with.

A related form of learning is organisational learning. It 'involves the aggregation of learning by multiple organisations and by multiple individuals acting either through organisations or independently of them'.[22] Governmental learning is a form that falls under such collective learning, as 'individually or collectively learned inferences from experience that get encoded into governmental institutions and decision-making procedures'. Governmental learning is more difficult than organisational learning according to Levy, 'because it involves the aggregation of learning by multiple organizations and by multiple individuals acting either through organisations or independently of them. Exactly how this works varies across different types of political systems.'[23] Post-mortems and public inquiries can be a good instrument for suggesting more encompassing lessons for organisations and systems of government to take on board, for creating cultures that encourage more dissent, challenge and diversity of thought as would be helpful in the EU or stronger mechanisms for organising analytical effort across government and defining foreign and security priorities as was recommended for Germany.

Finally, social learning concerns the modification of ideas and worldviews, ideas about the social construction of policy problems, the scope of policy, or policy goals.[24] Rather than the mere identification of lessons, social learning thus rather involves the establishment of 'relatively enduring alterations of thought or behavioural intentions concerned with the attainment (or revision) of policy objectives'.[25] This could be particularly relevant when surprises arose from socio-cultural blind spots rooted in deep-seated beliefs and assumptions derived from lessons learned from history or memories of more recent situations in the past.[26] In the case of the EU, we have seen how the European neighbourhood policy was strongly influenced by the success of the enlargement process and how the Commission struggled to systematically consider the inadvertent geopolitical risks and threats created by it. Or in the case of Germany, it would involve acknowledging the mistake of 'universalising lessons learnt from one's own history'[27] that create a proclivity to see progress towards peace and human rights and eschew the use of force when in reality the environment is becoming more hostile, material interests-based, and more actors regard the use of force as a first or second rather than last resort. For the UK, it might require rethinking the nature of the relationship with the United States, and in particular when to challenge the more senior partner when its intelligence is wrong and its policies are misguided and are inadvertently creating threats.

Even though the main empirical focus of this volume was not on the learning efforts post-2014, Chapters 5–7 make clear that learning efforts, particularly by the EU and Germany, have been limited, piecemeal and inadequate for the task of addressing the underlying problems. This is not entirely surprising in the light of the rather pessimistic conclusions of the wider literature on effective learning after crises, particularly after post-mortems or public inquiries of (foreign policy) crises.[28] Successful learning faces several obstacles: first, most people tend to confuse the identification of lessons with the actual learning of those lessons. Identifying lessons refers, usually, to the issuing of explicit recommendations that could improve individual or organisational performance. This frequently occurs after policy mistakes or crises. This transition from identifying what should happen to actually transposing these suggestions in practice poses many difficulties, as the implementation often reveals that such official lessons tend to be far removed from actual policy practice, leaving lessons on the shelf.[29] As argued in Chapter 1, instrumental policy learning or 'single loop learning' as the mere updating of processes and tools to improve performance is considered a form of learning that is comparatively the easiest to achieve.[30] 'As long as the learning does not question the fundamental design, goals, and activities of their organization', writes Argyris, lessons may be learned.[31] So-called 'double loop learning', which concerns changing fundamental aspects of the organisation or the policy design, is much more difficult.

Another important obstacle to the process of learning is the fact that in the three polities under study, various institutions are learning, at different levels. This means that for learning at the institutional level to take place, there needs to be both an individual process of learning and the aggregation of such learning. The cycle of learning thus involves multiple stages.[32] First, environmental feedback from crises or unforeseen events, analyses or social interaction should lead to individuals updating their beliefs about policy.[33] Second, these individuals need to undertake action to change organisational patterns. Third, these patterns need to be internalised and encoded into the institutions and organisations in question. Finally, these modified patterns should lead to a change in organisational behaviour. The transitions between these cycles all present possible barriers to learning.[34] As mentioned throughout this volume, the institutional specificities of the polities we studied may complicate such learning even more. At the European level, for example, there is no single EU agency responsible for EU foreign policy, nor is there a single policy domain to speak of, but rather a plethora of different bilateral and multilateral policies in external relations, development aid, crisis response and humanitarian action.[35] Who is to learn, and what exactly, and who is given the organisational responsibility to ensure that learning happens?

Institutions and governments need to have the capacity to learn. Drawing on the literature on policy learning in the field of public administration, Claire Dunlop proposed four types of capacity which are crucial in the process of learning and which, if they break down, may lead to a degeneration in the learning process.[36] First, there needs to be sufficient administrative and analytical capacity: individuals and units in the organisations must have sufficient resources and analytical capacity to produce knowledge and lessons for decision-makers. They need to know when decision-makers need to be informed about substantive trend breaks or risks regarding particular countries or threats. Few threats come as a 'bolt out of the blue' even though actors may be lulled into a sense of calm by hostile actors seeking to surprise. A key challenge is therefore to pick up on signals of change, especially unusual events, and then ask for additional resources to investigate further, namely to match resources to the pace of change/threat evolution on the ground – bringing in, if necessary, additional experts and joined up all-source intelligence. In Chapter 5 Paul Rimmer discussed how surprises are more likely in low-priority areas for intelligence collection, since analysts need to know the 'baseline for normal' in order to be able warn when things may go wrong, and that requires a long-term deep knowledge. He addressed how this was one of the problems in the UK's anticipation of the Arab uprisings. Awareness of the existing analytical capacity, and the willingness to increase this capacity when needed, is thus an important part of anticipatory foreign policy.

Second, organisations need to have the communicative capacity to convey such evidence and lessons towards decision-makers. This also requires a degree of internal organisational consensus around what lessons are legitimate and important to be learned.[37] An important issue this volume has identified is that of how to communicate unsolicited warnings that are neither purely strategic nor tactical – the difficult in-between – and the hindering influence of political prioritisation, national mood and hostile policy consensus on these warnings. Chapter 2 recounted how in the case of the

Arab uprisings, the warnings that were issued within the European Union came from wildly different places across institutions and lacked credible communicators and consistently open-minded recipients. One way of avoiding institutional bias suppressing 'unwelcome' news might be the creation of analytical challenge or alert channels particularly for junior officials and those in the field, which would be separate from the existing dissent channels focused on management or policy decisions.

Third, organisations as well as governments or institutions like the EU need to possess sufficient absorptive capacity: there need to be processes in place that allow decision-makers to absorb new information and warnings in order to learn any lessons. This also requires skills on the part of decision-makers. 'Only by attending to the cacophony of informational inputs (or policy chatter) can managers develop peripheral vision in the here and now as well as foresee problems as they emerge down the line.'[38] An issue is that, especially in crisis situations as in the cases under study, the degree of uncertainty surrounding developments and events is quite high. Because warnings tend to contain highly specialised information and may contain politically problematic messages, it is difficult for decision-makers to react to the knowledge they are receiving. Gerhard Conrad, assessing which instrumental and organisational lessons were key for the European Union in the wake of the strategic surprises discussed in this volume, concluded that the EU needs to have a dedicated independent assessment facility. He argues that, like Germany, the EU has too many different units that make assessments of the same situation, some of which are bound to institutional interests. What is lacking is a structure to systemically consider these views in order to reach a so-called final assessment as a basis for policy. Conrad argues that creating such an 'all-source situational awareness' would increase the EU's analytical and absorptive capacity.

Finally, an important obstacle to organisational and instrumental learning concerns institutional amnesia, or 'organisational forgetting'. Many of our interviewees and workshop participants stressed that a lesson from a particular case was actually not new, but similar mistakes had been made in earlier cases. Either these mistakes were not translated into lessons to be learned in the first place, or there was a tendency to forget lessons from previous episodes of surprise. Lessons, particularly instrumental and organisational learning processes, tend to be 'hardwired' into organisations through routines, programmes and standard operating procedures. Yet as the memory of the crises or triggers which created such routines and programmes fades, such lessons may be forgotten.[39] An important example of such institutional forgetfulness relates to the expertise of Russia and particularly the USSR accumulated prior to 1989, both in terms of the similar tactics the Soviet Union used and the flawed reasoning of Western analysts in the run up to the invasion of Czechoslovakia or Afghanistan. A longer view of Russian history might also have helped to understand why substantial parts of Russian foreign policy elites never accepted Ukraine as a sovereign country with its own national identity. The case of the Russo-Georgian War over South Ossetia in 2008 demonstrates the malleability of history and the lessons learned from it, as Eastern European and Baltic countries learned quite different lessons from the war than many Western diplomats. This partly explains the highly divergent warning and receptivity to warnings six years later in Ukraine. It may appear puzzling as to why the US government could still base its 2021 withdrawal plans from Afghanistan on over-optimistic assumptions about the capacities of the Afghan army despite experiencing the collapse of the US-trained Iraqi armed forces six years earlier when faced with ISIS. What is striking in the comparison of the ISIS 2014 and Taliban 2021 cases is not just the unexpected weakness of the US-trained national armies and the speed of conquest, but also the existence of a political mood hostile to estimative intelligence that questions the military withdrawal from both countries. Even though it was the United States which was primarily affected, interviewees concede that UK reporting about ISIS was also being coloured by so-called 'Iraq fatigue'.

Lessons for Future Research

The approach taken in this book highlights the benefits of conducting a dual comparison between cases and actors which could

Table 8.3 Examples of instrumental, organisational and social learning

	Instrumental learning	Organisational and governmental learning	Social learning
Requirements/ resourcing	Consider more frequently/systemically secondary and indirect consequences of conflict and crisis	Setting up new coordination mechanisms such as National Security Council for common assessment of intelligence requirements and threats	Substantially increase level of ambition for preventive foreign policy given more hostile environment vs. crisis management
Collection	Investment in technical tools monitoring local and social media sources	Changing demographic mix/diversity of analysts	Embrace more high-risk or contested intelligence collection methods
Analysis	Hiring or training more country experts with language skills in Arabic	Setting up structures for cross-cutting thematic or regional analyses to overcome country silos	Shift from probabilistic to more surprise-sensitive forecasting and contingency planning
Receptivity	Better training for ministers on intelligence use and more oral briefings and interactions	Creation of analytical dissent/alert channels that trigger automatic reviews	Creating clear points of accountability for acting or not acting such as NSCs
Learning and evaluation	Adjusting the rules and protocols for learning lessons after major decisions, surprises, failures or successes	Creating new units for cross-governmental identification, implementation and remembering of lessons	Change in learning and accountability structure via parliaments, news media and new legal instruments

be replicated by future research looking at the same or different actors and cases in order to test or develop new theories. The perspective also allowed us to see more clearly the interconnections between the three actors. For instance, a problematic bystander effect was when the UK deferred to US intelligence on key aspects such as the capacity of the Iraqi national army, when within the EU both Italy and France were seen as particularly credible because of their strong interests and links to MENA countries, or when both Germany and the UK did not look closely enough at geopolitical and security risks in Ukraine because this was seen as falling under the EU's responsibility. The literature on intelligence cooperation and sharing tends to focus within a rationalist framework on when and why specific intelligence products are shared among countries and allies with a strong focus on comparative advantages in collection and access or strong interests in a region.[40] However, what looks like a rational division of labour in terms of collection can become irrational because the partner country is not directing its resources to asking critical questions as a result of political, organisational or legal blind spots. We have seen that having strong political interests in a country can create source-selection biases in putting too much trust in local establishment actors and can also feed a soft politicisation of analysis given politically salient policies, preferences and agendas. Similarly problematic can be formal or informal prohibitions on analysing the unintended and potentially harmful effect of the government's or allies' policies or decisions. The intelligence and foreign policy literature is therefore well-advised to avoid underlaps and blind spots in the questions being asked among allies and partners and to explore how different levels of political engagement and national lenses can be an asset for better forecasting, preparedness and prevention. The literature in the political and administrative sciences as well as sociology on blind spots could be very useful here.[41]

Second, the comparison between quite different kinds of surprise shows substantial similarities in the performance of the three polities despite their significant strategic, organisational, cultural and resource differences. It shows that fundamental worldviews, assumptions and analytical methods were widely shared among the three actors and therefore produced common diagnostic challenges and performance problems. It points to the need for research on strategic surprise to go beyond generic cognitive biases and look more closely at cultural, institutional and professional biases that influence which questions are asked or omitted. Our research raises doubts over whether technical fixes and instrumental learning will be enough if the root cause of some of the diagnostic errors is to a large extent hardwired into Western models of training and recruitment into intelligence and diplomatic services. This is not the same as the much-cited group-think, but is a far less intangible, pervasive and transnational phenomenon. It chimes with the wider agenda in IR on local knowledge and grounded methodologies – including anthropology, sociology, or area and development studies – to understand what is happening behind foreign institutions that look superficially similar to Western ones, but do in fact work in radically different ways. This also relates to questions of how to treat state borders in intelligence analysis and to develop a better understanding of how new technologies and media platforms are changing the speed and impact of both political mobilisation as well as state surveillance and oppression. This means that intelligence studies needs to consider insights from communication, media and information technology studies more systematically, particularly, but not only with regard to renewed investment in OSINT.

Third, one of the great benefits of looking at European polities rather than the United States was to see more clearly how limited and, in some respects, unproductive the frequent analytical focus on intelligence versus policy failures is. While professional and political accountability for failures remains important, the reality is more frequently that surprises arise in the political, organisational and cultural 'in-between' of officials and decision-makers. This allows us to see helping and hindering factors for intelligence beyond 'politicisation', resulting not just from resource allocations and thematic and country priorities, but also the many subtle ways in which analysts and diplomats are sensitive to dominant political agendas and inferences about what kind of knowledge is welcome and what would be inconvenient. Even in political systems which place a considerable emphasis on containing analytical politicisation pressures such as the UK, we can see that the political climate can limit what questions are being asked, how early and in what way warnings happen. It also requires understanding professional cultures emphasising written over oral communication, consensus over minority opinions, or legal over moral and pragmatic arguments. Similarly, questions of career protection for civil servants, leadership styles and departmental cultures become highly relevant for understanding when and by whom warnings are being communicated, how minority views are being encouraged, and when senior officials can water down or change assessments of more junior analysts.[42] In the cases of Germany and the EU we learned how estimative intelligence is also related to the degree of risk-aversion and wishful thinking in foreign policy more broadly and how national and party-political perspectives can stifle the timely resourcing of intelligence collection of newly emerging problems as well as the communication of particularly inconvenient analytical judgements. This requires looking at intelligence as part and parcel of government knowledge production, which is itself embedded in analysis produced by a diverse and in some cases well-resourced and knowledgeable set of NGOs, think tanks and news media.

Finally, there is a substantial but currently underused literature on inquiries and learning in public policy that could help to explain better why some inquiries in matters of national security and intelligence have led to little change and why some polities are better at learning than others.[43] For this research agenda to work would require embracing a notion of learning as progress and enquire whether it improves performance in future similar cases, rather than the frequent use of learning as cognitive change in broader IR and foreign policy. The literature can help us to avoid unrealistically high expectations of learning in the view of the many obstacles identified, but also better make the case for fundamental reforms to the statutory, institutional and social mechanism available to promote deeper forms of learning among those polities with underdeveloped cultures and mechanisms for learning such as the EU and Germany. In the case of the UK, it requires understanding better how one can avoid attempts by politicians and bureaucracies to manage, control and delay public inquiries and to make sure that internal no-blame learning happens quickly enough to make a difference.

Notes

1. Bob De Graaf and James M. Nyce, eds, *The Handbook of European Intelligence Cultures* (London: Rowman & Littlefield, 2016); Richard J. Aldrich, 'Intelligence and the European Union', in *The Oxford Handbook of the European Union*, ed. Erik Jones, Anand Menon and Stephen Weatherill (Oxford: Oxford University Press, 2021).
2. For instance, the big data analytics company Palantir was only founded in 2003, partly with the help of the CIA.

3. Christoph O. Meyer and Ana Maria Albulescu, 'Britisches Vorbild: Was die nächste Bundesregierung vom Vereinigten Königreich über kritische Selbstreflexion und außenpolitisches Handeln lernen könnte', *Internationale Politik* (2021).

4. Former UK official, interview June 2021.

5. Rubén Arcos and José-Miguel Palacios, 'The Impact of Intelligence on Decision-Making: The EU and the Arab Spring', *Intelligence and National Security* 33, no. 5 (2018).

6. The content of the report, but not the report itself, was made available to: Andrew Higgins, 'Ukraine Upheaval Highlights E.U.'S Past Miscalculations and Future Dangers', *The New York Times*, 20 March 2014.

7. Christoph Meyer, Chiara De Franco and Florian Otto, *Warning About War: Conflict, Persuasion and Foreign Policy* (Cambridge: Cambridge University Press, 2020), 69.

8. William Shapcott, 'Do They Listen? Communicating Warnings: A Practitioners Perspective', in *Forecasting, Warning, and Responding to Transnational Risks*, ed. Chiara De Franco and Christoph O. Meyer (Basingstoke: Palgrave Macmillan, 2011).

9. Meyer, De Franco and Otto, *Warning About War: Conflict, Persuasion and Foreign Policy*, 52–89.

10. Sönke Neitzel and Bastian Matteo Scianna, *Blutige Enthaltung: Deutschlands Rolle Im Syrienkrieg* (Freiburg: Herder, 2021). Interview, 2020.

11. Meyer and Albulescu, 'Britisches Vorbild: Was die nächste Bundesregierung vom Vereinigten Königreich über kritische Selbstreflexion und außenpolitisches Handeln lernen könnte'.

12. Ibid.

13. Philip Tetlock and Dan Gardner, *Superforecasting: The Art and Science of Prediction* (London and New York: Random House, 2016).

14. Richard K. Betts, 'Warning Dilemmas: Normal Theory vs Exceptional Theory', *ORBIS* 26, no 4 (1983): 828–33.

15. Rob Johnston, *Analytic Culture in the US Intelligence Community: An Ethnographic Study* (Washington, DC: The Center for the Study of Intelligence, CIA, 2005).

16. Cynthia Grabo, *Handbook of Warning Intelligence: Assessing the Threat to National Security*, ed. Jan Goldman, vol. no. 12, Scarecrow Professional Intelligence Education Series (Lanham, MD: Scarecrow Press, 2010).

17. Michael F. Oppenheimer, *Pivotal Countries, Alternate Futures:*

Using Scenarios to Manage American Strategy (Oxford: Oxford University Press, 2016); William Ascher, *Forecasting: An Appraisal for Policy-Makers and Planners* (Baltimore, MD: Johns Hopkins Press, 1978); Myriam Dunn Cavelty and Victor Mauer, 'Postmodern Intelligence: Strategic Warning in an Age of Reflexive Intelligence', *Security Dialogue* 40, no. 2 (2009).

18. Oppenheimer, *Pivotal Countries, Alternate Futures.*
19. Florence Gaub, ed., *What If . . .? 14 Futures for 2024* (Paris: EU-ISS, 2020).
20. Chapter 10 in Meyer, De Franco and Otto, *Warning About War: Conflict, Persuasion and Foreign Policy.*
21. Lloyd S. Etheredge, 'Government Learning: An Overview', in *The Handbook of Political Behavior* (New York: Plenum Press, 1981); Peter J. May, 'Policy Learning and Failure', *Journal of Public Policy* 12, no. 4 (1992): 335.
22. Jack S. Levy, 'Learning and Foreign Policy: Sweeping a Conceptual Minefield', *International Organization* 48, no. 2 (1994): 289.
23. Ibid.
24. Hugh Heclo, *Modern Social Politics in Britain and Sweden; From Relief to Income Maintenance*, Yale Studies in Political Science (New Haven, CT: Yale University Press, 1974), 305; Paul A. Sabatier, 'An Advocacy Coalition Framework of Policy Change and the Role of Policy-Oriented Learning Therein', *Policy Sciences* 21, no. 2/3 (1988): 144; Peter Hall, 'Policy Paradigms, Social Learning, and the State: The Case of Economic Policymaking in Britain', *Comparative Politics* 25, no. 3 (1993): 278.
25. Heclo, *Modern Social Politics in Britain and Sweden; From Relief to Income Maintenance*, 306.
26. David Patrick Houghton, 'The Role of Analogical Reasoning in Novel Foreign-Policy Situations', *British Journal of Political Science* 26, no. 4 (1996).
27. Thomas Bagger, 'Germany, We Need to Talk', *Internationale Politik Quarterly*, 30 June 2021.
28. Sandra L. Resodihardjo, *Crises, Inquiries and the Politics of Blame* (London: Palgrave Macmillan, 2019), 41.
29. Alastair Stark, 'Left on the Shelf: Explaining the Failure of Public Inquiry Recommendations', *Public Administration* (2019).
30. May, 'Policy Learning and Failure'; Alastair Stark, *Public Inquiries, Policy Learning, and the Threat of Future Crises*, 1st edn (Oxford: Oxford University Press, 2018). Chris Argyris, 'Single-Loop and Double-Loop Models in Research on Decision

Making', *Administrative Science Quarterly* 21, no. 3 (1976): 367.

31. Argyris, 'Single-Loop and Double-Loop Models in Research on Decision Making', 367.

32. Levy, 'Learning and Foreign Policy: Sweeping a Conceptual Minefield', 288; James G. March and Johan P. Olsen, *Ambiguity and Choice in Organizations* (Bergen: Universitetsforlaget, 1976).

33. Claire A. Dunlop, Claudio M. Radaelli and Philipp Trein, 'Introduction: The Family Tree of Policy Learning', in *Learning in Public Policy: Analysis, Modes and Outcomes*, ed. Claire A. Dunlop, Claudio M. Radaelli and Philipp Trein, 1st edn (Cham: Springer International Publishing, 2018); Jeffrey T. Checkel, 'Why Comply? Social Learning and European Identity Change', *International Organization* 55, no. 3 (2001).

34. Chris Argyris and Donald A. Schön, *Organizational Learning*, Addison-Wesley OD Series (Reading, MA: Addison Wesley, 1978); John Lovell, '"Lessons" of U.S. Military Involvement: Preliminary Conceptualization', in *Foreign Policy Decision Making: Perception, Cognition, and Artificial Intelligence*, ed. Donald A. Sylvan and Steve Chan, New Dimensions in International Studies (New York: Praeger, 1984); B. Hedberg, *How Organizations Learn and Unlearn*, Working Papers (Stockholm: Arbetslivscentrum, 1979).

35. Michael E. Smith, 'Learning in European Union Peacebuilding: Rhetoric and Reality', *Global Affairs* 4, no. 2/3 (2018).

36. Claire A. Dunlop, 'Pathologies of Policy Learning: What Are They and How Do They Contribute to Policy Failure?', *Policy & Politics* 45, no. 1 (2017): 25.

37. Ibid., 25–33.

38. Claire A. Dunlop and Claudio M. Radaelli, 'Policy Learning and Organizational Capacity', in *The Palgrave Handbook of Public Administration and Management in Europe*, ed. E. Ongaro and S. Van Thiel (London: Palgrave Macmillan, 2018), 599.

39. Alastair Stark and Brian Head, 'Institutional Amnesia and Public Policy', *Journal of European Public Policy* 26, no. 10 (2018): 4, 7.

40. This strand of the literature on intelligence cooperation employs what Pepijn Tuinier calls 'a neorealist presumption', see Pepijn Tuinier, 'Explaining the Depth and Breadth of International Intelligence Cooperation: Towards a Comprehensive Understanding', *Intelligence and National Security* 36, no. 1 (2021); James Igoe Walsh, *The International Politics of Intelligence Sharing* (New York: Columbia University Press, 2009); Jennifer E. Sims, 'Foreign

Intelligence Liaison: Devils, Deals, and Details', *International Journal of Intelligence and Counterintelligence* 19, no. 2 (2006); H. Bradford Westerfield, 'America and the World of Intelligence Liaison', *Intelligence and National Security* 11, no. 3 (1996).

41. Tobias Bach and Kai Wegrich, eds, *The Blind Spots of Public Bureaucracy and the Politics of Non-Coordination* (London: Palgrave Macmillan, 2019); Eviatar Zerubavel, *Hidden in Plain Sight: The Social Structure of Irrelevance* (Oxford: Oxford University Press, 2015); Wayne Brekhus, 'A Sociology of the Unmarked: Redirecting Our Focus', *Sociological Theory* 16, no. 1 (1998).

42. Meyer, De Franco and Otto, *Warning About War: Conflict, Persuasion and Foreign Policy*, 52–89; Marc S. Gerstein and Edgar H. Schein, 'Dark Secrets: Face-Work, Organizational Culture and Disaster Prevention', in *Forecasting, Warning, and Responding to Transnational Risks: Is Prevention Possible?*, ed. Chiara De Franco and Christoph O. Meyer (Basingstoke: Palgrave Macmillan, 2011).

43. Stark, *Public Inquiries, Policy Learning, and the Threat of Future Crises*; Arjen Boin, Allan McConnell and Paul 't Hart, *Governing after Crisis: The Politics of Investigation, Accountability and Learning* (Cambridge and New York: Cambridge University Press, 2008).

References

Abdulrazaq, Tallha and Gareth Stansfield. 'The Enemy Within: Isis and the Conquest of Mosul', *The Middle East Journal* 70, no. 4 (2016): 525–42.

Abu Hanieh, Hassan and Mohammad Abu-Rumman. 'The "Islamic State" Organization: The Sunni Crisis and the Struggle of Global Jihadism', Amman: Friedrich Ebert Stiftung, 2015.

Adomanis, Mark. 'Confused About What's Happening in Ukraine?', *Forbes*, 2013.

Aldrich, Richard J. 'Intelligence and the European Union', in *The Oxford Handbook of the European Union*, edited by Erik Jones, Anand Menon and Stephen Weatherill, Oxford: Oxford University Press, 2021.

Allison, Roy. 'Russian "Deniable" Intervention in Ukraine: How and Why Russia Broke the Rules', *International Affairs* 90, no. 6 (2014): 1255–97.

Amnesty International. 'Syria: Rule of Fear: ISIS Abuses in Detention in Northern Syria', 19 December 2013: https://www.amnesty.org/en/documents/MDE24/063/2013/en/

Amrani, Issandr El. 'Human Rights: Reluctant to End Repression', *Financial Times*, 2010.

Amt, Auswärtiges. 'Grundprinzipien Deutscher Außenpolitik', 2019.

Arcos, Rubén and José-Miguel Palacios. 'The Impact of Intelligence on Decision-Making: The EU and the Arab Spring' [in En], *Intelligence and National Security* 33, no. 5 (2018): 1–18, 737–54.

Argyris, Chris. 'Single-Loop and Double-Loop Models in Research on Decision Making', *Administrative Science Quarterly* 21, no. 3 (1976): 363–75.

Argyris, Chris and Donald A. Schön. *Organizational Learning*, Addison-Wesley OD Series, Reading, MA: Addison-Wesley, 1978.

Ascher, William. *Forecasting: An Appraisal for Policy-Makers and Planners*, Baltimore, MD: Johns Hopkins Press, 1978.

Asseburg, Muriel. 'Proteste, Aufstände Und Regimewandel in Der Arabischen Welt', Berlin: SWP, 2011.

Assemblée Nationale. 'Les Printemps Arabes'. Commission Des Affaires Étrangères, 2012.

Auswärtiges Amt. ,Review 2014: Aussenpolitik weiter denken', 25 February 2015: https://www.bundesregierung.de/breg-de/service /publikationen/review-2014-aussenpolitik-weiter-denken-735224

Bach, Tobias and Kai Wegrich, eds. *The Blind Spots of Public Bureaucracy and the Politics of Non-Coordination*, London: Palgrave Macmillan, 2019.

Bagger, Thomas. 'Germany, We Need to Talk', *Internationale Politik Quarterly*, 30 June 2021.

Balfour, Rosa and Hanna Ojanen. 'Does the European External Action Service Represent a Model for the Challenges of Global Diplomacy?', Istituto Affari Internazionali, 2011.

Bar-Joseph, Uri. 'The Politicization of Intelligence: A Comparative Study', *International Journal of Intelligence and CounterIntelligence* 26, no. 2 (2013): 347–69.

Bara, Corinne. 'Forecasting Civil War and Political Violence', in *The Politics and Science of Prevision: Governing and Probing the Future*, edited by Andreas Wenger, Ursula Jasper and Myriam Dunn Cavelty, 177–93, Abingdon: Routledge, 2020.

Bareinske, Christian. 'Auslandsaufklärung', in *Handbuch des Rechts der Nachrichtendienste*, edited by Jan-Henrik Dietrich and Sven-R. Eiffler, 865–933, Stuttgart: Boorberg, 2017.

Barnea, Avner and Avi Meshulach. 'Forecasting for Intelligence Analysis: Scenarios to Abort Strategic Surprise', *International Journal of Intelligence and CounterIntelligence* (2020): 1–28.

Bauer, Wolfgang. 'Das Syrien-Drama: Assad weiß, wo sie sind', *Die Zeit*, 12 September 2013.

Bayat, Asef. 'The Arab Spring and its Surprises', *Development and Change* 44, no. 3 (2013): 587–601.

Beck, Martin. 'The Arab Spring as a Challenge to Political Science', in *The International Politics of the Arab Spring*, 9–36, 2014.

Becker, Petra. 'Syrian Muslim Brotherhood Still a Crucial Actor', SWP Comment 34, October 2013: https://www.swp-berlin.org/fileadmin /contents/products/comments/2013C34_bkp.pdf

Ben-Zvi, Abraham. 'Hindsight and Foresight: A Conceptual Framework for the Analysis of Surprise Attacks', *World Politics* 27, no. 3 (1976): 381–95.

Benmelech, Efraim and Esteban F. Klor. 'What Explains the Flow of

Foreign Fighters to ISIS?', *Terrorism and Political Violence* 32, no. 7 (2020): 1458–81, doi:10.1080/09546553.2018.1482214.

Bennett, Colin J. and Michael Howlett. 'The Lessons of Learning: Reconciling Theories of Policy Learning and Policy Change' [in En], *Policy Sciences* 25, no. 3 (1992): 275–94.

Beswick, Terri. 'EU Early Warning and Early Response Capacity for Conflict Prevention in the Post Lisbon Era', Clingendael, January 2012: https://www.clingendael.org/sites/default/files/2016-02/Early %20warning%20and%20early%20response%20capacity%20for %20conflict%20prevention%20in%20the%20post-Lisbon%20era _0.pdf

Betts, Richard K. 'Analysis, War and Decision: Why Intelligence Failures Are Inevitable', *World Politics* 31, no. 1 (1978): 61–89.

Betts, Richard K. *Enemies of Intelligence: Knowledge and Power in American National Security*, New York: Columbia University Press, 2007.

Betts, Richard K. *Surprise Attack: Lessons for Defence Planning*, Washington, DC: The Brookings Institution, 1982.

Betts, Richard K. (1983) 'Warning Dilemmas: Normal Theory vs Exceptional Theory', *ORBIS* 26, no 4 (1983): 828–33.

Bicchi, Federica. 'The EU as a Community of Practice: Foreign Policy Communications in the Coreu Network', *Journal of European Public Policy* 18, no. 8 (2011): 1115–32.

Bickel, Markus. 'Auf sich selbst zurückgeworfen', *FAZ*, 19 September 2013: https://www.faz.net/aktuell/politik/ausland/naher-osten/syriens -aufstaendische-auf-sich-selbst-zurueckgeworfen-12580131.html

Bickel, Markus. 'Der Diktator als Staatsmann', *FAZ*, 21 December 2013: https://www.faz.net/aktuell/politik/syrien-konflikt-der-diktator-als -staatsmann-12720785.html

Bickel, Markus. 'Der Krieg im Bürgerkrieg', *FAZ*, 22 November 2013: https://www.faz.net/aktuell/politik/ausland/naher-osten/syrien-der -krieg-im-buergerkrieg-12675253.html

Biscop, Sven. 'From ESDP to CSDP: Time for Some Strategy', *La revue géopolitique*, January 2010: https://www.diploweb.com/From-ESDP -to-CSDP-Time-for-some.html

Blockmans, Steven. 'The European External Action Service One Year On: First Signs of Strengths and Weaknesses', CEPS, January 2012: https://www.ceps.eu/ceps-publications/european-external-action-serv ice-one-year-first-signs-strengths-and-weaknesses/

Blockmans, Steven and Christoph Hillion, eds. 'EEAS 2.0. A Legal Commentary on Council Decision 2010/427/EU Establishing the

Organisation and Functioning of the European External Action Service', CEPS, 7 February 2013: https://www.ceps.eu/ceps-publica tions/eeas-20-legal-commentary-council-decision-2010427eu-estab lishing-organisation-and/

Blockmans, Steven and Ramses A. Wessel. 'The EEAS at Ten: Reason for a Celebration?', *European Foreign Affairs Review* 26, no. 1 (2021): 5–12.

Blair, David. 'Al-Qaeda is Thriving Amid the Chaos of Iraq', *The Telegraph*, 24 July 2013.

Blair, David. 'April Iraq's Deadliest Month in Almost Five Years', *The Telegraph*, 2 May 2013: https://www.telegraph.co.uk/news /worldnews/middleeast/iraq/10032814/April-Iraqs-deadliest-month -in-almost-five-years.html

Blome, Nikolaus et al. 'Bis jenseits der Grenze', *Spiegel*, November 2014.

Boin, Arjen, Allan McConnell and Paul 't Hart. *Governing after Crisis: The Politics of Investigation, Accountability and Learning*, Cambridge and New York: Cambridge University Press, 2008.

Boin, Arjen, Magnus Ekengren and Mark Rhinard. *Understanding the Creeping Crisis*, Springer Nature, 2021.

Boin, Arjen, Paul 't Hart, Eric Stern and Bengt Sundelius. *The Politics of Crisis Management: Public Leadership Under Pressure*, 1st edn, Cambridge: Cambridge University Press, 2005.

Börzel, Tanja, Assem Dandashly and Thomas Risse. 'Responses to the "Arabellions": The EU in Comparative Perspective – Introduction' [in En], *Journal of European Integration* 37, no. 1 (2015): 1–17.

Bossong, Raphael. 'Intelligence Support for EU Security Policy: Options for Enhancing the Flow of Information and Political Oversight', SWP Comment 2018/C 51, 3 December 2018: https://www.swp-berlin.org /en/publication/intelligence-support-for-eu-security-policy/

Boswell, Christina. 'The Political Functions of Expert Knowledge: Knowledge and Legitimation in European Union Immigration Policy', *Journal of European Public Policy* 15, no. 4 (2008): 471–88.

Boswell, Christina. *The Political Uses of Expert Knowledge: Immigration Policy and Social Research*, Cambridge: Cambridge University Press, 2009.

Brekhus, Wayne. 'A Sociology of the Unmarked: Redirecting Our Focus', *Sociological Theory* 16, no. 1 (1998): 34–51.

Brooks, Risa A. 2017. doi:10.1093/acrefore/9780190228637.013.26.

Brozus, Lars. *Fahren auf Sicht. Effektive Früherkennung in der politischen Praxis*, Berlin: SWP, 2018.

Bundesregierung. *Weissbuch zur Sicherheitspolitik und Zukunft der*

Bundeswehr. 13 July 2016: https://www.bundesregierung.de/resource /blob/975292/736102/64781348c12e4a80948ab1bdf25cf057 /weissbuch-zur-sicherheitspolitik-2016-download-data.pdf

Burgess, Adam. 'The Changing Character of Public Inquiries in the (Risk) Regulatory State', *British Politics* 6, no. 1 (2011): 3–29.

Burke, Edward. 'Running into the Sand? The EU's Faltering Response to the Arab Revolutions', *Centre for European Reform: Policy Brief* (2013): 1–17.

Busse, Volker. 'Organisation der Bundesregierung und Organisationsentscheidungen der Bundeskanzler in ihrer historischen Entwicklung und im Spannungsfeld zwischen Exekutive und Legislative', *Der Staat* 45, no. 2 (2006): 245–68.

Cavatorta, Francesco. 'The Failed Liberalisation of Algeria and the International Context: A Legacy of Stable Authoritarianism' [in En], *The Journal of North African Studies* 7, no. 4 (2002): 23–43.

Chadefaux, Thomas. 'Early Warning Signals for War in the News', *Journal of Peace Research* 51, no. 1 (2014): 5–18.

Checkel, Jeffrey T. 'Why Comply? Social Learning and European Identity Change', *International Organization* 55, no. 3 (2001): 553–88.

Chilcot Inquiry. 'Iraq Inquiry': http://www.iraqinquiry.org.uk

Chimelli, Rudolph. 'Drei-Fronten-Krieg gegen den Terror', *SZ*, 7 January 2014: https://www.sueddeutsche.de/politik/irak-syrien-libanon-drei-f ronten-krieg-gegen-den-terror-1.1856908

Chotiner, Isaac. 'How America Failed in Afghanistan', *The New Yorker*, 2021.

Christie-Miller, Alexander. 'Al-Qaeda Strives to Build Islamic State in Northern Syria', *The Times*, 26 October 2013: https://www.thetimes .co.uk/article/al-qaeda-strives-to-build-islamic-state-in-northern-syria -0sg3mtt6286

Christie-Miller, Alexander. 'Hanged and Beaten, but Syrian Activist Lived to Tell the Tale', *The Times*, 23 October 2013: https://www.thetimes .co.uk/article/hanged-and-beaten-but-syrian-activist-lived-to-tell-the -tale-97mvd3c6bmf

Clapper, James. 'DNI Clapper: Ukraine Intelligence "Not a Failure by Any Stretch"', news release, 10 March 2014: https://www.dni.gov /index.php/newsroom/speeches-interviews/speeches-interviews-2014 /item/1027-dni-clapper-ukraine-intelligence-not-a-failure-by-any -stretch

CNN. 'Woodward: Tenet Told Bush WMD Case a "Slam Dunk"', 2004.

Coghlan, Tom. 'Jihadist Groupies Flocking to Syria with Marriage in

Mind', *The Times*, 17 February 2014: https://www.thetimes.co.uk /article/jihadist-groupies-flocking-to-syria-with-marriage-in-mind -39jjnkrf03s

Colombo, Silvia and Nathalie Tocci. 'Re-Thinking Western Policies in Light of the Arab Uprising', 71–96, Rome: Istituto Affari Internazionali (IAI), 2012.

Committee of Privy Counsellors. 'The Report of the Iraq Inquiry. Executive Summary', House of Commons, 2016.

Connelly, Matthew, Raymond Hicks, Robert Jervis and Arthur Spirling. 'New Evidence and New Methods for Analyzing the Iranian Revolution as an Intelligence Failure', *Intelligence and National Security* (2021): 1–26.

Conrad, Gerhard. 'Europäische Nachrichtendienstkooperation – Entwicklungen, Erwartungen und Perspektiven', in *Reform der Nachrichtendienste zwischen Vergesetzlichung und Internationalisierung*, edited by Jan-Hendrik Dietrich et al., 161–73, Tübingen: Mohr Siebeck, 2019.

Conrad, Gerhard. 'Situational Awareness for EU Decision-making: The Next Decade', *European Foreign Affairs Review* 26, no. 1 (2021): 55–70.

Conrad, Gerhard, 'Warum wir einen Nationalen Sicherheitsrat brauchen', *Die Welt*, 26 November 2019.

Cordesman, Anthony H. and Sam Khazai. *Iraq in Crisis*, Lanham, MD: Rowman & Littlefield, 2014. https://csis-website-prod.s3.amazonaws .com/s3fs-public/legacy_files/files/publication/140513_Cordesman _IraqInCrisis_Web.pdf

Cordis. 'Political and Social Transformations in the Arab World': https:// cordis.europa.eu/article/id/203777-drivers-behind-the-arab-spring -unveiled

Coughlin, Con. 'Now Syria's Rebels are Fighting Each Other', *The Telegraph*, 19 September 2013.

Coughlin, Con. 'Syria is Now the Gravest Terrorist Threat to Britain', *The Telegraph*, 10 April 2014: https://www.telegraph.co.uk/news /worldnews/middleeast/syria/10757598/Syria-is-now-the-gravest -terrorist-threat-to-Britain.html

Coughlin, Con. 'The Syrian Civil War is Breeding a New Generation of Terrorist', *The Telegraph*, 3 December 2013: https://www.telegraph .co.uk/news/worldnews/middleeast/syria/10491523/The-Syrian-civil -war-is-breeding-a-new-generation-of-terrorist.html

Council of the European Union. 'EU Conflict Early Warning System: Objectives, Process and Guidance for Implementation', Joint Staff

Working Document, August 2017: https://ec.europa.eu/international -partnerships/system/files/swd-eu-conflict-early-warning-system -2017_en.pdf

Council of the European Union. 'Implementation Plan on Security and Defence', 14392/16, 14 November 2016: https://www.consilium .europa.eu/media/22460/eugs-implementation-plan-st14392en16.pdf

Cradock, Percy. *Know Your Enemy: How the Joint Intelligence Committee Saw the World*, London: John Murray, 2002.

Crofts-Gibbons, Catherine and Nikki Ikani. 'Timeline of Expert Claims and Responses for Ukraine Crisis Involving UK', 2021, INTEL website: https://www.kcl.ac.uk/eis/research/intel/intel-publications

Dahl, Erik J. *Intelligence and Surprise Attack: Failure and Success from Pearl Harbor to 9/11 and Beyond*, Washington, DC: Georgetown University Press, 2013.

Dahl, Eric J. 'Not Your Father's Intelligence Failure: Why the Intelligence Community Failed to Anticipate the Rise of ISIS', in *The Future of ISIS: Regional and International Implications*, edited by Faisal Al-Istrabadi and Sumit Ganguly, 41–65, Washington, DC: Brookings Institution, 2018.

Daragahi, Borzou. 'Al-Qaeda Affiliated Group Seizes Rebel-controlled Syrian Town', *Financial Times*, 19 September 2013: https://www.ft .com/content/706f1636-210f-11e3-a92a-00144feab7de

Daragahi, Borzou. 'Middle East: Three Nations, One Conflict', *Financial Times*, 27 May 2014: https://www.ft.com/content/b6f93e4e-e584 -11e3-8b90-00144feabdc0

Daragahi, Borzou. 'Surge in Iraq Violence Raises Fears of Return to Sectarian Civil War', *Financial Times*, 2 October 2013: https://www .ft.com/content/c9b483ce-2a7f-11e3-8fb8-00144feab7de

De Franco, Chiara and Christoph O. Meyer, eds. *Forecasting, Warning, and Responding to Transnational Risks*, Basingstoke: Palgrave Macmillan, 2011.

De Graaf, Bob and James M. Nyce, eds. *The Handbook of European Intelligence Cultures*, London: Rowman & Littlefield, 2016.

de Jouvenel, Bertrand. *L'Art de la conjecture*, Monaco: Editions du Rocher, 1964.

Debuysere, Loes and Steven Blockmans. 'Europe's Coherence Gap in External Crisis and Conflict Management. The EU's Integrated Approach between Political Rhetoric and Institutional Practice', Bertelsmann Stiftung, November 2019: https://www.bertelsmann -stiftung.de/fileadmin/files/BSt/Publikationen/GrauePublikationen /EZ_EU_Report_Weiss_ENG_4_2019.pdf

Dennison, Susi. 'The EU and North Africa after the Revolutions: A New Start or "Plus Ça Change"?' [in En], *Mediterranean Politics* 18, no. 1 (2013): 119–24.

Deutsche Welle. 'Al Qaeda Growing Stronger in Iraq and Syria', 4 January 2014: https://www.dw.com/en/al-qaeda-growing-stronger-in-iraq-and-syria/a-17340739

Deutscher Bundestag, 'Antwort der Bundesregierung auf die Große Anfrage der (. . .) Fraktion der FDP', Drucksache 19/13251, 4 September 2019.

Deutscher Bundestag. Antwort der Bundesregierung auf die kleine Anfrage der Abgeordneten Alexander Graf-Lambsdorff, Grigorios Aggelidis, Renata Alt, weiterer Abgeordneter und der Fraktion der FDP – Drucksache 15990 – ,Schaffung eines Nationalen Sicherheitsrates', 19, Wahlperiode, 19-16508, 15 January 2020.

Deutscher Bundestag. *Kleine Anfrage 18/1335*, 7 May 2014: http://dipbt.bundestag.de/doc/btd/18/013/1801335.pdf

Deutscher Bundestag. *Kleine Anfrage 18/1541*, 21 May 2014: http://dipbt.bundestag.de/doc/btd/18/015/1801541.pdf

Deutscher Bundestag. *Unterrichtung durch die Bundesregierung 18/933*, 27 March 2014: http://dipbt.bundestag.de/doc/btd/18/009/1800933.pdf

Deutscher Bundestag. Unterrichtung durch die Bundesregierung, 'Neufassung der Geschäftsordnung des Bundessicherheitsrates', 18, Wahlperiode, 18-5773, 13 August 2015.

Deutscher Bundestag, 'Vernetztes Handeln in der Außen-, Sicherheits- und Entwicklungspolitik stärken', Drucksache 19/8058, 27 February 2019.

Deutscher Bundestag Wissenschaftliche Dienste. *Sachstand: Strukturen der Krisenfrüherkennung in der deutschen Außen- und Sicherheitspolitik. WD 2 – 3000 – 070/20*, Berlin, 2020.

Diamond, Larry. 'Why Are There No Arab Democracies?', *Journal of Democracy* 21, no. 1 (2009): 93–112.

Diehl, Jörg and Christoph Sydow. 'Deutscher Salafist ruft zu Selbstmordanschlägen auf', *Der Spiegel*, 1 August 2013: https://www.spiegel.de/politik/deutschland/salafist-deso-dogg-ruft-in-hassvideo-zu-selbstmordanschlaegen-auf-a-914374.html

Dietrich, Jan-Hendrik and Satish Sule, eds. *Intelligence Law and Policies in Europa: A Handbook*, Munich: C. H. Beck, 2019.

Dietrich, Jan-Hendrik et al., eds. *Reform der Nachrichtendienste zwischen Vergesetzlichung und Internationalisierung*, Tübingen: Mohr Siebeck, 2019.

Dijkstra, Hylke. 'Solana and his Civil Servants: An Overview of Political-Administrative Relations', in *The High Representative for the EU Foreign and Security Policy – Review and Prospects*, edited by Gisela Müller-Brandeck-Borquet and Caroline Rüger, 35–63, Baden-Baden: Nomos, 2011.

Dijkstra, Hylke. 'The Council Secretariat's Role in the Common Foreign and Security Policy', *European Foreign Affairs Review* 13, no. 2 (2008): 149–66.

Doran, Charles F. 'Why Forecasts Fail: The Limits and Potential of Forecasting in International Relations and Economics', *International Studies Review* 1, no. 2 (1999): 11–41.

Dragneva, Rilka and Kataryna Wolczuk. 'The EU-Ukraine Association Agreement and the Challenges of Inter-Regionalism', *Review of Central and East European Law* 39 (2014): http://dx.doi.org/10.2139/ssrn.2604945

Duke, Simon. 'Under the Authority of the High Representative', in *The High Representative for the EU Foreign and Security Policy – Review and Prospects*, edited by Gisela Müller-Brandeck-Borquet and Caroline Rüger, 35–63, Baden-Baden: Nomos, 2011.

Dumitriu, Petru. Knowledge Management in the United Nations System, Joint Inspection Unit, JIU/REP/2016/10, 2016: https://www.unjiu.org/sites/www.unjiu.org/files/jiu_document_files/products/en/reports-notes/JIU%20Products/JIU_REP_2016_10_English.pdf

Dunlop, Claire A. 'Pathologies of Policy Learning: What Are They and How Do They Contribute to Policy Failure?', *Policy & Politics* 45, no. 1 (2017): 19–37.

Dunlop, Claire A. and Claudio M. Radaelli. 'Policy Learning and Organizational Capacity', in *The Palgrave Handbook of Public Administration and Management in Europe*, edited by E. Ongaro and S. Van Thiel, London: Palgrave Macmillan, 2018.

Dunlop, Claire A., Claudio M. Radaelli and Philipp Trein. 'Introduction: The Family Tree of Policy Learning', in *Learning in Public Policy: Analysis, Modes and Outcomes*, edited by Claire A. Dunlop, Claudio M. Radaelli and Philipp Trein, Cham: Springer International Publishing, 2018.

Dunlop, Claire A., Claudio M. Radaelli and Philipp Trein. *Learning in Public Policy: Analysis, Modes and Outcomes*, Cham: Springer International Publishing, 2018, doi:10.1007/978-3-319-76210-4.

Dunn Cavelty, Myriam and Victor Mauer. 'Postmodern Intelligence: Strategic Warning in an Age of Reflexive Intelligence', *Security Dialogue* 40, no. 2 (2009): 123–44.

Dyer, Geoff. 'Iraq's Under-resourced Army No Match for Sunni Insurgents', *Financial Times*, 11 June 2014.

Dyer, Geoff. 'US Alarmed at being Dragged into Fresh Iraq Conflict', *Financial Times*, 10 July 2014: https://www.ft.com/content/7e78e0fc -f0eb-11e3-8f3d-00144feabdc0

Dyson, Stephen B. and Paul 't Hart. 'Crisis Management', in *The Oxford Handbook of Political Psychology*, 2nd edn, edited by Leonie Huddy, David O. Sears and Jack S. Levy, 395–422, Oxford and New York: Oxford University Press, 2013.

The Economist. 'Russia and Georgia Rattle Sabres', 30 April 2008.

Economist Intelligence Unit. 'Après Ben Ali'.

Edwards, Geoffrey. 'The EU's Foreign Policy and the Search for Effect', *International Relations* 27, no. 3 (2013): 276–91.

Elliott, Dominic. 'The Failure of Organizational Learning from Crisis – A Matter of Life and Death?', *Journal of Contingencies and Crisis Management* 17, no. 3 (2009): 157–68.

Ensor, Josie. 'British Extremist in Syria Says "This is no Five-star Jihad"', *The Telegraph*, 21 April 2014.

Etheredge, Lloyd S. 'Government Learning: An Overview', in *The Handbook of Political Behavior*, 73–161, New York: Plenum Press, 1981.

EU High Representative. 'Shared Vision, Common Action: A Stronger Europe. A Global Strategy for the European Union's Foreign and Security Policy', Brussels: European Union, 2016.

European Council. 'Notice of Meeting and Provisional Agenda': https:// data.consilium.europa.eu/doc/document/CM-6114-2010-INIT/en /pdf

European Council. 'Press Release 3028th Council Meeting General Affairs European Council. "Statement of the Heads of State or Government on Ukraine." Brussels, 6 March 2014. Brussels': https:// data.consilium.europa.eu/doc/document/ST-12550-2010-INIT/en /pdf

European Institute. 'The European External Action Services Comes of Age', University of Maryland, December 2013: https://www .europeaninstitute.org/index.php/190-european-affairs/ea-december -2013/1826-the-european-external-action-service-comes-of-age-an -assessment

Evers, Erin. 'Executions Don't Make Iraq Safe', 11 October 2013: https:// www.hrw.org/news/2013/10/11/dispatches-executions-dont-make -iraq-safe

Evers, Erin. 'New Weapons Won't Address Iraq's Deeper Problems',

26 December 2013: https://www.hrw.org/news/2013/12/26/dis patches-new-weapons-wont-address-iraqs-deeper-problems

Fägersten, Björn. 'Bureaucratic Resistance to International Intelligence Cooperation – The Case of Europol', *Intelligence and National Security* 25, no. 4 (2010): 500–20.

Falkenrath, Richard A. 'The 9/11 Commission Report: A Review Essay', *International Security* 29, no. 3 (2005): 170–90.

Farson, Stuart and Mark Phythian. *Commissions of Inquiry and National Security: Comparative Approaches*, Santa Barbara, CA: Praeger, 2010.

FAZ. 'Dschihadisten stürmen Universität', 7 June 2014: https://www.faz.net/aktuell/politik/ausland/naher-osten/geiselnahme-im-irak-dsch ihadisten-stuermen-universitaet-12978017.html

FAZ. 'Im Irak gibt es keinen Staat', 28 April 2014: https://www.faz.net/aktuell/politik/ausland/asien/der-stellvertretende-irakische-minist erpraesident-salih-al-mutlaq-im-gespraech-12912844.html

Federal Foreign Office. Speech by Dr Frank-Walter Steinmeier, Federal Minister for Foreign Affairs, at the Handover Ceremony on 17 December 2013: https://www.auswaertiges-amt.de/en/newsroom /news/131217-bm-antrittsrede/258766

Federal Government. *Guidelines on Preventing Crises, Resolving Conflicts, Building Peace*, Berlin, 2017.

Federal Government, *Operations Manual: Interministerial Approach to Preventing Crises, Resolving Conflicts and Building Peace*, Berlin, 2019.

Financial Times. 'Iraq Needs a Future without Maliki', 30 April 2014: https://www.ft.com/content/a063fd7a-d05f-11e3-af2b-00144feab dc0

Financial Times. 'Multiple Car Bombs Kill Dozens across Iraq', 29 July 2013.

Fingar, Thomas. *Reducing Uncertainty: Intelligence Analysis and National Security*, Stanford, CA: Stanford University Press, 2011.

Focus. 'Waffenlieferungen nach Syrien geraten außer Kontrolle', 16 November 2013: https://www.focus.de/wissen/mensch/tid-32276 /nahost-experte-heiko-wimmen-warnt-waffenlieferungen-nach-syrien -geraten-ausser-kontrolle_aid_1038930.html

Ford, Harold P. *Estimative Intelligence: The Purposes and Problems of National Intelligence Estimates*, Lanham, MD: University Press of America, 1993.

Forsberg, Tuomas and Hiski Haukkala. *The European Union and Russia*, Basingstoke: Palgrave, 2016.

Frankel, Rebecca. 'The Failed States Index 2010', Foreign Policy: https:// foreignpolicy.com/2010/06/17/the-failed-states-index-2010/

Franks, Oliver and Privy Council. 'Falkland Islands Review: Report of a Committee of Privy Counsellors', Cmnd 8787, London: Her Majesty's Stationery Office, 1983.

Freedman, Lawrence. 'Ukraine and the Art of Crisis Management', *Survival* 56, no. 3 (2014): 7–42.

Freedman, Lawrence. *Ukraine and the Art of Strategy*, Oxford: Oxford University Press, 2019.

Gardham, Duncan. 'Lonely-hearts Blog for al-Qaeda Fighters', *The Times*, 20 January 2014: https://www.thetimes.co.uk/article/lonely-h earts-blog-for-al-qaeda-fighters-tg8ln8swqd5

Garthoff, Raymond L. *Intelligence Assessment and Policymaking: A Decision Point in the Kennedy Administration*, Washington, DC: The Brookings Institution, 1984.

Gaub, Florence. 'Understanding Instability: Lessons from the "Arab Spring". Report for the "History of British Intelligence and Security" Research Project', in AHRC Public Policy Series, Arts and Humanities Research Council, 2012.

Gaub, Florence, ed. *What If . . .? 14 Futures for 2024*, Paris: EU-ISS, 2020.

Gause, F. Gregory. 'Why Middle East Studies Missed the Arab Spring: The Myth of Authoritarian Stability', *Foreign Affairs* 90, no. 4 (2011): 81–90.

Gehring, Thomas, Kevin Urbanski and Sebastian Oberthür. 'The European Union as an Inadvertent Great Power: EU Actorness and the Ukraine Crisis', *Journal of Common Market Studies* 55, no. 4 (2017): 727–43.

George, Alexander L. 'Warning and Response: Theory and Practice', in *International Violence: Terrorism, Surprise and Control*, edited by Yair Evron, 12–24, Jerusalem: Hebrew University, Leonard David Institute, 1979.

German Foreign Office. 'Review 2014: Außenpolitik Weiter Denken: Krise – Ordnung – Europa', Berlin: Auswärtiges Amt, 2014.

Gerstein, Marc S. and Edgar H. Schein. 'Dark Secrets: Face-Work, Organizational Culture and Disaster Prevention', in *Forecasting, Warning, and Responding to Transnational Risks*, edited by Chiara De Franco and Christoph O. Meyer, Basingstoke: Palgrave Macmillan, 2011.

Gill, Peter. 'Sorting the Wood from the Trees. Were 9/11 and Iraq "Intelligence Failures"?', in *Strategic Intelligence: Understanding the*

Hidden Side of Government, edited by Loch K. Johnson, 151–68, 159, Westport, CT: Praeger Security International, 2007.

Gnad, Oliver. 'Wie strategiefähig ist deutsche Politik? Vorausschauende Regierungsführung als Grundlage zukunftsrobuster Entscheidungen', in *Internationale Sicherheit im 21. Jahrhundert. Deutschlands internationale Verantwortung*, edited by James Bindenagel, Matthias Herdegen and Karl Kaiser, 125–40, Bonn: Bonn University Press, 2016.

Gobe, Eric. 'The Gafsa Mining Basin between Riots and a Social Movement': https://halshs.archives-ouvertes.fr/halshs-00557826/document

Goodman, Michael S. *The Official History of the Joint Intelligence Committee. Volume I: From the Approach of the Second World War to the Suez Crisis*, London: Routledge, 2015.

Goodwin, Jeff. 'Why We Were Surprised (Again) by the Arab Spring' [in En], *Swiss Political Science Review* 17, no. 4 (2011): 452–6.

Götz, Elias. 'Putin, the State, and War: The Causes of Russia's near Abroad Assertion Revisited', *International Studies Review* 18, no. 4 (2016).

Grabo, Cynthia M. *Anticipating Surprise: Analysis for Strategic Warning*, Joint Military Intelligence College's Center for Strategic Intelligence Research, Washington 2002. https://www.ni-u.edu/ni_press/pdf/Anticipating_Surprise_Analysis.pdf

Grabo, Cynthia. *Handbook of Warning Intelligence: Assessing the Threat to National Security*, Scarecrow Professional Intelligence Education Series, edited by Jan Goldman, vol. no. 12, Lanham, MD: Scarecrow Press, 2010.

Grabo, Cynthia, with Jan Goldman. *Handbook on Warning Intelligence. Complete and Declassified Edition*, Lanham, MD et al.: Rowman & Littlefield, 2015.

Gruszczak, Artur. *Intelligence Security in the European Union: Building a Strategic Intelligence Community*, Basingstoke: Palgrave Macmillan, 2016.

Güssgen, Florian. 'Of Swiss Army Knives and Diplomacy. A Review of the Union's Diplomatic Capabilities', Jean Monnet Working Papers in Comparative and International Politics, April 2001: http://aei.pitt.edu/396/1/jmwp33.htm

Gusy, Christoph. 'Gesetz über den Bundesnachrichtendienst (BND-Gesetz – BNDG)', in *Sicherheitsrecht des Bundes*, edited by Wolf-Rüdiger Schenke, Kurt Graulich and Josef Ruthig, 1261–1303, München: C. H. Beck, 2014.

Guttmann, Aviva. 'Combatting Terror in Europe: Euro-Israeli Counterterrorism Intelligence Cooperation in the Club De Berne (1971–1972)', *Intelligence and National Security* 33, no. 2 (2018): 158–75.

Guttmann, Aviva. 'The Rise of ISIS as a Partial Surprise: An Open-source Analysis on the Threat Evolution and Early Warnings in the UK', forthcoming with *International Journal of Intelligence and CounterIntelligence*.

Guttmann, Aviva and Bahar Karimi. 'Timeline of UK Media and Middle East Experts' Anticipation of the Rise of ISIS and UK Government Reactions', June 2021: https://kclpure.kcl.ac.uk /portal/files/155074993/Timeline_of_UK_Media_and_GUTTMAN _PubJun2021_VoR.pdf

Hackensberger, Alfred. 'Al-Qaida schafft einen Gottesstaat im Niemandsland', *Die Welt*, 5 January 2014: https://www.welt.de/politik /ausland/article123560153/Al-Qaida-schafft-einen-Gottesstaat-im -Niemandsland.html

Hackensberger, Alfred. 'Die Kurden wollen weg von Bagdad', *Die Welt*, 29 April 2014: https://www.welt.de/politik/ausland/article127410744 /Die-Kurden-wollen-weg-von-Bagdad.html

Hall, Peter. 'Policy Paradigms, Social Learning, and the State: The Case of Economic Policymaking in Britain', *Comparative Politics* 25, no. 3 (1993): 275.

Handel, Michael. 'The Politics of Intelligence', *Intelligence and National Security* 2, no. 4 (1987): 5–46.

Hanieh, Hassan Abu and Mohammad Abu Rumman. *The 'Islamic State' Organization: The Sunni Crisis and the Struggle of Global Jihadism*, Amman: Friedrich Ebert Stiftung, 2015.

Haukkala, Hiski. 'A Perfect Storm; or What Went Wrong and What Went Right for the EU in Ukraine', *Europe-Asia Studies* 68, no. 4 (2016): 653–64.

Heclo, Hugh. *Modern Social Politics in Britain and Sweden; From Relief to Income Maintenance*, Yale Studies in Political Science, New Haven, CT: Yale University Press, 1974.

Hedberg, B. *How Organizations Learn and Unlearn*, Working Papers, Stockholm: Arbetslivscentrum, 1979.

Hedley, John Hollister. 'Learning from Intelligence Failures', *International Journal of Intelligence and CounterIntelligence* 18, no. 3 (2005): 435–50.

Heisbourg, François. 'A View from France: Not There Yet', in *Zeitenwende – Wendezeiten: Special Edition of the Munich Security*

Report, edited by Tobias Bunde, Laura Hartmann, Franziska Stärk, Randolf Carr, Christoph Erber, Julia Hammelehle and Juliane Kabus, 161–2, Munich: Munich Security Conference, 2020.

Helwig, Niklas. 'The High Representative of the Union: The Quest for Leadership in EU Foreign Policy', in *The European External Action Service: European Diplomacy Post-Westphalia*, edited by David Spence and Jozef Bátora, 87–104, London: Palgrave Macmillan, 2015.

Hemmer, Jort and Rosan Smits. 'The Early Warning and Conflict Prevention Capability of the Council of the European Union: A Mapping of the Pre-Lisbon Period', Clingendael, March 2010. https://www.clingendael.org/sites/default/files/pdfs/20100300_IfP -EW_report.pdf

Henökl, Thomas E. 'The European External Action Service: Torn Apart Between Several Principals or Acting as a Smart "Double-agent"?', *Journal of Contemporary European Research* 10, no. 4 (2014): 381–401. https://www.researchgate.net/publication/288689961_The _European_External_Action_Service_Torn_Apart_Between_Several _Principals_or_Acting_as_a_Smart_%27Double-agent%27

Herman, Michael. *Intelligence Power in Peace and War*, Cambridge: Cambridge University Press, 1996.

Hermann, Rainer. 'Ein Afghanistan am Mittelmeer', *FAZ*, 12 December 2013: https://www.faz.net/aktuell/politik/inland/deutsche-dschihadisten-ueber-die-a8-nach-aleppo-12717483.html?printPaged Article=true#pageIndex_3

Herrmann, Rainer. 'Kampfzone Levante', *FAZ*, 4 August 2013: https:// www.faz.net/aktuell/politik/ausland/naher-osten/naher-osten -kampfzone-levante-12310645.html

Hermann, Rainer and Christoph Ehrhardt. 'Zweifrontenkrieg gegen die Islamisten', *FAZ*, 6 January 2014: https://www.faz.net/aktuell/politik /ausland/naher-osten/irak-zweifrontenkrieg-gegen-die-islamisten -12739700.html

Herrmann, Richard K. and Jong Kun Choi. 'From Prediction to Learning: Opening Experts' Minds to Unfolding History', *International Security* 31, no. 4 (2007): 132–61.

Heuer, Richards J. and Randolph H. Pherson. *Structured Analytic Techniques for Intelligence Analysis*, 3rd edn, Thousand Oaks, CA et al.: CQ Press, 2021.

Heydemann, Steven. 'Explaining the Arab Uprisings: Transformations in Comparative Perspective', *Mediterranean Politics* 21, no. 1 (2015): 192–204.

Higgins, Andrew. 'Ukraine Upheaval Highlights E.U.'s Past Miscalculations and Future Dangers', *The New York Times*, 20 March 2014.

Hille, Kathrin and Roman Olearchy. 'Russia Rattles Sabre over Fate of Crimea': https://www.ft.com/content/84909a9e-9a55-11e3-8e06-00144feab7de

Hillion, Christophe and Steven Blockmans. 'From Self-Doubt to Self-Assurance', Report by the Task Force EEAS 2.0. January 2021. https://www.ceps.eu/download/publication/?id=32013&pdf=TFR_EEAS-2_0-From-self-doubt-to-self-assurance.pdf

Hilsman, Roger Jr. 'Intelligence and Policy-Making in Foreign Affairs', *World Politics* 5, no. 1 (1952): 1–45.

Hintjens, Helen M. 'Explaining the 1994 Genocide in Rwanda', *The Journal of Modern African Studies* 37, no. 2 (1999): 241–86.

HMG. 'Defence Reform', June 2011: https://assets.publishing.service.gov.uk/government/uploads/system/uploads/attachment_data/file/27408/defence_reform_report_struct_mgt_mod_27june2011.pdf

HMG. 'Government Response to the Intelligence and Security Committee's Annual Report 2011–2012', Cm8455, November 2012: https://assets.publishing.service.gov.uk/government/uploads/system/uploads/attachment_data/file/211566/Government-Response-2011-2012.pdf

HMG. 'Joint Forces Command is Now Called Strategic Command', no date: https://www.gov.uk/government/organisations/joint-forces-command

HMG. 'Joint Intelligence Committee', no date: https://www.gov.uk/government/groups/joint-intelligence-committee

HMG. 'Libya Crisis: National Security Adviser's Review of Central Coordination and Lessons Learned', 30 November 2011: https://assets.publishing.service.gov.uk/government/uploads/system/uploads/attachment_data/file/193145/Lessons-Learned-30-Nov.pdf

HMG. 'PM's Speech in Moscow', 12 September 2011: https://www.gov.uk/government/speeches/pms-speech-in-moscow

Holmes, Amy Austin and Kevin Koehler. 'Myths of Military Defection in Egypt and Tunisia', *Mediterranean Politics* 25, no. 1 (2018): 45–70.

Horowitz, Michael C. 'Future Thinking and Cognitive Distortions: Key Questions That Guide Forecasting Processes', in *The Politics and Science of Prevision: Governing and Probing the Future*, edited by Andreas Wenger, Ursula Jasper and Myriam Dunn Cavelty, 63–72, Abingdon: Routledge, 2000.

Houghton, David Patrick. 'The Role of Analogical Reasoning in Novel

Foreign-Policy Situations', *British Journal of Political Science* 26, no. 4 (1996): 523–52.

House of Commons. 'Coronavirus: Lessons Learnt to Date', 147, House of Commons: Health and Social Care, and Science and Technology Committees, 2021.

House of Commons Foreign Affairs Committee. 'British Foreign Policy and the "Arab Spring". Second Report of Session 2012–13', London, 2012.

House of Lords, European Union Committee. 'The EU and Russia: Before and Beyond the Crisis in Ukraine', London: House of Lords, 2015.

Howard, Michael. 'The Strategic Approach to International Relations', reprinted in *The Causes of Wars and other Essays. Second Edition*, 36–48, Cambridge, MA: Harvard University Press, 1983.

Howard, Philip N. and Muzammil M. Hussain. *Democracy's Fourth Wave?: Digital Media and the Arab Spring*, Oxford Studies in Digital Politics, Oxford and New York: Oxford University Press, 2013.

Howorth, Jolyon. 'Catherine Ashton's Five-Year Term: A Difficult Assessment', *Les Cahiers Européens de Sciences Po*, no. 3 (2014). https://www.sciencespo.fr/centre-etudes-europeennes/sites/sciencespo .fr.centre-etudes-europeennes/files/n%C2%B03_2014_Howorth %20v4.pdf

HRW. 'Iraq: Attacks Amount to Crimes Against Humanity, Authorities Should End Draconian Responses', 11 August 2013: https://www.hrw .org/news/2013/08/11/iraq-attacks-amount-crimes-against-humanity

HRW. 'Iraq: Harsh Tactics in Advance of Holy Month', 15 November 2013: https://www.hrw.org/news/2013/11/15/iraq-harsh-tactics -advance-holy-month

HRW. 'Iraq: Wave of Journalist Killings', 29 November 2013: https:// www.hrw.org/news/2013/11/29/iraq-wave-journalist-killings

Hughes, Thomas L. *The Fate of Facts in a World of Men: Foreign Policy and Intelligence-Making*, New York Foreign Policy Association, 1976.

Hulsman, John. 'Schlafwandelnd in Richtung Disaster', *SZ*, 1 September 2013: https://www.sueddeutsche.de/politik/usa-im-syrien-konflikt-schlafwandelnd-in-richtung-desaster-1.1759142

Hutchings, Robert and Gregory F. Treverton, eds. *Truth to Power. A History of the U.S. National Intelligence Council*, Oxford: Oxford University Press, 2019.

Ianchovichina, Elena. *Eruptions of Popular Anger: The Economics of the Arab Spring and its Aftermath*, World Bank MENA Development Report, Washington, DC: World Bank Group, 2018.

ICG. 'Anything But Politics: The State of Syria's Political Opposition',

Report 146, 17 October 2013: https://www.crisisgroup.org/middle
-east-north-africa/eastern-mediterranean/syria/anything-politics-state
-syria-s-political-opposition

ICG. Crisis Watch, July 2013: https://www.crisisgroup.org/crisiswatch
/july-2013

ICG. 'Make or Break: Iraq's Sunnis and the State', Report 144, 14 August
2013: https://www.crisisgroup.org/middle-east-north-africa/gulf-and
-arabian-peninsula/iraq/make-or-break-iraq-s-sunnis-and-state

ICG. 'Syria's Metastasising Conflicts', Report 143, June 2013: https://
www.crisisgroup.org/middle-east-north-africa/eastern-mediterranean
/syria/syria-s-metastasising-conflicts

Idris, Iffat. 'Analysis of the Arab Spring', Birmingham: GSDRC, 2016.

Ikani, Nikki. 'Change and Continuity in the European Neighbourhood
Policy: The Ukraine Crisis as a Critical Juncture', *Geopolitics* 24,
no. 1 (2019): 20–50.

Ikani, Nikki. *Crisis and Change in European Union Foreign Policy: A
Framework of EU Foreign Policy Change*, Manchester: Manchester
University Press, 2021.

Ikani, Nikki. 'Timeline of Expert Claims and Responses for the Arab
Uprising Involving UK', June 2021, INTEL website: https://www.kcl
.ac.uk/eis/research/intel/intel-publications

Ikani, Nikki and Ana Maria Albulescu. 'Timeline of Expert Claims and
Responses for the Arab Uprising Involving Germany and the EU',
June 2021, INTEL website: https://www.kcl.ac.uk/eis/research/intel
/intel-publications

Ikani, Nikki and Ana Maria Albulescu. 'Timeline of Expert Claims and
Responses for Ukraine Crisis Involving Germany and the EU', June
2021, INTEL website: https://www.kcl.ac.uk/eis/research/intel/intel
-publications

Ikani, Nikki, Aviva Guttmann and Christoph O Meyer. 'An Analytical
Framework for Postmortems of European Foreign Policy: Should
Decision-Makers Have Been Surprised?', *Intelligence and National
Security* 35, no. 2 (2020): 1–19, 197–215.

Intelligence and Security Commitee. 'Annual Report 2011–2012',
London: UK Stationary Office, 2012.

Intelligence and Security Committee of Parliament. 'Annual Report
2001–2002', Cm 5542, June 2002: https://isc.independent.gov.uk/wp
-content/uploads/2021/01/2001-2002_ISC_AR.pdf

Intelligence and Security Committee of Parliament. 'Annual Report
2002–2003', Cm 5837, June 2003: https://isc.independent.gov.uk/wp
-content/uploads/2021/01/2002-2003_ISC_AR.pdf

Intelligence and Security Committee of Parliament. 'Annual Report 2011–2012', Cm 8403, July 2012: https://irp.fas.org/world/uk/isc2011-12.pdf

Intelligence and Security Committee of Parliament. 'Annual Report 2012–2013', HC547, July 2013: https://assets.publishing.service.gov.uk/government/uploads/system/uploads/attachment_data/file/211553/31176_HC_547_ISC.PDF

Intelligence and Security Committee of Parliament. 'Annual Report 2015–2016', HC444, July 2016: https://isc.independent.gov.uk/wp-content/uploads/2021/01/2015-2016_ISC_AR.pdf

Intelligence and Security Committee of Parliament. 'Annual Report 2016–2017', HC655, December 2017: https://assets.publishing.service.gov.uk/government/uploads/system/uploads/attachment_data/file/727949/ISC-Annual-Report-2016-17.pdf

Intelligence and Security Committee of Parliament. 'Russia', HC 632, 21 July 2020: https://isc.independent.gov.uk/wp-content/uploads/2021/01/20200721_HC632_CCS001_CCS1019402408-001_ISC_Russia_Report_Web_Accessible.pdf

International Crisis Group. 'EU Crisis Response Capability – Institutions and Processes for Conflict Prevention and Management', Report No. 2, 26 June 2001: https://www.crisisgroup.org/europe-central-asia/eu-crisis-response-capability-institutions-and-processes-conflict-prevention-and-management

International Crisis Group. 'Popular Protest in North Africa and the Middle East', International Crisis Group, 2011.

International Staff and Office of Secretary General. 'NATO Restricted Engaging the New Ukraine', 25 February 2014, Document PO (2014) 0101.

Isaksen, Bjorn Gunnar M. and Ken R. McNaught. 'Uncertainty Handling in Estimative Intelligence – Challenges and Requirements from Both Analyst and Consumer Perspectives', *Journal of Risk Research* 22, no. 5 (2019): 643–57.

Jensen, Mark A. 'Intelligence Failures: What Are They Really and What Do We Do About Them?', *Intelligence and National Security* 27, no. 2 (2012): 261–82.

Jervis, Robert. 'Book Reviews', *Political Science Quarterly* 127, no. 1 (2012): 143–6.

Jervis, Robert. *Perception and Misperception in International Politics*, Princeton, NJ: Princeton University Press, 1976.

Jervis, Robert. 'Report, Politics and Intelligence Failures: The Case of Iraq', *Journal of Strategic Studies* 29, no. 1 (2006): 3–52.

Jervis, Robert. 'Why Intelligence and Policymakers Clash', *Political Science Quarterly* 125, no. 2 (2010): 185–205.

Jervis, Robert. *Why Intelligence Fails: Lessons from the Iranian Revolution and the Iraq War*, Cornell Studies in Security Affairs, Ithaca, NY: Cornell University Press, 2010.

Joffé, George. 'The Arab Spring in North Africa: Origins and Prospects', The Journal of North African Studies 16, no. 4 (2011): 507–32.

Johnson, Boris. 'We've Left it Too Late to Save Syria – This Conflict Can Never be Won', *The Telegraph*, 16 June 2013: https://www.telegraph .co.uk/news/worldnews/10123938/Weve-left-it-too-late-to-save-Syria -this-conflict-can-never-be-won.html

Johnson, Loch K. 'Sketches for a Theory of Strategic Intelligence', in *Intelligence Theory*, 47–67, Routledge, 2008.

Johnston, Rob. *Analytic Culture in the US Intelligence Community: An Ethnographic Study*, Washington, DC: The Center for the Study of Intelligence, CIA, 2005.

Joint Intelligence Committee. 'Iraq: How Important is Al Qaida in Iraq', JIC Assessment, 21 March 2007, declassified and released to the Chilcot Inquiry: https://webarchive.nationalarchives.gov.uk /20170831105159/http://www.iraqinquiry.org.uk/media/233625/20 07-03-21-jic-assessment-iraq-how-important-is-al-qaida-in-iraq .pdf?d=2007-03-21

Joint Intelligence Committee. 'Iraq, Insurgency, Sectarianism and Violence', JIC Assessment, 19 July 2006, declassified and released to the Chilcot Inquiry: https://webarchive.nationalarchives.gov.uk/ ukgwa/20171123123237/http://www.iraqinquiry.org.uk/media/211241/ 2006-07-19-jic-assessment-iraq-insurgency-sectarianism-and-viol ence.pdf

Jones, Chris. 'Secrecy Reigns at the EU's Intelligence Analysis Centre', *Statewatch* 22, no. 4 (2013). https://www.statewatch.org/media /documents/analyses/no-223-eu-intcen.pdf

Jones, Sam. 'Europe's Fears of Syria Blowback Soar in Wake of Museum Attack', *Financial Times*, 4 June 2014: https://www.ft.com/content /42c8022c-ebc8-11e3-ab1b-00144feabdc0

Kaim, Marcus and Ronja Kempin. 'A European Security Council. Added Value for EU Foreign and Security Policy?', SWP Comment no. 2, January 2019. https://www.swp-berlin.org/publications/products /comments/2019C02_kim_kmp.pdf

Kam, Ephraim. *Surprise Attack: The Victim's Perspective*, Cambridge, MA: Harvard University Press, 2013.

Kam, Ephraim. 'The Islamic State Surprise: The Intelligence Perspective',

Strategic Assessment 18, no. 3 (2015): 21–31. https://www.inss.org
.il/wp-content/uploads/systemfiles/adkan18_3ENG%20(4)_Kam.pdf

Kaplan, Rebecca. 'Rise of ISIS Poses Fresh Challenges for U.S. Intelligence
Community', CBS News, 27 June 2014: https://www.cbsnews
.com/news/rise-of-isis-poses-fresh-challenges-for-u-s-intelligence
-community/

Karolewski, Ireneusz Pawel and Mai'a K. Davis Cross. 'The EU's Power
in the Russia–Ukraine Crisis: Enabled or Constrained?', *JCMS:
Journal of Common Market Studies* 55, no. 1 (2017): 137–52.

Kass, Lani and J. Philipp London. 'Surprise, Deception, Denial and
Warning', *Orbis* 57, no. 1 (2013): 59–82.

Keohane, Daniel and Robert Grant. 'From Comprehensive Approach
to Comprehensive Action: Enhancing the Effectiveness of the EU's
Contribution to Peace and Security', Conference Report, Wilton Park,
December 2012: https://www.wiltonpark.org.uk/wp-content/uploads
/WP1202-final-report.pdf

Khalaf, Roula. 'The Costs of Clandestine Talks with Syria's Strongman',
Financial Times, 17 January 2014: https://www.ft.com/content
/9e99b7a0-7ede-11e3-a2a7-00144feabdc0

Kienle, Eberhard. 'Ambiguities and Misconceptions: European Policies
towards Political Reform in the Southern Mediterranean', in *Europe
and the Middle East. Perspectives on Major Policy Issues*, edited by
Al Siyassa Al Dawliya, 11–16, Cairo: Al Ahram Commercial Press,
2010. https://eeas.europa.eu/archives/delegations/egypt/documents
/syasah_dawlia_final_en.pdf

*Kleine Anfrage Der Abgeordneten Wolfgang Gehrcke, Dr. Diether
Dehm, Annette Groth, Heike Hänsel, Inge Höger, Andrej Hunko,
Niema Movassat, Dr. Alexander S. Neu, Alexander Ulrich, Kathrin
Vogler Und Der Fraktion Die Linke*, 2014.

Kofman, Michael, Katya Migacheva, Brian Nichiporuk, Andrew Radin,
Olesya Tkacheva and Jenny Oberholtzer. 'Lessons from Russia's
Operations in Crimea and Eastern Ukraine', 110, Santa Monica, CA:
RAND Corporation, 2017.

Krieger, Wolfgang. *Die deutschen Geheimdienste*, München: C. H. Beck,
2021.

Krieger, Wolfgang. 'German Intelligence History: A Field in Search of
Scholars', *Intelligence & National Security* 19, no. 2 (2004): 185–98.

Kroenig, Matthew. 'Facing Reality: Getting Nato Ready for a New Cold
War', *Survival* 57, no. 1 (2015): 49–70.

Kuipers, Sanneke, Ellen Verolme and Erwin Muller. 'Lessons from
the Mh-17 Transboundary Disaster Investigation', *Journal of*

Contingencies and Crisis Management 28, no. 4 (2020): 376–85.

Kuran, Timur. 'The Inevitability of Future Revolutionary Surprises', *American Journal of Sociology* 100, no. 6 (1995): 1528–51.

Kurtz, Gerrit S. and Christoph O. Meyer. 'Is Conflict Prevention a Science, Craft, or Art? Moving Beyond Technocracy and Wishful Thinking', *Global Affairs* 5, no. 1 (2018): 23–39.

Kuus, Merje. *Geopolitics and Expertise: Knowledge and Authority in European Diplomacy*, Chichester: Wiley Blackwell, 2013.

Kuzio, Taras. *Putin's War against Ukraine: Revolution, Nationalism, and Crime*, Toronto: CreateSpace, 2017.

Kuzio, Taras. 'The Crimea: Europe's Next Flashpoint?', in *The Jamestown Foundation Report*, Washington, DC: The Jamestown Foundation, 2010.

Latimer, Jon. *Deception in War*, New York: Abrams, 2003.

Lavoix, Hélène. 'Communication of Strategic Foresight and Early Warning', *Red Team Analysis*, 3 March 2021: https://redanalysis .org/2021/03/03/delivery-communication-strategic-foresight-early -warning-products/

Lavoix, Hélène. 'Revisiting Timeliness for Strategic Foresight and Warning and Risk Management', *Red Team Analysis*, 1 October 2018: https://redanalysis.org/2018/10/01/revisiting-timeliness-for-stra tegic-foresight-and-warning/

Lebow, Richard Ned. 'Generational Learning and Conflict Management', *International Journal* 40, no. 4 (1985): 555–85.

Lefebvre, Maxime and Christoph Hillion. 'The European External Action Service: Towards a Common Diplomacy?', *European Issue* 184, 25 October 2010: https://www.robert-schuman.eu/en/european-issues/0184-the-european-external-action-service-towards-a-comm on-diplomacy

Lehnguth, Gerold and Klaus Vogelgesang. 'Die Organisationserlasse der Bundeskanzler seit Bestehen der Bundesrepublik Deutschland im Lichte der politischen Entwicklungen', *Archiv des öffentlichen Rechts* 113, no. 4 (1988): 531–82.

Lesteven, Sandra. *La mise en place du service européen pour l'action extérieure. Cahier Thucydide* no. 11 (2011). https://www.afri-ct.org /wp-content/uploads/2012/03/11_SEAE.pdf

Levy, Jack S. 'Learning and Foreign Policy: Sweeping a Conceptual Minefield', *International Organization* 48, no. 2 (1994): 279–312.

Lippert, Barbara, Nicolai von Ondarza and Volker Perthes, eds. 'European Strategic Autonomy. Actors, Issues, Conflicts of Interests', German

Institute for International and Security Affairs, SWP Research Paper 4, March 2019: https://www.swp-berlin.org/publications/products /research_papers/2019RP04_lpt_orz_prt_web.pdf

Lledo-Ferrer, Yvan and Jan-Hendrik Dietrich. 'Building a European Intelligence Community', *International Journal of Intelligence and CounterIntelligence* 33, no. 3 (2020): 440–51.

Lovell, John. '"Lessons" of U.S. Military Involvement: Preliminary Conceptualization', in *Foreign Policy Decision Making: Perception, Cognition, and Artificial Intelligence*, edited by Donald A. Sylvan and Steve Chan, New Dimensions in International Studies, 129–57, New York: Praeger, 1984.

Lowenthal, Mark M. *Intelligence: From Secrets to Policy*, Thousand Oaks, CA: CQ Press, 2019.

Lowenthal, Mark M. 'The Intelligence Time Event Horizon', *International Journal of Intelligence and CounterIntelligence* 22, no. 3 (2009): 369–81.

Loyd, Anthony. 'Al-Qaeda Sets Up Sharia Courts in Key Syrian City', *The Times*, 3 May 2013: https://www.thetimes.co.uk/article/al-qaeda -sets-up-sharia-courts-in-key-syrian-city-v9w0f3wz7ks

Loyd, Anthony. 'Boy, 15, is Killed in Front of Parents for "Insulting Prophet"', *The Times*, 11 June 2013: https://www.thetimes.co.uk/article/boy-15- is-killed-by-islamist-rebels-for-insulting-prophet-h83cz669sx6

Loyd, Anthony, 'Boy of 16 is Whipped to Satisfy the Public Clamour for "Justice" – The Rebel Response to Crime and Disorder is Brutality in the Name of Sharia', *The Times*, 3 July 2013.

Loyd, Anthony. 'Face to Face with the New Enemy in Syria', *The Times*, 19 September 2013: https://www.thetimes.co.uk/article/face-to-face -with-the-new-enemy-in-syria-v7t772gkgph

Loyd, Anthony. 'Syrian War Revitalises al-Qaeda in Iraq', *The Times*, 12 December 2013: https://www.thetimes.co.uk/article/syrian-war- revitalises-al-qaeda-in-iraq-hdsrjknqfrk

Loyd, Anthony and Sheer Frenkel. 'Iraqi al-Qaeda Joins Syrian Rebels in Merger that will Alarm the West', *The Times*, 10 April 2013: https:// www.thetimes.co.uk/article/iraqi-al-qaeda-joins-syrian-rebels-in-mer ger-that-will-alarm-the-west-6nn25vl9kg5

MacFarlane, Neil and Anand Menon. 'The EU and Ukraine', *Survival* 56, no. 3 (2014): 95–101.

McCants, William F. *The Isis Apocalypse: The History, Strategy, and Doomsday Vision of the Islamic State*, New York: Picador/St. Martin's Press, 2016.

McFate, Jessica Lewis and Harleen Gambhir. 'ISIS's Global Messaging

Strategy Factsheet', Institute for the Study of War, December 2014.

Maddrell, Paul. *The Image of the Enemy: Intelligence Analysis of Adversaries since 1945*, Washington, DC: Georgetown University Press, 2015.

Malaniak, Daniel, Susan Peterson and Ryan Powers. 'Trip Snap Poll I: Nine Questions on Current Global Issues for International Relations Scholars' (2014): https://www.wm.edu/offices/global-research/trip/snap-polls/publications/trip-snap-poll-one-report-final.pdf

Malik, Shiv and Haroon Siddique. 'British Family Says Son has Died Fighting for Syria Jihadists', *The Guardian*, 21 November 2013.

Mansfield, Edward D. and Jack L. Snyder. *Electing to Fight: Why Emerging Democracies Go to War*. BCSIA Studies in International Security, Cambridge, MA: The MIT Press, 2005.

March, James G. and Johan P. Olsen. *Ambiguity and Choice in Organizations*, Bergen: Universitetsforlaget, 1976.

Marrin, Stephen. 'At Arm's Length or at the Elbow?: Explaining the Distance between Analysts and Decisionmakers', *International Journal of Intelligence and CounterIntelligence* 20, no. 3 (2007): 401–14.

Marten, Kimberly. 'Putin's Choices: Explaining Russian Foreign Policy and Intervention in Ukraine', *The Washington Quarterly* 38, no. 2 (2015): 189–204.

May, Peter J. 'Policy Learning and Failure', *Journal of Public Policy* 12, no. 4 (1992): 331–54.

Mearsheimer, John J. 'Why the Ukraine Crisis is the West's Fault: The Liberal Delusions that Provoked Putin', *Foreign Affairs* 93, no. 5 (2014): 77–89.

Meier-Klodt, Cord. *Einsatzbereit in der Krise? Entscheidungsstrukturen der deutschen Sicherheitspolitik auf dem Prüfstand*, SWP-Studie S34, Berlin: SWP, 2002.

Menon, Rajan and Eugene B. Rumer. *Conflict in Ukraine: The Unwinding of the Post-Cold War Order*, Cambridge, MA: The MIT Press, 2015.

Meyer, Christoph O. and Ana Maria Albulescu. ,Britisches Vorbild: Was die nächste Bundesregierung vom Vereinigten Königreich über kritische Selbstreflexion und außenpolitisches Handeln lernen könnte', *Internationale Politik*, 2021: 73–7.

Meyer, Christoph O., Chiara De Franco and Florian Otto. *Warning About War: Conflict, Persuasion and Foreign Policy*, Cambridge: Cambridge University Press, 2020.

Meyer, Christoph O., Eric Sangar and Eva Michaels. 'How Do Non-

Governmental Organizations Influence Media Coverage of Conflict? The Case of the Syrian Conflict, 2011–2014', *Media, War & Conflict* 11, no. 1 (2018): 149–71.

Meyer, Christoph, Nikki Ikani, Mauricio Avendano Pabon and Ann Kelly. 'Learning the Right Lessons for the Next Pandemic: How to Design Public Inquiries into the UK Government's Handling of Covid-19', London: King's College London, 2020.

Michaels, Eva. 'Germany's Anticipation of and Response to Isis' Rise to Power: Overview of Open-Source Expert Claims and Policy Responses', March 2021: https://www.kcl.ac.uk/eis/assets/newtimeline-germany -and-isis.pdf

Michaels, Eva. 'How Surprising was ISIS' Rise to Power for the German Intelligence Community? Reconstructing Estimates of Likelihood Prior to the Fall of Mosul', *Intelligence and National Security*, online first (2021).

Michaels, Eva and Bahar Karimi. 'Overview of Expert Claims and Eu Policy Responses to Isis' Rise to Power in Iraq and Syria', June 2021.

Miller, Bowman H. 'U.S. Strategic Intelligence Forecasting and the Perils of Prediction', *International Journal of Intelligence and CounterIntelligence* 27, no. 4 (2014): 687–701.

Missiroli, Antonio. 'The EU Foreign Service: Under Construction', RSCAS Policy Paper 2010/04: https://cadmus.eui.eu/bitstream/handle /1814/15282/RSCAS_PP_2010_04.pdf

Moore, David T. 'Species of Competencies for Intelligence Analysis', *American Intelligence Journal* 23 (2005): 29–43.

Morell, Michael and Bill Harlow. *The Great War of Our Time: The CIA's Fight against Terrorism – From Al Qa'ida to Isis*, New York: Grand Central Publishing, 2016.

Müller-Brandeck-Bocquet, Gisela and Carolin Rüger, eds. *The High Representative for the EU Foreign and Security Policy – Review and Prospects*. Baden Baden: Nomos, 2011.

Musiol, Lisa. 'Better Early than Sorry: How the EU Can Use its Early Warning Capacities to their Full Potential', International Crisis Group, 22 October 2019: https://www.crisisgroup.org/europe-central -asia/better-early-sorry-how-eu-can-use-its-early-warning-capacities -their-full-potential

NATO. 'NATO Nations Discuss Warning Intelligence Reform', 1 April 2019: https://www.nato.int/cps/en/natolive/news_165302.htm?select edLocale=en

NATO Development Concepts and Doctrine Centre (DCDC). 'A Guide to Red Teaming': https://www.act.nato.int/images/stories/events/2011/cde/rr_ukdcdc.pdf

Naumann, Klaus. 'Die Gewährleistung kohärenter Außenpolitik – Wie „vernetzt" man „Sicherheit"?', *Zeitschrift für Außen- und Sicherheitspolitik* 8 (2015): 157–71.

Neitzel, Sönke and Bastian Matteo Scianna. *Blutige Enthaltung: Deutschlands Rolle im Syrienkrieg*, Freiburg: Herder, 2021.

Nelson, Fraser. 'Terrorism in the UK: Social Media is Now the Biggest Jihadi Training Camp of Them All', *The Telegraph*, 25 April 2014: https://www.telegraph.co.uk/news/uknews/terrorism-in-the-uk/10786205/Terrorism-in-the-UK-Social-media-is-now-the-biggest-jihadi-training-camp-of-them-all.html

Neustadt, Richard E. and Ernest R. May. *Thinking in Time: The Uses of History for Decision-Makers*, New York: Free Press, 1986.

Nielsen, Harald. 'The German Analysis and Assessment System', *Intelligence and National Security* 19, no. 4 (1995): 54–71.

Nomikos, John M. 'European Union Intelligence Analysis Centre (INTCEN): Next Stop to an Agency?', *Journal of Mediterranean and Balkan Intelligence* 4, no. 2 (2014): 5–13.

Norheim-Martinsen, Per M. *The European Union and Military Force: Governance and Strategy*, Cambridge: Cambridge University Press.

Noutcheva, Gergana. 'Institutional Governance of European Neighbourhood Policy in the Wake of the Arab Spring', *Journal of European Integration* 37, no. 1 (2015): 19–36.

Nováky, Niklas. 'The Strategic Compass Charting a New Course for the EU's Security and Defence Policy', Martens Centre, December 2020: https://www.martenscentre.eu/wp-content/uploads/2020/12/CES_POLICY-BRIEF_TheStrategicCompass-V1.pdf

Office of the Federal President, 'Germany's Role in the World: Reflections on Responsibility, Norms and Alliances', speech by Federal President Joachim Gauck at the opening of the Munich Security Conference on 31 January 2014: https://www.bundespraesident.de/SharedDocs/Reden/EN/JoachimGauck/Reden/2014/140131-Munich-Security-Conference.html

Omand, David. *How Spies Think. Ten Lessons in Intelligence*, London: Penguin, 2020.

Omand, David. 'Means and Methods of Modern Intelligence and their Wider Implications', in *Intelligence Law and Policies in Europa: A Handbook*, edited by Jan-Hendrik Dietrich and Satish Sule, 38–64, Munich: C. H. Beck, 2019.

Omand, David. 'Reflections on Intelligence Analysts and Policymakers',

International Journal of Intelligence and CounterIntelligence 33, no. 3 (2020): 471–82.

Oppenheimer, Michael F. *Pivotal Countries, Alternate Futures: Using Scenarios to Manage American Strategy*, Oxford: Oxford University Press, 2016.

Oppermann, Kai. 'Deutsche Außenpolitik während der dritten Amtszeit Angela Merkels', in *Zwischen Stillstand, Politikwandel und Krisenmanagement. Eine Bilanz der Regierung Merkel 2013–2017*, edited by Reimut Zohlnhöfer and Thomas Saalfeld, 619–42, Wiesbaden: Springer VS, 2019.

Orenstein, Mitchell A. and R. Daniel Kelemen. 'Trojan Horses in EU Foreign Policy', *JCMS: Journal of Common Market Studies* 55, no. 1 (2017): 87–102.

Otto, Florian and Christoph O. Meyer. 'How to Warn: "Outside-in Warnings" of Western Governments About Violent Conflict and Mass Atrocities', *Media, War & Conflict* 19, no. 2 (2016): 198–216.

Palacios, José-Miguel. 'EU Intelligence: On the Road to a European Intelligence Agency?', in *Intelligence Law and Policies in Europa: A Handbook*, edited by Jan-Hendrik Dietrich and Satish Sule, 201–34, Munich: C. H. Beck, 2019.

Parker, Charles F. and Sander Dekker. 'September 11 and Postcrisis Investigation: Exploring the Role and Impact of the 9/11 Commission', in *Governing after Crisis*, edited by Arjen Boin, Allan McConnell and Paul 't Hart, 255–82, Cambridge: Cambridge University Press, 2008.

Peel, Michael. 'Syrian Rebel Infighting Grows as al-Qaeda Kills Rival Commander', *Financial Times*, 12 July 2013: https://www.ft.com/content/58a8f85e-eb05-11e2-bfdb-00144feabdc0

Perry World House. 'Keeping Score: A New Approach to Geopolitical Forecasting', White Paper, February 2021: https://global.upenn.edu/sites/default/files/perry-world-house/Keeping%20Score%20Forecasting%20White%20Paper.pdf

Perthes, Volker. 'Europe and the Arab Spring' [in En], *Survival* 53, no. 6 (2011): 73–84.

Philp, Catherine. 'Citizens Flee after Islamist Rebels Take Iraq's Second City', *The Times*, 11 June 2014: https://www.thetimes.co.uk/article/citizens-flee-after-islamist-rebels-take-iraqs-second-city-z92532l6s6k

Philp, Catherine. 'Dozens Killed as Wave of Bombings Hits Baghdad', *The Times*, 30 September 2013.

Philp, Catherine. 'Every US Soldier who has Fought There has the Same Question', *The Times*, 11 July 2014: https://www.thetimes.co.uk

/article/every-us-soldier-who-has-fought-there-has-the-same-question
-lklzv508z5n

Philp, Catherine. 'Islamic Insurgents Push Baghdad to the Brink', *The Times*, 12 June 2014: https://www.thetimes.co.uk/article/islamic-insurgents-push-baghdad-to-the-brink-mpm9q867fn9

Philp, Catherine. 'Pay Taxes in Gold or Die, Christians in Syria Told', *The Times*, 3 March 2014: https://www.thetimes.co.uk/article/pay-ta xes-in-gold-or-die-christians-in-syria-told-0205m87d9lg

Pillar, Paul R. *Intelligence and Us Foreign Policy: Iraq, 9/11, and Misguided Reform*, New York: Columbia University Press, 2011.

Pillar, Paul R. 'Predictive Intelligence: Policy Support or Spectator Sport', *SAIS Review* 27, no. 1 (2008): 25–35.

Political and Security Committee. 'Notice of Meeting and Provisional Agenda 14 January 2011': https://data.consilium.europa.eu/doc /document/CM-1136-2011-REV-1/en/pdf

Porteous, Tom. 'Sectarianism in the Muslim World is Dividing People who Have Lived Together for Centuries', 18 July 2013: https://www .hrw.org/news/2013/07/18/god-and-intolerance

Posner, Richard A. *Preventing Surprise Attacks: Intelligence Reform in the Wake of 9/11*, London: Rowman & Littlefield, 2005.

Prom-Jackson, Sukai and Eileen A. Cronin. 'United Nations Review of Change Management in UN System Organizations', JIU/REP/2019/4, 2019: https://www.unjiu.org/sites/www.unjiu.org/files/jiu_rep_2019 _4_english.pdf

Puglierin, Jana. 'Direction of Force: The EU's Strategic Compass', ECFR, 1 April 2021: https://ecfr.eu/article/direction-of-force-the-eus -strategic-compass/

Putin, Vladimir. 'Address by President of the Russian Federation', news release, 2014.

Putin, Vladimir. 'Direct Line with Vladimir Putin', Kremlin web page, 2014.

Rauwolf, Christian. 'Intelligence in EU-led Military Missions and Operations', in *Intelligence Law and Policies in Europa: A Handbook*, edited by Jan-Hendrik Dietrich and Satish Sule, 153–74, Munich: C. H. Beck, 2019.

Rehrl, Jochen, ed. *Handbook for Decision Makers. The Common Security and Defence Policy of the European Union*, Vienna, 2014. https://op.europa.eu/en/publication-detail/-/publication/07e87dbb -e9dd-11e6-ad7c-01aa75ed71a1

Rehrl, Jochen and Galia Glume, eds. *Handbook on CSDP Missions and Operations*, Vienna, 2015. https://eeas.europa.eu/archives/docs/csdp

/structures-instruments-agencies/european-security-defence-college
/pdf/handbook/final_-_handbook_on_csdp_missions_and_operations
.pdf

Resodihardjo, Sandra L. *Crises, Inquiries and the Politics of Blame*, London: Palgrave Macmillan, 2019.

Resodihardjo, Sandra L. 'Wielding a Double-Edged Sword: The Use of Inquiries at Times of Crisis', *Journal of Contingencies and Crisis Management* 14, no. 4 (2006): 199–206.

Rettmann, Andrew. 'Ashton Picks Finn to be EU "Spymaster"', Atlantic Council, 20 December 2010: https://www.atlanticcouncil.org/blogs /natosource/ashton-picks-finn-to-be-eu-spymaster/

Rettmann, Andrew. 'Competition Heating up for EU Intelligence Chief Job', *EU Observer*, 14 September 2010: https://euobserver.com /institutional/30794

Reuter, Christoph. 'Der Preis des Zögerns', *Der Spiegel*, 19 August 2012: https://www.spiegel.de/politik/der-preis-des-zoegerns-a-222411b7-0 002-0001-0000-000087818613?context=issue

Reuter, Christoph. 'Die schwarze Macht', *Der Spiegel*, 15 December 2013: https://www.spiegel.de/politik/die-schwarze-macht-a-9bf58f42 -0002-0001-0000-000123826502?context=issue

Reuter, Christoph. 'Disneyland für Dschihadisten', *Der Spiegel*, 7 July 2013: https://www.spiegel.de/politik/disneyland-fuer-dschihadisten-a -cf2fb99a-0002-0001-0000-000102241702?context=issue

Reuter, Christoph. 'Signal zum Aufstand', *Der Spiegel*, 12 January 2014: https://www.spiegel.de/politik/signal-zum-aufstand-a-3c2ada12-00 02-0001-0000-000124381324?context=issue

Reuters. 'Russia Starts Delivering $1 Billion Arms Package to Azerbaijan': http://www.reuters.com/article/2013/06/18/us-russia-azerbaijan -arms-idUSBRE95H0KM20130618

Reynolds, Paul. 'New Russian World Order: The Five Principles' (2008). http://news.bbc.co.uk/1/hi/world/europe/7591610.stm

Rezk, Dina. *Arab World and Western Intelligence: Analysing the Middle East, 1956–1981*, Edinburgh: Edinburgh University Press, 2017.

Rhinard, Mark. 'The Crisisification of Policy-Making in the European Union', *JCMS: Journal of Common Market Studies* 57, no. 3 (2019): 616–33.

Riddervold, Marianne, Jarle Trondal and Akasemi Newsome, eds. *The Palgrave Handbook of EU Crises*, Basingstoke: Palgrave Macmillan, 2021.

Roccu, Roberto and Benedetta Voltolini. 'Framing and Reframing the

EU's Engagement with the Mediterranean: Examining the Security-Stability Nexus Before and After the Arab Uprisings', *Mediterranean Politics* 23, no. 1 (2017): 1–22.

Roth, Andrew. 'Putin Tells European Official That He Could "Take Kiev in Two Weeks"', *The New York Times*, 2 September 2009: https://www.nytimes.com/2014/09/03/world/europe/ukraine-crisis.html

Roth, Florian and Michel Herzog. 'Strategische Früherkennung – Instrumente, Möglichkeiten und Grenzen', *Zeitschrift für Außen- und Sicherheitspolitik* 9 (2016): 201–11.

Roth, Kenneth. 'Time to Abandon the Autocrats and Embrace Rights. The International Response to the Arab Spring', Human Rights Watch, 2012.

Rovner, Joshua. *Fixing the Facts: National Security and the Politics of Intelligence*, Ithaca, NY: Cornell University Press, 2011.

Sabatier, Paul A. 'An Advocacy Coalition Framework of Policy Change and the Role of Policy-Oriented Learning Therein', *Policy Sciences* 21, no. 2/3 (1988): 129–68.

Sakwa, Richard. *Frontline Ukraine: Crisis in the Borderlands*, London: I. B. Tauris, 2016.

Sakwa, Richard. 'The Death of Europe: Continental Fates after Ukraine', *International Affairs* 91, no. 3 (2015): 553–79.

Salloum, Raniah. 'Irakische Qaida baut Macht im Norden Syriens aus', *Der Spiegel*, 9 November 2013: https://www.spiegel.de/politik/ausland/isis-in-syrien-wird-iraks-al-qaida-zu-einer-der-wichtigen-milizen-a-931017.html

Sanderson, Ian. 'Evaluation, Policy Learning and Evidence-Based Policy Making', *Public Administration* 80, no. 1 (2002): 1–22.

Schlie, Ulrich. 'Deutsche Sicherheitspolitik nach 1990: Auf der Suche nach einer Strategie', *Zeitschrift für Strategische Analysen* 4, no. 3 (2020): 304–14.

Schlie, Ulrich. 'Warum Deutschland künftig mehr denn je auf einen gesamtstrategischen Ansatz in der Außen- und Sicherheitspolitik angewiesen ist', in *Das Weißbuch 2016 und die Herausforderungen von Strategiebildung*, edited by Daniel Jacobi and Gunther Hellmann, 297–307, Wiesbaden: Springer VS, 2019.

Schmid, Martin. 'The HR/VP and the Organisation of the EEAS' Senior Management', in *The EU's External Action Service: Potentials for a One Voice Foreign Policy*, edited by Doris Dialer, Heinrich Neisser and Anja Opitz, 81–96, Innsbruck: Innsbruck University Press, 2014. https://www.uibk.ac.at/iup/buch_pdfs/eeas_bd3.pdf

Schockenhoff, Andreas. ‚Die Debatte ist eröffnet . . . und Streit erwünscht:

Warum Deutschland eine Sicherheitsstrategie braucht', *Internationale Politik* 5 (2008): 89–95.

Schoemaker, Paul J. H. 'Forecasting and Scenario Planning: The Challenges of Uncertainty and Complexity', in *Blackwell Handbook of Judgment and Decision Making*, edited by Derek J. Koehler and Nigel Harvey, 274–96, Wiley-Blackwell, 2004.

Seibel, Wolfgang. 'Arduous Learning on New Uncertainties? The Emergence of German Diplomacy in the Ukrainian Crisis', *Global Policy* 6, S1 (2015): 56–72.

Sénat. 'La Fonction "Anticipation Stratégique": Quel Renforcement Depuis Le Livre Blanc?', 2011.

Sénat. 'Le Renforcement De La Fonction D'anticipation Stratégique Depuis Les Livres Blancs De 2008', Commission des Affaires Étrangères, de la Défense et des Forces Armées, 2011.

Sénat. 'Les Relations Avec La Russie: Comment Sortir De L'impasse?', Paris: French Senate, 2015.

Sénat. 'Rapport D'information Déposé En Application De L'article 145 Du Règlement Par La Commission Des Affaires Étrangères En Conclusion Des Travaux D'une Mission D'information Constituée Le 4 Mars 2015 (1) Sur La Crise Ukrainienne Et L'avenir Des Relations Entre La Russie Et L'union Européenne Et La France', Assemblée Nationale Constitution Du 4 Octobre 1958 Quatorzième Législature, 2016.

Sénat. 'Rapport D'information No 585 Au Nom De La Commission Des Affaires Étrangères, De La Défense Et Des Forces Armées (1) Sur Le Renforcement De La Fonction D'anticipation Stratégique Depuis Les Livres Blancs De 2008': http://www.senat.fr/rap/r10-585/r10-5851.pdf

Seyfried, Pia. 'A European Intelligence Service? Potentials and Limits of Intelligence Cooperation at EU Level', BAKS Working Paper 20/2017: https://www.baks.bund.de/en/working-papers/2017/a-european-intelligence-service-potentials-and-limits-of-intelligence

Shapcott, William. 2011. 'Do They Listen? Communicating Warnings: A Practitioners Perspective', in *Forecasting, Warning, and Responding to Transnational Risks*, edited by Chiara De Franco and Christoph O. Meyer, 117–26, Basingstoke: Palgrave Macmillan.

Sherlock, Ruth. 'Al-Qaeda Recruits Entering Syria from Turkey Safehouses', *The Telegraph*, 30 October 2013: https://www.telegraph.co.uk/news/worldnews/middleeast/syria/10415935/Al-Qaeda-recruits-entering-Syria-from-Turkey-safehouses.html

Sherlock, Ruth. 'Al-Qaeda Training British and European "Jihadists" in

Syria to Set Up Terror Cells at Home', *The Telegraph*, 19 January 2014: https://www.telegraph.co.uk/news/worldnews/middleeast/syria/ 10582945/Al-Qaeda-training-British-and-European-jihadists-in-Syria-to-set-up-terror-cells-at-home.html

Sherlock, Ruth. 'Islamist Rebels Seize Key Syrian Helicopter Base, Boosting Hardliners' Influence', *The Telegraph*, 5 August 2013: https://www.telegraph.co.uk/news/worldnews/middleeast/syria /10225207/Islamist-rebels-seize-key-Syrian-helicopter-base-boosting -hardliners-influence.html

Sherlock, Ruth. 'Syria: Al-Qaeda-linked Rebels Execute Regime "Militia Men" in Front of Children', *The Telegraph*, 13 September 2013: https://www.telegraph.co.uk/news/worldnews/middleeast/syria /10308808/Syria-Al-Qaeda-linked-rebels-execute-regime-militia-men -in-front-of-children.html

Simpkins, Brian Keith. 'How Intelligence Failures Contributed to ISIS Territorial Gain in Iraq', American Military University, 24 July 2017.

Sims, Jennifer E. 'Foreign Intelligence Liaison: Devils, Deals, and Details', *International Journal of Intelligence and Counterintelligence* 19, no. 2 (2006): 195–217.

Single Analysis Capacity. 'Worst Case Scenarios for the Narrower Middle East', 2007.

SIPRI. 'Sipri Yearbook 2015 – the Ukraine Conflict and its Implications', 2015.

Smith, Julianne. 'Eine Frage der Staatskunst. Deutschland sollte erneut über einen Nationalen Sicherheitsrat nachdenken', *Internationale Politik* January/February (2019): 92–8.

Smith, Martin and Linda Hirsch. 'The Rise of ISIS', written and produced by Martin Smith, Frontline, 2014: https://www.pbs.org/wgbh /frontline/film/rise-of-isis/transcript/

Smith, Michael E. 'Learning in European Union Peacebuilding: Rhetoric and Reality', *Global Affairs* 4, no. 2/3 (2018): 215–25.

Soldt, Rüdiger and Reiner Burger. 'Über die A8 nach Aleppo', *FAZ*, 18 December 2013: https://www.faz.net/aktuell/politik/inland/deut sche-dschihadisten-ueber-die-a8-nach-aleppo-12717483.html?print PagedArticle=true#pageIndex_3

Solomon, Erika. 'Islamist Insurgents Seize Iraqi City of Mosul', *Financial Times*, 10 June 2014.

Spence, David. 'The Early Days of the European External Action Service: A Practitioner's View', *The Hague Journal of Diplomacy*, no. 7 (2012): 115–34.

Spencer, Richard. 'Al-Qaeda's Syrian Wing Takes Over the Oilfields once Belonging to Assad', *The Telegraph*, 18 May 2013: https://www.telegraph.co.uk/news/worldnews/middleeast/syria/10065802/Al-Qaedas-Syrian-wing-takes-over-the-oilfields-once-belonging-to-Assad.html

Spencer, Richard. 'Five Killed in Gunfight During Raid on Home of Iraqi MP', *The Telegraph*, 28 December 2013: https://www.telegraph.co.uk/news/worldnews/middleeast/iraq/10540382/Five-killed-in-gunfight-during-raid-on-home-of-Iraqi-MP.html

Spencer, Richard. 'Iraq Crisis Q & A: Who or What is ISIS? Is it Part of al-Qaeda?', *The Telegraph*, 11 June 2014: https://www.telegraph.co.uk/news/worldnews/middleeast/iraq/10892898/Iraq-crisis-Q-and-A-Who-or-what-is-ISIS-Is-it-part-of-al-Qaeda.html

Spencer, Richard. 'Syria: The Jihadi Town Where "Brides" are Snatched from Schools', *The Telegraph*, 29 March 2014: https://www.telegraph.co.uk/news/worldnews/middleeast/syria/10731665/Syria-the-jihadi-town-where-brides-are-snatched-from-schools.html

Stares, Paul B. *Preventive Engagement: How America Can Avoid War, Stay Strong, and Keep the Peace*, New York: Columbia University Press, 2018.

Stark, Alastair. 'Left on the Shelf: Explaining the Failure of Public Inquiry Recommendations', *Public Administration* (2019): 1–16, 609.

Stark, Alastair. *Public Inquiries, Policy Learning, and the Threat of Future Crises*, 1st edn, Oxford: Oxford University Press, 2018.

Stark, Alastair. *Public Inquiries, Policy Learning, and the Threat of Future Crises*, Oxford University Press, USA, 2019.

Stark, Alastair and Brian Head. 'Institutional Amnesia and Public Policy', *Journal of European Public Policy* 26, no. 10 (2018): 1521–39.

Stedman, Stephen John. 'Alchemy for a New World Order: Overselling "Preventive Diplomacy"', *Foreign Affairs* 74, no. 3 (1995): 14–20.

Stein, Janice Gross. 'Building Politics into Psychology: The Misperception of Threat', *Political Psychology* (1988): 245–71.

Stein, Shimon. 'One Year of the Arab Spring: The European Union and the Arab Spring', Institute for National Security Studies, 2012.

Steinberg, Guido. 'Der Irak und der syrische Bürgerkrieg', *SWP Aktuell* 46 (2013): https://www.swp-berlin.org/fileadmin/contents/products/aktuell/2013A46_sbg.pdf

Steinberg, Guido. 'Irak: im Zangengriff der Konfessionen', *Welt-Sichten*, 5 December 2013: https://www.welt-sichten.org/artikel/19637

Stepka, Maciej. 'EU Crisis Management and Conflict Prevention:

Identifying Institutional Constraints for Early Warning Analysis Utilization', *Politeja*, no. 49 (2017): 127–42.

Stern, Eric and Bengt Sundelius. 'Crisis Management Europe: An Integrated Regional Research and Training Program', *International Studies Perspectives* 3, no. 1 (2002): 71–88.

Stern, Jessica and J. M. Berger. *The State of Terror*, New York: HarperCollins, 2015.

Stewart, Susan. 'The EU, Russia and a Less Common Neighbourhood Lessons Reinforced by the Vilnius Summit', Berlin: SWP Comment, 2014.

Strachan-Morris, David. 'Threat and Risk: What is the Difference and Why Does it Matter?', *Intelligence and National Security* 27, no. 2 (2012): 172–86.

Tagesschau. 'Baghdad ist auf der Kippe', 12 June 2014: https://www.tagesschau.de/ausland/irak-isis-102.html

Tagliavini report. 'Independent International Fact-Finding Mission on the Conflict in Georgia (IIFFMCG)', Brussels: Council of the European Union, 2009. http://news.bbc.co.uk/1/shared/bsp/hi/pdfs/30_09_09_iiffmgc_report.pdf

Taleb, Nassim and Mark Blyth. 'The Black Swan of Cairo: How Suppressing Volatility Makes the World Less Predictable and More Dangerous', *Foreign Affairs* 90, no. 3 (2011): 33–9.

Tankel, Stephen. *With Us and Against Us: How America's Partners Help and Hinder the War on Terror*, New York: Columbia University Press, 2018.

Task Force 'EEAS 2.0'. 'From Self-Doubt to Self-Assurance: The European External Action Service as the Indispensable Support for a Geopolitical EU', edited by Pierre Vimont, Christophe Hillion and Steven Blockmans, Brussels: CEPS, SIEPS, FES, 2021. http://library.fes.de/pdf-files/bueros/bruessel/17378.pdf

Tetlock, Philip and Dan Gardner. *Superforecasting: The Art and Science of Prediction*, London and New York: Random House, 2016.

Teutmeyer, Benjamin. 'Die Rolle der NATO in der Ukraine-Krise', *Zeitschrift für Außen- und Sicherheitspolitik* 7 (2014): 431–40.

The Telegraph. 'Iraqi Forces by Numbers: Who Has the Biggest Army?', 12 June 2014: https://www.telegraph.co.uk/news/worldnews/middleeast/iraq/10894811/Iraqi-forces-by-numbers-who-has-the-biggest-army.html

The Telegraph. 'Iraqis Blame Government for Lack of Protection as al-Qaeda Claim Responsibility for Deadly Attacks', 12 August 2013: https://www.telegraph.co.uk/news/worldnews/middleeast/iraq/10236785/

Iraqis-blame-government-for-lack-of-protection-as-al-Qaeda-claim-responsibility-for-deadly-attacks.html

The Telegraph. 'Wave of Violence Sees at Least 47 Killed Across Iraq', 26 August 2013: https://www.telegraph.co.uk/news/worldnews/middleeast/iraq/10265935/Wave-of-violence-sees-at-least-47-killed-across-Iraq.html

The White House. 'Remarks by President Biden on the Drawdown of U.S. Forces in Afghanistan', 2021.

The White House, Office of the Press Secretary. Remarks by the President at the National Defense University, Washington, DC, 23 May 2013: https://obamawhitehouse.archives.gov/the-press-office/2013/05/23/remarks-president-national-defense-university

Tomlinson, Hugh. 'Jailbreaks and Suicide Bombers Push Iraq Back Towards Anarchy', *The Times*, 23 July 2013: https://www.thetimes.co.uk/article/jailbreaks-and-suicide-bombers-push-iraq-back-towards-anarchy-vk3j8753lnf

Tomlinson, Hugh. 'Rush-hour Suicide Bomb Attacks Kill 71 in Baghdad', *The Times*, 28 August 2013: https://www.thetimes.co.uk/article/rush-hour-suicide-bomb-attacks-kill-71-in-baghdad-pssfftwsmfw

Trenin, Dimitri. 'Why Russia Won't Interfere', *The New York Times*, 23 February 2014: https://www.nytimes.com/2014/02/24/opinion/why-russia-wont-interfere.html

Tuinier, Pepijn. 'Explaining the Depth and Breadth of International Intelligence Cooperation: Towards a Comprehensive Understanding', *Intelligence and National Security* 36, no. 1 (2021): 116–38.

UK Ministry of Defence. 'Defence in a Competitive Age', CP 411, March 2021: https://assets.publishing.service.gov.uk/government/uploads/system/uploads/attachment_data/file/974661/CP411_-Defence_Command_Plan.pdf

UK Ministry of Defence. 'Global Strategic Trends', 2018.

UK Parliament. 'British Foreign Policy and the "Arab Spring"', Foreign Affairs Committee – Second Report, House of Commons, 3 July 2012: https://publications.parliament.uk/pa/cm201213/cmselect/cmfaff/80/8002.htm

UK Parliament. 'Review of Intelligence on Weapons of Mass Destruction', Report of a Committee of Privy Counsellors, HC898, London: The Stationery Office, 14 July 2004: https://fas.org/irp/world/uk/butler071404.pdf

US Department of Defense. 'Directive 3115.16', dated 5 December 2013, updated 10 August 2020: https://fas.org/irp/doddir/dod/d3115_16.pdf

US Department of Defense. 'News Briefing with Gen. Odierno from the Pentagon', 4 June 2010: http://www.defense.gov/ transcripts/transcript.aspx?transcriptid=4632

US Senate Select Committee on Intelligence and US House Permanent Select Committee on Intelligence. 'Joint Inquiry into Intelligence Community Activities before and after the Terrorist Attacks of September 11, 2001: Hearings before the Select Committee on Intelligence, US Senate and the Permanent Select Committee on Intelligence, House of Representatives', US Government Printing Office, 2004.

Valbjørn, Morten. 'Reflections on Self-Reflections – On Framing the Analytical Implications of the Arab Uprisings for the Study of Arab Politics', *Democratization* 22, no. 2 (2015): 218–38.

Van Puyvelde, Damien. 'European Intelligence Agendas and the Way Forward', *International Journal of Intelligence and Counter Intelligence* 33, no. 3 (2020): 506–13.

Vanhoonacker, Sophie and Karolina Pomorska. 'The European External Action Service and Agenda-Setting in European Foreign Policy' [in En], *Journal of European Public Policy* 20, no. 9 (2013): 1316–31.

Voeten, Eric. 'Who Predicted Russia's Military Intervention?', *The Washington Post*, 12 March 2014: https://www.washingtonpost.com /news/monkey-cage/wp/2014/03/12/who-predicted-russias-military -intervention-2/

Vogel, Toby. 'Ashton Names Team to Advise on EEAS. Senior Officials will Help Set Up External Service as MEPs are Left Out of Preparatory Team', *Politico*, 21 January 2010: https://www.politico.eu/article /ashton-names-team-to-advise-on-eeas/

Walsh, James Igoe. *The International Politics of Intelligence Sharing*, New York: Columbia University Press, 2009.

Walters, Simon. 'Revealed: Boris Johnson Scrapped Cabinet Ministers' Pandemic Team Six Months before Coronavirus Hit Britain', *Daily Mail*, 12 June 2020.

Warrick, Joby. *Black Flags: The Rise of ISIS*, London: Bantam, 2015.

Webber, Mark and James Sperling. 'NATO and the Ukrainian Crisis: Collective Securitisation', *European Journal of International Security* 2, no. 1 (2016): 19–46.

Werkner, Ines-Jacqueline. 'Die Verflechtung innerer und äußerer Sicherheit. Aktuelle Tendenzen in Deutschland im Lichte europäischer Entwicklungen', *Zeitschrift für Außen- und Sicherheitspolitik* 4 (2011): 65–87.

Westerfield, H. Bradford. 'America and the World of Intelligence Liaison', *Intelligence and National Security* 11, no. 3 (1996): 523–60.

Weyland, Kurt. 'The Arab Spring: Why the Surprising Similarities with the Revolutionary Wave of 1848?', *Perspectives on Politics* 10, no. 4 (2012): 917–34.

Whiteman, Hilary. 'Lone Wolf? Australian Police Shoot Dead Teen "Terror Suspect"', CNN, 25 September 2014: https://edition.cnn.com /2014/09/24/world/asia/australia-terror-shooting-laws/index.html

Whitesmith, Martha. *Cognitive Bias in Intelligence Analysis: Testing the Analysis of Competing Hypotheses Method*, Edinburgh: Edinburgh University Press, 2020.

Whitman, Richard G. and Ana E. Juncos. 'The Arab Spring, the Eurozone Crisis and the Neighbourhood: A Region in Flux' [in En], *JCMS: Journal of Common Market Studies* 50 (2012): 147–61.

Whitson, Sarah Leah. 'Letter to President Obama Regarding the Visit of Iraqi Prime Minister Nuri al-Maliki', 29 October 2013: https://www .hrw.org/news/2013/10/29/letter-president-obama-regarding-visit-ira qi-prime-minister-nuri-al-maliki

Wiegand, Gunnar and Evelina Schulz. 'The EU and its Eastern Partnership: Political Association and Economic Integration in a Rough Neighbourhood', in *Trade Policy between Law, Diplomacy and Scholarship: Liber Amicorum in Memoriam Horst G. Krenzler*, edited by Christoph Herrmann, Bruno Simma and Rudolf Streinz, London: Springer, 2015.

Wiegel, Michaela. ‚Ein Fahndungserfolg aus purem Zufall‘, *FAZ*, 2 June 2014: https://www.faz.net/aktuell/politik/ausland/attentat-in-bruessel -ein-fahndungserfolg-aus-purem-zufall-12968612.html

Wilson, Andrew. *Ukraine Crisis: What It Means for the West*, New Haven, CT and London: Yale University Press, 2014.

Winkler, Heinrich August. *Die Geschichte des Westens, Band 4: Die Zeit der Gegenwart*, Munich: C. H. Beck, 2016.

Wirtz, James J. 'The Art of the Intelligence Autopsy', *Intelligence and National Security* 29, no. 1 (2014): 1–18.

Wirtz, James J. 'The Intelligence-Policy Nexus', in *Strategic Intelligence: Understanding the Hidden Side of Government*, edited by Loch K. Johnson, 139–50, Westport, CT: Praeger Security International, 2007.

Wirtz, James J. 'When Do You Give It a Name? Theoretical Observations about the ISIS Intelligence Failure', in *The Future of ISIS: Regional and International Implications*, edited by Faisal Al-Istrabadi and Sumit Ganguly, 67–85, Washington, DC: The Brookings Institution, 2018.

Wittkowsky, Andreas, Wanda Hummel and Tobias Pietz. '"Vernetzte Sicherheit": Intentionen, Kontroversen und eine Agenda für die Praxis', *Zeitschrift für Außen- und Sicherheitspolitik* 5 (2012): 113–26.

Wohlstetter, Roberta, *Pearl Harbor. Warning and Decision*, Stanford, CA: Stanford University Press, 1962.

Wolfsfeld, Gadi, Elad Segev and Tamir Sheafer. 'Social Media and the Arab Spring', *The International Journal of Press/Politics* 18, no. 2 (2013): 115–37.

Wright, Nicholas. 'No Longer the Elephant Outside the Room: Why the Ukraine Crisis Reflects a Deeper Shift Towards German Leadership of European Foreign Policy', *German Politics* 27, no. 4 (2018): 479–97.

Yarhi-Milo, Keren. *Knowing the Adversary*, Princeton, NJ: Princeton University Press, 2014.

Zähle, Kai. 'Der Bundessicherheitsrat', *Der Staat* 44, no. 3 (2005): 462–82.

Zandee, Dick, Adája Stoetman and Bob Deen. 'The EU's Strategic Compass for Security and Defence. Squaring Ambition with Reality', Clingendael Report, 31 May 2021: https://www.clingendael.org/sites /default/files/2021-05/Report_The_EUs_Compass_for_security_and _defence_May_2021.pdf

Zekri, Sonja. 'Abschreckendes Beispiel Irak', *SZ*, 4 September 2013: https://www.sueddeutsche.de/politik/moeglicher-militaereinsatz-in-syrien-abschreckendes-beispiel-irak-1.1761923

Zekri, Sonja. '50.000 Islamisten sagen sich von Übergangsregierung los', *SZ*, 25 September 2013: https://www.sueddeutsche.de /politik/opposition-in-syrien-50-000-islamisten-sagen-sich-von-ueber gangsregierung-los-1.1780675

Zerubavel, Eviatar. *Hidden in Plain Sight: The Social Structure of Irrelevance*, Oxford: Oxford University Press, 2015.

Zimmermann, Hubert. 'Neorealism', in *The Palgrave Handbook of EU Crisis*, edited by Marianne Riddervold, Jarle Trondal and Akasemi Newsome, 99–113, Basingstoke: Palgrave, 2020.

Index